Insurance Law in China

Edited by
Johanna Hjalmarsson and
Dingjing Huang

Contemporary Commercial Law

Insurance Law in China
by
Johanna Hjalmarsson and Dingjing Huang
(2015)

Causation in Insurance Contract Law
by
Meixian Song
(2014)

Insurance Law in China

Edited by

Johanna Hjalmarsson
Informa Senior Research Fellow in Maritime and Commercial Law at the University of Southampton

and

Dingjing Huang
Postgraduate Researcher at the University of Southampton

Routledge
Taylor & Francis Group
LONDON AND NEW YORK

First published 2015 by Routledge

2 Park Square, Milton Park, Abingdon, Oxon, OX14 4RN
711 Third Avenue, New York, NY 10017

Routledge is an imprint of the Taylor & Francis Group, an Informa business

First issued in paperback 2020

British Library Cataloguing in Publication Data
A catalogue record for this book is available from the British Library

Library of Congress Cataloging in Publication Data
Insurance law in China / edited by Johanna Hjalmarsson, Dingjing Huang.
pages cm. – (Contemporary commercial law)
Summary: "The book seeks to present and discuss current topics in Chinese insurance law and regulation to an English-speaking audience knowledgeable of common law insurance law and international insurance business" – Provided by publisher.
ISBN 978-1-138-78509-0 (hardback) – ISBN 978-1-315-76802-1 (ebook) 1. Insurance law – China. 2. Insurance – State supervision – China. I. Hjalmarsson, Johanna, editor. II. Huang, Dingjing, editor.
KNQ998.I59 2015
346.51'086 – dc23
2014025094

ISBN 978-1-138-78509-0 (hbk)
ISBN 978-0-367-73887-7 (pbk)

Typeset in Plantin
by Florence Production Ltd, Stoodleigh, Devon, UK

Contents

Foreword

On behalf of the University of Southampton Confucius Institute, I am pleased to offer a short foreword to these proceedings. Our key mission as a Confucius Institute is to deliver Chinese language learning and cultural events at the university, schools, colleges and in the wider community. However, we also take great pleasure in supporting the academic work undertaken by our colleagues in partnership with Chinese universities. We have funded conferences and symposiums in various subject areas and this was our first joint activity with the Southampton Law School.

The Chinese and English Insurance Law Conference was ambitious, with two full days of presentations and discussion featuring eminent academics and leading practitioners from China and the UK. Delivered on consecutive days at the University of Southampton and Lloyd's of London, the conference attracted a mixed audience of academics, legal practitioners, researchers and students. The event was an outstanding success, a rare opportunity for intercultural communication and knowledge that was well received by all participants.

The quality of the presentations is best appreciated in the proceedings.

Mark Cranshaw
Director, University of Southampton Confucius Institute

Foreword

The significance of China as both a market for and a supplier of financial services cannot be overstated. With China's status as a maritime power and a major exporter, many risks in China have traditionally found their way to the London market, either in the form of direct insurance or in the form of reinsurance of local carriers. In recent years, with the gradual liberalisation of Chinese trading laws and the reception of institutions such as Lloyd's, the insurance industry in China has become of increasing interest to Europe and all points west. However, Chinese law remains a mystery to many. It is not sufficiently understood that it is impossible to divorce legal principles from Chinese culture, and that Chinese law more closely resembles civil rather than common law systems with its use of codes and an absence of precedent in the courts.

The Confucius Institute has long been working to make Chinese principles more accessible to others. Its recent collaborations with the Law School at the University of Southampton has led to two important conferences with academic and practitioner representatives from both jurisdictions. This work is a collection of the papers presented at the first conference in April 2013. The papers cover a wide range of general topics: the history and structure of Chinese law; the operation of insurance law in China; access to the Chinese insurance market; the role of brokers in the Chinese market; the complex relationship between competition law and financial services; the regime for the protection of intellectual property rights; and the realities of dispute resolution in China. Specific areas of insurance law are also analysed: liability insurance; catastrophe insurance; the structure of the law relating to marine insurance; liability for oil pollution with insurance arrangements covering such liability; cargo insurance; limitation of liability for maritime claims; and lessons for China from the current proposals for reform in the UK.

The papers are of an unwavering high standard, unsurprising given that they have been presented by leading academics and practitioners from China and Europe, coupled with students who have taken their studies to PhD level and beyond and are now either practising or teaching. There have, in the past, been books in English on Chinese insurance law, but the treatment of substantive issues has been cursory. This collection is perhaps the most important work on the subject to appear in print in England. All who wish to understand more about the Chinese legal system and substantive law will find this book invaluable. The editors are to be congratulated for organising the conference and seeing its great contribution to knowledge onto the printed page.

Rob Merkin
University of Exeter, DLA Phillips Fox

Preface

The Chinese insurance market is expanding enormously as risk aversion takes hold in the economy while the role of the State as guarantor of commerce is gradually reduced. Insurance is a heavily regulated field with detailed contract law stipulations. An introduction to regulation and contract law and an understanding of current issues is essential for someone seeking to do business in the Chinese market. Insurance law is a field that translates well from one jurisdiction to another, and academics will be interested in understanding how issues are dealt with in another jurisdiction. Against this background, this book seeks to present and discuss current topics in Chinese insurance law and regulation to an English-speaking audience knowledgeable of common law insurance law and international insurance business. The editors hope to contribute to an improved understanding and well-informed discussion of the many aspects of insurance law addressed in the book.

This work sprang from the Chinese-English Insurance Law Conference held in April 2013, and started life as a project to collect and publish the papers presented. The conference was organised by the Insurance Law Research Group at Southampton Law School in collaboration with the Confucius Institute at the University of Southampton. There are a number of people to whom special thanks are due for the success of the conference: the directors and former director of the Confucius Institute, Mark Cranshaw, Dr Xueyi Zhu and Professor Siyi Fu, who generously sponsored and supported the conference; Dr Meixian Song, Dr Miao Li and Yiqing Yang, for their part in creating the successful funding proposal; and Jingbo Zhang and Haihua Song, who offered great effort in organising the conference together with the editors. The conference was generously supported by Lloyd's Market Association Academy with an excellent venue at Lloyd's of London. Gratitude is owed to David Kendall, chairman of the British Insurance Law Association, for chairing the London event and to Professor Rob Merkin for support at several crucial junctures along the way.

Several of the papers presented at the conference have been included in this book and have been updated with new legislation issued after the conference. Through the conference, we met further authors who agreed to contribute to the book. Two papers presented at the conference are already available in important journals: Dr Zhen Jing's article 'The insured's post-contract duty of notification of increase of risk: a comparative perspective', available at *Journal of Business Law*, 2013, pp 842–867, and Professor James Davey's article 'Remedying the remedies: the shifting shape of insurance contract law', available at *Lloyds Maritime and Commercial Law Quarterly*, 2013(4), pp 476–495. We are grateful to them and to Julian Burling, Dr Adolfo Paolini Pisani and Professor Hongjun Shan for their excellent presentations at the conference, and congratulate them on the publication of their papers elsewhere.

The book is divided into three parts and offers a mixture of introductory, comparative and in-depth studies. In Part I, 'Principles of insurance', Dr Meixian Song and Yiqing Yang provide an introduction on the history and development of Chinese insurance industry and insurance law; Professor Tingzhong Fu introduces the legal requirements for accessing the Chinese insurance market in view of China's WTO commitments; Dr Miao Li focuses on the law of insurance brokers, giving an insight into insurance brokers' legal responsibility under Chinese law; Dr Andrea Lista provides detailed analysis on theoretical reflections on the application of competition law to the insurance sector in EU and China; Professor Beiping Chu discusses several hot topics and the most recent developments in Chinese insurance law; and Dr Wenhao Han summarises Chinese law on jurisdiction, applicable law and dispute resolution from an insurance law perspective.

In Part II, 'Specific forms of insurance', a comprehensive discussion on liability insurance in China is given by Dr Tao Yu; legal issues on intellectual property and insurance in the Chinese legal system are discussed by Dr Lena Todd (Hua Li); and catastrophe insurance in China is reviewed by Johanna Hjalmarsson and Mateusz Bek.

Part III offers a comprehensive look at marine insurance. First, Professor Pengnan Wang gives a general introduction to the law and practice of Chinese marine insurance; Professor Lixin Han and Ke Wei deal with civil liability insurance for ship source oil pollution damage in China, considering China's implementation of the Civil Liability Convention 1992 and the Demonstration Project of Blanket Civil Liability Insurance for Coastal Ships' Oil Pollution Damage; Jingbo Zhang considers cargo insurance documents under the letter of credit framework; Dingjing Huang compares English law and Chinese law in respect of insurer's limitation of liability; and last but not least, Dr Meixian Song reviews the UK Law Commission's reform on insurance contract law with regard particularly to marine insurance law, looking for lessons valuable to Chinese marine insurance law.

The appendices are the Chinese Insurance Act 2009 and Chapter 12 of the Chinese Maritime Code 1992 regulating marine insurance contracts. The Chinese Insurance Act 2009 has been translated by Dingjing Huang and Haihua Song with critical assistance from Johanna Hjalmarsson. A guide to the translation is provided in a foreword to the translation.

We also need to thank Alexia Sutton at Routledge for her patience and all the members of the Insurance Law Research Group and Southampton Law School who have contributed in unseen ways to the making of this book, particularly Dr Aysegul Bugra for her crucial help and contribution. Last but not least, we thank our families for their patience and generosity.

The endeavour has been to state the law as at May 2014.

Johanna Hjalmarsson and Dingjing Huang
Southampton, June 2014

Author biographies

EDITORS

Johanna Hjalmarsson
Johanna is the Informa Senior Research Fellow in Maritime and Commercial Law at Southampton Law School, University of Southampton. She is the Director of the Insurance Law Research Group and a Member of the Institute of Maritime Law. Having served as a Junior Judge in her native Sweden, she worked for many years for the United Nations and the Office of the High Representative in Bosnia and Herzegovina, specialising in law reform. She has published several books and articles and is the Editor of *Shipping and Trade Law* and *Lloyd's Law Reporter*, as well as the IML publication *The Ratification of Maritime Conventions*. She is a Founder and General Editor of the free web resource AviationLaw.EU and teaches insurance and marine insurance law.

Dingjing Huang
LLM (University of Southampton), LLB (Shanghai Maritime University, China). Dingjing Huang is a PhD candidate at the University of Southampton. His research is on limitation on liability and maritime liens. He is a tutor in admiralty law at Southampton Law School and a member of the Insurance Law Research Group. He was a member of the organising committee for the Chinese-English Insurance Law Conference in 2013 and the Chinese-English Maritime Law Conference in 2014, also securing the funding for the latter.

CONTRIBUTORS

Mateusz Bek
Mateusz Bek graduated from the University of Southampton with an LLB (Hons) degree and subsequently an LLM Maritime Law (Distinction) degree. He is currently a Senior Researcher at the Institute of Maritime Law, University of Southampton, and will commence a training contract with a leading international shipping law firm in 2016.

Professor Beiping Chu

Beiping Chu is a Professor and Doctoral Supervisor at the Law School of Dalian Maritime University, and lectures mainly on marine insurance law, international maritime arbitration, ship collision law and shipping law. He is the Dean of DMU Law School, Deputy Secretary General and Executive Director of China Insurance Law Association, Director of Institute of Marine Insurance Law of DMU, Supporting Member of London Maritime Arbitrators Association (LMAA), Member of China Maritime Arbitration Commission (CMAC) Panel of Arbitrators and Member of Dalian Arbitration Commission of PRC Panel of Arbitrators.

Professor Tingzhong Fu

Tingzhong Fu is a Professor of Maritime Law at Tsinghua University School of Law, Beijing, China, as well as a Guest Professor at Dalian Maritime University and Shanghai Maritime University. He is also an Arbitrator with the China Maritime Arbitration Commission.

Professor Lixin Han

Lixin Han is a Professor of Maritime Law and Marine Environmental Law at Dalian Maritime University. Lixin is also the Vice-Dean of Law School, Dalian Maritime University, Guest Professor at East China University of Political Science and Law and an Arbitrator of CMAC & CIETAC.

Dr Wenhao Han

Wenhao Han is a Chinese and English dual-qualified dispute resolution lawyer specialising in shipping, insurance and reinsurance. Wenhao had worked in Shanghai and Hong Kong before relocating to London in 2012. Wenhao is an associate at Norton Rose Fulbright LLP. Wenhao assists insurers, P&I clubs and shipowners in both pursuing and defending all types of shipping and insurance claims in China. Wenhao also has experience in ship finance and international trade. Wenhao also regularly contributes to publications. He has contributed book chapters to *Reinsurance Practice and Law* (2009), *Colinvaux' Law of Insurance in Hong Kong* (2009) and *Research Handbook on International Insurance Law and Regulation* (2011). Wenhao has a PhD in insurance law from University of Southampton (2006) and an LLM in maritime law from Dalian Maritime University (2002).

Dr Hua Li (Lena Todd)

Hua Li studied Information Science in East China Normal University, Shanghai, and taught IP law and international private law for six years in China. She got her doctorate in legal comparative study in Cardiff University. She now lives in Hampshire, working as a freelance researcher.

Dr Miao Li

Miao Li graduated from University of Southampton with a doctorate in insurance law and a Master's degree in maritime law. She is a qualified solicitor in England and Wales and a qualified lawyer in China. She has practised law in London, Hong Kong and mainland China.

Dr Andrea Lista

Andrea Lista, Dott. Giur. LLD (Italy), LLM (Soton), PhD (London), is a Legal Consultant, Senior Lecturer in Commercial Law, and the Director of LLM Programmes, School of Law, University of Southampton. Andrea has notably worked as a legal advisor to a multinational enterprise leading in underwater technology and has been a legal consultant to the European Parliament. He has lectured for several years in various areas of commercial law (international trade, competition law, internal market law and corporate law) in Southampton and London, and he is an active legal consultant.

Dr Meixian Song

PhD (University of Southampton), LLM (University College London), LLB (Dalian Maritime University). She is a Lecturer in Maritime Law at the Law School of the University of Exeter, specialising in Maritime and Commercial Law, is a qualified lawyer in China, and is the author of *Causation in Insurance Contract Law* by Informa Law from Routledge.

Professor Pengnan Wang

Pengnan Wang is the senior partner of Wang Pengnan & Co, Dalian, and has been the youngest Professor of Maritime Law in Dalian Maritime University since 1996. He is a leading specialist in the research of law of marine insurance in China, and is a member of International Working Group on Marine Insurance in CMI (Committee Maritime International). He has been awarded as the leading Chinese lawyer in shipping and marine insurance in China by Chambers Asia Pacific, Global Legal Expert and Legal's Finest 200.

Ke Wei

Ke Wei is an Underwriter and Risk Management Specialist with the Special Risk Division, PICC P&C (Dalian Branch International Department). He is involved with special risk projects, including Air Insurance, Hull Insurance for ocean engineering vessels, and Nuclear Insurance. He is also the Project Manager of the Shipping Risk Research & Management Team and successfully leads the Marine Security General Insurance project, which occupies 100 per cent of the market share in China.

Yiqing Yang

Yiqing Yang is a PhD Candidate at Exeter University, where her main research interests are insurance law concerning the principle of good faith and fair dealing in England, China and Australia.

Dr Tao Yu

Tao Yu is a Lecturer at the University of International Business and Economics, as well as a Visiting Scholar at the Insurance Law Centre of Uccon Law School. Tao Yu is also a Consultant on Insurance Law to the China Insurance Regulatory Commission.

Jingbo Zhang

Jingbo Zhang is a Lecturer in Commercial and Maritime Law at the School of Law, University of Southampton. She is also a member of the Southampton Institute of Maritime Law. She coordinated the Chinese-English Insurance Law Conference in April 2013 and the Chinese-English Maritime Law Conference in April 2014.

Table of cases

UNITED KINGDOM CASES
(including Canada and New Zealand)

EU CASES

CHINESE CASES
(including Taiwan)

Table of judicial interpretations and other court instructions

Table of legislation

UNITED KINGDOM

CHINESE LEGISLATION

MISCELLANEOUS

Table of decisions, directives, regulations, treaties, conventions, standard contract terms, guidelines and reports

Part I

Principles of insurance

1 Introduction to Chinese insurance law

Dr Meixian Song[1] *and Yiqing Yang*[2]

This chapter reviews the history of the Chinese insurance industry and introduces current legislation applicable to insurance contracts and their administration. The process of forming and developing the insurance industry, along with the applicable legislation, has involved a significant legal transplantation from common law, particularly English common law, into Chinese legislation. Nonetheless, Chinese insurance law has developed independently and improved rapidly during this period of legislative reform.

1 Brief history of the Chinese insurance industry

1.1 Pre-1949: before the People's Republic of China

Insurance in China has a long history. Thousands of years ago, businessmen traded food and goods between inland China and its coastal cities and conducted freight on the Yangtze River. To prevent the total loss of any one shipment, the businessmen established 'collective agreements' to share the economic losses resulting from any vessel sinking, rapids, bandits or pilferage.[3]

Long before modern insurance formally established itself in China, the relief material reserve system and the idea of sharing losses already existed. The origins of insurance can be traced back to the time of the pre-Qin period.[4] The modern insurance industry, however, was not established until the end of the Qing dynasty (1644–1911),[5] China's last feudal dynasty.

1 Lecturer in Maritie Law at University of Exeter, PhD (Southampton Law School), LLM (UCL), LLB of Dalian Maritime University (China).
2 PhD Candidate (University of Exeter), LLM (Southampton Law School), LLB of Peking University (China).
3 Jennifer A. Meyer, 'Let the buyer beware: economic modernization, insurance reform, and consumer protection in China', 1994, 62 *Fordham L. Rev.* 2125, p 2136.
4 Dongzhou (700–256 BC) had the Spring and Autumn Period and the Warring States Period. The Spring and Autumn Period represents an early formation of the State of China.
5 Fang Su and Jinliang Xu, *The Insurance* [*Bao Xian Xue*], 2003–2004, Beijing: Tsinghua University Press, p 32.

Initially, the Qing dynasty pursued a 'closed-door' policy, resulting in serious troubles both at home and abroad. With the economic expansion of modern foreign capitalist countries, the weak and corrupted Qing government was compelled to accept trade, thus the modern insurance system was first introduced by the British merchants of the East India Company at the beginning of the nineteenth century.[6] In 1805, the Canton Insurance Company was established in Guangzhou by a British businessman.[7] The first Chinese insurance company, the Insurance Capital-Attracting Agency, was founded in Shanghai by China Merchants' Steam Navigation Company on 28 December 1875.[8] After the collapse of the Qing dynasty and the nationalists' rise to power in 1911, the Chinese conducted their insurance business primarily to support foreign trade.[9] The insurance industry retained this structure through the Second World War and the Civil War, until the establishment of the People's Republic of China.

1.2 1949–1979

Until the beginning of the twentieth century, the Chinese insurance industry was dominated by foreign companies. Most insurers were large foreign companies that left China entirely after 1949, though some retreated to Hong Kong.

On 20 October 1949, the Financial Committee of the State Council formed a State-owned enterprise, the People's Insurance Company of China (PICC), in Beijing.[10] The establishment of the PICC marked a crucial development in China's insurance industry. In its first decade of operation, the PICC made rapid and steady progress by setting up regional branches and offices in all of China's provinces, autonomous regions and municipalities.[11] PICC developed a mission to 'protect State assets, ensure industry safety, promote materials flow, provide stability' and, more importantly, to 'collect surplus funds and enriching State assets'.[12]

In 1959, insurance operations were abolished in China, except for foreign (marine and aviation) insurance needs. In the same year, the PICC became a department of the central bank.[13]

6 Dongxia Yang, *Zhong Guo Jin Dai Bao Xian Fa Yi Zhi Yan Jiu*, 2009, Beijing: Law Press China, pp 23–25.

7 Ibid.

8 Ying He and Haitao Zhai, 'Textual research on the first insurance company established by Chinese in China', 2005, 3, Historical Archives.

9 Jennifer A. Meyer, 'Let the buyer beware: economic modernization, insurance reform, and consumer protection in China', 1994, 62 *Fordham L. Rev.* 2125, p 2137.

10 Min Chang, *The Insurance Law*, 2011, Beijing: Law Press China, p 9.

11 'Company History' section, PICC official website, available at: www.picc.com (accessed 14 May 2014).

12 Dingfu Wu, *Development and Reform Report on China Insurance Industry (1979-2003)*, 2004, Beijing: China Economic Publishing House, p 4.

13 'Company History' section, PICC official website, available at: www.picc.com (accessed 14 May 2014).

1.3 1979–2000: economic reforms and China's insurance industry

In 1978, as part of the Deng Xiaoping-initiated economic reforms and open-door policies, in conjunction with the Four Modernisations, China resumed its foreign trade and investment activities, thus the insurance industry began to resume through the re-establishment of the People's Insurance Company of China (PICC). In 1996, the PICC was restructured as PICC Group, as a holding company for its life, property and reinsurance operation, named People's Insurance Company of China Holding Limited. In 1998 the PICC Group was disbanded and the three PICC companies were renamed:[14]

(1) PICC (Life) Insurance Company Limited;
(2) PICC Property Insurance Company Limited; and
(3) PICC Reinsurance Company Limited.

The PICC enjoyed a monopoly position in China's emerging insurance market. This monopoly, however, ended in 1985 with the passage of the Provisional Regulations Regarding the Administration of Insurance Enterprises. These Regulations opened the domestic market to other Chinese insurers. In 1987, the Bank of Communications of China (BOCOM) was authorised to set up insurance business departments in its sub-branches of the different districts. Based on its original insurance business, the new insurance company was formally named the China Pacific Insurance Company (CPIC). From the beginning of 1991 to the end of 1996, CPIC had become a nationwide joint-stock company, with 58 sub-branches in China and two subsidiaries overseas.[15]

Ping An Insurance Company of China (hereinafter PAICC) was the first joint-stock enterprise. It was established by China Merchants' Steam Navigation in Shenzhen, Guangdong province, in March 1988. In September 1992, PAICC, authorised by the People's Bank of China, opened for business throughout China. Since then, PAICC has developed from a regional company into the third national insurance company, and was allowed to handle all types of risks, including international reinsurance business. In 1994, it became the second largest insurance company in China.[16]

In addition, many smaller insurance companies have been established in recent years, including New China Life Insurance Company Ltd, Tai Kang Life Insurance Company Ltd, China United Insurance Company, Yongan

14 Ibid.
15 Jianhua Yuan, *A Brief Introduction of Insurance*, 2005, Chengdu: Southwest University of Finance and Economics Publishing House.
16 Ibid.

Property Insurance Company Ltd, Huatai Insurance Company of China Ltd and Dazhong Insurance Company Ltd. Most of them have developed into nationwide insurance companies. Domestic competitors in the marketplace have gradually eroded the PICC monopoly. Rapid growth in foreign-related insurance business and foreign-owned insurance companies can also be observed during this period.

Economic reforms led foreign enterprises to play a role in the revival of China's insurance industry beginning in 1992. In September 1992, the People's Bank of China granted American Insurance Group[17] (hereinafter AIG) a licence to begin selling individual life and property insurance in Shanghai. Until 1995, the PICC owned nine foreign-related and overseas insurance institutions, some of which were holding companies or group companies.

From 1992 to 2000, China gradually approved the re-entry of 16 additional leading foreign insurers. Economic reforms have increased foreign participation in the insurance industry in China.[18]

1.4 Present potential of China's insurance industry

Since the reforms and opening up, and especially since the 16th National Congress of the Communist Party of China in 2002, China's insurance industry has grown quickly: the range of services on offer has been expanded, the market system has been gradually perfected, laws and regulations have been completed step by step and the supervision level has improved.

1.5 Today's PICC and China Re

With 60 years of operating history, the PICC brand enjoys a prominent reputation in the Chinese insurance market, as well as in the international insurance market. The People's Insurance Company (Group) of China Limited is the largest insurance and financial services provider in China, with 11 subsidiaries, namely PICC Property and Casualty Company Limited, PICC Asset Management Company Limited, PICC Health Insurance Company Limited, China Life Insurance (Group) Company, PICC Investment Holding Company Limited, the People's Insurance Company of China (Hong Kong) Limited, PICC Investment and Asset Management Company Limited, Beijing No. 88 West Changan Road Development Company Limited, Zhongshen International Insurance Brokers Company Limited, China Insurance Brokers Company Limited and

17 American Insurance Group (AIG) of the United States was founded in Shanghai in 1919.

18 'Company History' section, PICC official website, available at: www.picc.com (accessed 14 May 2014).

PIBC.[19] Two of the flagship subsidiaries are introduced below, as is China Reinsurance (Group) Corporation.

1.5.1 PICC Property and Casualty Company Ltd

PICC Property and Casualty Company Ltd (PICC P&C), as the largest property insurance company in mainland China, was established by the People's Insurance Company (Group) of China Limited (previously known as PICC Holding Company, hereinafter referred to as PICC Group) in July 2003, under the validation of the State Council and approval of the China Insurance Regulatory Commission (CIRC), with a registered capital of CNY 12.25598 billion.[20] It was once the People's Insurance Company of China, which was founded by the People's Bank of China under the approval of the Committee of Finance and Economy of the Central Government on 20 October 1949.

PICC P&C is a flagship subsidiary of the PICC Group and a Fortune 500 company.[21] On 6 November 2003, the company successfully launched its IPO in Hong Kong, becoming the first large Chinese State-owned financial enterprise to go public overseas. In 2012, the company collected more than CNY 190 billion of premium. It has a steady ranking of number one in Asia, and is in second place among the single-branded property insurance companies in the world.[22]

1.5.2 China Life Insurance (Group) Company[23]

China Life Insurance (Group) Company, headquartered in Beijing, is a large State-owned financial and insurance company. In 1995, China's first Insurance Act came into force. In 1996, according to the requirements of the Insurance Act, non-life insurance and life insurance should be operated separately. PICC (Life) Co. Ltd was set up by taking over the existing life insurance business from PICC and by reorganising 17 local life insurance companies, entering an era of separate operation.

In March 1999, PICC (Life) Co. Ltd was renamed China Life Insurance Company and became a solely State-owned corporation under the direct leadership of the State Council. Since then, China Life has provided life

19 'Group Introduction' section ('Corporate Profile' section), PICC official website, available at: www.picc.com (accessed 14 May 2014).
20 See www.picc.com (accessed 14 May 2014).
21 See PICC P&C official website, available at: www.piccnet.com.cn/cn/gywm/gsjj/index.shtml (accessed 14 May 2014).
22 Ibid.
23 See the official website of China Life, 'History & Culture' section, available at: www.chinalife.com.cn/publish/yw/584/index.html (accessed 14 May 2014).

insurance coverage to millions of Chinese people, assuming the duty of serving economic development and safeguarding social stability. With the approval of the State Council and the China Insurance Regulatory Commission, the former China Life Insurance Company was restructured as China Life Insurance (Group) Company in 2003. It includes the subsidiaries China Life Insurance Company Limited, China Life Asset Management Company Limited, China Life Property & Casualty Insurance Company Limited, China Life Pension Company Limited, China Life Insurance (Overseas) Company Limited, China Life Investment Holding Company Limited and Insurance Professional College. Its business covers life insurance, property and casualty insurance, pension plans (corporate annuity), asset management, industrial investment and overseas operations. Through capital operation, it has invested in several banks, security firms and other non-financial institutions.

1.5.3 China Re[24]

The China Re Group originated from the People's Insurance Company of China (PICC), which was established in October 1949. In 1996, PICC Reinsurance Company Limited was founded on the basis of the reinsurance department of PICC, filling the blank in China's insurance history of not having a reinsurance company. On 18 March 1999, the China Reinsurance Company was set up, which was a historical transition in becoming a modern commercial reinsurance company. On 22 December 2003, China Reinsurance Company was restructured into China Reinsurance (Group) Company, which marked the beginning of group management and separate operation of life and P&C business in China's reinsurance industry. In October 2007, China Reinsurance (Group) Company was restructured into China Reinsurance (Group) Corporation, moving into a brand new era of group management, professionalised and internationalised operation.

Along with several significant transformations, China Re Group has played a positive part in cultivating China's reinsurance industry, facilitating the growth of the direct insurance market and supporting social and economic development. As the insurer of insurers, China Re Group has taken on a dominant and leading role in China's insurance market. As a leading company in China's reinsurance industry, China Re Group has also played an increasingly important role in the international reinsurance market.

Through its six subsidiaries (China Property & Casualty Reinsurance Company Ltd, China Life Reinsurance Company Ltd, China Continent Property & Casualty Insurance Company Ltd, China Re Asset Management Company Ltd, China Insurance Media Company Ltd and Huatai Insurance

24 See the China Re official website, available at: www.chinare.com.cn;http://eng.chinare.com.cn (English) (accessed 14 May 2014).

Agency & Consultant Service Ltd), China Re Group provides comprehensive products and services including not only reinsurance, but also direct insurance, asset management, insurance brokerage and insurance media service.

2 Insurance organisations and legal sources

2.1 Insurance organisations

Once the domestic business of PICC had been fully reactivated in 1980, at the end of 1982 PICC was reformed into a State-owned corporation directly governed by the State Council and officially detached from the People's Bank of China from 1 January 1984. Nevertheless, the People's Bank of China remained the supervision institution of the insurance industry until 1998.

On 18 November 1998, the China Insurance Regulatory Commission (CIRC), 中国保险监督管理委员会, was established and authorised by the State Council to conduct administration, supervision and regulation of the Chinese insurance market, and to ensure that the insurance industry operates stably in compliance with the law.[25] This institution was created with the purpose of taking over the role hitherto played by the People's Bank of China in supervising the insurance industry. The specified major responsibilities of the CIRC include making policies and drafting laws, examining and approving qualifications of the relevant participants of the industry, approving or filing the premium rates and the clauses, supervising the market conduct of insurance companies and the management of prudential funds, investigating and imposing penalties on certain types of irregularities and other duties authorised by the State Council. It is noteworthy that the CIRC also supervises the overseas insurance organisations established by domestic insurance and non-insurance organisations according to the law.[26]

The Insurance Association of China (IAC), 中国保险行业协会, was set up on 23 February 2001. It represents the collective interests of China's insurance industry and it is run under the supervision of the CIRC. The association makes statements on issues of common interest, promotes exchange at the international level and also acts as an advocate for high standards of customer service in the insurance industry. The IAC has five working committees, namely the Life Insurance Working Committee, the Property Insurance Working Committee, the Insurance Agency & Broker

25 For a general introduction of the CIRC, see: http://english.gov.cn/2005-10/01/content_74050.htm (accessed 14 May 2014).

26 For the details of the major responsibilities, see the government official website translation, available at: http://english.gov.cn//2005-10/01/content_74051.htm (accessed 9 April 2013).

Working Committee, the Actuarial Working Committee and the Corporate Governance Special Committee. So far, its membership consists of 150 insurance companies, 37 agencies and brokerages and 36 local insurance associations.[27]

The Chinese Insurance Law Society, 中国保险法学研究会, was set up in March 2011. This is a nationwide academic community dedicated to theoretical research and legal practice in the insurance law field. The newly established organisation is quite different from the British Insurance Law Association, which plays a comprehensive and far-reaching role in its field.

2.2 Chinese insurance law sources

Unlike England, the Chinese mainland operates a civil law system. Legislation, rather than case law, is the primary legal source. In contrast to some legislation adopted in common law countries, notably the English Marine Insurance Act 1906, Chinese legislative instruments are created to make law prospectively, rather than as a statement of currently existing good law. Among the promulgated legislative instruments in China, the Civil Law Code contains a couple of provisions regulating general issues of insurance contract law. Moreover, the Chinese Contracts Act also provides some principles and default rules on the basis of contract law theories in order to fill any legal voids arising from the absence of specific provision in the Chinese Insurance Act. As to marine insurance law, Chapter 12 of the Chinese Maritime Code (CMC Art 216–Art 256) (see Appendix II) provides rules applicable particularly to marine insurance contracts. The CMC came into effect in November 1992, in response to the rapid expansion of marine insurance business and the dramatic improvements of non-marine insurance law. The reforms to the chapter on marine insurance were subject to heated discussion at the proposal stage.

Besides commercial insurance, social insurance is also a key part of the insurance industry and legal regime in China. The Social Insurance Act 2011 was adopted on 28 October 2010, and became effective from 1 July 2011. This is the first national law in China's social welfare system that covers pension, basic medical insurance, unemployment insurance, work-related injury insurance and maternity insurance. It clearly states that non-nationals who work in China must participate in all aforementioned aspects.

2.2.1 Chinese Insurance Act 1995

The Chinese Insurance Act is the most important piece of legislation on general insurance contracts and insurance industry administration. The first

27 See the official website of IAC, available at: www.iachina.cn/01/01/ (accessed 14 May 2014), translated by the author.

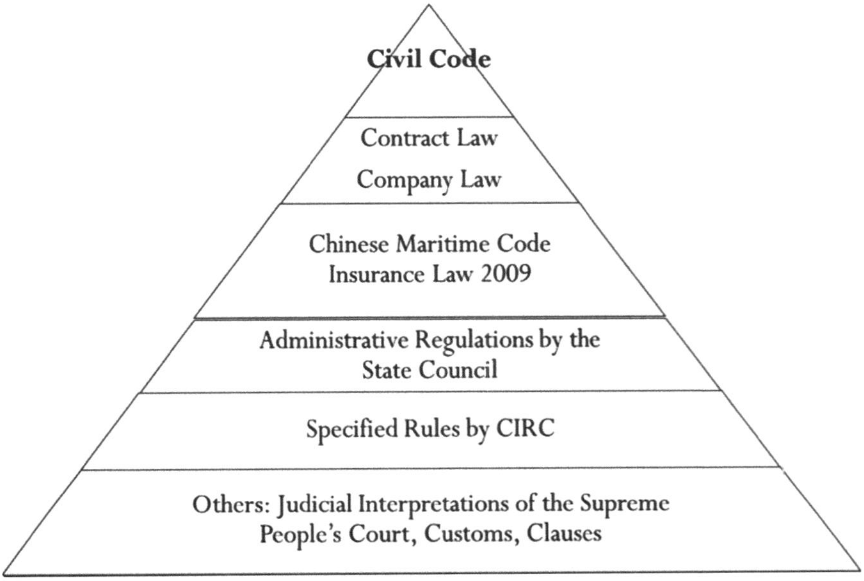

Figure 1.1 Structure of legal sources of Chinese insurance law

attempt to draft independent and complete legislation on insurance was made by the People's Bank of China in 1991, primarily purporting to put in place a more workable and solid legal foundation for the insurance industry. As a result, the Chinese Insurance Act first came into effect in October 1995 (hereinafter the Insurance Act 1995). This Act regulates both insurance contracts and insurance industry administration, and consists of eight chapters and 152 articles. Chapter 1, 'General provisions', contains rules universally applied throughout the Act. Chapter 2, consisting of 60 articles, sets out principles of insurance contract law and specific issues of property insurance and life insurance. The remaining chapters are concerned with insurance companies, agencies and brokerage, operational rules and supervision of the Chinese insurance market.

2.2.2 Chinese Insurance Act 2002

In response to China's commitments in relation to the accession to the WTO at the end of 2001, and due to the rapid expansion of the Chinese insurance industry, the first reform of the Insurance Act 1995 took place in October 2002, and the revised Insurance Act came into effect on 1 January 2002 (hereinafter the Insurance Act 2002). This Act retained the original structure of the Insurance Act 1995. As to the content, this reform focused primarily on the openness and supervision of the market. The parts pertaining to insurance contract law were almost untouched except for an added emphasis on utmost good faith.

With respect to the openness of the market, the Insurance Act 2002 mildly reduced some restrictions. For instance, it had been strictly provided that an insurance company must not concurrently underwrite property insurance business and life insurance business. The Insurance Act 2002 allowed property insurance companies to sell short-term health insurance and accidental injury insurance. Moreover, the Insurance Act 2002 was made applicable to foreign-invested insurance companies, either solely or jointly invested, and branches of foreign insurance companies.[28]

As the CIRC was set up in 1998, the Insurance Act 2002 affirmed and emphasised the CIRC's function of supervising the insurance industry in statutory form. On the one hand, the law authorised the CIRC to exercise most of the functions mentioned above and also to impose more severe penalties on the irregularities. On the other hand, the CIRC was no longer permitted to interfere in the concrete operations of insurance companies in making clauses and fixing premium rates. The CIRC was merely entitled to decide whether to approve the rate or clauses submitted by the companies in the case of insurance involving public policy or compulsory insurance. In other cases, the CIRC should only file the reported items.

Overall, the first revision was not a dramatic reform to the Insurance Act 1995. It mainly enhanced the legal basis to administrate the entire insurance industry in the context of the gradual opening up of the market.

2.2.3 Chinese Insurance Act 2009

The second reform to the Insurance Act 1995 was carried out in 2009 in the context of challenges presented by the global economic recession. The Insurance Act 2009 retains the original structure with minor changes to individual chapters. Unlike the previous revision, however, this revision is regarded as a major reform, such that almost every Article is revised to some extent. The emphasis of the reforms is on insurance contract law.

Taking two notable examples, first, insurable interest is now stated differently in relation to life and property insurance. In compliance with Article 12, the assured under a policy of life insurance must have an insurable interest both at the time of concluding the insurance contract and at the time of loss or damage, whereas property assureds are only required to have an insurable interest at the time of loss. Moreover, the term is given a wide definition, namely any legitimate form of interest recognised by law in the subject matter insured. It should also be noted that Article 48 provides that a lack of insurable interest in property insurance contracts does not go to

28 For further discussion of the distinctions between forms of undertakings, see Chapter 2.

the root of the effect of contracts, but is merely a precondition for claiming the indemnity. In relation to marine insurance, due to the absence of provisions in the Chinese Maritime Code, the Insurance Act 2009 is the direct and primary legal authority.

Second, unlike in English insurance law, breaches of utmost good faith in Chinese insurance law are not neatly categorised into non-disclosure and misrepresentation. Article 16 of the Insurance Act 2009 clarifies that the assureds shall answer the questions of the insurers on the basis of actual facts. A particularity of this Article is that it places a time limit on the insurer to exercise the right of termination, namely within 30 days from the date of receipt of information about breaches, or within two years after the conclusion of the insurance contract. First, unlike in the English Marine Insurance Act, the language used in the Insurance Act 2009 is 'termination' rather than avoidance in terms of the validity of the contract. Second, on the expiry of those time limits, insurers will be liable for the indemnity. In English law, the remedies available to insurers are waiver by election or estoppel, and no time bar applies.

2.2.4 Regulations and rules

Supplementary to the law made by the legislative authority, the State Council produces many administrative regulations. The CIRC, as the supervision institution, also has the power to make relevant regulatory stipulations.[29] These Regulations and Rules are important for the operation of insurance in China. More importantly, the State Council and the CIRC have promulgated some specific legal instruments on foreign-invested insurance companies.

Following China's accession to the WTO on 11 December 2001, the Chinese insurance market has gradually opened up to foreign insurers and insurance-related service providers. Foreign life insurers have been permitted to provide property insurance and insurance of persons since 2002, and group life insurance, health insurance and annuity and other pension-like products since 11 December 2004. Exactly two years later, foreign insurance brokers were permitted to set up wholly owned subsidiaries in China by the CIRC. Compulsory motor third party liability (MTPL) insurance has been open to foreign-invested insurance companies since 1 May 2012.

There are two administrative Regulations of the State Council particularly relating to insurance issues, namely Regulations on Administration of

29 See: www.circ.gov.cn/web/site0/tab5176/ (accessed 14 May 2014). These regulations and rules can be found at the CIRC official website, although currently only versions in Chinese are available.

Foreign-Invested Insurance Companies[30] (中华人民共和国外资保险公司管理条例) ('the Regulations') and Measures on Compulsory Motor Vehicle Accident Liability Insurance (机动车交通事故责任强制保险条例) ('the Measures'). The Regulations came into effect on 1 February 2002. Article 5 states that foreign-funded insurance companies shall abide by the laws and regulations of China and shall not infringe upon the social and public interests of China. The Regulations cover the following issues: set-up and registration, business scope, supervision and administration, termination and liquidation, and legal liabilities. As to the Measures, they were first enacted in March 2006. However, the 2006 Measures provided that only domestic insurance companies were allowed to underwrite such business. The first amendment to the Measures, which was effected on 1 May 2012, states that any insurance company can insure such risks with the approval of the CIRC. The second amendment was effected on 1 March 2013, just adding a new Article 43.[31]

With respect to the departmental rules enacted by the CIRC, they are mostly made in the form of CIRC orders, which constitute the main portion of the legal instruments applicable to the insurance industry. These rules mainly cover the administration of insurance business, insurance organisation, the use of insurance funds etc.[32] Finally, it is worth mentioning here the Rules on Implementing Regulations on Administration of Foreign-Invested Insurance Companies (中华人民共和国外资保险公司管理条例实施细则). The Rules, which entered into effect on 15 June 2004, provide further guidance on the establishment and operation of foreign-invested insurance companies, elaborating on the Regulations mentioned above by the State Council. The Rules particularly further clarify the equity and capital, and the application requirements.[33]

30 The English translation of the full text is available at: www.china.org.cn/business/laws_regulations/2007-06/22/content_1214775.htm (accessed 14 May 2014).

31 This new Article is regarding the insurance liability between trailer and tractor. A trailer is not required to have insurance, but the insurance on the tractor shall be liable to the insured loss.

32 Guojian Xu *et al.*, *Insurance Law in China*, 2008, Hong Kong: CCH Hong Kong Limited, p 13.

33 The English translation of the full text is available at: http://english.wzj.saic.gov.cn/nd/nd_2004052502.html (accessed 27 May 2014).

2 The law relating to access to insurance markets in China

Professor Tingzhong Fu[1]

1 Introduction

'Access to the market' refers to the conditions and procedures applicable to an entity wishing to enter into the market of one country. The standards applicable to access for foreign capital to the market of another country depends on the commitments made by the government in its protocol on accession to the WTO. The acceding WTO member, in promising to open the domestic market to insurance services, should ensure that any treatment of foreign suppliers in future shall not be less favourable than that which has been promised in the letter of commitment.

Since the 1980s, a policy of reform and openness to the outside world has been implemented in China. This reform has entailed abolishing the original economical system so as to change the planned economy into a market economy, while openness refers to the opening of the gates of our country to promote economic coordination with foreign countries and to encourage foreign capital or modern science and technology.

Under the planned economy, which had been implemented for more than 40 years, all problems could be solved by the government of the State. When a certain enterprise suffered serious losses due to natural calamities or accidents, the government could, by virtue of its power, concentrate the materials of certain districts or even the whole country for remedial action so as to recover its production and assist the return to daily life. Under such a system, the function of insurance is not obvious. However, under the system of a market economy, the government is not entitled to interfere with the production or activities of management; the deficits of individual enterprises shall be borne by the enterprises themselves. Only at this stage do the role and function of commercial insurance become evident. In order to protect the construction of the market economy, it is imperative to develop

1 Professor, School of Law, Tsinghua University, Beijing, China; Guest Professor, Dalian Maritime University (Dalian, China) and Shanghai Maritime University (Shanghai, China).

commercial insurance. Against this background, the first Insurance Act was issued in 1995. In this sense, the introduction of the Insurance Act constitutes one of the important milestones showing that the economic system of China has been turned towards the direction of a market economy. However, at the time when the Insurance Act 1995 was promulgated, China was at the initial stage during which the economic system was being transformed from a planned economy. Furthermore, China was at that time not a member of the WTO and its market (including the insurance market) had not been opened to the outside world. For this reason, some imprints of the old period would unavoidably feature in the law. In 2001, China accessed the WTO, and in that connection the Chinese government made certain commitments in the Accession Protocol. In order to meet those commitments and to effect normalisation in the management of the market, the 'Regulations Regarding the Management of Foreign Capital Insurance Companies' (the 'Regulations') were issued by the State Council on 12 December 2001[2] and on 13 May 2004, the 'Rules for the Implementation of the Regulations' (the 'Rules') were issued by the China Insurance Regulatory Commission under the authorisation of the State Council. The Rules provided a fully detailed legal basis for foreign insurance companies' accession to the market of China.

2 Definition of foreign capital insurance company

In the light of concepts defined in the Regulations, the foreign capital insurance company is a general concept that refers to joint-venture insurance companies, exclusive investment companies and the branches of foreign insurance companies established within the territory of China.[3] In view of the fact that the legal systems of Hong Kong, Macau and Taiwan are different from that of the Chinese mainland, the legal framework stipulated for foreign insurance companies entering into the market of China shall apply equally to applicants from the above jurisdictions.[4]

2.1 Sino-foreign joint-venture insurance companies

Joint-venture insurance companies, as the term suggests, refers to companies that are jointly invested by insurance companies or financial organisations of China and of foreign countries in accordance with Chinese legislation. Such companies have an absolute status as legal persons that

2 The 'Regulations' were revised by the State Council in May 2013 and the revised 'Regulations' came into force on 1 August 2013. Only Article 7 of the old 'Regulation' was revised.

3 Article 2 of the 'Regulations'.

4 Article 39 of the 'Regulations'.

can independently enjoy rights and bear legal liabilities. This mode of organisation is conducive to accession of insurance companies to the international market, but the proportion of foreign capital is limited to the legal standard. More specifically, the proportion of foreign capital is not allowed to exceed 50 per cent; this proportion applies not only to joint-venture companies engaged in property insurance, but also to those engaged in life insurance.[5]

2.2 Exclusive investment company

'Exclusive investment company' refers to insurance companies that are invested in wholly by foreign insurance companies themselves and established through lawful registration within the territory of China. By the end of 2012, 21 foreign insurance companies in which the investment is exclusively by foreign insurance companies have been registered in China; among them, 20 companies are engaged in original insurance of property and only one company carries on life insurance.

2.3 Branch office

Branch office, as the term suggests, refers to a branch corporation established in the host country by foreign insurance companies. As a component part of the company, the branch office has no qualification of independent subject in the sense of civil legislation. While it is entitled to operate certain business within the scope approved and permitted by the government of the host country, the services performed by the head office include acceptance of business and settlement of claims, and liabilities shall be borne by its head office. Since the viability and stable management of a branch depends on the supervision of the head office by the authorities of its home country, once the head office has gone bankrupt due to deficient supervision, the consequences will certainly affect its branch. In other words, China will be at risk in permitting this type of organisation to access the market of China. For this reason only, the examination and permission performed by the Chinese government for this mode of organisation should be very strict.

3 The commitments made by the Chinese government at the time of accession to the WTO

The commitment to market access is set out in Part Three (Specific Commitments) of the General Agreement on Trade in Services (GATS).

5 Article 3 of the 'Rules'.

This means that the opening of the market is not a general or absolute obligation; only when it is listed in the Schedules of Commitments through negotiation does it have legal force in relation to its members. There is no exception to trade in insurance services. The Chinese government has made commitments on the relevant trade in services (including insurance) in Appendix 9 (Schedules of specific commitments), which is annexed to the Protocol on the Accession. The commitments in respect of insurance (including life insurance, health insurance, annuity insurance, property insurance, reinsurance and other subsidiary service of insurance) are as follows.

3.1 The scope of insurance commitments

The commitments made by the Chinese government on the service of cross-border supply of insurance includes: reinsurance, international marine insurance, brokers' services for large-scale commercial activity and brokers' services for international maritime transport and air transport.

3.2 The commitments on type of organisation of foreign capital insurance companies

With reference to the opening of the insurance market, China has drawn on the experience of many developing countries. The specific commitments are given item by item. Under the commitments, the particular area and schedule for opening is conclusively defined. In the first place, China chose the sections or areas to which the impact will not be serious. Furthermore, various limitations were attached to the commitments, including limitation on the progress of opening markets, amendments to the law, the quota and the proportion of the service:

(1) From the date of accession, any foreign property insurance companies are allowed to establish a branch office or joint-venture companies in China. The proportion of shares possessed by foreign capital may reach 51 per cent.
(2) Within two years after China's accession to the WTO, foreign property insurance companies are allowed to set up a subsidiary corporation with exclusive investment within the territory of China. The subsidiary corporations are independent legal persons for the purposes of Chinese legislation, but remain under the control of the company's head office. Therefore, the government of China is entitled to adopt measures similar to those applicable to Chinese native companies so as to ensure that the operation of the business can be carried out under the condition of safety and stability. Due to this reason, the Chinese government would be willing to accept foreign insurance companies in the form of subsidiaries to enter into its market.

(3) From the date of accession, foreign life insurance companies are allowed to establish joint-venture companies in China, the capital share under foreign ownership may reach 50 per cent and they can also freely choose the partners for joint ventures instead of obtaining a nomination by government.
(4) In the field of brokers, foreign companies are allowed to set up joint-venture companies to operate a broker's business for reinsurance, international maritime transport, air transport and land transport. The share owned by foreign capital in the joint-venture company is not allowed to exceed 50 per cent; nevertheless, the proportion of shares can be raised to 51 per cent within three years after China's accession to the WTO. In addition to the above, it is permitted to set up a subsidiary office within five years after China's accession. With regard to other brokering services, no commitments have been made.
(5) The limitation of areas of service is to be phased out and the establishment of branches within the company is permissible under such conditions.

3.3 Commitments on scope of region

Under the policy of market economy, China is to progressively open the market of insurance, or, in other words, China will open the market by means of a step-by-step process. Under this principle, foreign insurance companies may only be established in the districts nominated by the regulatory authority (the China Insurance Regulatory Commission) and a branch office could only operate business within the administrative districts (including provinces, autonomous regions or municipalities directly under the Central government) in which the company is situated. If a joint-venture company or exclusive investment company wants to operate business beyond its region of service, then a branch office should be established in that district.[6] In particular, the commitments in relation to the scope of business are as follows:

(1) From the date of accession, it was permissible for foreign life insurance companies, property insurance companies and the insurance broker companies to provide insurance services in Shanghai, Guangzhou, Dalian, Shenzhen and Foshan of Guangdong province. All these cities are situated in coastal areas.
(2) Within two years after accession, foreign life insurance companies, property insurance companies and insurance broker companies were able to provide insurance services in Beijing, Chengdu, Chongqing,

6 Article 27 of the 'Rules'.

Fuzhou, Suzhou, Xiamen, Ningbo, Shenyang, Wuhan and Tianjin. That is to say, the scope of services could be extended to inland cities.

(3) Three years after accession, the regional limitations were abolished.

3.4 Commitments about the scope of business

Foreign companies are entitled to provide insurance services wholly or partly within the scope of business approved by the China Insurance Regulatory Commission:

(1) At the time of China's accession to the WTO, foreign capital insurance companies engaged in non-life insurance were permitted, without geographical limitation, to provide the service of 'large-scale commercial insurance' and the service of 'Master Policy', which covers different subject matters insured of the same legal person. Such insurance companies were also permitted to provide the service of non-life insurance for overseas enterprises, as well as the services of property insurance, liability insurance and credit insurance for foreign investment enterprises located in the territory of China.

(2) Two years after China's accession to the WTO, foreign non-life insurance companies were permitted to provide a 'comprehensive service' of non-life insurance for Chinese and foreign customers.

(3) From the date of China's accession to the WTO, licences may be conferred upon foreign companies for providing reinsurance services for life or property by means of the establishment of branch offices, joint-venture companies or exclusive investment companies, and there are no limitations upon the region of service or the quantity of licences to be issued.

4 Qualifications of foreign insurance companies

4.1 Property requirements

The investor should be an insurance company that has been engaged in commercial insurance for more than 30 years. Its capital by the end of year before the application was submitted should not be less than USD 500,000,000. As to the broker company of insurance, its whole value of property should be more than USD 500,000,000. The purpose in requiring such credentials and qualities is to perform the selection necessary so as to encourage powerful companies of high quality to enter into the market of China.

4.2 The representative office

The foreign company investing to establish a company in China should have a representative office that has been working in China for two years without interruption. Since the representative office is an administrative office of the head office abroad, it has no qualification to be engaged in insurance or investment or other insurance business, except to maintain business relationships with the consumers of its head office and exploring commercial opportunities for it. The functions of the representative office include: (1) getting in touch with the government or business circles of the host country on behalf of the head office; (2) to be a guide for the establishment of the company in the host country; and (3) to implement management or control of overseas organisations of the company. Since the activities of the representative office are not in the nature of actual access to the market, the scrutiny of the China Insurance Regulatory Commission is relatively relaxed.

4.3 Sufficient registered capital

The registered capital of foreign companies should not be less than that of the legal standard. The minimum capital of a joint-venture company or exclusive invested company is RMB 200,000,000 or monies equivalent to this sum. If a foreign company is planning to set up a branch office in China, the head office should allot as operating bankroll not less than RMB 200,000,000 or monies equivalent to this sum with freely exchanged currency.[7] For a company established before the 'Regulations' became effective, if the capital and bankroll is less than RMB 200,000,000, the difference should be replenished. If the scope of business or the scale of management is extended, the China Insurance Regulatory Commission should increase the minimum amount of registered capital or bankrolls mentioned above. The 'registered capital' should be money that can be actually paid.[8]

4.4 Well-developed insurance supervision system

Foreign insurance companies must prove in their application that: (1) there is a well-developed legal system in respect of supervision of insurance in the home country; (2) the company is subject to effective supervision by the authorities of its home country; (3) the application for establishment of an insurance company in China has been approved by its home country; and (4) the company is in conformity with prudential requirements stipulated by the Insurance Regulatory Commission.[9] The prudential requirements in the sense of the 'Regulation' consist of five conditions, namely: reasonable framework for governing the legal person; a stable system

7 Article 6 of the 'Regulations'.
8 Article 5 of the 'Regulations'.
9 Article 8 of the 'Regulations'.

for controlling risks; a well-developed system in respect of internal supervision of the company; an effective system of information management; and good order and condition of the management, there being no record of grave activities of violation of law in the history of the company.[10]

5 National treatment for foreign companies

5.1 Compulsory insurance

'Compulsory insurance' refers to insurance that is mandatory in accordance with an administrative order or regulations for particular groups of people or enterprises. In China, compulsory insurance is at present limited to the scope of liability insurance for motorised vehicles covering third party liability, endowment insurance, unemployment insurance and the insurance of common reserved funds for housing. The essence of compulsory insurance is to impose the will of government compulsively on the people; therefore, the principle of freedom of contract is necessarily limited to some extent. Strictly speaking, compulsory insurance is not in the nature of a commercial activity, precisely for this reason. It is provided in the Insurance Act (2009) that insurance companies or any other organisations should not compel any persons to sign an insurance contract.[11]

5.2 Reinsurance

From the date of China's accession to the WTO, foreign insurance companies within the territory of China are required to arrange reinsurance for the whole business by Chinese insurance companies nominated by the authorities. The proportion of reinsurance is to be gradually reduced to 20 per cent for the first year, 15 per cent for the second year, 10 per cent for the third year and 5 per cent for the fourth year. However, any compulsory reinsurance should be cancelled in the fifth year. The reinsurance mentioned above is aimed at the basic risks of all business.

6 Procedure for application

6.1 Application

An applicant who wants to establish an insurance company in China should submit an application in written form, attaching a copy of the business licence issued by the authority of its home country; a certificate showing that the company satisfies the solvency standard; the statement issued

10 Article 11 of the 'Rules'.
11 Article 11 of the Insurance Act 2009.

by authority of its home country, the function of which is to certify that the authority of its home country has approved its application for establishment of an insurance company in China; the company's constitution; the annual reports for the last three years; a research report demonstrating practicability and the scheme for preparation of establishment; the list of persons in charge of preparation with their curricula vitae and certificates of qualification attached; the background materials about the Chinese partner investor if the company is in the nature of a joint venture; and other relevant materials as stipulated by the China Insurance Regulatory Commission.[12]

6.2 Examination

The China Insurance Regulatory Commission should carry out a preliminary examination of the application as soon as it has been received and decide within six months whether or not the application can be accepted. For an application that has been accepted, a formal application form should be issued to the applicant. A motivated notice in written form should be given when an application is rejected.

6.3 Preparation of establishment

Preparations should be completed within one year from the date of receipt of the formal application form. If for legitimate reasons the work cannot be completed within the stipulated period, the deadline can be extended by three months. However, if the preparations cannot be completed within the extended deadline, the decision of acceptance made by the China Insurance Regulatory Commission automatically becomes invalid.

6.4 Approval

Once preparations for establishment have been completed, the applicant should submit the filled out application form and other relevant documents to the Insurance Regulatory Commission for final approval. The documents to be attached to the application form include: a report on the preparations; the constitution of the company to be established; the investor and the sum of its investment; a capital verification certificate issued by a statutory capital verification institution; a certificate of authorisation for responsible persons issued by the head office; a list of high ranking managerial staff; their curricula vitae and certificates of qualification; the business plan and reinsurance programme of the proposed company for the first three years; the insurance clauses to be applied in China; the method of calculation of

12 Article 9 of the 'Regulations'.

premium rates and reserves for liabilities; and information about the place of business and facilities of the company to be established. For the branch office of a company, the head office should also provide a letter of guarantee undertaking the liabilities of paying tax and debt; as for a joint-venture company, the contract of joint management is also needed, as well as other relevant documents required by the regulatory authority.[13]

The China Insurance Regulatory Commission should decide in accordance with the 'Regulation' whether or not the application can be approved. The decision should be made within 60 days from the date of receipt of the full set of materials and the business licence should be issued if the application is approved. As for applications that are not approved, notice in written form explaining the reasons should be given to the applicant. The establishment of a branch office in China by a foreign capital company should also be examined by the Insurance Regulatory Commission according to the relevant Regulations.[14]

6.5 Registration

If an application for establishment of an insurance company has been approved by the regulatory authority, the applicant should submit its business licence to the Industrial and Commercial Bureau for registration so as to obtain a business licence.[15]

6.6 Drawing the cash deposit

Foreign capital insurance companies should draw a cash deposit of 20 per cent from the total sum of its registered capital or working capital. The cash deposit should be reserved in the bank nominated by the Insurance Regulatory Commission for the purpose of clearing debts in the case of liquidation of the company.[16]

7 Supervision and management of foreign capital insurance companies

7.1 Prohibition of illegal associated transactions

An 'associated transaction', as the term suggests, is a transaction conducted between associated enterprises. According to Article 20 of the 'Regulation', associated enterprises refers to companies that have some connection in

13 Article 11 of the 'Regulations'.
14 Article 14 of the 'Regulations'.
15 Article 12 of the 'Regulations'.
16 Article 13 of the 'Regulations'.

economic interests. This includes three types of circumstances as follows: (1) relation of control in respect of shareholding or investment; (2) shares and investments are under the control of the same person; (3) other connection of economic interests.[17]

Associated transactions are unavoidable under the market economy paradigm. The advantage of associated transactions is that by virtue of the administrative power of the head office, commercial contracts concluded by associated companies can be fulfilled preferentially so as to save on transaction costs that would arise in ordinary transactions. Their disadvantages are also obvious. Associated companies may use administrative powers to promote transactions, which may easily lead to unfairness in respect of price or mode of transaction in circumstances of lack of competition, thus the benefit of some shareholders could be compromised and creditors may also be disadvantaged. For this reason, it is provided in the 'Regulation' that any business of reinsurance and other associated transactions in respect of purchases and sales of property must be approved by the China Insurance Regulatory Commission.

7.2 Management reporting[18]

Foreign capital insurance companies must, within three months of the end of the year, submit their annual report in written form to China Insurance Regulatory Commission so as to make it public. If any of the following circumstances have occurred in the head office, the branch corporation should, within 10 days from the date of the event, submit a report in written form to the Insurance Regulatory Commission:

(1) change of company's name, main responsible person or place of registration;
(2) change of capital;
(3) change in shareholders holding more than 1 per cent of the total sum of share capital of the company;
(4) adjustment of the scope of business;
(5) any penalty imposed by the authority of its home country;
(6) serious deficit;
(7) separation, merger, dissolution, revocation or bankruptcy according to the law; and
(8) other circumstances provided for by the CIRC.[19]

17 Article 20 of the 'Regulations'.
18 Articles 21 and 22 of the 'Regulations'.
19 Article 22 of the 'Regulations'.

7.3 Winding up and liquidation of foreign capital companies

The winding up of a company refers to activities and procedures for settlement of every kind of legal relations after the dissolution of a company so as to eliminate the personality of the company. Winding up is to take place in the following circumstances:

(1) The company is dissolved with the approval of the authority owing to the occurrence of separation, combination and other events regulated in the constitution of the company. If a foreign capital insurance company is dissolved, then a liquidation committee should be organised for clearing its debts, while a foreign capital insurance company engaged in life insurance cannot be dissolved except in the event of separation or combination.
(2) The company is revoked owing to violation of law and administrative regulations. In this case, a public announcement of liquidation should be made through the newspapers at least three times from the date of the organisation of the liquidation committee. The contents of the public announcement should be ratified by the Insurance Regulatory Commission.
(3) The company is announced to be bankrupt by the court since it has no financial ability to pay its debts as they fall due. During the period from the announcement of the bankruptcy to the date of liquidation, none of its property may be moved overseas.

7.4 Legal liabilities[20]

A company that violates the law or regulations of the host country should bear administrative liability or even criminal liability in case it has committed a criminal offence.

7.4.1 Administrative liability

Administrative penalties apply to activities violating supervisory regulations, namely: if the operation has exceeded the scope of business; not drawing the deposit according to regulations or misappropriating the deposit; engaging in associated transactions prohibited by the 'Regulation'; failing to replenish the registered capital or working capital in the event that the capital is insufficient under the Regulations; evading the supervision of the authority by providing false documents, materials or reports; and refusing or hindering administrative inspections. The various forms of penalty

20 Article 30 of the 'Regulations'.

include a fine, confiscation of illegal income, suspension of business, prevention from accepting new business or even revocation of the business licence.

7.4.2 Criminal liability

Potential related criminal offences in the field of insurance include the offence of establishment of a financial organisation without authorisation and the crime of unauthorised operation.

8 An evaluation of the system in respect of access to the market of China

Generally speaking, as a result of China's accession to the WTO, the opportunities for access by foreign capital to the Chinese markets have improved gradually in accordance with the requirements of the General Agreement on Trade in Services. Nevertheless, the system still operates with some defects, as will be noted in the following.

8.1 There are no regulations in respect of access to China's market by means of a share purchase

Market access is only considered from the perspective of establishing a new organisation, but there are no provisions regarding access to the market by means of a purchase of shares to become a shareholder in an existing company.

8.2 There is an omission in the procedural rules

The procedure for access to the Chinese market is adapted purely for foreign capital insurance companies, but there are no provisions regarding the administrative liabilities to be imposed in the event of breach of the 'Regulations' by the authority; for example, by delay or rejection of applications without lawful reasons.

8.3 There are no provisions regarding coordination between the host country and the home country of foreign insurers

Supervision of market access is a complicated project that not only relates to the interests of the host country, but also involves benefits for the home country. Therefore, it is necessary to strengthen the coordination between these two countries. Nevertheless, in the 'Regulations' and their 'Rules' for implementation, there is only a requirement for a well-developed system in respect of financial supervision in the home country of foreign applicants, but there are no requirements for coordination between the organisations of the two countries.

In the author's opinion, in the market economy paradigm, the insurance legislation of China has come a long way in a short period of time. However, by comparing with the comparable legislation of advanced countries, it is irrefutable that there is room for further improvement as mentioned above. Therefore, it is necessary for China to learn from the experience of advanced countries so as to extract and adopt best practice.

3 Insurance brokers under Chinese law

Dr Miao Li[1]

1 Background

There are three broad categories of insurance intermediaries in China. They are insurance brokers, insurance agents and insurance assessors. Insurance brokers and insurance agents are usually involved in the process of concluding insurance contracts, while insurance assessors are responsible for assessing the risks and/or values of the insured subject matter before or after the conclusion of the insurance contract.

According to the Insurance Act of the People's Republic of China 2009 (the Chinese Insurance Act 2009), an insurance broker is an entity which, based on the interests of proposers, provides intermediary services for proposers and insurers to enter into insurance contracts, and charges commissions according to law.[2]

An insurance agent is an entity or individual that has been authorised by an insurer to transact insurance business on its behalf within the scope of authorisation and gets in return agent's handling fees to be collected from the insurer.[3]

It can be seen from these two definitions that an insurance broker acts on behalf of the proposer,[4] while an insurance agent acts on behalf of the insurer.

In this chapter, the discussion will focus on the law relating to insurance brokers.

1 PhD (Southampton Law School).

2 Article 118, Chinese Insurance Act 2009. This author uses the word 'proposer' per context and corresponding English usage. The Chinese Insurance Act 2009 uses a word which in the rest of this work has been translated as 'assured'; see Appendix I. Some translations use 'applicant'.

3 Article 117, Chinese Insurance Act 2009.

4 Article 10 of the Chinese Insurance Act 2009 provides: 'An assured refers to a party who enters into an insurance contract with an insurer and who is obliged to pay the premium in accordance with the contract.'

2 The development of insurance broking in China

2.1 The general market

The insurance broking industry in China has a very short history. Only in 1993 was the first insurance broker company, Huatai Insurance Broker Company, licensed by the governing authority at that time.

In the same year, Sedgwick Group, once a very large British insurance broker firm, acquired a licence to do consultancy work in relation to risk management. In 1998, Sedgwick was acquired by Marsh & McLennan and the consultancy licence was transferred to Marsh. This can be said to be the first stage of the development of the insurance broking industry.

From 2000 to 2002, the government imposed strict control over market access. Licences were awarded on a case-by-case basis. In 2000, only three insurance broker companies were awarded licences; four companies were given their licences in 2001 and only six companies in 2002.

From 2003, the governing authority set up application standards and made the market more accessible. The number of companies obtaining their licences for insurance broking from 2003–2007 are as follows:

Table 3.1 Companies obtaining insurance licences, 2003–2007

Year	2003	2004	2005	2006	2007
Numbers	67	116	77	56	38

According to the latest statistics from the China Insurance Regulatory Commission ('the Commission'), until the end of the first quarter of 2013 there were 433 insurance broker companies in China.

2.2 The admittance of foreign insurance broker companies

Joining the WTO encouraged the opening of the Chinese insurance broking market to the world. China became a WTO member in December 2001. The commitment regarding the insurance industry made by the Chinese government was that:

(1) As from the entry into the WTO, insurance broking companies could be set up as Sino-foreign joint ventures in Shanghai, Guangzhou, Dalian, Shenzhen and Foshan. The foreign investors could not hold shares exceeding 59 per cent of the total.
(2) Three years after entry, the area restriction was abolished, and foreign investors could not hold shares exceeding 51 per cent of the total.
(3) Five years after China's entry into the WTO, insurance broker companies could be wholly owned by foreign investors.

Willis and Aon first obtained access to the Chinese market by setting up joint ventures with Chinese investors. In 2005, Willis increased its shareholding from 50 per cent to 51 per cent, and became the first foreign-holding insurance broker company in China. In 2006, Marsh became the first insurance broker company that was wholly owned by foreign investors.

3 The requirements to set up a broker firm in China

3.1 The business form

According to Article 6 and Article 92 of the Rules on Administration of Insurance Broker Institutions 2009 (the 2009 Rules),[5] insurance broker entities may take the form of companies or partnerships.

3.2 The minimum share capital

According to Article 8 of the old 2009 Rules, it was stated that the minimum registered share capital (RSC) for setting up an insurance broker company is RMB 50 million, and it must be paid-up capital in cash.[6]

3.3 The reserve fund or professional indemnity insurance

Insurance broking companies must purchase professional indemnity insurance or set up a reserve fund within 20 days from the date of registration with the bureau of industry and commerce.[7]

3.3.1 Professional indemnity insurance

If the insurance broking company purchases professional indemnity insurance, the amount of indemnity should not be lower than RMB 5 million for a single event. For a policy fixed for a one-year period, the amount of indemnity should not be lower than RMB 10 million and it should not be lower than twice that of the business income of the previous year.[8]

When the amount of indemnity reaches RMB 50 million, there is no requirement to increase.[9]

5 The 2009 Rules were revised by the China Insurance Regulatory Commission and the new Rules were issued on 27 April 2013. Article 8 of the 2009 Rules was revised and Article 13 of the 2009 Rules was deleted. The 2013 Rules came into effect on the day they were issued.

6 This Article was revised in the 2013 Rules. For the amendments, see '6 Recent developments' below.

7 Article 39 para 1 of the 2009 Rules (Article 38 of the 2013 Rules).

8 Article 40 para 2 of the 2009 Rules (Article 39 of the 2013 Rules).

9 Ibid.

3.3.2 Reserve fund

If the insurance broking company sets up a reserve fund, the amount of the fund should be 5 per cent of the registered share capital. When the insurance broking company increases the registered share capital, the reserve fund should also increase. When the reserve fund reaches RMB 1 million, there is no requirement to increase.[10]

The reserve fund should take the form of a deposit in a bank, or other forms recognised by the Commission.

When the reserve fund is set up, the insurance broking company cannot use the fund, unless:[11]

(1) the share capital is reduced;
(2) the licence is revoked;
(3) a professional indemnity insurance is purchased; and
(4) in other situations where the Commission so permits.

3.4 The branches

An insurance broker company set up at the minimum registered share capital (RMB 10 million) can set up three branches. If more branches need to be set up, further capital money needs to be invested. The current rate is RMB 200,000 for each further branch. If the share capital of the insurance broker company is RMB 20 million, no additional capital needs to be invested for additional branches.[12]

3.5 Foreign-invested broker firms

A foreign broker company who wishes to set up a foreign-invested insurance broker company in China should apply to the China Insurance Regulatory Commission for a practising licence. The licence is valid for three years. The company should apply for an extension no later than 30 days before the end of the third year.[13]

When a foreign broker company applies to the Commission for permission to set up a foreign-invested broker firm in China, the following requirements should be satisfied:[14]

(1) the applicant must have been engaged in insurance business for more than 30 years in a WTO Member State;

10 Article 41 of the 2009 Rules (Article 40 of the 2013 Rules).
11 Article 42 of the 2009 Rules (Article 41 of the 2013 Rules).
12 Article 13 of the 2009 Rules. This article is deleted in the 2013 Rules.
13 Articles 11, 15 and 20 of the 2009 Rules (Articles 11, 14 and 19 of the 2013 Rules).
14 Administrative Licensing Handbook: 'the approval of setting up foreign-invested insurance broker company and branches'.

(2) the applicant must have a representative office established in China for more than two years; and
(3) the applicant's total assets shall be no less than USD 200 million.

4 Activities of a licensed insurance broker company

According to Article 30 of the 'Rules', the following activities can be carried out by a licensed insurance broker company:

(1) draft the insurance plan, choose the insurance company and make proposals on behalf of the applicant;
(2) assist the assured or beneficiary in claiming;
(3) reinsurance broking;
(4) risk assessment and risk management consultancy work; and
(5) other activities permitted by the China Insurance Regulatory Commission.

5 Duties under the current law and regulation

The following legislation and regulations are relevant to insurance brokers:

(1) Insurance Act of the People's Republic of China 2009 (Insurance Act 2009).
(2) The First Judicial Interpretation on the Insurance Act of the People's Republic of China 2009 (the first interpretation).
(3) Order No. 6 [2009] of the China Insurance Regulatory Commission – Rules on the Regulation of Insurance Brokerage Institutions (the 2009 Rules).
(4) Agency law under the Chinese Civil Code 1987.

5.1 Duty of disclosure

Under the UK Marine Insurance Act 1906, where insurance is effected for the assured by an agent, the agent must disclose to the insurer:

(1) Every material circumstance which is known to himself, and an agent to insure is deemed to know every circumstance which in the ordinary course of business ought to be known by, or to have been communicated to him.
(2) Every material circumstance which the assured is bound to disclose, unless it comes to his knowledge too late to communicate it to the agent.[15]

15 Section 19 of Marine Insurance Act 1906.

That means the broker not only has a duty to forward the material facts disclosed by the assured, but he also has an independent duty to disclose material facts within his own knowledge, even if this information is unknown to the assured.

As a consequence, the insurers are entitled to avoid the insurance contract if the broker has failed to disclose material facts, even if the assured himself is unaware of the circumstances in question.

However, under Chinese law, only the proposer has a duty of disclosure when asked by the insurer. Article 16 of the Insurance Act 2009 states that 'In concluding an insurance contract, the insurer may inquire about the relevant circumstances concerning the subject matter of the insurance or the insured. The applicant shall make an honest disclosure'. Chapter 12 of the Chinese Maritime Code includes several Articles governing marine insurance contracts.[16] There is a similar Article to section 18 of the UK Marine Insurance Act 1906, which sets out the assured's duty of disclosure.[17] But there is no Article in that chapter referring to the broker's duty of disclosure.

However, this does not mean that brokers do not have any duty of disclosure at all. According to the Insurance Act 2009 and general agency law in the Chinese Civil Code, the agent is liable to his principal, the proposer, for any loss or damage caused by the agent's breach of his duty.[18] If a broker has failed to pass on to the insurer the material information disclosed by the applicant, he will be held liable for any loss or damage suffered by the applicant.

5.2 Premium

Under English law, if a marine policy is effected through a broker, the broker is directly responsible for the payment of the premium: 'Unless otherwise agreed, where a marine policy is effected on behalf of the assured by a broker, the broker is directly responsible to the insurer for the premium'.[19]

Under Chinese law, all the premiums are payable by the proposer, whether under a marine or a non-marine policy.

Article 14 of the Insurance Act 2009 stipulates that 'Where an insurance contract is concluded, the proposer shall pay the premiums as agreed and the insurer shall begin to undertake the insurance liability from the agreed time'.

16 See Appendix II.

17 Article 222 of the Chinese Maritime Code: 'the assured must disclose to the insurer, before the contract is concluded, every material circumstance which is known to the assured, and the assured is deemed to know every circumstance which, in the ordinary course of business, ought to be known by the assured.'

18 Article 128 of the Chinese Insurance Act 2009; Article 66(2) of the Chinese Civil Code.

19 Section 53 of the Marine Insurance Act 1906.

According to Article 216 of the Chinese Maritime Code:

> a contract of marine insurance is a contract whereby the insurer undertakes, as agreed, to indemnify the loss of the subject matter insured and the liability of the insured caused by perils covered by the insurance against the payment of an insurance premium by the insured.

5.3 Commission

Under Chinese law, commission should only be paid to agents and brokers who have been legally recognised, and no other person can receive such remuneration.[20]

The effect of Article 130 of the Insurance Act 2009 is that a firm that is not authorised by the Commission will not be authorised to receive commission from the insurer. It will only be allowed to receive payments in the nature of consultancy fees from the proposer. This makes a big difference in terms of the income received by the firm. The average commission received by a broker firm is about 10–15 per cent of the premium, whereas the consultancy fee is only about 2–5 per cent of the premium.

5.4 Prohibited activities

When transacting insurance business, no insurance agents or brokers may commit any of the following acts:[21]

(1) deceiving the insurer, proposer, insured or beneficiary;
(2) concealing material information with respect to the insurance contract;
(3) preventing the proposer from fulfilling his obligation of making a full and accurate disclosure, or inducing the proposer not to fulfil his obligation of making a full and accurate disclosure;
(4) promising to give the proposer, the insured or the beneficiary benefits other than the ones provided for in the insurance contract;
(5) by taking advantage of the administrative powers and position, or of the occupational facilities, or by employing other illegitimate means, coercing or inducing the proposer to enter into an insurance contract;
(6) forging or altering the insurance contract with no authority, or providing falsified documents for either party of the insurance contract;
(7) misappropriating, retaining for his own use or peculating premium or loss money;

20 Article 130 of the Chinese Insurance Act 2009.
21 Article 131 of the Chinese Insurance Act 2009.

(8) abusing of his position to gain profit for other person or institution;
(9) making fraudulent claims in complicity with the proposer, the assured or the beneficiary; and
(10) revealing confidential business information obtained during the transactions done for insurer, proposer or the assured.

6 Recent developments

In June 2012, the China Insurance Regulatory Commission (CIRC) sent out a circular to the local licensing authorities on Further Regulation on the Admission of Insurance Intermediaries, in which the licensing authorities were temporarily requested to only accept applications for setting up insurance agent or insurance broker companies from insurance intermediary group companies, vehicle manufacturing, selling and repairing companies, banks, post offices and insurance companies, with a minimum registered share capital not less than RMB 50 million, as well as applications for setting up branches of national insurance intermediary companies. All other applications were suspended; for example, applications for setting up small regional insurance intermediary companies or applications for setting up insurance intermediary companies with a registered share capital lower than RMB 50 million.

The background of the launching of this new policy was that the insurance intermediary market was very young, the levels of professionalism and specialism of the insurance intermediaries were low, the capability to manage risks was weak, the service could not meet the customers' needs and many small intermediary companies that did not have a good management structure were inclined towards misconduct in the performance of their business. The policymaker suggested that the low threshold for admission to the market is one of the main reasons that caused these problems. The aim of the new policy was to promote insurance intermediary companies with large-scale and/ or specialised services, to control both the quality and quantity of new intermediaries.

With this big change in policy, the insurance intermediary market keeps growing steadily. The statistics show that the premium received through insurance intermediaries has risen by 10.76 per cent and business income has risen by 20.44 per cent. The quantity and quality of new insurance intermediaries were properly controlled.

In April 2013, the CIRC made a resolution to amend the Rules on the Regulation of Insurance Broker Institutions 2009 (the Rules 2013). The new amendment has increased the registered share capital for new insurance intermediary companies from RMB 10 million to RMB 50 million.[22]

22 Another amendment made by the Rules 2013 was that Article 13 of the Rules 2009, which regulates the setting up of branches of insurance broking institutions, was deleted. All other Articles of Rules 2009 remain the same.

To assist the implementation of the new Rules, the CIRC sent out another circular, which gives directions on setting up new branches by the insurance brokers formed before the new Rules were in force. The requirements are:

(1) Insurance broker companies that were formed before the new Rules came into effect, and with a registered share capital lower than RMB 50 million, can only apply to set up new branches within the province in which the company was registered.
(2) Insurance broker companies that were formed before the new Rules came into effect, and with registered share capital lower than RMB 50 million, can apply to set up new branches within another province if they already had a branch registered in that province.

The circular also directed that online insurance broking service companies should also have a minimum of RMB 50 million registered share capital, unless they were formed before the new Rules came into force.

The effect of the new Rules and the circular is that there are two categories of insurance broker companies in the market. One is the kind that has a minimum of RMB 50 million registered share capital, which was set up according to the new or the old Rules. They can set up any new branches within the country provided all other requirements for new branches are satisfied. The other type of insurance broking companies are those insurance broking companies set up according to the old Rules with a registered share capital lower than RMB 50 million. For these companies, they are allowed to carry on business and are not requested to increase their registered share capital. However, they can only set up new branches within the province where they have already established registered offices. If they intend to establish new offices outside the existing areas, they need to increase the registered share capital to RMB 50 million.

The aim of the new policy was to enhance the standards of the market, control both the quantity and quality of the new intermediaries and promote better services provided by insurance intermediary companies. The current trend indicates that for a new insurance broking company to be welcomed by the authorities and the market, it must be capable of good management, professionalism and specialisation.

4 Faraway, so close

Some theoretical reflections on the application of competition law to the insurance sector in EU and China

Dr Andrea Lista[1]

1 Introduction

Competition law is an extremely complex area of law in constant evolution, and whose underpinning principles cross paths with economic and market theories. Its pervasive effects embrace every aspect of the market economy, including the insurance sector. The application of competition law to this sector has always posed serious questions, due to the atavistic need for cooperation between insurers in the form of joint statistical studies, co-insurance and reinsurance of large risks and the provision of standardised conditions for insureds. While the EU framework has developed gradually over some time, in China, competition regulation is a very recent phenomenon, which nevertheless poses the very same questions when it comes to its application to the insurance sector.

The regulation of forms of cooperation between insurers under Article 101 of the Lisbon Treaty (Foundation Treaty of European Union, hereafter TFEU) and Article 14 of the Chinese Anti-Monopoly Law arguably represents one of the paramount and most intricate aspects of the application of the competition rules to the insurance sector, and it shall therefore occupy a preponderant space in this chapter. This is due to the fact that the insurance industry historically has been characterised by intense forms of horizontal cooperation between undertakings, deemed necessary for the correct functioning of the financial services industry.

Due to its more extensive historical and legal background, the EU scenario will take the lion's share of the legal and teleological analysis.

1 Associate Professor in Commercial Law, Law School, University of Southampton, UK. The author is particularly grateful to Ms Johanna Hjalmarsson, Senior Research Fellow at Law School, University of Southampton, for her invaluable comments, and to Mr James Dingjing Huang, PhD Candidate at Law School, University of Southampton, for his help with the research of sources on Chinese law. The usual disclaimer applies.

However, the considerations made in relation to the application of competition law to European insurers will prove perfectly valid and relevant also for the Chinese insurance industry. The reason for this lies with the fact that, as will be readily appreciated, the current Chinese antitrust regulatory framework has been structured and moulded on the basis of the EU competition rules enshrined in the TFEU.

Due to the lack of case law pertaining to the Chinese scenario, emphasis will be put on the extensive EU jurisprudence on the application of competition law to the insurance industry, the critical analysis of which gives rise to critical considerations directly relevant for the Chinese insurance industry.[2]

2 Overview of the EU and China competition regulatory framework

EU competition law includes four main policy areas arising from the treaty rules:

(1) The control of any type of cartels, or control of collusion and other anticompetitive practices that have an effect on the EU (Article 101 TFEU).
(2) The prohibition of monopolies, or of any abuse of dominant market positions (governed by Article 102).
(3) The control of direct and indirect aid given by EU member states to companies (State aid, covered under Article 107).[3]
(4) The control of proposed mergers, acquisitions and joint ventures involving companies having a defined amount of turnover in the EU/EEA (governed by Article 102 and by Council Regulation 139/2004 EC, the Merger Regulation).

If the EU competition rules have been developed since the outset of the European Community, the People's Republic of China has only in recent times introduced a comprehensive competition regulatory framework with the enactment of the Anti-Monopoly Law on 1 August 2008. The 2008 Anti-Monopoly Law prohibits 'monopolistic conducts', which can be divided into the following subcategories:

(1) anticompetitive ('monopoly') agreements between undertakings;
(2) abuse of dominant position; and

2 As will be readily appreciated, the Chinese Anti-Monopoly Law derives its underpinning principles from the experience of EU competition law. The lessons learned from the application of EU competition rules to the European insurance industry can thus be applied, *mutatis mutandis*, to the Chinese insurance market.

3 State aid, a component – or anomaly, some may say – of the EU competition regulatory framework, shall not be taken into account due to the lack of cross-reference elements with the Chinese scenario.

(3) mergers that may have the effect of eliminating or restricting competition.

Thus far, enforcement emphasis has been placed on control of mergers and acquisitions, although the Chinese Anti-Monopoly Committee has also recently turned its attention to anticompetitive behaviours, with investigations initiated by the relevant authorities and private actions brought before courts.

Before analysing individual elements of competition regulation in Europe and China and their reflection on the respective insurance industries, attention must be paid to general issues arising from the application of competition law to the insurance sector.

3 The application of competition law to the insurance industry: general issues and background

Economic doctrine generally distinguishes the insurance industry from other sectors of the economy on the basis of the idea that the insurance business is primarily to be considered as an instrument of risk management.[4] It has been correctly noted that the peculiarity of the insurance industry indeed 'lies in uncertainty'.[5] In order to foresee the future cost of claims and thus to be in the position to determine the premium,[6] insurers need to rely on meaningful statistics concerning the 'probability of realisation of the insured event and the foreseeable extent of the loss'.[7]

Cooperation would therefore seem a natural and essential component of the insurance industry, and would play a paramount role in the provision

4 See G. Faure, T. Hartlief, 'Insurance and expanding systemic risks', in *Policy Issues in Insurance*, 2003, Paris: OECD, p 12. For a detailed analysis of the nature of business insurance, see E. G. Vaughan and M. Vaughan, *Fundamentals of Risk and Insurance*, 2008, 10th edition, Hoboken, NJ: John Wiley & Sons.

5 See M. Faure, 'Insurance and competition law: balancing the conflicts', *Global Issues in Insurance Regulation*, London, 17–18 April 2002, p 6, available at: www.nottingham.ac.uk/business/cris/papers/Grif%20%20Michael%20Faure.pdf (accessed 3 July 2011). On this point, see also G. Faure and R. Van Den Bergh, 'Competition on the European market for liability insurance', 2002, p 12, available at: http://arno.unimaas.nl (accessed 18 June 2014).

6 The final price of insurance comprises the 'risk premium' covering the cost of the insured product, a security charge, overheads and profit. The risk premium itself can be subdivided in two components: (a) net premiums, aiming at covering the cost of the product insured on the basis of past statistical evidence (frequency and scale of claims); and (b) a second component that levels the net premium either upwards or downwards according to predictions relating to the future (i.e. circumstances likely to happen capable of having an impact on the frequency or scale of claims).

7 See M. Faure, 'Insurance and competition law: balancing the conflicts', p 6.

and access to information sufficiently general to enable the calculation of average values, of crucial importance in order to determine insurance premiums. More specifically, economists maintain that, especially when claims are relatively infrequent and risk categories are relatively numerous, large statistics identified on the basis of information exchange between insurance undertakings would allow better actuarial calculations based on internal claims experience.[8] This would result in a clear incentive for insurance firms either to merge or to cooperate in the pooling of claims.[9]

Horizontal agreements would thus represent a fundamental feature of the insurance sector at any level (i.e. direct insurance, in which customers are the end users, reinsurance, whereby insurers are themselves the end users of policies subscribed with other insurers, and retrocession, through which providers of reinsurance obtain coverage for their own risks).

If horizontal agreements on joint determination of risk would seem an essential component of the business of direct insurance, cooperation in the form of co-insurance and reinsurance is also considered necessary to meet the needs of the modern insurance markets, whenever the entity of the risk to cover considerably exceeds the assets of an individual insurer.[10]

In addition to the above forms of cooperation, a further peculiarity of the insurance industry would be represented by an overall lack of transparency, which would thwart the capacity of consumers to compare insurance policies offered by competing insurers.[11] This information deficiency would revert against the functioning of the insurance market mechanisms, leading to inefficient results. That is the reason why standardisation of policy terms has been traditionally considered as 'the correct regulatory answer to an alleged market failure'.[12]

Several aspects of the insurance business may thus seem to be characterised by an inherently monopolistic nature difficult to reconcile with Article 101 of the TFEU or Article 13 of the Chinese Anti-Monopoly Law, which prohibit agreements between undertakings, decisions by associations of undertakings and concerted practices that have as their object or effect the prevention, restriction or distortion of competition within a market.

The application of Article 101 of the TFEU and Article 13 of the Chinese Anti-Monopoly Law to the insurance industry indeed poses serious

8 See G. Faure and T. Hartlief, 'Insurance and expanding systemic risks', p 26.

9 See G. Faure and R. Van Den Bergh, 'Competition on the European market for liability insurance', p 23.

10 See M. Faure, 'Insurance and competition law: balancing the conflicts', p 11. On this point, see also G. Faure and T. Hartlief, 'Insurance and expanding systemic risks', p 26. See also M. Faure and R. Van Den Bergh, 'Restrictions of competition in the insurance markets and the applicability of EC law', 1995, *Kiklos*, vol 48, Fasc I, pp 65–85, available at: http://arno.unimaas.nl/show.cgi?fid=4627 (accessed 3 July 2011).

11 See M. Faure, 'Insurance and competition law: balancing the conflicts', p 17.

12 See M. Faure, 'Insurance and competition law: balancing the conflicts', p 11.

questions; forms of cooperation in the form of joint determination of risk, co-insurance, reinsurance and the standardisation of policy terms represent the sort of quintessentially anticompetitive activities against which Article 101 and Article 13 were specifically designed. It is not surprising, therefore, that the insurance industry has traditionally vehemently rejected the idea of being subject to the application of antitrust forms of Regulation.[13]

Are we faced with two irreconcilable positions, then? Not necessarily. In Europe, the way out can be found in Article 101 itself. The third paragraph of this Article permits the possibility of an exemption for anticompetitive agreements that contribute to improving the production or distribution of goods or to promoting technical or economic progress, while allowing consumers a fair share of the resulting benefit, without resulting in the elimination of competition. Article 101(3) represents the basis for the adoption of the insurance block exemption Regulations that will be the subject of analysis in the following, together with considerations on the Chinese scenario.

Similarly, in China, all horizontal and vertical agreements caught under Articles 13 and 14 of the Anti-Monopoly Law may be exempted under Article 15 if they satisfy exemptions, which, as outlined in the following, are extremely similar in nature to the ones enshrined in Article 101(3).

4 Article 101 of the TFEU and Article 13 of the Chinese Anti-Monopoly Law: the control of collusive behaviours

4.1 Article 101 of the TFEU

Article 101 of the TFEU is the provision of the Lisbon Treaty related to anticompetitive behaviours representing the outcome from collusion among undertakings. It prohibits all agreements between undertakings, decisions by associations of undertakings and concerted practices that may affect trade between member states and that have as their object or effect the prevention, restriction or distortion of competition within the common market.

The provision is structured into three paragraphs. The first paragraph lays down a general prohibition of any collusive behaviour between undertakings having as object or effect the restriction, prevention or distortion of competition in the market. This prohibition has a vast scope of application, which includes both informal agreements (gentlemen's agreements) and concerted practices (i.e. forms of practical collusion) where undertakings adopt the same behaviour, raising or lowering prices at the same time in absence of a formal agreement (i.e. without having physically agreed to do so).

13 See Case C-45/68 *Verband der Sachversicherer* [1987] ECR 405, 449 Commission Decision '*Nuovo Cegam*', 11/04/84 OJ L99/29.

Further, Article 101 covers both horizontal agreements (agreements between undertakings occupying the same position in the production or distribution chain) (e.g. agreements between retailers) and vertical agreements (between undertakings having a different position in the production or distribution chain) (e.g. agreements between retailers and suppliers), effectively outlawing the operation of cartels within the EU.

Horizontal agreements represent the most serious threat to competition, and include the 'hard-core' restrictions (i.e. price-fixing, establishment of quotas and market sharing). Information exchange agreements are another very controversial form of horizontal agreements due to their capability of facilitating collusive conduct among competing firms, as such agreements are likely to enhance the possibility of monitoring competitors' conduct. Vertical agreements are also seen as a possible danger to competitive markets as they tend to lead to 'market foreclosure' (i.e. the side effect of exclusive agreements between a producer and certain distributors to sell only its brand of a specific product).

The second paragraph of Article 101 provides that any arrangement prohibited by Article 101(1) is prohibited and automatically void. Finally, the third paragraph of Article 101 lays down an 'exemption' mechanism permitting an arrangement within the meaning of Article 101(1), which would otherwise be prohibited by Article 101(2). In practice, Article 101(3) provides for an exemption for any collusive practice capable of impairing competition insofar as it creates efficiencies that outweigh the restriction of competition, consumers obtain a fair share of those benefits, there are no less restrictive means of achieving the efficiencies and competition is not eliminated altogether.[14] Article 101(3) constitutes the basis for the 'block exemption regulations' that have been introduced by the Commission over the years in order to grant exemption on a large scale to specific kinds of agreements.

4.2 Anticompetitive ('monopoly') agreements under Chinese law

According to Article 13 of the Anti-Monopoly Law, any of the following monopoly agreements among competing business operators shall be prohibited:

(1) fixing or changing prices of commodities;
(2) limiting the output or sales of commodities;
(3) dividing the sales market or the raw material procurement market;
(4) restricting the purchase of new technology or new facilities or the development of new technology or new products;

14 See Article 101(3) of the TFEU.

(5) making boycott transactions; and
(6) other monopoly agreements as determined by the Anti-Monopoly Authority under the State Council.

For the purposes of this section, 'monopoly agreements' refers to agreements, decisions or other concerted actions that eliminate or restrict competition. As with the EU regime, exemptions from the prohibition enshrined in Article 13 are possible. The criteria are laid down by Article 15. Under Article 15, an agreement among business operators shall be exempted from application of Articles 13 and 14 for the purpose of: (1) improving technologies, researching and developing new products; (2) upgrading product quality, reducing cost, improving efficiency, unifying product specifications or standards or carrying out professional labour division; (3) enhancing operational efficiency and reinforcing the competitiveness of small and medium-sized business operators; (4) achieving public interests such as conserving energy, protecting the environment and relieving the victims of a disaster and so on; (5) for the purpose of mitigating serious decrease in sales volume or obviously excessive production during economic recessions; (6) for the purpose of safeguarding the justifiable interests in the foreign trade or foreign economic cooperation; or (7) other circumstances as stipulated by laws and the State Council.

Where a monopoly agreement is in any of the circumstances stipulated in items (1) to (5), business operators must additionally prove that the agreement can enable consumers to share the interests derived from the agreement, and will not severely restrict the competition in the relevant market.

Article 15 embeds the same doctrine of 'legal applicable exceptions' as in Article 101(3) of the EU Treaty. Nevertheless, unlike with EU competition law, where the EU Commission has promulgated and implemented various specific Regulations for the purpose of implementing and enforcing Article 101(3), in China, several fundamental issues, such as the specific contents and criteria of the 'legal exceptions' enshrined in Article 15, or who has the authority to stipulate the implementing rules, still remain unclear.

By the same token, within the context of private enforcement, the extent and criteria of the burden of proof for obtaining an exemption on the basis of a 'reasonable cause' also remain unclear. Furthermore, there will also be the need to clarify whether the assessment and comparison between pro-competition and anti-competition factors is limited within the preset scope of application of Article 15 of the Anti-Monopoly Law, or could include further reasonable causes not listed therein.[15]

15 See Article 15 of the China Anti-Monopoly Law.

5 Regulation of forms of horizontal cooperation between insurers in Europe and China

5.1 Forms of horizontal cooperation between insurers in China

In the absence of a block exemption, Chinese insurance undertakings are fully exposed to the application of Article 13 of the Anti-Monopoly Law, which, as established in the above, prohibits price-fixing agreements, or any other form of horizontal cooperation between insurers capable of restricting or affecting competition.

Nevertheless, differently from the European insurance market, which has been subject to a series of legislative initiatives analysed in the above, the regulation of the insurance industry in China has started in recent times with the introduction of the Chinese Insurance Act in 2009. According to section 67 of the Act, the establishment of an insurance company is subject to the approval of the insurance supervision and regulation authority of the State Council.

When examining the application for the establishment of an insurance company, the insurance supervision and regulation authority of the State Council shall take into consideration the development of the insurance industry and the need for fair competition.

The concept of fair competition is therefore embedded into the Chinese Insurance Act, which, under section 115, also compels insurance companies to operate their business according to the principle of fair competition, and warns them not to commit unfair competition.

We have seen that just like with the EU scenario, under Article 15 of the Chinese Anti-Monopoly Law, an agreement among business operators shall be exempted from application of Articles 13 and 14 of the Chinese Anti-Monopoly Act for the purpose of, inter alia, upgrading product quality, reducing cost, improving efficiency, unifying product specifications or standards, or carrying out professional labour division, enhancing operational efficiency and reinforcing the competitiveness of small and medium-sized business operators.

As established in the above, these redemptive factors appear to be modelled after EU law, but without the requirement of 'indispensability', which is embedded in Article 101(3) of the TFEU. This potentially makes resorting to the exemptions easier compared to the European scenario, where insurers seeking individual exemption are required to prove that a proposed agreement capable of hindering competition is indispensable in order to achieve one of the grounds for exemption listed by Article 101(3) of the TFEU (e.g. technical and economic progress, etc.).

Exchange of information between Chinese insurers would therefore need to be justified under one of the grounds listed by Article 15 of the Chinese Anti- Monopoly Law. A possible ground for exemption would lie with the concepts of 'improved efficiency' and the enhancement of 'operational efficiency'. Exactly like in Europe, under Article 15 of the Anti-Monopoly Law efficiency gains attained by information exchanges between insurers must be passed on to consumers. This means that Chinese insurers will need to prove that the exchange of information has a beneficial impact on end users.

As we are about to discover, the same considerations that are thereafter expressed in relation to the European scenario apply also to the Chinese insurance industry; it is submitted that the lower the market power of the parties involved in the information exchange, the more likely it is that the efficiency gains would be passed on to consumers to an extent that outweighs the restrictive effects on competition. Small insurers (and new market entrants) are thus subject to a lower burden of proof compared to larger or more established market players.

By the same token, in order to be consistent with Article 15, agreements on standard policy conditions, co-insurance/reinsurance pools and safety equipment will need to create efficiencies that outweigh the restriction of competition, and see that consumers obtain a fair share of those benefits. Just like their European counterparts, Chinese insurers will have a higher possibility to succeed if they can prove that some leeway is granted in terms of the possibility to deviate from the status quo of the agreement, providing alternative conditions or the possibility to co-insure/reinsure outside the pool. In the case of standard policy conditions, an agreement binding only on specific predetermined terms leaving the freedom to provide diverse conditions in relation to remaining provisions will be likely to benefit from an individual exemption. Conversely, agreements that will not confer any degree of freedom to provide alternative conditions will be considered anticompetitive unless beneficial for consumers. Under such circumstances, individual exemptions may be granted to standardisation agreements that effectively render particularly hermetic policy conditions accessible for consumers.

As just established, the similarities in relation to the competition assessment of forms of horizontal cooperation between EU and Chinese insurers are many. Nevertheless, it deserves to be outlined that a number of provisions in the Anti-Monopoly Law differ quite significantly from the EU competition regulatory framework, reflecting the importance of the socialist heritage of China's market economy.

Declared aims of the Anti-Monopoly Law include, inter alia, the protection of public interest and the promotion of the socialist market economy. Protecting market competition and the legitimate interests of consumers are also listed as legislative purposes in Article 1 of the Anti-Monopoly Law. Article 4 provides that 'the State formulates and implements competition rules compatible with the socialist economy, strengthens and perfects macro regulation and control, and completes a unified, open, competitive and orderly market system'. Such statements of principle confer a high degree of discretion in the application of competition rules to the insurance sector, and could be used to curb competition between insurers where needed.

Furthermore, one should also consider the interface between the Anti-Monopoly Law, trade associations and industry self-discipline. Trade associations traditionally often control the behaviour of many Chinese industries, with specific reference to those dealing with export trade. Article 16 of the Anti-Monopoly Law states that 'Industry associations shall not organize the business operators in their industry to engage in the monopolistic conducts prohibited by this Chapter'.

Nevertheless, Article 11 provides that 'trade associations shall strengthen self-discipline of the industries, provide guidance for enterprises in their industries to compete lawfully, and protect the order of market competition'. This could ignite competition concerns, as trade associations (traditionally a common instrument for price-fixing) are clearly tasked with the duty to enhance the overall power and international competitiveness of Chinese industry, and this may justify the use of domestic cartels in the name of responding to competitive pressures from foreign competitors.

This is particularly relevant for the Chinese insurance industry, as under the World Trade Organization Chinese insurance industry framework, the Chinese government lowered entry barriers to foreign insurers, allowing them to establish joint-venture insurance firms in China.[16]

Due to the lack of case law in relation to forms of horizontal cooperation between insurers in China, the analysis shall now focus on the European scenario. The similarities between the competition frameworks of the two continents render the considerations and suggestions for alternative regulatory paradigms made in the following of direct relevance for the Chinese scenario.

5.2 The EU scenario

The European Commission had claimed from the outset that the EU competition law framework found full application to the insurance industry.[17] Nevertheless, both the European Commission and European courts soon acknowledged the structural peculiarities of the insurance industry giving rise to a wave of individual exemptions to forms of horizontal cooperation between insurers involving, inter alia, information exchange agreements,[18]

16 On this point, see Chapter 2.

17 As early as 1972, the Commission stated that the EC Treaty competition rules fully applied to the insurance industry (see, inter alia, the *Commission Report on Competition Policy*, 1972 (vol. II) points 51–57).

18 Case C-45/68 *Verband der Sachversicherer* [1987] ECR 405, 449, Commission Decision '*Nuovo Cegam*', 11/04/84 OJ L99/29.

co-insurance[19] and reinsurance[20] forms of collaboration and standard policy conditions.[21] After a first generation of insurance cases and individual exemptions, the Commission decided to introduce a block exemption through Council Regulation 3932/92,[22] for agreements between insurance undertakings related to: (1) cooperation with respect to the establishment of common risk premium tariffs based on collectively ascertained statistics or the number of claims; (2) the establishment of common standard policy conditions; (3) the common coverage of certain types of risks; and (4) the testing and acceptance of security devices. Regulation 3932/92 was followed by Regulation 358/2003,[23] subsequently replaced by Regulation 267/2010,[24] the current block exemption regulation.[25]

The introduction of the current block exemption regulation[26] was preceded by a Commission report, the *Report on the Insurance Block Exemption*.[27] In the report, the Commission came to the preliminary conclusion that agreements on cooperation in the area of joint calculations, tables and studies should be facilitated and that the block exemption in this area deserved continuity of application. The same considerations arose in relation to insurance pools. Finally, it was maintained that two of the constitutive elements of the old regime, namely standard policy conditions and security devices, should be completely removed from the scope of the block exemption, whereas the exchange of statistical information for risk calculation and the creation of insurance pools should continue to benefit

19 Commission Decision, '*Nuovo Cegam*', 11/04/84 OJ L99/29.

20 Commission Decision, *Technisches Kontor fuer die Maschinen-B-U-Versicherung (TEKO)*, 20/12/89 OJ L13/34.

21 Commission Decision, *Concordato Incendio* 1990 OJ L15/25.

22 Commission Regulation (EEC) No 3932/92 of 21 December 1992 on the application of Article 85(3) of the Treaty to certain categories of agreements, decisions and concerted practices in the insurance sector. Official Journal L 398, 31.12.1992.

23 Commission Regulation (EC) No 358/2003 of 27 February 2003 on the application of Article 81(3) of the Treaty to certain categories of agreements, decisions and concerted practices in the insurance sector.

24 Commission Regulation (EU) No 267/2010 of 24 March 2010 on the application of Article 101(3) of the Treaty on the Functioning of the European Union to certain categories of agreements, decisions and concerted practices in the insurance sector (OJ L 83/1, 30.3.2010).

25 The legal basis for the adoption of the EU block exemption Regulations is Article 101 of the TFEU, by virtue of which all agreements satisfying its terms are fully exempted without the need for individual notification.

26 Commission Regulation (EU) No 267/2010 of 24 March 2010 on the application of Article 101(3) of the Treaty on the Functioning of the European Union to certain categories of agreements, decisions and concerted practices in the insurance sector (OJ L 83/1, 30.3.2010).

27 Commission Report on the Insurance Block Exemption, 24 March 2009, available at: http://ec.europa.eu/competition/sectors/financial_services/insurance_ber_report_ep.pdf (accessed 18 June 2014).

from immunity. Starting from March 2010, only agreements on joint compilations, tables and studies of risk and co-insurance and reinsurance pools continue to benefit from a general exemption, whereas agreements on standard policy conditions and on minimum specifications for security devices are no longer sheltered by the shield of a block exemption, and are consequently fully exposed to the application of Article 101 of the Lisbon Treaty.

5.2.1 The new regime for joint compilations, tables and studies under Regulation 267/2010

The block exemption continues to cover agreements on joint compilations, tables and studies, as the Commission still acknowledges the importance of cooperation between insurance undertakings in this area.[28] Nevertheless, there is a significant change compared to the previous regime. The new block exemption crucially requires calculations and studies to be made available not only to all insurance companies, but also to consumer and customer organisations that request them.[29] This represents a welcome change, as the requirement of disclosure may work as a deterrent for insurance undertakings to avoid forms of information exchanges related to the actual insurance premium. Nevertheless, if on the one hand this requirement is designed to enhance the obligation to share information beyond the previous regime, single individuals are not in a position to have access to this data. Further, the requirement enshrined in Article 3(2)(e) is subject to an exemption on the basis of public security issues,[30] and the concept of public security remains yet to be clarified.

On the basis of the block exemption regime, insurers are allowed to share information and statistics in order to jointly determine the risk premium. The line of reasoning behind the block exemption appears to embrace the 'premium calculation argument'.[31] This claim relates to the determination of premiums by insurance companies, with the rationale that deficiencies in the individual statistics prevent insurers from attaining an accurate rating of risks. Cooperation among undertakings would therefore seem necessary in order to ensure that income and expenses are balanced, the insolvency

28 Ibid., recital no 9.

29 Ibid., Article 3(2)(e). Single individuals are not in the position to have access to these data. Further, the requirement enshrined in Article 3(2)(e) is subject to an exemption on the basis of public security issues.

30 Ibid., Article 3(2)(d).

31 For a detailed analysis of the 'premium calculation argument', see M. Faure, 'Insurance and competition law: balancing the conflicts', p 22. See also M. Faure and R. Van den Bergh, 'Restrictions of competition on insurance markets and the applicability of EC antitrust law', *Kyklos*, 1995, p 65.

risk is contained and the 'moral hazard problem' is adequately faced.[32] The premium calculation argument furthermore posits that cooperation between insurance undertakings in relation to risk premium calculation is vital in order to improve the conditions of the service, and thus worthy of an exemption under Article 101(3) of the treaty.

Prima facie, this argument appears to be accurate. It has been correctly noted that the peculiarity of the insurance business lies in uncertainty.[33] In order to accurately project the exact cost of claims and thus to be able to determine the premium, insurers need to rely upon forecasts relating to the probability of the insured event and the foreseeable extent of the loss.[34] Such assessment entails the need to have access to meaningful statistics, with cooperation thus necessary to generate the statistical data necessary in order to enable insurers to calculate the premiums.[35] Nevertheless, economic doctrine has identified at least two main idiosyncrasies in relation to the premium calculation argument.[36] *In primis*, insurers are not the only undertakings dealing with uncertainty, as uncertainty represents a normal business risk shared by any entrepreneur carrying on an economic activity and cannot justify, per se, the existence of cartels.[37] Second, the premium calculation argument as enshrined in the current block exemption regulation

32 See M. Faure, 'Insurance and competition law: balancing the conflicts'. For a comprehensive examination of the moral hazard problem, see M. V. Pauly, 'The truth about moral hazard and adverse selection', *Syracuse University Journal*, no 36, 2007, available at: www-cpr.maxwell.syr.edu/pbriefs/pb36.pdf (accessed 3 July 2011). See also M. V. Pauly, 'The economics of moral hazard: comment', *The American Economic Review*, vol 58, no 3, part 1, June 1968, pp 531–537, available at: www.jstor.org/stable/1813785?origin=JSTOR-pdf (accessed 3 July 2011). Moral hazard is defined by economists as 'behaviours that can lead to asymmetric information between market participants' (see A. Sagi and E. Patiki, 'Consumer behaviour and asymmetric information theory', available at: www.bmf.hu/ (accessed 3 July 2011). In insurance, moral hazard is believed to occur when 'the expected loss from an adverse event increases as insurance coverage increases' (M. V. Pauly, 'The economics of moral hazard: comment', p 533). According to M. V. Pauly, moral hazard can be defined as 'the effect of having an insurance and insured's incentives to reduce expected losses' (M. V. Pauly, 'The economics of moral hazard: comment', p 534). Moral hazards problems arise whenever one market participant has no responsibility for the consequence of its actions. A person covered by an insurance policy is thus less likely to take efficient care; in other words, once insured, people are more prone to take actions that result in a claim on their policy.

33 See M. Faure, 'Insurance and competition law: balancing the conflicts', p 3.

34 Ibid.

35 The need for large statistics studies is considered particularly stringent in case of relatively infrequent claims and relatively numerous risk categories. For an overview of these issues, see J. Finsinger, 'European integration of insurance markets. Preliminary but novel perspectives', Working Paper, Universitat Luneburg, no 75, 1989, pp 70–92.

36 These considerations are based on the criticisms formulated by M. Faure in 'Insurance and competition law: balancing the conflicts', p 23.

37 On this point, see also J. Finsinger and F. A. Schmidt, 'Prices, distribution channels and regulatory intervention in European insurance markets', p 12.

appears to be formulated in excessively generic terms. The doctrine has distinguished between different classes of insurance: '*Zufallsrisiken*' (risk determined by coincidence) and '*Änderungsrisiken*' (risks relating to a change of the dangerous situation itself).[38] While the latter are very difficult, if not impossible, to predict accurately, the former can be easily determined on the basis of the law of the large numbers without the need for any joint form of cooperation.[39] Among this category of risks, difficulties may nevertheless arise in the determination of 'one-off risks', such as catastrophe risks, which are extremely difficult to determine.

The difficulties arising in relation to *Zufallsrisiken* have been considered instead to be mainly related to the incompatibility between competition law and the long duration of insurance contracts used to insure them, rather than to the nature of the risks per se.[40] While long-term contracts are believed by the insurers to be an essential form of cooperation, especially in the field of prevention, it is rather difficult to justify their exemption under Article 101(3).[41] Forms of joint cooperation in the field of prevention are allegedly considered worthy of exemption, as they are deemed to allow a substantive reduction of claims, which would consequently lead to a reduction of premiums, ultimately beneficial to consumers.[42] Contrary to these opinions, the Commission regards long-term insurance contracts as a threat to competition as they reduce the possibility of access to the market by new insurers.[43]

38 See W. Moschel, 'Kommentar zum Kartellgesetz', Munich: Beck, 1981, pp 20–24, as quoted in M. Faure, 'Insurance and competition law: balancing the conflicts', p 7.

39 See M. Faure, 'Insurance and competition law: balancing the conflicts', p 7.

40 Ibid. At p 9, M. Faure points out that in many classes of insurance access to the relevant statistical data can be easily obtained. For instance, he emphasises that elaboration of mortality data does not require cooperation since statistical analyses of life expectancies of people are widely available to the general public. He also points out that statistical data related to the frequency of illnesses and accidents are also of easy access.

41 See Comments of Assuralia on the Commission inquiry into the European business insurance sector, available at: http://ec.europa.eu/competition/sectors/financial_services/inquiries/replies_interim_report/17_assuralia.pdf (accessed 17 June 2014).

42 For a general overview of insurance cooperation in the field of prevention, see A. W. Whitney, 'Insurance and prevention', available at: www.casact.org/pubs/proceed/proceed22/22264.pdf (accessed 17 June 2014). For instance, preventive work on a large scale is being carried on by the fire insurance companies, and to some extent by the life insurance companies. More recently, the stock casualty insurance companies have also come to the conclusion that they must attack the problem of the automobile hazard and have taken positive steps in that direction.

43 See the Commission's Business Insurance Sector Inquiry Interim Report of 21 January 2007, p 47. Here, in case of repeal of the current block exemption, the English market, with its annually renewable contracts, may have a competitive head start compared to markets characterised by longer-term contracts, such as France, Austria or Italy. On the structure of the UK insurance industry, see P. Hardwick and M. Guirguis, 'The UK insurance industry: structure and performance', in *Huebner International Series on Risk, Insurance and Economic Security*, 2007, New York: Springer, available at: www.springerlink.com/ (accessed 18 June 2014).

Overall, uncertainties relating to the calculation of premium risks might be overcome by other legal means than premium fixing agreements. In the current situation, when consumers in mass insurance markets buy insurance, they are charged on the basis of the risk premium calculated by the insurers through the use of significant statistics and historical data relating to the past frequency and entity of claims. These statistics tend to strike a balance between consumers having a historical record full of claims and others having no claims or small entity claims. In substance, the risk premium calculated on the basis of these statistics represents the average premium.[44]

If insurers could not rely on the current block exemption on joint calculations and studies of risks, the main question would arise in relation to the determination of the risk premium. An alternative to joint cooperation could be represented by the introduction by law of 'tailor-made' insurance policies.[45] When customers wish to shift between insurance providers, the latter could be obliged by law to provide the existing insured with a personal certificate or register showing the insured's past record of claims. By virtue of this system, the new insurer would then be in a position to calculate the risk premium on the basis of the personal record of the new customer.[46]

This system arguably presents two beneficial features. First, it represents an efficient form of information sharing between insurers, allowing them to pass on information on risks that generally promote competition rather than limiting it by cartel agreements on premiums. Second, this system might also enhance competition among insurers, allowing customers to change insurance providers without being obliged (as often happens today) to start at the high beginner's premium with their new insurer. Objections may arise in relation to new customers (i.e. consumers buying insurance for the very first time) and in relation to insureds with a personal record of frequent and expensive claims. The scenario theorised above would see the former unable to provide the required data to insurers, and therefore potentially subject to unduly high-cost policies. The same applies to the latter, who will be penalised by the past frequency of their claims and thus may even be unable to find insurance companies prepared to offer services to them at an affordable price. For both categories of insureds, fear on the part of public policymakers may arise due to the risk that a segment of consumers remain without insurance due to their inability to afford high premium costs or the refusal of undertakings to insure them.

44 The personal record of claim of the actual consumer comes into play only to a limited extent (i.e. a discount in case of no claim during the past years).

45 This idea has been formulated in the doctrine by W. Moschel, 'Kommentar zum Kartellgesetz', 1981, Munich: Beck, pp 20–24, as quoted in. M. Faure, 'Insurance and competition law: balancing the conflicts', p 23.

46 See M. Faure, 'Insurance and competition law: balancing the conflicts', p 24.

These concerns deserve consideration and appear to cast some doubts on this alternative regulatory framework to the current regime. In response, it seems possible to claim that replacing the existing block exemption with a 'tailor-made insurance system' could arguably lead to a diversification of prices and of competition, beneficial also for first-time buyers and consumers with personal statistics showing a high number of past claims.

The reason is simple: if insurers are no longer able to jointly determine the risk premium, the competition among them would be mainly based on an element of price diversification by virtue of which some undertakings, particularly new market entrants, will try to attract new customers on the basis of tariffs that are very convenient for first-time buyers, while others will provide attractive packages for consumers with a claims-intensive past.

As established in the above, absent a block exemption for the joint determination of risks, difficulties for insurers could arise in relation to the calculation of one-off risks (e.g. fire and operational failure) and no-fault-based risks. Nevertheless, many statistical data (e.g. mortal car accidents rather than average life statistics) are nowadays widely available and do not require the need for cooperation. These data are, in fact, also often accessible for no-fault-based risks (e.g. flooding of a particular property) and may equally represent the basis for the calculation of the individual risks although they are not linked with the behaviour of the insured.[47]

In the case of liability insurance, the theorised individual system of calculation of risks might not only represent a suitable alternative to the current block exemption regime, but may also lead to the creation of market efficiencies. The doctrine has identified the creation of a linkage between the premium and the behaviour of the insured as an efficient way to face the moral hazard problem.[48] For instance, in the case of fault-based insurance, where policies are solely determined on the basis of the conduct of the individual concerned, competition is in fact deemed to ensure the creation of an optimal scenario whereby the premium perfectly reflects the behaviour of the insured, and, as a consequence, the moral hazard problem is efficiently faced. A competitive insurance market could therefore arguably

47 Some of these statistics are available at governmental links, such as: www.statistics.gov.uk/cci/nugget.asp?id=881 (accessed 3 July 2011).

48 As mentioned before, once insured, people are more willing to take actions that result in cashing in their policy. In seminal economic studies of accident law, 'liability rules are seen as instruments to achieve reduction of accident costs'. See S. Shavell, *Economic Analysis of Accident Law*, 1987, Cambridge, MA: Harvard University Press, p 36. M. Faure (in 'Insurance and competition law: balancing the conflicts', p 23) points out that liability rules could therefore act as deterrent and give incentives to insureds to avoid risks. Nevertheless, this scenario changes drastically if insurers do not bear losses because they are insured. At this point, insurance undertakings should take over the deterrent function of liability rules and the only possibility for them to face the moral hazard problem would be to cooperate in the calculation of risks.

not only have a positive effect on moral hazard issues, as it is allegedly deemed to enable the narrowing of the need for risk pools, but is also considered crucial in order to avoid the risks of moral hazard and adverse selection.[49] In any event, just as with the repeal of the block exemption related to standard policy conditions and safety equipment, a further repeal of the remaining pillars of the block exemption would surely be accompanied by specific guidelines. For the time being, the theoretical full application of Article 101 to the insurance industry will now be considered in light of the EU Commission's guidelines on horizontal cooperation agreements.[50]

5.2.2 Assessment of information exchange in light of the EU Commission's guidelines on horizontal cooperation agreements

In the absence of a block exemption, any exchange of information between insurance undertakings would be capable of infringing Article 101 and should be carefully weighed beforehand in order to avoid severe sanctions. According to the Commission's guidelines, the exchange of market information may lead to restrictions of competition, in particular in situations where it is liable to enable undertakings to be aware of the market strategies of their competitors.[51] When it comes to the insurance industry, the exchange of relevant statistical data between insurers can indeed qualify as an exchange of market strategies information, as joint statistical data are used in order to determine insurance premiums, which can be defined as the quintessential market strategy tool for insurers.

The guidelines acknowledge that information exchange is a common feature of many competitive markets and may generate various types of efficiency gains and help to solve problems of information asymmetries.[52] Moreover, the Commission also sees information exchange as beneficial for consumers in case they reduce end users' search costs and improve their choice.[53]

In absence of a block exemption, exchange of information between insurers would need to be self-assessed vis-à-vis the application of Article 101. The starting point is that any information exchange can only be addressed under Article 101 if it establishes or is part of an agreement, a

49 Ibid.

50 The Commission's Guidelines on the applicability of Article 101 of the Treaty on the Functioning of the European Union to horizontal cooperation agreements, 2011/C 11/01, 14/01/2011, available at: http://eur-lex.europa.eu/LexUriServ/LexUriServ.do?uri=OJ:C:2011:011:0001:0072:EN:PDF (accessed 17 June 2014).

51 See the Commission's Guidelines on the applicability of Article 101 of the Treaty on the Functioning of the European Union to horizontal cooperation agreements, para 58.

52 Ibid., para 57.

53 Ibid.

concerted practice or a decision by an association of undertakings. Even in the absence of an official agreement between insurers, the exchange of information may still be caught by Article 101 if it amounts to a concerted practice. The guidelines on horizontal cooperation point out that in line with the case law of the Court of Justice of the European Union, the concept of a concerted practice refers to a form of coordination between undertakings by which, without it having reached the stage where an agreement properly so-called has been concluded, practical cooperation between them is knowingly substituted for the risks of competition.[54] The concept of concerted practice is a broad concept that includes even a hypothetical scenario where only one insurance undertaking discloses statistical information to its competitor(s).[55]

The next analytical step in the assessment of the exchange of information between insurers is the identification of the nature of the exchange. As established above, not all practices are considered harmful under the guidelines, which, in particular, look favourably upon the exchange of historic data. According to the guidelines, the exchange of historic data is unlikely to lead to a collusive outcome as it is unlikely to be indicative of the competitors' future conduct or to provide a common understanding on the market.[56]

When it comes to the insurance sector, the main question is whether joint statistics could qualify as historical data. On an abstract level, the answer to this question is affirmative; joint statistical data on the frequency of claims do have the character of historical information. Nevertheless, it is the opinion of this author that the concept of historical data needs to be assessed in relation to the nature of a specific market. In a market such as the insurance industry, the exchange of historic data regarding frequency of claims and other relevant statistics, despite the declarations of principle of the Commission guidelines, can have an impact on future behaviours of insurers and provide an understanding of the market. The reason for this is that, let us not forget, the exchange of historical data in the insurance industry leads to the determination of insurance premiums, having severe market implications in terms of the conduct of insurance undertakings.

Where would all this leave insurers in the case of a complete repeal of the current block exemption? The only possible way for insurers to circumvent the application of Article 101 would be to prove that the

54 Ibid., para 60. For the definition of a concerted practice, see, inter alia, Case C-8/08, *T-Mobile Netherlands*, para 26; Joined Cases C-89/85 and others, *Wood Pulp*, [1993] ECR 1307, para 63.

55 See the Commission's Guidelines on the applicability of Article 101 of the Treaty on the Functioning of the European Union to horizontal cooperation agreements, para 62. See Joined Cases T-25/95 and others, *Cimenteries*, [2000] ECR II-491, para 184.

56 See the Commission's Guidelines on the applicability of Article 101 of the Treaty on the Functioning of the European Union to horizontal cooperation agreements, para 90.

information exchange may lead to efficiency gains within the meaning of Article 101(3). According to the guidelines, information about competitors' costs can enable companies to become more efficient if they benchmark their performance against best practice in the industry and design internal incentive schemes accordingly.[57] Most importantly, the guidelines explicitly refer to exchange of consumer data between companies in markets with asymmetric information about consumers (such as the financial services market).[58] The Commission points out that within the financial services market, keeping track of the past behaviour of customers in terms of accidents or credit defaults provides an incentive for consumers to limit their risk exposure.[59] Moreover, according to the guidelines, information about consumers' past behaviour also makes it possible to detect which consumers carry a lower risk and should benefit from lower prices. In this context, information exchange can also reduce consumer lock-in, thereby inducing stronger competition, since the information is generally specific to a relationship and consumers would otherwise lose the benefit from that information when switching to another company.[60]

The guidelines appear therefore to offer a possibility for individual exemption under Article 101(3) of the TFEU. Nevertheless, it needs to be emphasised that restrictions that go beyond what is necessary to achieve the efficiency gains generated by an information exchange do not fulfil the conditions of Article 101(3).[61] In order to fulfil the condition of indispensability, insurers will need to prove that the data's subject matter, aggregation, age, confidentiality and frequency, as well as coverage of the exchange, are of the kind that carries the lowest risks indispensable for creating the claimed efficiency gains.[62]

In case of a complete repeal of the insurance block exemption, this concept of indispensability of the exchange of information will assume a completely different role in view of the adoption or not of possible ancillary measures. If the repeal of the current regime is not to be accompanied by the introduction of alternative means of information sources for insurers about insureds (such as the introduction of consumer 'passports' containing individualised historic statistical data theorised above), then the guidelines will represent an interesting platform for obtaining individual exemption of information exchange agreements.

Conversely, if the repeal of the current block exemption regulatory framework will be accompanied by the enactment of a 'tailor-made

57 Ibid., para 95.
58 See the Commission's Guidelines on the applicability of Article 101 of the Treaty on the Functioning of the European Union to horizontal cooperation agreements, para 97.
59 Ibid.
60 Ibid.
61 Ibid., para 101.
62 Ibid.

insurance system', the element of the indispensability of the exchange of information will be an arduous burden of proof for insurers to overcome.

In any case, it deserves to be pointed out that according to the guidelines, efficiency gains attained by indispensable restrictions must be passed on to consumers to an extent that outweighs the restrictive effects on competition caused by an information exchange.[63] This means that insurers will ultimately be subject to the burden of proof that the exchange of information has a beneficial impact on end users. Interestingly, the guidelines indicate that the lower the market power of the parties involved in the information exchange, the more likely it is that the efficiency gains would be passed on to consumers to an extent that outweighs the restrictive effects on competition.[64] For small insurers (and new market entrants), the burden of proof would be considerably lower compared to larger or well-established market players.

5.2.3 The current EU regime for co-insurance and reinsurance pools

The current regime retains the block exemption for pools that cover 'new risks' and for other pools subject to certain market share thresholds. In line with the previous regime, pools covering new risks are exempted for a three-year period, regardless of the participants' market share.[65] The risk must be genuinely new or, exceptionally, a risk the nature of which has, on the basis of an objective analysis, changed so materially that it is not possible to know in advance what subscription capacity is necessary in order to cover such a risk.[66] The concept of risk changed on the basis of object criteria is new and will have to be further elaborated. Nevertheless, this new concept may represent an important tool for the Commission in order to assess the effective necessity of the coverage of specific risks through pools.

There are also changes in respect of pools covering existing risks. If, under the previous regime, market share thresholds were considered in relation to the turnover of the pool, from now on the possibility of benefiting from the exemption will depend on the turnover of all participating companies on the relevant market, regardless of the fact that the turnover is achieved inside or outside the pool.[67] This narrows down the scope of application of the exemption considerably, and arguably will ignite a certain degree of uncertainty. This new scenario would be, in fact, particularly delicate for larger insurers, as uncertainty shall inevitably arise in relation to the calculation of market shares for all undertakings participating in the pool.

63 See the Commission's Guidelines on the applicability of Article 101 of the Treaty on the Functioning of the European Union to horizontal cooperation agreements, para 103.

64 Ibid.

65 Ibid., Article 6(1).

66 Ibid., Article 1(6)(b).

67 Ibid., Article 6(3)(c).

For the first time, ad hoc co-insurance and co-reinsurance agreements will fall outside the application of the block exemption.[68] Ad hoc co-reinsurance agreements on the subscription market are defined by the Regulation as agreements whereby a certain part of a given risk is covered by a lead insurer and the remaining part of this risk is covered by follow insurers who are then invited to cover that remainder in order either to: (1) reinsure mutually all or part of their liabilities in respect of a specified risk category; or (2) incidentally accept, in the name and on behalf of all the participants, the reinsurance of the same category of risks.[69] This means that insurance undertakings participating in ad hoc agreements will be fully exposed to the EU competition rules. Overall, the new regime for pools represent an important step forward if compared to the old status quo.

The need for insurers to cooperate by means of coinsurance and reinsurance appears to be, prima facie, another essential element of business insurance, and represents the most extensive form of cooperation among competing insurers. The idea that cooperation between insurers is crucial and, to some extent, required by the modern insurance markets has been endorsed by both the US and European insurance regulatory frameworks.[70]

Coinsurance and co-reinsurance groups ('pools') are risk-sharing joint ventures among insurers or reinsurers otherwise acting as independent undertakings.[71] They are typically created in order to diversify and share exceptionally large, ultra-hazardous or uneven risks. Each undertaking participating in the pool benefits from the profits of the pool or bears its losses pro rata (i.e. in proportion to the quota owned).

There are two main forms of pools: (1) co-insurance pools; and (2) reinsurance pools. The former are created by direct insurers in order to jointly cover specific types of risks (e.g. environmental, nuclear risks or terrorism). The foremost aim of the latter is instead to enable the diversification of very large loss risks across national or international insurance markets.[72] In the modern economy, insurance undertakings are under an enormous amount of pressure to cover risks of a magnitude that often go above and beyond the financial means of an individual insurer.[73] If insurers

68 Ibid., Article 1(5)(b).

69 Ibid., Article 1(4)(a) and Article 1(4)(b).

70 See R. Havens and M. Theisen, 'The application of United States and EEC antitrust laws to reinsurance and insurance pooling arrangements', *The Antitrust Bulletin*, 1986, pp 1300–1301. Currently, both the McCarran-Ferguson Act and Commission Regulation 267/2010 grant a block exemption for the cooperation of insurance undertakings in the form of co-insurance and reinsurance.

71 See the Commission's Business Insurance Sector Inquiry Interim Report of 25 January 2007, p 26, available at: http://ec.europa.eu/competition/sectors/financial_services/inquiries/interim_report_24012007.pdf (accessed 3 July 2011).

72 The availability of reinsurance provides insurers with increased capacity and flexibility, enabling coverage of risks for which cover could otherwise not be obtained.

73 See M. Faure, 'Insurance and competition law: balancing the conflicts', p 9. See also J. Finsinger, 'European integration of insurance markets: preliminary but novel perspectives',

are not in the position to diversify risks within their internal organisational structures, the natural tendency is then to cooperate with other undertakings in co-insurance or reinsurance pools;[74] this tendency of insurers to cooperate has been considered one of the several aspects rendering business insurance a 'naturally monopolistic' activity.[75]

Pooling arrangements for the joint coverage of ultra-hazardous risks and reinsurance are thus deemed to be beneficial for the competition in the insurance sector, and even necessary in order to provide the insurance service in relation to peculiar types of risk. As a matter of fact, some authors have emphasised that risks that are not readily diversifiable in the long term are inevitably subject to more expensive insurance policies or to limited coverage availability for policyholders.[76]

Such arrangements would then allegedly allow small insurance undertakings to enter into and be part of specialised markets. According to these theories, allowing small insurers to pool would therefore result in an enhancement of competition, as in the absence of cooperation, only very large insurance undertakings (and sometimes not even them) would be able to offer coverage for particular risky activities.[77]

Pooling is also deemed to facilitate the purchase of reinsurance, and through reinsurance the capacity to insure is meant to increase in a sort of beneficial circle for the insurance industry, which ultimately would also help to stabilise operating results.[78]

In line with the aforementioned economic theories, the new Regulation treats insurance pools favourably as they allow a greater number of insurers to enter the market, consequently increasing the opportunity of covering particular risks that would otherwise remain uncovered. Despite such declarations of principle, the Commission did point out that pools may not always be justified, especially in case there is enough capacity for multiple pools to cover any given risk, and in the absence of an exhaustive

Working Paper, Universitat Luneburg, no 75, 1989, pp 70–72.

74 See M. Faure, 'Insurance and competition law: balancing the conflicts', p 10. See also OECD, Policy Roundtables, 'Competition and related regulation issues in the insurance industry', 1998, available at: www.oecd.org/dataoecd/34/25/1920099.pdf. (accessed 3 July 2011).

75 Ibid., p 9. It is interesting to note that, until not long ago, in several Member States (e.g. Italy), the insurance industry was actually a State monopoly.

76 See Patricia M. Danzon, *The McCarran-Ferguson Act: Anticompetitive or Procompetitive?*, p 24.

77 See R. Havens and M. Theisen, 'The application of United States and EEC antitrust laws to reinsurance and insurance pooling arrangements', pp 1300–1301. See also J. Finsinger, 'Verbraucherschutz auf Versicherungsmarkten', 1988, Munich: Florentz, pp 70–72.

78 See R. Havens and M. Theisen, 'The application of United States and EEC antitrust laws to reinsurance and insurance pooling arrangements', pp 1300–1301. See also M. Faure, 'Insurance and competition law: balancing the conflicts', p 10.

ready-made list of risks that require joint coverage.[79] Thus, from an antitrust perspective, co-insurance and reinsurance groups raise a very important question: is it really possible to determine when a pool is necessary in order to cover a specific risk? In theoretical terms, the answer is yes. Assuming that insurers endeavour to achieve an optimal balance between premiums and losses, the more the risks are homogeneous and the higher the number of insured related to that risk, the lower the spread between premium and losses.[80] Insurers who do not cover large numbers of homogeneous risks effectively have three options in order to spread the risks: reinsure individually, join a co-insurance pool or become part of a co-reinsurance group.[81] The first option is the safest from a compliance perspective as it does not entail any form of joint determination of risk premium. Consequently, joint co-insurance or reinsurance should be allowed only in extreme cases when forms of individual reinsurance are not sufficient to spread risks. As often happens with theoretical legal arguments, the practical aspects are far more intricate. It is very difficult in practice to adopt specific criteria to ascertain how many homogeneous risks need to be insured before an acceptable spread is reached by insurers without the need to reinsure or to join co-insurance or reinsurance pools. It is equally arduous to determine when individual reinsurance practices represent an optimal and more efficient way to minimise risk rather than the use of pools.[82]

Regulation 267/2010 would therefore, prima facie, represent the optimal regulatory framework for co-insurance and reinsurance pools (although doubts do arise in relation to the extent of the current block exemption). The doctrine has emphasised that inefficiencies may indeed arise under the current block exemption regime in relation to pool agreements, especially in the case of powerful lobbies characterising specific insurance segments.[83]

79 See the Commission's Business Insurance Sector Inquiry Interim Report of 25 January 2007, p 82.

80 This point was formulated by L. Gyselen, 'EU antitrust law in the area of financial services', Fordham Corporate Law Institute, 23rd Annual Conference on International Antitrust Law and Policy', New York, 1996, p 34, available at: http://europa.eu.iny/comm/competition/speeches/text/sp1997_005_en.html (accessed 3 July 2011). For instance, in the case of third-party liability car insurance, the accuracy of the calculation of the risk premium will increase considerably in relation to the degree of homogeneity of the risk insured (e.g. utility cars driven by women up to 40 years old vis-à-vis all types of cars driven by people of all ages).

81 This analysis is based on the theories elaborated by L. Gyselen, 'EU antitrust law in the area of financial services'.

82 An attempt to do this was made in vain by L. Gyselen, 'EU antitrust law in the area of financial services', p 45.

83 See M. Faure and R. Van den Bergh, 'Liability for nuclear accidents in Belgium from an interest group perspective', *International Review of Law and Economics*, 1990, pp 241–254. See also M. Faure, 'Insurance and competition law: balancing the conflicts', p 11. M. Faure and R. Van den Bergh have identified examples of such inefficiencies in the field

Moreover, the Commission itself emphasises that the need for co-insurance and reinsurance pools depends mainly on the frequency of claims and diversification of risks.[84]

These considerations revert the analysis to the rationale for allowing the block exemption of pools. If pooling is only justified under the belief that it leads to increased competition and creates efficiencies, the assumption would be that without pooling, only a limited number of insurers could provide coverage for certain types of risks.[85] Without any form of co-insurance or reinsurance practice, competition would thus be too limited. Conversely, if despite the existence of a block exemption pooling causes a high degree of consolidation on insurance markets, the end result is obviously not efficient and doubts inevitably arise in relation to the current status quo.

Apart from issues relating to deficiencies and inefficiencies (which are likely to arise with or without a block exemption), the arguments pro and contra block exemption need to be carefully counterbalanced in view of the possibility to identify valid regulatory alternatives. The current EU block exemption generally allows the possibility for insurers to cooperate in order to insure or reinsure any risks; from this perspective, a blanket exemption in relation to all classes of risk may not be optimal.[86]

A valid alternative could be then to allow pooling arrangements for joint insurance and reinsurance only in relation to catastrophic, ultra-hazardous or uneven risks (e.g. nuclear, environmental, aviation risks and terrorism). In other words, the idea would be to confine the block exemption to risks that otherwise would remain uncovered due to the impossibility for single insurers to diversify them internally. A suitable suggestion could therefore be to restrict the block exemption to the above-mentioned specific types of risk and to maintain the current thresholds enshrined in Regulation 267/2010 as they represent a safe harbour against excessive concentration. New risks and other peculiar situations could be covered by individual exemptions, and, most of all, the need for pools could be reduced by the abolition of the block exemption for joint calculation of premiums.

As previously mentioned, in a perfectly competitive insurance market characterised by an effective linkage between insured behaviour and risk premium, the moral hazard problem could be adequately faced in an optimal

of nuclear insurance: as a result of the lobbying power of the Belgian nuclear insurance industry, the nuclear insurance and reinsurance pool agreements led to high premiums, a low availability of insurance capacity and low financial limits on the liability of the licensee of a nuclear power plant.

84 See the Commission's Business Insurance Sector Inquiry Interim Report of 25 January 2007, p 64.

85 See M. Faure, 'Insurance and competition law: balancing the conflicts', p 10.

86 On this point, see the observations made by M. Faure, 'Insurance and competition law: balancing the conflicts', p 10.

way, narrowing the need for risk pools. A teleological link therefore arguably exists between the joint calculation of premiums and the cooperation in the form of co-insurance and reinsurance.

5.2.4 Agreements on standard policy conditions

Cooperation on the design of policy forms was generally considered acceptable as it was deemed to facilitate price comparisons for consumers.[87] Considering that the supply of insurance services traditionally lacks transparency, in granting a block exemption the Commission took into consideration that non-binding standard policy conditions allegedly procured efficiencies for insurance undertakings and could have benefits for consumer organisations and brokers.

Exactly as with any kind of service industry, consumers need to have access to information in order to determine which service provider is most suitable for them. Information deficiencies are theoretically capable of deterring the functioning of the market, leading to ineffective results.[88] A block exemption relating to the standardisation of policy conditions was therefore considered the correct regulatory response to an 'alleged market failure'.[89]

As from 24 March 2009, the scenario is radically different. The new Regulation represents a weighty rebuttal of the above approach and the end of the block exemption in this area. The Regulation does not regard standard policy conditions as a sufficiently sector-specific feature to merit special treatment by way of block exemption coverage. The removal of standard policy wording from the comfort zone of a block exemption is significant news and is likely to create legal uncertainty for the industry, which may soon have to assess the competition law sensitivity of each standardisation agreement.[90]

The rationale for this radical change of policy appears to be that in the absence of a block exemption for standard terms, competition would allegedly be enhanced by virtue of the fact that insurers could supply a

87 See P. M. Danzon, 'The McCarran-Ferguson Act: anticompetitive or procompetitive?', p 28. On this point, see also M. Faure, 'Insurance and competition law: balancing the conflicts', available at: www.nottingham.ac.uk/business/cris/papers/Grif%20-%20Michael%20Faure.pdf (accessed 3 July 2011).

88 See M. Faure, 'Insurance and competition law: balancing the conflicts', p 11. On this point, see also P. M. Danzon, 'The McCarran-Ferguson Act: anticompetitive or procompetitive?', p 28.

89 See M. Faure, 'Insurance and competition law: balancing the conflicts', p 11.

90 As recently happened in connection with the abolition of the Council Regulation (EEC) No 4056/86 OJ L 378/4, 22/12/1986, which provided a block exemption for the maritime sector, the Commission will issue guidelines in order to help insurers verify the validity of their agreements on policy conditions vis-à-vis Article 101.

greater variety of policies. In the past, the *raison d'être* supporting the current block exemption for standard policy conditions had been criticised for being erroneous both in formulation and in the proposed remedy.[91] In particular, the claim that consumers are not capable of estimating the contents of insurance contracts is perhaps formulated in excessively generic terms.

It is appropriate to distinguish between different classes of insurance. In the case of mass consumer insurance, it has been correctly noted that policies containing sharply drafted exclusion clauses, the implications of which can only be assessed by a specialised lawyer, may be difficult to understand for consumers.[92] On the contrary, according to economic doctrine, in the field of commercial and industrial insurance, the commercial awareness of the typology of customers does not appear to require specific legal protection.[93] Since the problem seems thus to arise mainly in relation to non-commercial buyers, it has been argued that the repeal of the block exemption should be confined to this area and the role of insurance brokers could be emphasised as a means of consumer protection.[94]

Clearly this was not the intention of the Commission, which, with Regulation 267/2010 envisaged a complete repeal of the block exemption related to standard policy conditions. As we have established, the rationale for this decision is to be found in the assumption that the use of standard policy conditions was not a peculiarity of the insurance industry and thus did not deserve special consideration. Standard policy conditions are indeed of common use in trade; nevertheless, they do give rise to competition concerns. On a general level, problems occur whenever an association of undertakings imposes on its members an obligation to use common terms and conditions of sale and purchase. This inevitably reverts against competition as in the first place it limits the freedom of the undertakings involved to provide conditions that vary from the one imposed upon them. Most importantly, consumers may also be harmed by such practices as their choice of service providers is inevitably narrowed down.

91 On this point, see M. Faure, 'Insurance and competition law: balancing the conflicts', p 15.

92 Ibid., p 12.

93 Ibid.

94 See M. Faure, 'Insurance and competition law: balancing the conflicts', p 12. A competitive supply of insurance brokers could indeed assist consumers in finding an insurance policy that fits their preferences as far as premium and policy conditions are concerned. The Commission itself recently emphasised that insurance brokers have increased their role in most member states, and that the role of insurance brokers can be used to strengthen the bargaining position of consumers, acting as a countervailing force to the increased bargaining power of large insurers and reinsurers. See the Commission's Business Insurance Sector Inquiry Final Report of 25 September 2007, available at: http://ec.europa.eu/competition/sectors/financial_services/inquiries/final_report_annex.pdf (accessed 1 July 2011).

Conversely, standard policy conditions are less likely to have a detrimental impact on competition where members retain the freedom to adopt dissimilar conditions if they wish to do so. Under the current regime, the freedom to implement diverse conditions is, as previously established, an essential condition for the exemption. Notwithstanding, standard policy conditions can still have an adverse effect on competition if a large proportion of the insurance undertakings adopt the same policy conditions. Thus, the theoretical freedom to adopt different standard policy conditions does not represent, in this case, a safety net, as customers may be left with little or no choice in practice.

A scenario without a block exemption will also inevitably give rise to the need to identify suitable ways to regulate the flow of information related to insurance policies.[95] The key here will be the identification and enactment of valid forms of consumer protection. In order to protect consumers, some member states[96] have already enacted a system of *ex post* control of policy conditions through courts or relevant independent authorities. Such systems appear to suggest a valid alternative in order to shield consumers against hostile policy conditions while granting competition between insurance undertakings.

Apart from issues related to consumer protection, the repeal of the block exemption for standard policy conditions creates a scenario where agreements between insurance undertakings will need to be assessed on a case-by-case basis vis-à-vis Article 101(3). On the basis of Article 101(3), individual exemptions will be granted if specific conditions apply: agreements on standard policy conditions will qualify for exemption insofar as they create efficiencies that outweigh the restriction of competition, consumers obtain a fair share of those benefits, there are no less restrictive means of achieving the efficiencies, and competition is not eliminated altogether. In order to be consistent with Article 101(3), it will need to be proven that agreements on standard policy conditions grant some leeway to the undertakings concerned in terms of the possibility to deviate from the status quo of the agreement providing alternative conditions. For instance, an agreement binding only on specific predetermined terms leaving the freedom to provide diverse conditions in relation to remaining provisions will be likely to benefit from an individual exemption. Conversely, agreements that will not confer any degree of freedom to provide alternative conditions will be considered anticompetitive unless beneficial for

95 See R. Eisen, P. Zweifel and W. Muller, 'Unternehmerische Versicherungswirtschaft: Konsequenzen Der Deregulierung Fur Wettbewerbsordnung Und Unternehmensfuhrung', 1993, Munich: Florenz, pp 17–18. See also M. Faure, 'Insurance and competition law: balancing the conflicts', p 12.

96 Inter alia, Italy and France, where the relevant competition authorities are tasked with the duty to monitor and review insurance standard policy conditions.

consumers. Under such circumstances, individual exemption may be granted to standardisation agreements that effectively render particularly hermetic policy conditions accessible for consumers.[97] Agreements on standard policy conditions could also possibly be exempt if a linkage exists with agreements on joint calculations of risks. The reason for this is that the original idea of the Commission was to provide a block exemption only for standard policy conditions related to joint calculation of risks.[98] This idea was ultimately abandoned, but, considering that the joint calculation of risks will still be part of the new block exemption regime, it is perhaps not unreasonable to foresee a favourable treatment of standard policy conditions linked with agreements on joint calculation of risks.

5.3 Joint determination of approved safety equipment in the EU

Under the current regime, agreements between insurers on technical specifications for security equipment no longer benefit from the block exemption. In the course of preparations of Regulation 267/2010, the original idea of the Commission was to introduce a new condition for exemption of agreements between insurers on approved security equipment.[99] According to a proposed draft, the condition for exemption was to be that technical specifications, rules, procedures or codes of practice adopted by national associations of insurance or reinsurance undertakings in other member states must have been explicitly recognised as equally valid by an association or associations of insurance or reinsurance undertakings in one or several member states.[100] The same rationale applied to any approval of a security device or installing and maintenance undertaking issued by an association of insurance or reinsurance undertakings in another member state.[101]

97 After the decentralisation process of the enforcement of the EC competition rules introduced by Regulation 1/2003 on the implementation of the rules on competition laid down in Articles 81 and 82 of the Treaty (OJ 2003 L 1/1), the Commission is no longer the only body entitled to grant individual exemption. National competition authorities and national courts are also currently involved in checking the validity of co operation agreements vis-à-vis Article 101(3) of the Treaty. The burden of proof is high and lays on the applicants.

98 See the Draft Commission Regulation (EU) No 267/2010, available at: http://ec.europa.eu/comm/competition/antitrust/others/regulation_en.pdf (accessed 3 July 2011).

99 Ibid.

100 See the proposed Commission Regulation (EU) No 267/2010, Article 9(n).

101 Ibid., Article 9(m). Moreover, the draft Regulation did not offer any exemption to technical specifications, rules, procedures or codes of practice adopted by an association or associations of insurance or reinsurance undertakings in one or several member states if there was equivalent technical specifications, rules, procedures or codes of practice at European level.

Under the past block exemption regime, security devices used to be exempt insofar as the technical specifications and compliance assessment procedures are 'precise, technically justified and in proportion to the performance to be attained by the security device concerned'.[102] The exemption found application whenever the rules for the evaluation of installation undertakings and maintenance undertakings are 'objective, relate to their technical competence and are applied in a non-discriminatory manner'.[103] Such specifications and rules were required to be established and distributed with an accompanying statement that insurance undertakings are 'free to accept for insurance, on whatever terms and conditions they wish, other security devices or installation and maintenance undertakings which do not comply with these technical specifications or rules'.[104]

Just as with standard policy conditions, the new Regulation draws the finishing line for the exemption of joint determination of safety equipment. Security devices are no longer considered sufficiently sector-specific to merit special treatment and will be removed from the block exemption framework.

6 Abuse of dominant position in EU and China

6.1 Article 102 of the TFEU: abuse of dominant position and mergers regulation in the EU

6.1.1 Article 102: meaning and issues

Article 102 of the TFEU prohibits the abuse of dominant position by one or more undertakings within the common market or in a substantial part as incompatible with the common market insofar as it may affect trade between member states. The essence of Article 102 is to control market power. The prohibition on abuses of dominant position provided by Article 102 incorporates three cumulative elements. First, one or more undertakings need to acquire a dominant position within the common market or in a substantial part thereof. The concept of dominance does not exist in the abstract, but only in relation to a particular market, intended as a clearly defined geographical area where a product is marketed and where the conditions of competition are sufficiently homogeneous for the effect of the economic power of the undertaking to be evaluated. The relevant market needs thus to be identified in its geographical and product dimensions prior to the assessment of dominance, which is mainly based on the analysis of the share of the market occupied by a specific undertaking in conjunction

102 See Commission Regulation (EU) No 267/2010, Article 9(a).
103 Ibid., Article 9(b).
104 Ibid., Article 9(c).

with the assessment of the market share of its nearest competitor. Nevertheless, it needs to be emphasised that a dominant position within a market is not illicit in itself; it is the abuse of that position that is illegitimate. Accordingly, in order to trigger the application of Article 102, the undertaking or undertakings concerned must have abused that position of dominance.

The concept of dominance does not exist in the abstract, but in relation to a particular market.[105] Thus, the first stage in order to ascertain the existence of a position of dominance is the identification of the concept of relevant market. The court, in *United Brands v Commission*,[106] stated that it is necessary to define the relevant market both on its product and its geographical dimensions.[107] The concepts of the relevant product market and the geographical market will now be considered in turn.

6.1.2 The relevant product market

The approach behind the definition of the relevant product market offered by the Commission and the court has been to focus upon the notion of interchangeability (i.e. the extent to which the goods or services under scrutiny are interchangeable with other products). The notion of interchangeability entails the analysis of 'cross-elasticities' of one specific product. The existence of high cross-elasticity indicates that the products are interchangeable. The more products tend to be interchangeable, the more are the probabilities that, in practice, they belong to the same relevant market.

6.1.3 The relevant geographic market

The court, in *United Brands v Commission*, described the concept of geographic market as a 'clearly defined geographic area where a product is marketed and where the conditions of competition are sufficiently homogeneous for the effect of the economic power of the undertaking to be evaluated'.[108]

The legal elements and concepts enshrined into Article 102 of the TFEU represent the foundations for the antitrust assessment of mergers and acquisitions in Europe considered at a later stage of this chapter.

105 Ibid., paragraph 26.
106 *United Brands v Commission* Case 27/76 [1978] ECR 207.
107 Ibid., paragraph 11.
108 See *United Brands v Commission*, para 43.

6.2 The EU Merger Regulation regime

The foremost aim of the EU Merger Regulation is to monitor and regulate mergers and concentrations having 'community dimensions'.[109] A concentration is defined as a change of control on a lasting basis resulting from: (1) the merger of two or more previously independent undertakings; or (2) the acquisition of one or more persons already controlling at least one undertaking, or by one or more undertakings, whether by purchase of securities or assets, by contract or by any other means, of direct or indirect control of the whole or parts of one or more other undertakings.[110]

The creation of a joint venture performing on a lasting basis all the functions of an autonomous economic entity also constitutes a concentration.[111]

The concept of 'community dimension' is delineated by worldwide and EU-wide turnover of the undertakings concerned. Concentrations are of a 'community dimension' where the merging parties' (the 'undertakings concerned'):

> (i) combined world-wide turnover is superior to €5 billion and each of at least two of the merging parties realized superior to €250 million turnover in the EU, unless each of the merging parties obtains more than 2/3 of its EU turnover in one and the same Member State, or;
>
> (ii) combined world-wide turnover is superior to €2.5 billion; in each of at least three Member States, the combined turnover of the merging parties is superior to €100 million; in each of those three Member States, the turnover of each of at least two of the merging parties is superior to €25 million; the Community wide turnover of each of at least two of the merging parties is superior to €100 million; unless each of the merging parties obtains more than 2/3 of its EU turnover and the same Member State.[112]

109 See Council Regulation (EC) No 139/2004 of 20 January 2004 on the control of concentrations between undertakings (the EC Merger Regulation), Official Journal L 24, 29.01.2004, p 1, Article 3.

110 Ibid., Article 4.

111 Ibid., Article 5.

112 Ibid., Article 1. Turnover is defined by the Regulation as 'the amounts derived by the undertakings concerned in the preceding financial year from the sale of products and the provision of services falling within the undertakings' ordinary activities after deduction of sales rebates and of value added tax and other taxes directly related to turnover' (Article 5). Where parts only of an undertaking are to be acquired, then only the turnover attributable to the parts being acquired will be taken into account in order to determine whether the thresholds are met (Article 5(2)).

The Regulation adopts different criteria for credit or financial institutions and insurance undertakings. In relation to insurance undertakings in place of turnover, the following must be used:

> the value of gross premiums written which shall comprise all amounts received and receivable in respect of insurance contracts issued by or on behalf of the insurance undertakings, including also outgoing reinsurance premiums, and after deduction of taxes and parafiscal contributions or levies charged by reference to the amounts of individual premiums or the total volume of premiums.[113]

In determining the €250 million turnover threshold within the EU, gross premiums income received from European Union residents must be applied, and in relation to the application of the two-thirds concentration rates mentioned above, gross premiums received from European residents and from residents of one member state, respectively, must be taken into account.[114] The provenance of the premium rather than the place of receipt is thus relevant in order to determine the relevant thresholds.

The relevant thresholds, either based on turnovers, gross premiums or other criteria, are not confined to the undertakings directly concerned in the concentration, but are extended to groups of undertakings. The Regulation identifies the undertakings to be treated as forming part of the same group as parent, subsidiary or associated companies, or companies linked by a relationship of effective management control.[115]

Adopting the phraseology of Article 102, the Regulation prohibits a concentration in case it 'would significantly impede effective competition, in the common market or in a substantial part of it, in particular as a result of the creation or strengthening of a dominant position'.[116]

However, in assessing the impact of the concentration on the market, the Commission may also take into account, in the first place:

> the need to maintain and develop effective competition within the common market in view of, among other things, the structure of all the markets concerned and the actual or potential competition from undertakings located either within or outwith the Community.[117]

The Commission may also consider the market position of the undertakings concerned and their economic and financial power, the alternatives

113 See Council Regulation (EC) No 139/2004, Article 3(b).
114 Ibid., Article 5(3b).
115 Ibid., Article 5(4).
116 Ibid., Article 2(3).
117 Ibid., Article 2(1).

available to suppliers and users, their access to supplies or markets, any legal or other barriers to entry, supply and demand trends for the relevant goods and services, the interests of the intermediate and ultimate consumers, and the development of technical and economic progress provided that it is to consumers' advantage and does not form an obstacle to competition.[118]

6.3 Abuse of dominant position and mergers regulation in China

6.3.1 Article 17 of the China Anti-Monopoly Law: the abuse of dominant position

The provisions of the Anti-Monopoly Law that deal with abuse of dominant position are modelled on Article 102 of the TFEU. Article 17 prohibits undertakings holding dominant market positions from selling commodities at unfairly high prices or buying commodities at unfairly low prices; selling commodities at prices below cost without justifiable reason; refusing to enter into transactions with their trading counterparts without justifiable reasons; allowing their trading counterparts to make transactions exclusively with themselves or with the undertakings designated by them, without justifiable reasons; conducting tie-in sales of commodities or adding other unreasonable trading conditions to transactions, without justifiable reasons; without justifiable reasons, applying differential prices and other transaction terms among their trading counterparts who are on an equal footing; or other acts of abuse of dominant market positions confirmed as such by the authority for enforcement of the Anti-Monopoly Law under the State Council.

For the purposes of the Anti-Monopoly Law, dominant market position means a market position held by undertakings that are capable of controlling the prices or quantities of commodities or other transaction terms in a relevant market, or preventing or exerting an influence on the access of other undertakings to the market.

Under Article 18, the dominant market position of an undertaking shall be determined on the basis of the following factors:

(1) its share on a relevant market and the competitiveness on the market;
(2) its ability to control the sales market or the purchasing market for raw and semi-finished material;
(3) its financial strength and technical conditions;
(4) the extent to which other business mangers depend on it in transactions;
(5) the difficulty that other undertakings find in entering a relevant market; and

118 Ibid.

(6) other factors related to the determination of the dominant market position held by an undertaking.

Article 19 lays down the criteria for assessment, stating that the conclusion that an undertaking holds a dominant market position may be deduced from: (1) the market share of one undertaking accounts for half of the total in a relevant market; (2) the joint market share of two undertakings accounts for two-thirds of the total, in a relevant market; or (3) the joint market share of three undertakings accounts for three-quarters of the total in a relevant market.

Under the circumstance specified in (2) or (3) of the preceding paragraph, if the market share of one of the undertakings is less than one-tenth of the total, the undertakings shall not be considered to have a dominant market position. Where an undertaking that is considered to hold a dominant market position has evidence to the contrary, he shall not be considered to hold a dominant market position.

The above provisions are unusually strictly reliant on market shares in order to create a presumption of collective dominance. In Europe, complex evidence such as contractual agreements or structural market factors are required in order to prove collective dominance under Article 102 of the TFEU.

6.3.2 The Chinese mergers regulatory regime

According to Article 20 of the Anti-Monopoly Law, concentration of undertakings entails mergers of undertakings, control over other undertakings gained by an undertaking through acquiring their shares or assets, and control over other undertakings or the ability to exert a decisive influence on the same gained by an undertaking through signing contracts or other means.

According to Article 21, when their intended concentration reaches the threshold level as set by the State Council, undertakings shall declare in advance to the authority for enforcement of the Anti-Monopoly Law under the State Council; they shall not implement the concentration in the absence of such declaration.

Article 22 lays down the circumstances under which undertakings may dispense with declaration to the authority for enforcement of the Anti-Monopoly Law under the State Council, which are as follows: (1) one of the undertakings involved in the concentration owns 50 per cent or more of the voting shares or assets of each of the other undertakings; or (2) one and the same undertaking not involved in the concentration owns 50 per cent or more of the voting shares or assets of each of the undertakings involved in the concentration.

As in the EU, financial undertakings such as insurers and banks are subject to special turnover thresholds as criteria for mergers and acquisitions. The anti-monopoly rules state that once all the various income elements belonging to the financial institutions involved in a merger are aggregated, only 10 per cent of the aggregate will be taken into account for the purpose of turnover thresholds.

7 Mergers and acquisitions in the Chinese insurance market

It has been noted that cross-border mergers and acquisitions in the Chinese insurance sector have been on the rise in the last decade, with a consolidated trend of foreign enterprises participating in the insurance market via joint-venture arrangements or wholly foreign-owned enterprises.[119]

The Chinese authorities have very recently relaxed the application of their mergers and acquisitions rules to the insurance sector in an attempt to promote the creation of a stronger and more competitive insurance market, as well as expanding the footprint of private capital, including the domestic and China-based foreign-funded insurance firms.[120]

A series of measures have been designed by the Chinese Insurance Regulatory Commission in order to broaden the availability of financing sources for insurers. According to Article 30 of the Measures,[121] investors in merger and acquisitions activities revolving around insurance companies may raise funds from merger and acquisition loans or by other means, provided that the amount of said loans does not exceed 50 per cent of the total monetary consideration. This is a significant change as, under the previous regime, the China Insurance Regulatory Commission did not allow shareholders of insurance undertakings to benefit from banking loans or other financial leverages for merger and acquisitions in the insurance market.

Compared to the past, shareholder requirements are now more relaxed. Article 2(4) of the Notice of the China Insurance Regulatory Commission on Issues concerning Article 4 of the Measures for the Administration of Equity in Insurance Companies[122] used to require that a shareholder of an insurance company who contributes over 20 per cent (exclusive) of the total capital of the insurance company or holds more than 20 per cent (exclusive) of its shares shall have been investing in the insurance company for three years or longer.

119 See W. Han, 'China: developments in insurance law and regulation in the People's Republic', in J. Burling and K. Lazarus, *Research Handbook on International Insurance Law and Regulation*, 2011, Cheltenham: EE Publishing, p 723.

120 See: www.circ.gov.cn/Default.aspx?alias=www.circ.gov.cn/english (accessed 18 June 2014).

121 The Measures are available at: www.circ.gov.cn/Default.aspx?alias=www.circ.gov.cn/english (accessed 18 June 2014).

122 See Article 4 of the Measures for the Administration of Equity in Insurance Companies.

This is no longer the case, as Article 29 of the new measures exempts the shareholders from the Article 2(4) requirement on the basis of the China Insurance Regulatory Commission's prior approval.

Further, according to Article 21 of the Measures, acquirers are now allowed to control two insurance companies engaging in the same type of business after the completion of acquisition, subject to the China Insurance Regulatory Commission's *bene placit*. It is submitted that this provision is expected to encourage a wave of mergers and acquisitions in the Chinese insurance industry, especially by investors with the availability of large capital. The approval of the China Insurance Regulatory Commission entails the possibility for the regulatory authority to shape insurance mergers and regulate the market with a high degree of discretion.

It needs to be emphasised that this scenario is not too distant from the EU scenario, where clearance of the EU Commission is sometimes needed. The main discerning element lies with the different interest of the China Insurance Regulatory Commission, which could be moved by the need to protect and enhance the Chinese domestic insurance market in making its decisions.

The new measures are expected to be allegedly beneficial for both large and small-sized insurance firms. The current scenario sees large insurance firms having the lion's share of the Chinese market, with the rest of the market highly cellular and fragmented among smaller players.[123]

The Measures could see joint efforts and mergers by small insurance firms competing in the same segment of the market, in the attempt of gaining market strength in order to face larger competitors. Meanwhile, with the restructuring of the insurance sector facilitated by the Measures, the thrusting out of smaller firms could mitigate the pressure of price war initiated by smaller firms upon the large market incumbents. This is not necessarily a positive thing, as the creation of more large conglomerates could lead to a weak competitive environment with standardised rates.

While relaxing the merger and acquisition criteria for the insurance sector, the China Insurance Regulatory Commission maintains its regulatory position in relation to the task of mitigating information asymmetry. The new measures strengthen and highlight information disclosure and the independent role of intermediary service agencies.

To this end, Article 23 of the Measures provides that 'where the parties to the M&A activities of insurance companies fail to perform the obligations of reporting, announcement or notification as required, or are found to have false records, misleading statements or material omissions in reports,

123 For instance, in 2013 the five largest life insurance companies accounted for 69.5 per cent of the market, and the five largest casualties and property insurance companies' market shares reached 74.3 per cent. However, the rest of the market is divided by nearly 100 insurers, and most of them have less than 1 per cent of market shares.

announcements and other documents, the China Insurance Regulatory Commission' shall be entitled to order the said parties to 'make correction, and arrange regulatory talks with or issue regulatory letters to the parties concerned, order the parties concerned to suspend or stop the M&A activities, and take other regulatory measures'.

Article 24 further strengthens the 'watchdog' position of the China Insurance Regulatory Commission by allowing it to restrict shareholders' rights, order the transfer of equity or take other measures, in case the parties to the M&A activities of insurance companies fail to truthfully report the information on the actual controller and the relationship of affiliation, or fall under the circumstances of holding equity on behalf of others, which has a material impact on the M&A activities.

Article 25 of the Measures goes even further than that by empowering the China Insurance Regulatory Commission to set up credit files, and restrict a professional service intermediary failing to comply with the M&A procedures of insurance companies from participating in the M&A of insurance companies within three years.

Along the same lines, Article 26 of the Measures stipulates that during the M&A process of insurance companies, the China Insurance Regulatory Commission may communicate and coordinate with the Ministry of Commerce, the People's Bank of China, the China Banking Regulatory Commission and the China Securities Regulatory Commission, as well as administrations for industry and commerce and tax authorities, to verify the completeness, truthfulness and accuracy of the information submitted.

The Measures also set up a transitional period and a lockup period in order to ensure sustainable operation of the acquired insurance company. Article 11 of the Measures provides that the period from the conclusion of an equity transfer agreement, capital contribution agreement or share subscription agreement to the completion of the ownership transfer of relevant equity or shares shall be the acquisition transition period. During the acquisition transition period, except for the purpose of rescuing the target insurance company facing serious financial difficulties, the acquirer concerned shall not propose to re-elect the board of directors of the target insurance company, and the target insurance company shall not engage in investment, and purchase and sale of assets that have a material impact, or engage in transactions with the acquirer and its affiliated parties.

Article 12 provides that, except under special circumstances such as risk disposal or transfer between different parties under the control of the same controller, an acquirer shall undertake, in writing, not to transfer its holdings of the equity or shares in the target insurance company within three years from the completion of the acquisition.

Interestingly, concentration filing is expressly provided for the first time by Article 4, which states that whenever industry entry, application for the concentration of business operators, transfer of State-owned equity and other relevant matters are involved in the M&A of insurance companies, as a result of which the approval from relevant departments of the State shall be obtained, the M&A activities shall be carried out only after the required approvals have been obtained.

Just as has been done above in relation to the antitrust assessment of forms of horizontal cooperation between insurers, the analysis shall now turn to the European insurance mergers regulatory approach. Yet again, the similarities between the two regimes and the absence of jurisprudence related to mergers and acquisitions between Chinese insurers render the below analysis and critical considerations particularly valuable for the Chinese insurance industry.

8 The regulation of EU insurance mergers

Under EU law, the assessment of insurance mergers is based on the identification of the relevant geographic market, product market and on an assessment of possible dominance considered in the following.

8.1 EU insurance mergers and the analysis of the relevant geographic market

The relevant geographic market of insurance sector mergers has been largely considered to be confined within the territory of single member states.[124]

The reasons for this have been identified for the first time by the Commission in its decision *Commercial Union/General Accident*.[125] In *Commercial Union/General Accident*, it was held that the insurance industry relevant geographic market can, on a general level, be identified mainly at national level in view of 'the established insurance market structure, the need for adequate distribution channels, fiscal constraints in some cases and differing national systems of regulatory supervision'.[126]

The national dimension of the relevant geographic market in the insurance sector was further emphasised in *AXA/UAP*,[127] in which the Commission identified in the consumer behaviour another element rendering the geographic market mainly a national *affaire*.[128]

124 See J. Faull and A. Nikpay (eds), *The EC Law of Competition, Second Edition*, New York and Oxford: Oxford University Press, 2007, p 681. Only in the lines of reinsurance and direct insurance of large commercial risks has the relevant geographical market been identified at community level. The creation and extension of a dominant position within the territory of single member states are still subject to the merger regulation as long as they are capable of potentially affecting competition at community level. See Case T-219/99 *British Airways plc v Commission* [2004] 4 CMLR 1008.

125 Commission Decision, *Commercial Union/General Accident* (Case IV/M.11420) 1988.

126 Ibid., para 9.

127 Commission Decision, *AXA/UAP* (Case IV/M.862) 1996.

128 Ibid., para 13. In this case, the Commission, considering inter alia that the low degree of cross-border insurance service provision effectively obliges consumers to buy insurance mainly at national level, did not feel the need to investigate the relevant geographical market as the proposed concentration was not capable of having an impact on the common market or a substantial part of it.

These findings are in line with earlier decisions in the cases *Codan/Hafnia*[129] and *Fortis/La Caixa*.[130] This approach was confirmed by relatively recent merger decisions; in *AXA/Winterthur*,[131] the Commission found that the relevant geographical markets for life and non-life insurance can still be considered confined mainly at national level.[132] Also, in *Aviva/Ark Life*,[133] life insurance was considered by the Commission in line of principle essentially national in scope[134]due to national regulatory issues that constitute a material barrier to international supply in the production of life insurance products; the life insurance sector is indeed circumscribed mainly at national level.[135]

At first glance, this approach appears to be justified; it is indeed true that the insurance industry is still mainly confined to a national dimension. Nevertheless, the restriction of the relevant geographic market to the territory of single member states has led to a series of consolidations in the insurance market. These 'national' mergers, despite being considered by the Commission incapable of affecting the internal market as such, encouraged, as a matter of fact, a series of recent concentrations also at European level.[136]

It is interesting to note that the aforementioned approach of the Commission to the relevant geographic market is partially different when it comes to the line of credit insurance.

In *Allianz/Vereinte*,[137] the Commission in first instance considered the relevant geographic dimension of credit insurance as confined to the

129 Commission Decision, *Codan/Hafnia* (Case IV/M.344) 1993. Also in this case, the Commission, considering the low level of intra-community competition between insurance undertakings, found geographic markets to be mostly national in view of differences in distribution channels, consumer preferences and public regulation. See para 7.

130 Commission Decision, *Fortis/La Caixa* (Case IV/M.254) 1992. In this case, the Commission emphasised the national dimension of the geographic market in relation to the remarkable differences existing between the insurance products in different member states. Once again, the lack of harmonisation in the insurance industry is adducted as one of the main reasons for the relegation of the relevant geographical market at national level.

131 Commission Decision, *AXA/Winterthur* (Case No COMP/M.4284) 2006.

132 Ibid., para 18.

133 Commission Decision, *Aviva/Ark Life* (COMP/M.4047) 2006.

134 See Commission Decision, *Aviva/Ark Life* (COMP/M.4047) 2006, para 15.

135 See *Aviva/Ark Life* (COMP/M.4047) 2006, para 13. See also Case COMP/M.2491, *Sampo Storebrand Decision* 27 July 2001; Case COMP/M.2343, *Toro Assicurazioni/Lloyd Italico Decision*, 15 March 2001; Case No COMP/M.2400, *Dexia/Artesia Decision*, 14 June 2001; and Case COMP/M.2225, *Fortis/ASR Decision* 13 December 2000.

136 The high degree of consolidation at community level of the insurance industry has been emphasised testified by the Commission's Business Insurance Sector Inquiry Report of September 2007 (see the Commission's Business Insurance Sector Inquiry Report of September 2007, p 40).

137 Commission Decision, *Allianz/Vereinte* (Case IV/M.812) 1996.

national level due to the market structure of credit insurance, its distribution channels, consumer preferences and national legislation.[138] Nevertheless, in the subsequent decision *Allianz/AGF*,[139] the Commission found that, especially for industrial and commercial policies, insurance markets were becoming more and more open to intra-community competition.[140] This trend of internationalisation became particularly strong due to customers' needs, suppliers' interests and the nature of credit insurance business.[141]

Furthermore, always in *Allianz/AGF* it was held that multinational corporations indeed require a wider geographical scope in terms of servicing their group-wide operations, as they have an interest in optimising coverage and benefits from scale effect.[142] Policies designed for multinational companies have to provide worldwide buyer and political cover on a group-wide basis from a single source.

Moreover, according to the Commission, markets in recent years have become more international due to the liberalisation of European insurance markets, the worldwide reinsurance structures and the growing internationalisation of the business.[143]

This element of 'internationality' characterising the credit insurance market should therefore, per se, be capable of affecting trade between member states engaging the application of Regulation 139/2004.

The international dimension of credit insurance is nevertheless counter-balanced, according to the Commission, by a strong national element. Policies are indeed still mainly contracted on a local basis because detailed information is needed on the business of the insured, the financial situation of the customers and local economic structures. Especially the *del credere* insurance market (with specific reference to the segment of export credit insurance), notwithstanding the growing internationalisation, is characterised by a national dimension due to the characteristics of its product.[144]

138 Ibid., para 11.
139 Commission Decision, *Allianz/AGF* (Case IV/M.1082) 1998.
140 Ibid., para 26.
141 Ibid., para 26.
142 See *Allianz/AGF* (Case IV/M.1082) 1998, para 27.
143 Ibid., para 27.
144 See *Allianz/AGF*, para 27. '*Del credere*', or credit insurance in the narrow sense, as it is called, includes three types of insurance policies: domestic credit insurance, export credit insurance and capital goods insurance. Domestic credit insurance and export credit insurance protect the policyholders against insolvency of their clients in the domestic market and abroad. Export credit insurance can be further divided according to the kind of risks covered. In particular, political risks are covered by special policies managed on behalf of the State acting as a reinsurer. In numerous countries (e.g. Italy, France, Germany), this kind of policy is only offered by one specialised company. See *Allianz/AGF*, para 18.

Del credere insurance therefore requires local support; small and medium-sized clients usually seek credit insurance with domestic companies, and policies are thus still mainly contracted on a local basis because detailed information is needed on the business of the insured, the financial situation of the customers and local economic structures. That is the reason why, in *Allianz/AGF*, the Commission emphasised that local insurers, as a general rule, are better equipped to meet these requirements than their foreign competitors.[145]

Large groups such as Allianz and Coface, which are present worldwide, also fulfil these criteria.[146] In sum, the Commission concluded that domestic and export credit insurance represent a driving force in internationalisation and concentration of the market.[147]

The same conclusion was reached in *Hermes/Sampo/FGB-FCIC*.[148] In this case, the Commission emphasised that the credit insurance market is in constant evolution and that there is an increasing number of foreign insurers who offer insurance policies to national policyholders, also cross-border.[149] However, the fact that Hermes was seeking a local alliance in the Finnish market was considered to be in line with the Commission's previous findings indicating that market entry may still require operating together with a local player.[150] *Hermes/Sampo/FGB-FCIC* yet again reiterated the Commission's idea that the line of credit insurance, despite its undeniable international dimension, is still mainly confined at national level, leaving no space for the application of Regulation 139/2004.

A field considered by the Commission to have international and global geographical dimensions is the field of reinsurance. The reasons for this are to be found in the first place in relation to the fact that reinsurance products are traded between industry specialists and not sold to the general public. Consequently, controls by national authorities over the conduct of reinsurance tend to be much less extensive than those over direct insurance.[151]

Another reason for the global character of the reinsurance business is, according to the Commission, the fact that the reinsurance business can be readily conducted across national borders (e.g. by telephone).[152] The

145 See *Allianz/AGF* (Case IV/M.1082) 1998, para 26.
146 Ibid., para 27.
147 Ibid., para 28. The final definition of geographical markets, however, was left open because the Commission, for the purposes of the case *Allianz/AGF*, had only to appraise the effects of the concentration on any alternative market affected.
148 Commission Decision, *Hermes/Sampo/FGB-FCIC* (Case IV/M.1101) 1998.
149 Ibid., para 33.
150 Ibid., para 33.
151 See Commission Decision, *Mederic/URRPIMMEC/CRI/Munich Re* (Case IV/M.949) 1997, para 13.
152 Ibid., para 13.

existence of a world market is also evidenced by the presence of international broking firms that mediate reinsurance on a worldwide scale.[153]

9 The analysis of the relevant product market

The concept of 'substitutability' or 'interchangeability' is the key element for the identification of the relevant product market. This concept is exactly the same used by the Commission and the European courts in order to determine the relevant product market in case of application of Article 102 of the Treaty.[154]

The idea here is that the more products are interchangeable/substitutable with one another, the more likely it is that they do belong to the same market. The determination of the relevant product market is entirely based on a specific economic analysis aiming to identify the consumer behaviour in case of impossibility of accessing a particular product.

For instance, what is going to happen if consumers cannot buy life insurance? Are they going to buy motor insurance instead? If so, life insurance would be interchangeable with motor insurance, and the two products would be considered part of the same market. Due to their discerning and distinguished aims and the peculiarity of their characteristics, different types of insurance are separate product markets. Consequently, life and non-life insurance can indeed be distinguished into as many product markets as there are insurances covering different kinds of risk.

It has been noted how the rationale lying beyond the Commission's approach in determining the relevant product market in relation to mergers and acquisitions in the insurance sector shows a remarkable degree of consistency.[155] Since the outset, the Commission has distinguished between life insurance, general insurance and reinsurance.

More specifically, according to the Commission, life and non-life insurance can be divided into as many product markets as there are insurances covering different kinds of risk;[156] on a general level, the Commission is thus inclined to differentiate the insurance industry into as many product markets as there are insurances for different kinds of risks. However, in *AXA/UAP*, the Commission outlined that under specific circumstances, it is also possible to regroup risks in a single category;[157] for instance, different types of personal risks (labour accidents, professional illnesses and accidents occurring in private life) could be brought back

153 Ibid., para 13. Within the European Union, freedom of establishment to provide reinsurance services was enacted by Directive EEC 225/64.

154 See, inter alia, *United Brands v Commission*, Case C-27/76 [1978] 1 CMLR 429

155 See Faull and Nikpay, 'The EC law of competition', p 679.

156 See Commission Decision, *Sun Alliance/Royal Insurance* (Case IV/M.759) 1996, para 7.

157 See Faull and Nikpay, 'The EC law of competition', p 680.

according to the French insurance practice under the same insurance category of '*accidents corporels*', as well as 'general health risks'.[158]

9.1 The definition of the relevant product market in the EU insurance sector

On a general level, it has been contested that the Commission did not define precisely the relevant product market in relation to mergers and acquisitions in the insurance sector.[159] In the aforementioned case law, the Commission offered generic guidelines for the determination of the relevant product market in insurance mergers, leaving, nevertheless, the identification of the actual product market open in all the cases, since no significant competition concerns arose.[160] This assertion is fundamentally correct; nevertheless, the Commission's identification of the relevant product market tends indeed to be very specific, especially as far as the lines of credit insurance and reinsurance are concerned.

Credit insurance is generally acknowledged as a means of protection for suppliers of goods and services against insolvency of a debtor or extended late payments.[161] In *Allianz/Vereinte*[162] and *Allianz/Hermes*,[163] the Commission took the demand-side position adopted in *AG/Amev*, claiming that life and non-life insurance could be segmented into as many product markets as there are different types of risk.

Reinsurance is another field that has been the object of specific analysis relating to the relevant product market. The purpose of reinsurance is to spread the risks between insurers. Reinsurers accept either the whole or part of the risk insured by another insurer and thereby provide the primary insurer with the ability to increase the amount of insurance underwritten, and to diversify risk over time and geographic area.[164] Thus, the reinsurance product is traded between industry specialists; it is written only with other insurance companies, no premium income is derived from reinsurance sales to the public and no channels for retail distribution are therefore required.[165]

Accordingly, the reinsurance business must, according to the Commission, be considered as distinct from direct insurance. This was the rationale

158 See Commission Decision in *AG/Amev*, para 10. On this point, see also Faull and Nikpay, 'The EC law of competition', p 680.

159 See Faull and Nikpay, 'The EC law of competition', p 679.

160 The definition of the relevant product market is utterly superfluous if the Commission does not consider a specific merger/acquisition capable of threatening competition at community level.

161 See the Commission Decision in *Hermes/Sampo/ FGB/FCIC* (Case IV/M.1101) 1998, para 25.

162 *Allianz/Vereinte* (Case IV/M.812) 1996.

163 Ibid.

164 Ibid., para 7.

165 Ibid., para 7.

in *ERC/NGR Victory*,[166] where it was held that the business of reinsurance represents a specialist form of insurance, and this line of reasoning was reiterated in subsequent decisions.[167] Yet again, the Commission did not feel the need to specify the precise definition of the relevant product market neither in the reinsurance mergers. The Commission's application of the concept of 'interchangeability/substitutability' in assessing the relevant insurance product market appears to be, prima facie, coherent. In general, the Commission suggests the existence of as many relevant service markets as there are insurances for different kinds of risk.

This approach has been confirmed in the recent past by the decision in *Axa/Winterthur*,[168] where it was reiterated that life and non-life insurance can be divided into as many product markets as there are different kinds of risks covered, given that their characteristics, premiums and purposes are distinct and that there is typically no substitutability from the consumers perspective between certain different risks insured.[169]

It is indeed true that, due to their different aims and the peculiarity of their characteristics, different types of insurance (e.g. life insurance and non-life insurance) operate in separate product markets. It is also possible, of course, to further divide a line of insurance (e.g. credit insurance) into subcategories according to the specific risk that is the object of the insurance. What is not entirely convincing are the results of such an approach: such narrow definitions could lead to the insurance market being considered as a market characterised by niche subcategories, allowing a high degree of consolidation among undertakings.

The consideration of the relevant product market is, as a matter of fact, crucial in order to assess the creation or the enhancement of a dominant position and its possible impact on the internal market or a substantial part thereof; the narrower the relevant product market, the less likely that a merger between insurance undertakings would pass the thresholds established by Regulation 139/2004, giving rise to competition concerns.

Only recently does the Commission appear to have acknowledged this risk. In the above-mentioned decision *Axa/Winterthur*, the Commission indeed recognised that from a supply-side perspective the conditions for insurance of different types of risk are quite similar and most large insurance

166 *ERC/NGR Victory* (Case IV/M.433) 1994.

167 See, inter alia, Commission Decisions in *General Re/Kolnische Ruch* (Case IV/M.491) 1994; *Employers Reinsurance/Frankona Ruckversicherungs AG* (Case IV/M.600) 1995; *Employers Reinsurance/Aachener Ruckversicherungs-Gesellschafts AG* (Case IV/M.601) 1995; and *Schweizer Ruck/Mercantile & General Reinsurance Company* (Case IV/M.828) 1996.

168 Commissions Decision, *Axa/Winterthur* (Case Comp/M.4284) 2006.

169 Ibid., para 8. For example, life individual, life group and unit linked for life insurance; motor, fire, transport, health, property, general civil liability, casualty, litigation, working accidents, etc. for non-life insurance.

companies are active in several types of risk. This suggests that different types of non-life insurance could be included in the same product market.[170] The Commission, applying this line of reasoning, *mutatis mutandis*, also considered that a similar approach might apply to life insurance.[171]

This change of approach of the Commission was necessary in light of the gradual consolidation in the insurance sector characterising the internal market, as acknowledged by the Commission itself in its *Business Insurance Sector Inquiry Interim Report* of January 2007.[172]

10 The assessment of dominance

The last step in order to evaluate mergers and acquisitions is to assess whether, as a result of the merger, the insurance undertakings involved in the transaction would obtain a dominant position in the insurance sector capable of affecting the internal market or a substantial part of it.

The assessment of dominance is the result of economic analysis that takes into account in first place the market shares of the undertakings. As previously mentioned, under Regulation 139/2004, the calculation of the market shares is based on the value of gross premiums written. This comprises all amounts received and receivable in respect of insurance contracts issued by or on behalf of the insurance undertakings, including also outgoing reinsurance premiums, and after deduction of taxes and parafiscal contributions or levies charged by reference to the amounts of individual premiums or the total volume of premiums.[173]

Despite the specific guidelines laid down by the merger regulation, the Commission did not always explain the calculation of the market shares in the insurance mergers/acquisitions.[174] It has been noted that, overall, the calculation is based on the total premiums earned during a year period;[175] nevertheless, with specific reference to life insurance, the Commission has attempted to 'refine the calculation of the market shares to get a better proxy of market'.[176] In *Abeille Vie/ Viagere/Sinafer*,[177] for instance, the calculation of the market shares was carried out by the Commission taking into account the new policies issued.[178] In a similar way, in *Allianz/Vereinte*, the

170 See Commission Decision in *Axa/Winterthur*, para 3.

171 Ibid., para 9.

172 See the Commission Business Insurance Sector Inquiry Interim Report of January 2007, p 37, available at: www.ec.europa.eu/competition/sectors/financial_services/inquiries/ (accessed 29 August 2014).

173 See Council Regulation (EC) No 139/2004, Article 3(b).

174 See Faull and Nikpay, 'The EC law of competition', p 683.

175 Ibid., p 683.

176 Ibid., p 683.

177 *Abeille Vie/Viagere/Sinafer* (Case IV/M.919) 1997.

178 See Commission Decision in *Abeille Vie/ Viagere/Sinafer*, para 17. On this point, see Faull and Nikpay, 'The EC law of competition', p 683.

determination of the market shares in the line of health insurance was considered the result of not only current market performance, but rather of the turnover made on the basis of long-term contracts often stipulated a long time in advance.[179] On a general level, a market share in the region of 30 per cent in relation to a specific insurance line has not been considered a symptom of appreciable dominance able to hinder competition.[180]

The Commission's permissive approach in allowing forms of consolidation in the insurance industry gives rise to some scepticism; as previously mentioned, doubts arise in relation to every single aspect of the procedure for the assessment of mergers. First, in relation to the identification of the geographical dimension of the market, we have seen how the Commission considers the relevant geographical markets for life and non-life insurance as mainly a national *affaire*.[181] It has been also already outlined that this approach appears to be confirmed by recent merger decisions[182] (although the Commission has also recognised that especially the credit insurance markets nowadays tend to be more European because of the liberalisation of European insurance markets, the worldwide reinsurance structures and the growing internationalisation of the business).[183]

The Commission has permitted a number of insurance consolidations within the territory of individual Member States, by virtue of the fact that they are unlikely to represent a threat to competition in the internal market or a substantial part of it. All this seems idiosyncratic and has proven to be counterproductive. In spite of the fact that insurance distribution channels still remain mainly confined to a national level, it is very difficult indeed to disentangle the impact of concentrations taking place at the national level from the internal market. The first reason for this is that consolidations at national level often represent the platform for future cross-border mergers and acquisitions.[184] Second, the Commission's approach in considering the possible impact of a position of dominance arising within the territory of a single member state on the internal market is idiosyncratic in comparison to the assessment of abuse of dominant position under Article 102 of the Treaty[185] made by the Commission and the Court of

179 See Commission Decision in *Allianz/Vereinte*, para 21. On this point, see also Faull and Nikpay, 'The EC law of competition', p 683.

180 See Commission Decision in *AXA/Winterthur* (Case No COMP/M.4284) 2006, para 3.

181 The life insurance market, especially, is considered by the Commission, in principle, national in scope. See Commission Decision, *Aviva /Ark Life*, para 18.

182 See Commission Decision in *AXA/Winterthur* (Case No COMP/M.4284) 2006.

183 Ibid., para 27.

184 On this point, see 'The Financial Services M&A Review', 2005, Pricewaterhouse Coopers, p 24.

185 According to Article 82 of the Treaty, 'any abuse by one or more undertakings of a dominant position within the common market or in a substantial part of it shall be prohibited as incompatible with the common market insofar as it may affect trade between Member States.'

First Instance.[186] According to the European Courts, an abuse of dominant position is caught by the EU competition framework if it is capable of restricting competition, or, in other words, if the conduct of a dominant undertaking is capable of having, or likely to have, such an effect.[187] The potential impact on the internal market of an abuse of dominant position taking place within the territory of a single member state is considered sufficient in order to trigger the application of the EU antitrust regulatory framework.

On the contrary, when it comes to mergers and acquisitions in the insurance industry, the rationale of the Commission results seem to be subverted: even a concentration of 80 per cent in a national insurance market does not give rise to competition concerns at community level.[188] The assessment of an abuse of dominant position is indeed radically different from the evaluation of a consolidation; nevertheless, it is necessary to bear in mind that we are considering an industry that benefits from a block exemption. In other words, allowing the possibility of consolidation at national level between undertakings perfectly allowed to cooperate in order to determine the risk premiums, without considering the impact, even only potentially, on the internal market does not seem to be after all a great idea.

It is interesting to note that the Commission, with a rather far-fetched approach, has allowed mergers and acquisitions in the insurance industry taking into account potential competition coming from different geographic markets from the ones actually considered in specific cases.[189] Potential competition is taken into account although belonging to another geographic market, whereas the potential impact of a dominant national position on the internal market is completely disregarded. For as long as insurance undertakings will have the possibility to benefit from a block exemption system, it would perhaps be advisable to consider the potential impact of national consolidation in line with the Commission's approach relating to the assessment of abuse of dominant position.[190]

The assessment of the relevant product market gives rise to similar concerns. We have seen that the general tendency of the Commission is to leave open the determination of the relevant product market.[191]

186 See Commission Decision in *Allianz/AGF*, para 29.

187 See Case T-219/99 *British Airways plc v Commission* [2004] 4 CMLR 1008, at point 293 of the judgment.

188 See Commission Decision in *Allianz/AGF*, para 27.

189 See, inter alia, Commission Decisions in *Sun Alliance/Royal Insurance*; *Allianz/Vereinte*; *AXA/UAP*; and *GRE/PPP*.

190 See Commission Decisions in *Abeille Vie/ Viagere/Sinafer* (Case IV/M.919) 1996.

191 In many decisions on mergers and acquisitions relating to the insurance industry (see, inter alia, *General Re/Kolnische Ruch*; *Employers Reinsurance/Frankona Ruckversicherungs*; *Employers Reinsurance/Aachener Ruckversicherungs-Gesellschafts*; and *Schweizer Ruck/ Mercantile & General Reinsurance Company*), the Commission does not consider it necessary to identify the relevant product market on the basis of an alleged no risk for competition.

In spite of this, in several decisions the Commission suggests in terms of general guidelines the existence of as many relevant service markets as there are insurances for different kinds of risks.[192] We also saw how the Commission stretched the differentiation of the relevant product market in the insurance industry even further, envisaging narrower segmentations: for instance, distinctions could be drawn between the different methods of distribution (e.g. direct sale, or sale through agents, brokers or other intermediaries) or the breakdown of distribution arrangements for individual products.[193]

In sum, the Commission's approach in relation to the determination of the relevant product market seems to be ambivalent; either the specification of the relevant product market is left open, or it tends to be indeed very specific with a considerable segmentation of the different types of insurance products (especially as far as the lines of credit insurance and reinsurance are concerned).[194]

Either way, many uncertainties arise: first, the Commission seemed precipitous in avoiding to define the relevant product market whenever it considered the presence of potential competitors enough to justify forms of consolidation at national level without, in practice, assessing their possible impact on the internal market.

Second, the general guidelines and tendency of the Commission to narrow down the definition of the relevant product market is not particularly convincing. It is indeed true that, on the basis of the concept of substitutability, different lines of insurance are not interchangeable with one another and therefore represent different product markets.[195] It is also true that the general market of life insurance and non-life insurance might be narrowed down in relation to specific kinds of risks.[196]

Nevertheless, envisaging narrower segmentations in relation to the different methods of distribution or the breakdown of distribution arrangements for individual products appears to be overstated; such an approach could result in the potential permissibility of any possible insurance merger or acquisition.

Two other important factors need to be taken into account: first, although the insurance industry tends to be very specialised, insurer undertakings generally provide a wide range of services. This is to say that allowing a consolidation between insurers on the basis of a relevant product market

192 See Commission Decision in *AG/Amev*.

193 See Commission Decision in *Abeille Vie/ Viagere/Sinafer*, para 12.

194 See, inter alia, Commission Decisions in *Allianz/Vereinte*; *Allianz/Hermes*; and *AG/Amev*.

195 For instance, it is not possible to claim that the life insurance market is the same market as the non-life insurance one.

196 In the field of non-life insurance, for example, it is possible to distinguish between motor insurance, home insurance, etc.

considered in the narrowest possible way could be in practice misleading if the undertakings involved provide different types of insurance services.

The second element to be considered is yet again the block exemption system. If insurers are already in a position to cooperate and to jointly determine the risk premium, a more careful assessment of the consequences of a merger would be advisable.

A possible solution could be to go beyond the formal concept of substitutability (in *extrema ratio* even not to apply it), and to jointly consider the segments of the insurance market in which the undertakings involved in the consolidation operate. A global analysis of the post-merger scenario in terms of relevant product market that goes beyond any type of formalistic approach appears to be the only means by which to assess the real impact of insurance mergers within the internal market, and to evaluate their conformity with the EU competition rules.

Finally, the assessment of dominance is not free from criticism either. It has already been noted that, in general, the Commission did not consider a market share in the region of 30 per cent of the market enough to lead to the creation or reinforcement of a dominant position.[197]

The Commission seems, therefore, to have adopted a loose approach in assessing the market share element of mergers and acquisitions in the insurance sector. We have already seen how different reasons have been formulated in order to justify such an approach.

Especially in relation to the non-life insurance sector, the Commission contested a high degree of supply-side substitutability in terms of common set of skills relating to risk assessment, administration and claims management.[198] The general idea is that insurance companies specialised in one or more insurance products are capable of reapplying those skills in order to provide other lines of insurance.[199] According to the Commission, this high degree of supply-side substitutability characterising the insurance industry would result in an enhancement of competition in potential terms; consequently, a market share concentration in the region of 30 per cent would not lead to a threat to competition.[200]

As previously mentioned, another frequent argument put forward by the Commission in order to justify insurance mergers and acquisitions is to be

197 See, inter alia, Commission Decisions in *Coda/Afnia*; *Sun Alliance/Royal Insurance*; *Allianz/Vereinte*; *AXA/UAP*; *Allianz/AGF*; *GRE/PPP*; and *Hermes/Sampo/ FGB/FCIC*.

198 On this point, see Faull and Nikpay, 'The EC law of competition', p 684. In relation to Commission Decisions, see, inter alia, *Commercial Union/General Accident* and *Sun Alliance/Royal Insurance*.

199 See, inter alia, Commission Decisions in *Sun Alliance/Royal Insurance*. On this point, see Faull and Nikpay, 'The EC law of competition', p 684.

200 See, inter alia, Commission Decisions in *Coda/Afnia*; *Sun Alliance/Royal Insurance*; *Allianz/Vereinte*; and *AXA/UAP*.

found in the low barriers to entry due to the EU liberalisation movement and the creation of new channels of distributions such as brokers, online selling, and marketing by banks and supermarkets.[201]

Finally, we have already seen how the Commission, in order to evaluate the impact of insurance mergers and acquisitions is inclined to consider the potential competitors operating in the insurance market, even in relation to other relevant product and geographical markets.[202] This line of reasoning has been stretched by the Commission up to a point at which even a consolidation within the region of 80 per cent of the market is not enough to represent a threat to competition in the light of the presence of potential competition.[203] It goes without saying that such an approach could lead to dangerous consequences. We already saw how detrimental the impact of consolidation in the insurance market can be and that one of the main reasons for mergers and acquisitions activities is to counteract competitive forces by redistributing market share.

It is very interesting to note that, on the contrary, the Commission considers the argument of the low barriers to entry into the market as a rationale to allow consolidation in the insurance industry. In other words, while the consolidation in the insurance market can indeed be seen as a reaction to fresh competitive forces mainly deriving from the new technology that opened the door to new channels of distribution, the Commission's tendency to allow mergers in the light of the new competition and channels of distribution is counterintuitive and difficult to understand.

Another discrepancy can be found in the fact that in assessing mergers in the insurance field, the Commission has considered the risk of the creation or strengthening of a dominant position of a collective entity only on very few occasions.[204] This is only partly related to the doubts arising regarding the effective power of the Commission to evaluate mergers and acquisitions in light of the concept of 'collective dominance'. These doubts have been discarded by the ECJ in the case *French Republic, SCPA and EMC v Commission*,[205] in which it has been held that the Commission is entitled to assess mergers and acquisitions also under a collective dominance

201 See Faull and Nikpay, 'The EC law of competition' p 684. See, inter alia, Commission Decisions in *Coda/Afnia*; *Sun Alliance/Royal Insurance*; *Allianz/Vereinte*; *AXA/UAP*; *Allianz/AGF*; and *Hermes/Sampo/FGB/FCIC*.

202 See, inter alia, Commission Decisions in *Coda/Afnia*; *Sun Alliance/Royal Insurance*; *Allianz/Vereinte*; *AXA/UAP*; *Allianz/AGF*; and *Hermes/Sampo/ FGB/FCIC*.

203 See Commission Decisions in *Allianz/AGF*.

204 See, inter alia, Commission Decision in *UAP/Vinci* (Case IV/M.384) 1993.

205 Joined Cases C-68/94 and C-30/95 *French Republic, SCPA and EMC v Commission* [1988] ECR I-1375.

perspective (i.e. a dominant position held by the parties to the concentration together with an entity not a party thereto).[206]

10.1 In defence of the concept of 'collective dominance': a possible valid alternative for the assessment of EU insurance mergers and acquisitions?

Even after *French Republic, SCPA and EMC v Commission*,[207] the Commission's analysis of mergers and acquisitions in the insurance industry reverts mainly only to the creation of a dominant position of a single entity[208] (i.e. an individual dominant position held by the parties to the concentration resulting from the mergers). A collective dominant position in the insurance industry deriving from the various synergies arising from the consolidation is therefore very rarely taken into account by the Commission.

It is interesting to note that, on the contrary, following the case *French Republic, SCPA and EMC v Commission*, the issue of collective dominance

206 Ibid., para 168. Doubts were raised in relation to Council Regulation (EEC) No. 4064/89 of 21 December 1989 on the control of concentrations between undertakings (now repealed by Council Regulation (EC) No. 139/2004 of 20 January 2004). In particular, the issues in dispute were related, in the first place, to the wording of the Regulation which is silent in regard to any type of referral to the concept of dominant positions. Second, it was contested that there was nothing in the legislative history of the Regulation to support the view that the legislature intended it also to cover collective dominant positions. The ECJ rejected these arguments. Referring to the wording of the Regulation, it was outlined how the Regulation does not exclude its being used also to prevent the creation or strengthening of collective dominant positions. In particular, Article 2(3) of the Regulation links the dominant position to the concentration, not to the undertakings concerned, and refers to the consequences of the proposed concentration for the structure of competition, thus referring to an objective situation. Furthermore, the ECJ stated that it cannot be deduced from the wording of Article 2 of the Regulation that only concentrations which create or strengthen an individual dominant position, that is, a dominant position held by the parties to the concentration, come within the scope of the Regulation. In particular Article 2, in referring to 'a concentration which creates or strengthens a dominant position', does not in itself exclude the possibility of applying the Regulation to cases where concentrations lead to the creation or strengthening of a collective dominant position, that is, a dominant position held by the parties to the concentration together with an entity not a party thereto.
Moreover, it was emphasised that the use of Article 2 in conjunction with Articles 87 (now Article 83) and 235 (now Article 229) of the Treaty as the legal basis of the Regulation showed that its objective is to fill in a lacuna in competition law left by Articles 85 (now Article 81) and 86 (now Article 82) of the Treaty, with reference to the control of oligopolistic dominant positions. Finally, the ECJ noted that nothing in the '*travaux préparatoires*' permits the conclusion to be drawn that the Council intended to exclude the use of the Regulation to prevent collective dominant positions on the market, that is, situations of dominance linked to the presence of several strongly interdependent economic entities.

207 Joined Cases C-68/94 and C-30/95 *French Republic, SCPA, and EMC v Commission (Kali + Salz)* [1998] ECR I-1375.

208 On this point, see Faull and Nikpay, 'The EC law of competition', p 685.

has in fact been taken into account by the Commission in relation to other industries. In its decision in *Gencor/Lonrho*,[209] the Commission, in rejecting the merger, observed that despite the low market share of the new entity in the common market (in relation to the market for platinum), by virtue of the creation of powerful commercial synergies, the commercial entities involved in the merger would have been in the position to influence the determination of the platinum price in Europe.[210] The same line of reasoning can be found in *Price Waterhouse/Coopers & Lybrand*.[211] This time, the Commission found a consolidation in the audit and accounting market resulting in no more than 40 per cent of the market share potentially harmful for competition; the new entity would have been, in fact, capable of influencing the level of post-merger supply such as to create a situation of collective dominance.[212]

The Commission appears largely to reject the possibility to apply on a large scale the concept of collective dominance to the insurance industry, forgetting the synergies created by the block exemption system and the consequent power that insurance undertakings have to jointly determine the risk premium. The co-insurance and insurance pools arrangements deriving from the current EU insurance regulative framework have been recognised as creative of 'structural links between insurance companies'.[213] This results to be in line with the concept of collective dominance analysed by the Commission in other sectors.

Apart from its decision in *UAP/Vinci*, the analysis of collective dominance has been taken into account only in two other circumstances. It has been correctly noticed that in *Allianz/AGF*, although without any explicit referral, the Commission considered the concept of collective dominance in relation to the line of '*del credere*' credit insurance.[214] In this sector, Allianz and AGF had, according to the Commission, respectively 60 per cent of the Italian market, 50 per cent of the UK market and 40 per cent of the Belgian, French and German market. Notwithstanding such high market shares, the Commission did not consider this scenario a consolidation of dominance due to the particular structure of the '*del credere*' credit insurance market, and the potential competition. At European level, the Commission considered that evidence of instances of recent entry into the market by new competitors (although a third of the size of the undertakings involved in the actual merger) was sufficient in order to dismiss the risk of the

209 Commission Decision, *Gencor/Lonrho* (Case IV/M.619) 1996.
210 See Commission Decision in *Gencor/Lonrho*, para 206.
211 *Price Waterhouse/Coopers & Lybrand* (Case IV/M.1016) 1998.
212 Ibid., para 107.
213 On this point, see Faull and Nikpay, 'The EC law of competition', p 685.
214 Ibid., p 685.

determination of a dominant position potentially capable of threatening competition.[215]

Having come to this conclusion, the analysis of the Commission went on to focus on the synergies and the structural links between AGF and two of its subsidiary companies, Coface and Euler. Significant doubts with regard to the creation or strengthening of a dominant position arose, especially considering the above-described scenario in conjunction with the synergies with two other undertakings operating the same lines of insurance. Such circumstances, de facto, were capable of reducing the number of existing competitors and/or discouraging competition between them.

Nevertheless, even in the presence of such a critical scenario, and the relatively serious issues relating to the effective creation of a situation of collective dominance, the Commission did not find any threat to competition and cleared the merger.[216]

A similar line of reasoning emerges from the Commission's decision in *AXA/GRE*.[217] The decision concerned a merger in the field of non-life insurance business taking place between AXA and the UK undertaking GRE. This merger analysis pertained mainly to the Luxembourg market, where AXA had a prominent role. The Commission noted that the Luxembourg market was already highly concentrated with only three significant players: La Foyer having a market share in the region of 50 per cent of the market, la Luxembourgeoise, which held 25 per cent of the market, and AXA holding 20 per cent. The new scenario arising from the merger resulted in the creation of a link between AXA and La Foyer by virtue of new complex synergies triggered by the merger between AXA and GRE.

In light of the concept of collective dominance, the Commission considered this link between AXA and La Foyer, although the latter was not officially involved in the notified merger. By virtue of these synergies, the new entity AXA/GRE, together with La Foyer, were to control almost 80 per cent of the Luxembourg market regarding motor insurance, casualty and property insurance. Even this high concentration was not considered by the Commission capable of creating or enhancing a dominant position in light of the sale of part of GRE's shares in La Foyer to buyers not directly or indirectly connected to AXA.[218]

215 See Commission Decision in *Allianz/AGF*, para 44. On this point, see Faull and Nikpay, 'The EC law of competition', p 686.

216 The Commission held that 'after the execution of the undertakings proposed by the parties, the remaining links between Coface and AGF will in their present state [did] not in themselves constitute obstacles to effective competition on the common market or a substantial part of it.' See Commission Decision in *Allianz/AGF*, para 76.

217 Commission Decision *AXA/GRE* (Case IV/M.1453) 1999.

218 In substance, the merger in the case *AXA/GRE* was cleared by the Commission under Article 6(1)(b) of Regulation 138/2004, which states that: 'where the Commission finds that the concentration notified, although falling within the scope of this Regulation, does not raise serious doubts as to its compatibility with the common market, it shall decide not to oppose it and shall declare that it is compatible with the common market.'

Among relatively recent decisions,[219] the Commission analysed the concept of collective dominance only in *AXA/Winterthur*.[220] The decisions concerned the market of non-life insurance and the relevant geographic market was identified as mainly the Belgium and Luxembourg markets, although the undertakings involved in the merger operated on a large scale across the internal market.[221]

The Commission took into account the links and synergies that both AXA and Winterthur had in terms of participation in brokers within the relevant geographic market.[222] Nevertheless, in the Commission's view, the transaction was very unlikely to give rise to any conglomerate effects, and in particular portfolio effects, that could have led to a significant impediment of competition.[223]

11 The way forward: a possible different regime for mergers and acquisitions in the EU insurance sector?

The Commission's approach in assessing mergers and acquisitions in the insurance industry has been analysed in detail. The attitude of the Commission in allowing consolidation in the insurance industry can be characterised as rather loose and *laissez-faire*. All this can lead (and to some extent already has) to detrimental consequences for the markets in this sector.[224]

The next step is to endeavour to suggest a way forward and a different approach in assessing consolidations relating to the insurance industry. In the first place, consolidations, mergers and acquisitions often represent means used by companies in order to expand their operations and increase long-term profitability. In other words, mergers and acquisitions as phenomena are integral parts of the modern market economy. Notwithstanding, corporate mergers may indeed be aimed at reducing market competition, and are very often driven by the need to limit competition. Accordingly, the purpose of merger control regimes is to monitor the market and avoid situations of dominance that may have a detrimental impact on the economy.

219 See, inter alia, Commission Decision in *Aviva/ARK Life* (Case Comp/M.4047) 2006.

220 *AXA/Winterthur* (Case Comp/M.4284) 2006.

221 Ibid., para 20.

222 See Commission Decision in *AXA/Winterthur*, para 30. Within the Belgian and Luxemburg markets, AXA and Winterthur were also present in the outward insurance distribution market via their participation in brokers. In particular, Winterthur owned Atelia and had a 60 per cent stake in VJL and AXA-owned Viaxis. Each of these three companies, however, represented less than 1 per cent of the total insurance broking in Belgium.

223 See Commission Decision in *AXA/Winterthur*, para 33.

224 We have seen also how negative the impact of mergers and acquisitions is on the insurance markets in terms of competition and consumer protection.

At European level, the system of merger control is implemented through Regulation 139/2004. The Regulation applies generally to any kind of mergers, regardless of the sector or market involved in the transactions; the only differentiation in terms of regulation in relation to the insurance industry is related to the calculation of the turnover of the entities involved in the mergers.[225]

The Commission's attitude in assessing mergers and acquisitions in the insurance industry is characterised by a rather singular approach. Since the outset, the Commission has been very keen on acknowledging the *sui generis* characteristics of the insurance industry in terms of analysis of the relevant geographic and product markets. Despite the recognition of the international level of specific lines of insurance,[226] the relevant geographic market is considered to be mainly confined to the national level in view of 'the established insurance market structure, the need for adequate distribution channels, fiscal constraints in some cases and differing national systems of regulatory supervision'.[227]

In terms of relevant product market, the Commission claims the existence of as many relevant service markets as there are types of insurance for different kinds of risks. Stretching this line of reasoning further, the Commission envisages even narrower segmentations; for example, distinctions could be drawn between the different methods of distribution (e.g. direct sale, or sale through agents, brokers or other intermediaries) or the breakdown of distribution arrangements for individual products.[228]

If, on one hand, the recognition of the insurance industry as an area mainly confined at national level and the fragmentation of the relevant product market are, in principle, correct, the impact of such concepts on the assessment of insurance mergers and acquisitions resulted, on the other hand, in a *laissez-faire* approach on the Commission's part that acknowledged consolidation in the insurance market.

In other words, the object of criticism is not the line of reasoning applied by the Commission in the identification of the relevant geographic and product markets per se, rather it is its application in relation to the assessment of the mergers and acquisitions in the insurance market.

225 See Council Regulation (EC) No. 139/2004, Article 3(b). In relation to insurance undertakings, the turnover is calculated basically in relation to 'the value of gross premiums written which shall comprise all amounts received and receivable in respect of insurance contracts issued by or on behalf of the insurance undertakings, including also outgoing reinsurance premiums, and after deduction of taxes and parafiscal contributions or levies charged by reference to the amounts of individual premiums or the total volume of premiums.'

226 For instance, reinsurance.

227 See Commission Decision in *Commercial Union/General Accident*, para 9.

228 See Commission Decision in *Abeille Vie/ Viagere/Sinafer*, para 12.

It is undoubtedly true that the lack of harmonisation at community level and the peculiar distribution channels characterising the insurance industry render its geographic dimension mainly confined to a national level. In the same way, it is incontestable that the insurance market can be divided into as many relevant service markets as there are insurances for different kinds of risks.

The problem arises when these concepts are applied in an assessment of insurance mergers and acquisitions. If the relevant geographic market is mainly represented by the territory of single Member States, it is very rare that insurance mergers are capable of engaging the inter-state element necessary in order to claim the application of the merger regulation. Equally, if the relevant product market is narrowly fragmented, it would be very difficult that the requirement of the creation or the enhancement of a position of dominance is fulfilled as per Regulation 139/2004[229] and, consequently, that consolidation in the insurance market is caught by the merger control framework.

In addition to these elements, the assessment of dominance is not free from criticism either; the Commission tends to evaluate insurance mergers and acquisitions only in relation to the individual dominant position held by the parties to the concentration resulting from the mergers. The collective dominance perspective (i.e. a dominant position held by the parties to the concentration together with an entity not a party thereto) is rarely taken into account.

There would be the need to disentangle these concepts from the concrete assessment of mergers and acquisitions. Yet again, a parallel with the Commission's approach in assessing abuse of dominant position seems interesting.

In assessing the abuse of dominant position, the Commission takes into account several elements, such as the possibility for an undertaking to control both production and distribution, and the position of economic strength in the market.

Similarly, the Commission, in assessing insurance mergers and acquisitions, should take into account in the first place the existence of the block exemption framework allowing insurance undertakings to cooperate and share information; this capacity enhances the position of economic strength of insurers operating within the internal market considerably.[230]

The benefits derived by insurance undertakings from the block exemption regulation should be assessed in conjunction with other important elements that the Commission does not seem currently to consider.

229 See Council Regulation (EC) No 139/2004, Article 2.

230 It has already been noticed how different the assessment of an abuse of dominance position is from the evaluation of mergers and acquisitions. Nevertheless, the presence of the block exemption regulation system must be taken into account.

First, in relation to the relevant geographic market, after having acknowledged that the insurance business relevant geographic market remains mainly confined to national level, it would still be possible to consider the potential impact of national consolidation on the internal market.[231] The potential effect on the internal market of insurance mergers at national level could be taken into account, in conjunction with the ample scope for cooperation under the block exemption system. This would result in triggering the engagement of the application of the merger regulation.

In relation to the determination of relevant product market, having identified the specific line of insurance involved in the transaction, the Commission could also take into account the participation of the insurance undertakings implicated in the merger in relation to different lines of insurance, so as to assess the dominance in light of a more comprehensive scenario.[232]

Alternatives can also be suggested in terms of assessment of dominance. The current trend is to consider concentration of market shares within the region of 40 per cent, 50 per cent (even 80 per cent!)[233] of the market not likely to raise concerns in relation to a possible detrimental impact on competition. It is very difficult to suggest specific thresholds, as the concrete scenarios may vary considerably from case to case. Yet again, a parallel with the assessment of abuse of dominant position may be drawn. The suggested approach would be to consider a threshold in the region of 30/40 per cent a generic indication of a potential dominance to be assessed, of course, also in relation to the market shares of the nearest competitors.

The analysis of collective dominance deserves a specific mention. We have seen that the analysis of collective dominance entails the consideration of possible synergies between the entities involved in the merger and third parties. It has also been outlined that the Commission rarely takes this concept into account in assessing insurance mergers and acquisitions. Especially in light of the block exemption system and the active cooperation between insurers, it would be advisable to always consider possible links or synergies of the insurers involved in the transaction with third parties in order to assess a possible risk of dominance in the form of oligopoly.

231 The potential effect of dominance is taken into account by the Commission whenever it assesses an abuse of dominant position, which, although taking place within the territory of a single member state, will be caught by the European competition regulatory framework (specifically by Article 82 EC), if capable of having an impact on trade between member states. See Case T-219/99 *British Airways plc v Commission*.

232 In case the insurance undertakings involved in a merger deal only with a single type of insurance service, this analysis would not of course be possible. Nevertheless, although insurers tend nowadays to be very specialised, it is common that they provide simultaneously different types of insurance services.

233 See Commission Decision in *Allianz/AGF*.

12 Conclusive remarks

The application of competition law to the insurance sector has always been, and will always be, controversial. We have seen that some aspects of the sophisticated structure of this sector of the economy are indeed difficult to reconcile with antitrust principles.

Nevertheless, it is the opinion of this author that the ramifications of the insurance industry and its deep synergies with the other sectors of the economy call for competition regulation and vigilant antitrust scrutiny.

This chapter has embarked on a journey that aimed at exploring the most controversial issues revolving around the application of competition law to the EU and Chinese insurance sectors, with the view of proposing, where possible, suggestions for further developments. We have seen that the main problematic issues surround forms of horizontal cooperation between insurers and mergers and acquisitions.

The exploration of the Chinese scenario has produced some interesting discoveries in terms of similarities with the EU competition regulatory framework. This, nevertheless, does not come as a surprise since, as established in the above, the Chinese Anti-Monopoly Act has been largely structured on the basis of the relevant competition law provisions of the EU Treaty. What was interesting to note is a possible lenient attitude towards forms of horizontal cooperation and mergers and acquisitions between insurers arising from Chinese competition law and insurance sector-specific regulation, and the recognised need to foster the domestic market vis-à-vis foreign competition.

In line with the considerations made in relation to the European scenario, it is submitted that a systematic grant of exemptions and a relaxed approach to mergers and acquisitions could lead to a highly consolidated market, with the relative negative consequences to be borne by end users, and it is not advisable. A different legislative approach could be based on the aforementioned theorised suggestions for the competition assessment of forms of horizontal cooperation and mergers and acquisitions between insurers in Europe, which are perfectly viable also for the Chinese scenario.

More specifically, a careful scrutiny of forms of joint cooperation on statistical data, agreements on co-insurance and reinsurance, to be exempted only under extreme circumstances, could create a more efficient and balanced paradigm.

By the same token, a strict assessment of mergers and acquisitions between insurers based on the concept of collective dominance theorised in the above could work efficiently and become an effective counterbalancing factor vis-à-vis excessive consolidation in the insurance industry, the negative consequences of which could reverberate against end users.

5 Current issues and developments in Chinese insurance law

Professor Beiping Chu[1]

1 Introduction

With a view to ensuring that courts correctly apply the Insurance Act 2009 and to unify the adjudication criteria, in addition to the promulgation of the *Interpretation on Certain Issues concerning the Application of the Insurance Act of the PRC (I)*,[2] the Supreme Court of China has begun to deliberate on a second judicial interpretation, namely *Interpretation II to the Insurance Act*, of which a draft for comments was announced to the public in 2012, focusing on controversial issues in relation to the chapter on insurance contracts under the Insurance Act. In such circumstances, considering the large number of controversial issues arising out of judicial practice in the hearing of marine insurance cases in China, the Supreme Court has been considering whether another judicial interpretation in respect of trial of marine insurance cases shall be made. For this purpose, the Supreme Court, through higher courts and maritime courts, and the China Maritime Law Association, through its marine insurance sub-commission, launched an investigation on the focal controversies as appeared in the court, raised by practitioners in insurance or law firms, as well as academics across China. The final version of *Interpretation II* came into force on 8 June 2013.[3] In this chapter, the author will discuss several current issues.

1 Doctor and Professor of Maritime Law, Doctoral Supervisor of Law School, Dalian Maritime University (Dalian, China); Dean of Law School, Dalian Maritime University.

2 Interpretation No. 12 [2009] of the Supreme People's Court.

3 Interpretation II of the Supreme People's Court on Several Issues concerning the Application of the Insurance Act of the People's Republic of China (Interpretation No. 14 [2013]) was adopted at the 1577th meeting of the Judicial Committee of the Supreme People's Court on 6 May 2013 and came into force on 8 June 2013.

2 Insurable interest

2.1 The test of insurable interest

Paragraph 6 of Article 12 of the Insurance Act 2009[4] requires that the insurable interest must be a legal interest. Nevertheless, there are some scholars supporting a twin-track test for the insurable interest, so that the insurable interest in property insurance should be a legal one, whereas in personal insurance, only assureds who have a specified relationship with the insured shall be deemed to have an insurable interest.

Paragraph 6 of Article 12 of the Insurance Act emphasises the legal relationship between the insured and the subject matter insured.[5] In judicial practice, the courts have also adopted different tests in determining the existence of an insurable interest. The Higher Court of Shandong Province applied a 'legal relationship' test in the case *M/V Rong Sheng*, while Dalian Maritime Court applied an 'economic relationship' test in the case *M/V Yu Hang*.[6] The former test, which is similar to the 'narrow and strict approach' in English law, focuses on the legal relationship between the party and the subject matter insured. Such a test is arguably too conservative in the modern economy. The latter test, which is similar to the 'wide and liberal approach', focuses on the economic relationship between the insured and the subject matter insured, which is also in line with introducing the concept of 'insurable interest' into insurance law for the purpose of preventing gambling by insurance. The use of the 'economic relationship' test has been confirmed in both an early *Interpretation of the Supreme Court on the Relevant Issues concerning the Application of the Insurance Laws of PRC (Draft for Comments)* and the *Research Program on the Amendments to the Maritime Laws*. In light of the above, the Chinese legislator generally tends to adopt the 'wide and liberal approach' as the test of insurable interest. Such an approach was also adopted in the *Interpretation II of the Supreme Court on the Relevant Issues concerning the Application of the Insurance Laws of PRC (Draft for Comments)*, which provided that 'an insurable interest includes a current interest and any other legally recognised interest such as liabilities, expectation interests as produced by the current interests'.[7]

4 Paragraph 6 of Article 12 of the Insurance Act 2009 provides: 'An insurable interest means a lawful interest which the insured or the assured has in respect of the subject matter insured.'

5 Ibid.

6 Si Yuzhuo, *Maritime Law Monograph*, 2007, Beijing: China Renmin University Press, p 399.

7 This provision is contained in Article 1 of the Draft for Comments issued in March 2012. The full text of this draft is available in Chinese at: www.court.gov.cn/gzhd/zqyj/201203/t20120322_175287.htm (accessed 21 May 2014). However, no such provision is included in the final draft of the Interpretation II as it was subsequently enacted.

2.2 Who must possess an insurable interest?

There are three views on this issue. The first is that the assured must have an insurable interest. This view was adopted by the Insurance Act 1995 and the Insurance Act 2002. The second view is that both the assured and the insured must have an insurable interest. The third is that only the insured needs to have an insurable interest. The Insurance Act 2009 provides for a compromise between the above views, and provides definitions of the concepts 'assured' and 'insured'.[8] Such an approach increases the number of persons that could have an insurable interest and allows more entities possessing an interest to participate in the insurance contract. This can help stimulate the development of the insurance market.

2.3 The time when the insurable interests should be at hand in property insurance

Article 12 of the Insurance Act 2009[9] addresses this issue. Paragraph 2 of this Article provides that, under a property insurance policy, the insured must have an insurable interest in the subject matter insured when the insured event occurs. In the meantime, it provides, in paragraph 1 of the same Article, that the insured under a personal insurance contract must possess an insurable interest when the personal insurance contract is concluded.[10] These provisions are well suited to the different natures of both personal insurance and property insurance, and should prove straightforward to implement in practice.

However, after the entry into force of the Insurance Act 2009, there remained some contentious issues in insurance practice. The author has selected the following key issues for discussion:

(1) Under a marine cargo insurance policy where the period of liability is usually from warehouse to warehouse, if an insured event occurs in the period between the warehouse and the cargo holds, does the insured (the buyer) in a sale on FOB terms have an insurable interest?

The general view is that the insured does not have an insurable interest.

8 Article 12 of the Insurance Act 2009.

9 Paragraph 2 of Article 12 of the Insurance Act 2009 provides: 'The insured under property insurance shall have an insurable interest in the subject matter when an insured event occurs.'

10 Paragraph 1 of Article 12 of the Insurance Act 2009 provides: 'when entering into an insurance contract, the assured under personal insurance shall have an insurable interest in the insured person.'

(2) Can an insurable interest be assigned as a result of the assignment of the insurance contract?

The general view is that the insurable interest is assignable subject to the mutual agreement of the parties and in conjunction with assignment of the insurable contract.[11] However, there is also another view that, although the contract of carriage of goods by sea is freely assignable without the consent of the insurer, assignment of the insurance policy to third parties requires endorsement. This view is affirmed in the arbitration case of *M/V Shui Cheng* on cargo damage/shortage.[12]

(3) If there is no insurable interest under an insurance contract, is that contract an invalid contract, or is it still a valid contract but the insured has no right to claim from the insurer when the insured event occurs?

According to Article 48 of the Insurance Act, the existence of an insurable interest is a condition of the insured's entitlement to claim from the insurer rather than a condition of the validity of the insurance contract.[13]

3 Causation

3.1 The current rules on causation in Chinese insurance law

In China, insurance transactions are regulated by two statutes: Chapter 12, entitled 'Contract of Marine Insurance' of the Chinese Maritime Code (the 'Maritime Code') regulates marine insurance while the Insurance Act regulates other forms of insurance. The principle of causation is regulated by the same two statutes. The legislation on causation has the following characteristics:

(1) There is no express provision regarding the principle of causation in Chinese insurance law.

Neither the Insurance Act nor the Maritime Code expressly sets out the principle of proximate cause or other principles of causation.

(2) The principle of causation lacks clarification in Chinese law.

11 Chengjie Zhou and Jun Liu, 'A study on the insurable interest in marine insurance', *Chinese Water Transportation*, 2003(8), p 45.
12 See: www.ccmt.org.cn/ (accessed 21 May 2014).
13 See Chapter 14 of this work; for an earlier text in Chinese, see Meixian Song, 'The UK's Law Commission's reform project in respect of marine insurance', *Chinese Journal of Maritime Law*, 2012(1).

Although no explicit provision in the Chinese statutes requires a causal link between the risk and the loss, there is an implied[14] principle of causation in the Chinese statute. Article 2 of the Insurance Act provides that:

> 'Insurance' in this Act refers to a commercial insurance transaction whereby an assured, in accordance with the terms and conditions of a contract, pays a premium to an insurer, and the insurer undertakes to indemnify the insured where property loss or damage is *caused as a result of* the occurrence of an insured event, or to pay an indemnity upon the occurrence of death, injury, or illness of the insured or the attainment of a certain age, time limit or other requirements agreed upon in the contract.
>
> (emphasis added)

The term 'caused as a result of' in Article 2 shows the implication of the principle of causation. Article 216(1) of the Maritime Code provides that:

> [a] contract of marine insurance is a contract whereby the insurer undertakes, as agreed, to indemnify the loss to the subject matter insured and the liability of the insured *caused by* perils covered by the insurance against the payment of an insurance premium by the insured.
>
> (emphasis added)

The term 'caused by' in Article 216(1) also implies the principle of causation. In addition to the above, the term 'caused by' is also found in many other Articles of the Maritime Code conveying the intention to require the causation in the insurance laws.[15]

3.2 Problems in practice

As the legislation does not provide any specific test to determine the causation, to some extent there exists ambiguity for practitioners and courts to deal with this issue, as is demonstrated by the following points:

(1) It is unclear what specific test should be applied in determining causation.

In practice, tests that are often discussed are the main cause, the direct cause, the proximate cause, etc., among which the proximate cause is perhaps best supported. However, there is no widely accepted opinion on what the proximate cause is and how to apply that test.

14 Editors' note: 'Implied' is here used in the non-legal sense, not in the common law contract law sense.

15 See Articles 237, 238, 239, 242, 243, 244 and 252 of the Maritime Code 1992.

(2) The question how the policy should respond where there are concurrent causes is undetermined.

If the loss is caused by more than one event, especially in circumstances where the causes of damage consist of covered risks and uncovered risks, or simultaneously include covered risks and exempted risks, there is widespread controversy among theorists and practitioners on how to determine the insurer's liability for compensation.

3.3 Current trends

(1) The legislator has attempted to adopt the principle of proximate cause, but the principle has not yet been enshrined in statute.

Article 19 of the Interpretation on Certain Issues concerning the Trial of Insurance Disputes (Draft for Comments) issued by the Supreme Court in December 2003 provides that '[t]he insurer's argument that its liability shall be limited to the loss proximately caused by the insured perils should be granted by the court'. The principle of proximate cause was proposed again in the third draft of the Interpretation on Certain Issues concerning the Application of the Insurance Law of the PRC (Draft for Comments), which is an early version of the Interpretation I of the Supreme Court on Certain Issues concerning the Application of the Insurance Law of the PRC (Draft for Comments) 2003.[16] However, considering the complications arising from the principle of proximate cause and the potential incompatibility attributed to the legal transplantation of the doctrine of proximate cause – which is supported by the common law precedents – into the statutes of the civil law system, this proposal has been dismissed.

(2) The principle of proportional causation is now under consideration.

Article 22 of Interpretation II (Draft for Comments) issued by the Supreme Court in March 2012 provides that '[w]here the loss is caused by multiple causes, including perils covered and perils uncovered, the court can determine the insurer's liability according to the proportion or degree of perils covered to all the causes'.

16 See Articles 30, 31 and 32 of Interpretation on Certain Issues concerning the Application of the Insurance Law of the PRC (Draft for Comments) (3).

4 Utmost good faith

4.1 There are concepts of good faith in Chinese law, but no concept of utmost good faith

The principle of good faith is always regarded as 'an imperial rule' of civil law systems. Since China is also a country embracing a civil law system, the General Principles of the Civil Law 1986 and the Insurance Act 2009 both contain provisions on the specific doctrine of the good faith with which the parties must comply in civil transactions. Article 4 of General Principles of the Civil Law provides that '[i]n civil activities, the principles of voluntariness, fairness, making compensation for equal value, good faith shall be observed'. Article 5 of the Insurance Act 2009 provides that 'Parties to insurance activities shall observe the principle of good faith in exercising their rights and fulfilling their obligations'. However, there is no concept of *utmost* good faith in the Insurance Act. Even the Maritime Code, which is deeply influenced by English law, does not contain provisions of utmost good faith nor does it have any provision of the principle of good faith as do the General Principles of the Civil Law and the Insurance Act. Nevertheless, the Maritime Code is not only an important legal branch in Chinese civil laws, but also a special legislation subsidiary of the insurance law. According to Article 184 of the Insurance Act, '[m]arine insurance shall be governed by the relevant provisions of the Maritime Code of the People's Republic of China; for matters not covered by the Maritime Code, the relevant provisions of this Act shall apply'. Therefore, the principle of good faith, which has been provided in the Insurance Act, does apply to marine insurance.

4.2 The principle of good faith in China shares its core connotation with utmost good faith

Though there are provisions on the principle of good faith under the General Principles of Civil Law and the Insurance Act, such general provisions on the principle of good faith can hardly meet the requirements of marine insurance practice where the parties are required to subject to a higher and stricter level of general good faith. For such reasons, both the Insurance Act and the Maritime Code contain stricter, more specific and operational provisions on good faith than the general provisions on the principle of good faith. Such provisions mainly relate to the obligation of disclosure, which is also the core obligation of utmost good faith in English insurance law. Article 16 of the Insurance Act provides the details of the obligation of disclosure by the assured and the legal effects if the assured fails to comply with its obligations.[17] Article 6 of Interpretation II of Supreme Court on

17 See Article 16 of the Chinese Insurance Act 2009, Appendix I in this work.

the Relevant Issues concerning the Application of the Insurance Laws of PRC (Draft for Comments) explicitly provides the scope of disclosure that:

> [a]n insurer shall make definite and specific inquiries against an insurance applicant at the time of execution of an insurance contract. The information related to the subject matter insured or the insured which the insurance applicant knows or should have known shall fall into the information under Paragraph 1 of Article 16 of the Insurance Law that 'shall be disclosed faithfully' by the insurance applicant.[18]

Article 222 of the Maritime Code provides the obligation of disclosure in marine insurance that:

> Before the contract is concluded, the insured shall truthfully inform the insurer of the material circumstances which the insured has knowledge of or ought to have knowledge of in his ordinary business practice and which may have a bearing on the insurer in deciding the premium or whether he agrees to insure or not.

Article 223 further provides the legal effects if the insured fails to comply with such obligation.[19]

It is noteworthy that the standard of disclosure of the Maritime Code is stricter than that of the Insurance Act. The Maritime Code adopts a subjective standard while the Insurance Act requires the insurer to inquire. In such circumstances, it is clear that Chinese marine insurance law substantially contains the principle of utmost good faith, although there is no express provision setting out a concept of utmost good faith.

The main issue for both scholars and practitioners relating to the obligation of disclosure is the scope of disclosure in marine insurance; for example, how to define the concepts 'material circumstance' and 'knowledge of circumstances which ought to be known to the insured', and whether marine insurance should adopt unlimited disclosure, thus departing from what applies to other forms of commercial insurance.

18 This provision is included as Article 5 of the final draft of the Interpretation II with minor changes.

19 See Article 223 of the Maritime Code in Appendix II, p 361.

5 Limitation of action in subrogation and liability insurance

5.1 Subrogation

The basis of the doctrine of subrogation differs between the civil law system and common law, as the civil law system adopts a theory of statutory assignment of claim while the common law employs a theory of legal subrogation of claim. Most civil law jurisdictions adopt the former theory, viz. the statutory assignment; for instance, Article 170 of Chapter 5 of the German Insurance Contracts Act 2008,[20] Article 662 of the Japan Commercial Code,[21] Article 1916(1) of the Italian Civil Code,[22] Article 682 of the Korean Commercial Code[23] and Article 53 of the Taiwan Insurance Law.[24] Scholars and practitioners in civil law jurisdictions also support this approach. For instance, some scholars are of the view that the right to claim is automatically transferred to the insurer from the time when the insurer pays the compensation without any requirement upon the insured to

20 Section 170 of Chapter 5 Life Insurance: 'Right of Subrogation: (1) If attachment is executed on the insurance claim or compulsory execution has been carried out or insolvency proceedings are opened against the assets of the policyholder, the designated beneficiary may, with the consent of the policyholder, subrogate to the contract of insurance. Where the beneficiary subrogates, he must satisfy the demands of the creditor initiating the proceedings or of the insolvency estate up to the amount of the payment which the policyholder could demand from the insurer in the event of the termination of the contract of insurance. (2) Where no beneficiary is designated or named, the policyholder's spouse or life partner or children shall be entitled to the same right. (3) The subrogation is effected by giving notice thereof to the insurer. The notification may only be made within one month after the time when the person entitled to subrogate learns of the attachment or after the insolvency proceedings have been opened.'

21 Article 662 of Japanese Commercial Code: '(1) In case a loss is caused by a third person, if the insurer pays the whole amount of indemnity to the insured, he acquires the rights of the insurance applicant or the insured against the third person up to the limit of the amount paid by him. (2) If the insurer pays part of the amount of indemnity to the insured, he can exercise his right against the third person only so far as the right of the insurance applicant or the insured is not injured.'

22 Article 1916(1) of Italian Civil Code: 'The insurer who has paid the insurance money shall subrogate insured's claim for indemnity against the third party within the extent of the indemnity amount.'

23 Article 682 of Korean Commercial Code: 'In case damages is caused by a third person, if the insurer pays indemnities, he acquires the right of claim of insured against the third person up to the limit of the amount paid by him. If the insurer pays part of the amount of indemnity to the insurance applicant of insured, he can exercise his right against the third person only so far as the right of the subrogation or the insured is not injured.'

24 Article 53 of Taiwan Insurance Law: 'In case a loss is caused which is included in insured liability and insured has the right of claim against the third person, if the insurer pays the indemnities, he acquires the right of subrogation against the third party up to the limit of amount paid by him.'

separately assign the right of claim.[25] In Judgment No 923 (69 Year) of the Taiwan Supreme Court, it is held that 'the statutory subrogation has an effect of assignment of the creditor's right. The insured's right of claim would be transferred to the insurer after the compensation has been paid'.[26]

Like other civil law jurisdictions, mainland China adopts the theory of statutory assignment of claim in the legislation on subrogation, and Article 60 of the Insurance Act 2009 also evinces such adoption.

5.2 Commencement of limitation of action for subrogation

The starting point for the limitation of action for subrogation is not explicitly provided by Chinese statutes. But there are several theories concerning this issue. The first view is that the limitation of action shall begin to count when the insurer is aware of the existence of any obligor who is liable for the loss/damage insured. Professor Gui Yu and Professor Yuan Zongwei are the advocates of this view.[27] The second view is that it commences when the assured is aware of the existence of any obligor who is liable for the loss/damage insured. Professor Wensen Shi takes this view.[28] Practitioners in Taiwan have also adopted this view.[29] The third theory is that the limitation counts from the date of the occurrence of the insured event.[30] The fourth theory is that it counts from the date when the insured

25 Chaoguo Jiang, *The Basic Theories of Insurance Law*, 2002, Beijing: China University of Political Science and Law Press, p 298.

26 Wensen Shi, *Insurance Law Thesis (Volume 1)*, 1985, Taiwan: Wu-Nan Book Inc., p 143.

27 Yuxian Liang, *The New Study on Insurance Law*, 2004, Beijing: China Renmin University Press, p 137.

28 Wensen Shi, *Study on Judgment on the Basis of Insurance Law*, Wu-Nan Book Inc., Taiwan, 1980. In Chapter 5, Section 6 of the book, he says: first, the insurer is not deprived of its lawful right of subrogation by legally stipulated time bars. Second, subject to the principle that no one can effectively transfer that which does not belong to them, the insurer's right of subrogation allows it to succeed to but also limits the recovery rights of the assured against the third party' (original in Chinese).

29 'The third seminar held by the Taiwan Judicial Court discussed the starting point for the time bar of insurer's rights of subrogation under Article 53 of the Taiwan Insurance Law. The First Court proposed that given that it is accepted that the insurer's right of subrogation under Article 53 constitutes a type of legal transfer of creditor's rights, and that therefore the insurer may exercise the insured's rights to claim compensation against the third party by subrogation in its own name, meaning that it essentially succeeds to the insured's rights to claim against the third party. The limitation of action begins when the insured was able to exercise its right to claim. This view of limitation of action is arguably consistent with the substance of the principle of subrogation. There is a further explanation by the Ministry of Finance of Taiwan that because the insurer's subrogated rights derive from the insured, the limitation of action should begin when the insured could first exercise its right to claim' (original in Chinese).

30 In a relevant case on the website of Jiangsu Court, the insurer did not have reasons to suspend limitation of action, and the time to litigate from the event accrued had exceeded the period, then the plaintiff had no right to win, whose claim should be overruled.

could exercise its right of claim (i.e. the time when the insured knew or should have known of the occurrence of the insured event).[31] The fifth theory suggests that the time limitation shall begin from the date when the insurer has paid the indemnity to the insured.

It is generally accepted that the commencement of the limitation of action for subrogation should be based on the legal relationship between the insured and the third party. From the legal perspective, the relationship between the insured and the third party is either one based on tort or one based on contract. In both types of relationship, the limitation of action will be determined in accordance with Article 137 of General Principles of the Civil Law, under which the limitation for action shall be counted from the time when the claimant knows or should have known that its right was being infringed, provided there is no specific rule in special legislation. Most scholars in China hold this view.[32] Article 17 of the Interpretation II (Draft for Comments) has also provided that the limitation of action for subrogation shall be counted from the time when the insured knew or should have known that its right was being infringed by a third party.[33] In fact, the courts have adopted this test in their practice.[34]

5.3 Limitation of action in respect of liability insurance

The determination of the commencement of the limitation of action in liability insurance is one of the most controversial issues in Chinese insurance law. To have a better understanding of the issue, it might be necessary to review the relevant provisions of the Maritime Code, the Insurance Act and the General Principle of the Civil Law.

Articles 264 and 267 of the Maritime Code provide that the limitation of actions with regard to contracts of marine insurance is two years, counting from the date on which the peril insured occurred. The limitation of action shall be discontinued as a result of bringing an action or submitting the case for arbitration by the claimant, or the admission to fulfil obligations by the person against whom the claim was brought. However, the limitation of action will not be discontinued if the claimant withdraws his action or

31 Task Group of Shanghai Supreme Court, 'Applicable law studies on disputes of insurance subrogation rights', *Applicable Law*, 5, 2011, p 25.

32 Aidong Cui, *Study on the System of Insurance Subrogation*, 2012, Doctoral Dissertation, Ji Lin University.

33 Paragraph 2 of Article 17, Interpretation II (Draft for Comments). However, Article 16 of the enacted Interpretation II provides that the time bar for subrogation shall be counted from the time when the insured's right is subrogated to the insurer.

34 *Nipponkoa Insurance Co. Ltd v Zhenjiang Shipyard Co. Ltd, Tonghua Container Transportation Co. Ltd*; *Hushu branch in Hangzhou of the Chinese people's property insurance Co. Ltd v Xu Zhiwei, Song Pingping*; and *Mitsui Sumitomo Insurance v Zhenjiang Shipyard Co. Ltd, Tonghua Container Transportation Co. Ltd.*

his submission for arbitration, or his action is rejected by a decision of the court.

In the meantime, Article 26 of the Insurance Act provides that the limitation period for an insured or beneficiary in any insurance other than life insurance to claim indemnity or insurance money against the insurer shall be two years, which commences from the day when the insured or beneficiary knows or should have known of the occurrence of the incident insured.

The general provisions on the limitation period were contained in Articles 135, 137, 139 and 140 of General Principles of Civil Law. Article 135 provides, 'Except as otherwise provided by law, the limitation period for bringing actions to the court for protection of civil rights shall be two years'.[35] Article 137 provides, 'The limitation period of action shall begin when the entitled person knows or should have known that his rights have been infringed upon'.[36] Article 139 provides:

> A limitation of action shall be suspended during the last six months of the limitation if the plaintiff cannot exercise his right of claim because of force majeure or other obstacles. The limitation shall resume on the day when the grounds for the suspension are eliminated.[37]

Article 139 continues, 'The limitation shall be resumed on the day when the grounds for the suspension are eliminated'.[38] Article 140 provides, 'And the limitation period of action shall be discontinued if a suit is brought or if one party makes a claim for or agrees to fulfil obligations',[39] and continues, 'A new limitation period shall be counted from the time of such discontinuance'.[40]

Therefore, the provisions of the Maritime Code are obviously different from the provisions of the General Principles of the Civil Law in respect of the commencement point of limitation of action and the events to discontinue the period. Presently, it is generally accepted that such provisions of the Maritime Code are rules specifically for marine insurance. Moreover, the view of the Supreme Court has also been presented in the Symposium of Presiding Judges of the Maritime Court held on 20 July 2001. According to the minutes of the symposium, it is clarified that the provisions on the limitation of action in the Maritime Code form an independent and complete system. Hence, in respect of the limitation period of action of marine insurance, the provisions of the Maritime Code shall prevail.

35 Article 135 of the General Principles of Civil Law.
36 Article 137 of the General Principles of Civil Law.
37 Article 139 of the General Principles of Civil Law.
38 Ibid.
39 Article 140 of the General Principles of Civil Law.
40 Ibid.

However, some scholars in China are of the opinion that it deviates from the general principles of law to use the date of the occurrence of the events insured as the starting point for the limitation of action in marine insurance claims, and their reasons are mainly as follows:[41]

(1) The occurrence of the peril insured and the infringement on the insured's rights under the marine insurance are not necessarily relevant.
(2) The insured does not have the right of suit against the insurer before the insurer rejects the claim.
(3) If the insured actively claims an indemnity after the occurrence of an insured event, it will be unjust for the insured to sustain the negative consequence of 'idleness in exercising its rights' when he, in fact, does not idly exercise its right.

In practice, there are some judgments in China supporting the above views that the limitation of action shall begin from the day when the insured receives the notice of rejection to compensate, instead of the day when the accident occurred; for instance, the judgment of the appeal case *China Pacific Insurance (Group) Co. Ltd ZheJiang Branch v Longteng Trading Co. Ltd.*[42]

Although there are heated arguments on the limitation period, as mentioned above, it will be very difficult to unify or to fundamentally alter the provisions of the Maritime Code and the Insurance Act in a short time. However, as to the limitation period of action in liability insurance, it is widely accepted that there should be a specific litigation distinguished from other general insurance contracts. This view can be observed in Article 18 of Interpretation II (Draft for Comments), which reads that 'the limitation period of action for the insured under a liability insurance contract shall be counted from the date on which the civil liability of the insured is ascertained'.[43]

6 Direct action against P&I Club

6.1 Whether a P&I Club is a commercial insurance organisation

The Maritime Code has no clear provisions on whether the cover provided by P&I Clubs or other mutual insurance organisations falls to be classed as

41 Cui Meng and Mao Lin, 'The understanding and application of the limitation of action for insurance contract: reflection on Article 264 of Maritime Code of the PRC', *Chinese Journal of Maritime Law*, 2012(3), p 54.
42 (2009) Hu Hai Fa Shang Chu Zi No. 325 before the Shanghai Maritime Court; (2009) Hu Gao Min Si Hai Zhong Zi No. 214 before the Shanghai Higher Court.
43 This provision is included in the final draft of the Interpretation II as Article 16.

marine insurance contracts; while Article 6 of the unrevised Insurance Act provides that an insurance company engaged in commercial insurance business must be established in accordance with the law, other organisations and individuals are forbidden from engaging in commercial insurance business.[44] Accordingly, insurance companies are the only entities that could engage in commercial insurance.

However, Article 6 of the Insurance Act 2009 provides that the insurance business may only be operated by insurance companies established in accordance with the Act and by other insurance organisations as determined by applicable law and administrative regulations, and no other entities or individuals may operate such business. This means that insurance businesses can also be operated by insurance organisations other than insurance companies. Further, Article 183 of the Insurance Act also provides that the Act applies to the commercial insurance business engaged in by insurance organisations that are established in accordance with the law. Though P&I Clubs may be categorised as 'other insurance organisations' than insurance companies, it is still worthwhile to discuss whether the cover provided by P&I Clubs belongs to commercial insurance business.

Though the insurance industry traditionally opines that the aim of commercial insurance business is to make benefits and to acquire the biggest profits, the rules of a P&I Club may provide that it is a not-for-profit organisation. It has therefore been generally acknowledged within the insurance industry that the business carried out by P&I Clubs was not 'commercial insurance business'. In 2003, the China Insurance Regulatory Commission (the 'CIRC') replied to the Hubei Higher Court that, pursuant to Articles 2 and 9 of the Insurance Act 2002 and the Regulations of Notice about the Establishment of the China Insurance Regulatory Commission, the CIRC is responsible for the supervision and administration of the commercial insurance industry within the nation, while the business engaged in by P&I Clubs does not fall within the scope of the commercial insurance business stipulated in Article 2 of the Insurance Act 2002, and consequently is not subject to the supervision of the CIRC.[45] In addition, with reference to the question whether a P&I insurance contract concluded between a P&I Club and its members is a marine insurance contract, the Supreme Court expressed its view in a reply to the Hubei Higher Court that the China Shipowners Mutual Assurance Association (the 'CPI') is not a commercial insurance company in the sense of the Insurance Act, and the insurance contracts entered into between the CPI and its member are therefore not a commercial insurance. As a result, contract law and other relevant regulations should be applied to these contracts instead of the

44 Article 6 of the Chinese Insurance Act 1995.

45 See the China Insurance Regulatory Commission's Reply as to the question of the China Shipowners Mutual Assurance Association [Baojianhan (2003) No. 78].

Insurance Act.[46] It will be seen from the above that the Chinese courts have attached great importance to the question of whether the business conducted by P&I Clubs is commercial insurance.

If profitability is accepted as the standard to distinguish between commercial insurance and other activities, the business of a P&I Club is not commercial insurance.[47] However, if a P&I Club provides its members with fixed premium hull insurance or oil pollution liability insurance, this will exceed the scope of mutuality, in which circumstance it is probable that such business transactions of the P&I Club will be defined as for-profit transactions. As provided by Article 53 of the Regulation on the Prevention and Control of Marine Pollution from Ships, which came into effect on 1 March 2010, 'The owner of a vessel navigating on the sea areas under the jurisdiction of the People's Republic of China shall acquire the coverage of civil liability insurance against vessel-induced oil pollution damage or corresponding financial securities'. The relevant authority of China had approved 23 insurance institutions, including 12 overseas P&I Clubs, one Chinese P&I Club and 10 insurance companies, to cover such risks. The requirements of the Regulation do not differ between P&I Clubs and insurance companies for the purpose of providing the relevant insurances on civil liability. In addition, the relevant authority of China had obtained the CIRC's opinion before approving the above 23 insurance institutions. Therefore, it is likely that the P&I Club will be defined as 'other commercial insurance institutions', as provided in Article 183 of the Insurance Act, which should be supervised by State authority.[48]

6.2 Direct actions against P&I Clubs

Article 65 of the Insurance Act sets out the protection of the aggrieved third party:

> The insurer may directly indemnify a third party for losses or damages caused by the assured of liability insurance in accordance with law and provisions in the contract.

46 See the Supreme Court's reply as to the governing law regarding the case on appeal between the *China Shipowners Mutual Assurance Association v Nanjing Hongyou Shipping Co. Ltd* [4th Civil Court Reply (2003) No. 34].

47 The P&I Clubs in the UK were usually registered as companies limited by guarantee without share which means the members of them are not shareholders, and will not contribute to share capital. The members of a P&I Club form the network of reciprocal guarantees and will not gain profit from the Club. See S. J. Hazelwood, *P&I Clubs Law and Practice*, LLP, 2000, p 13.

48 Article 183 of the Insurance Act 2009 provides: 'Commercial insurance businesses operated by legally established insurance organisations other than insurance companies shall be governed by this Act.'

> Where the insured under liability insurance causes losses or damages to a third party and the liability for compensation to the third party is ascertained, the insurer shall, upon the request of the insured, make the indemnity payment directly to the third party. Where the insured is negligent in making such a request, the third party is entitled to claim directly against the insurer for its portion of the compensation.

If a P&I Club is deemed to be a commercial insurance organisation per the Insurance Act, an injured third party can file a lawsuit against the P&I Club directly, relying on the above provision of the Insurance Act, although the Maritime Code contains no provisions in respect of liability insurance. Otherwise, the Insurance Act will not govern P&I insurance contracts, and, as a result, it seems that there is no legal ground for a third party to claim against the P&I Club or other mutual insurance organisations directly. However, the nature of the right of a third party to claim an indemnity from the liability insurer directly is similar to the right of subrogation defined by the Contracts Act. In the event that the members are reluctant to request their mutual insurance organisations to pay an indemnity that has fallen due, the aggrieved third party shall be entitled to claim directly against the mutual insurance organisation by taking the position of the members. There is no legislation similar to the Third Parties Rights Against Insurers Act 2010 of the United Kingdom, nor any case precedents such as *The Fanti and The Padre Island (No 2)*[49] in China. Therefore, disputes regarding the right of subrogation are governed by Interpretation I of the Supreme Court on Certain Issues concerning the Application of the Contract Law. Article 18 of this interpretation provides that 'the defences to which the sub-debtor is entitled against the debtor can be invoked by the sub-debtor against the creditor in the subrogation litigation'. The provision should be construed as legal confirmation of the rights of the sub-debtor when defending a claim against a third party in a subrogation action. In such a circumstance, there is still a chance for the 'pay to be paid' clause in the P&I Club insurance contracts or mutual insurance contracts to be applied.

7 Summary

Although marine insurance is no longer as special a form of insurance as it once was, it is still necessary to maintain its relative independence because of its special history, internationalism, special value orientation and the self-contained nature of maritime laws, as well as particular loss management mechanisms such as general average, constructive total loss, abandonment, etc. Therefore, it is reasonable for the Chinese legislator to stipulate the provisions of marine insurance in the Maritime Code instead of in the insurance law. Now, amendments to the Maritime Code are arguably a

49 *The Fanti* and *The Padre Island* (No. 2) [1990] 2 Lloyd's Rep 191.

better way to coordinate the differences between the Maritime Code and the Insurance Act, especially taking into account the fact that the Insurance Act was amended as recently as 2009, while the Maritime Code has yet to be modified since its publication.

6 Jurisdiction, applicable law and dispute resolution

Dr Wenhao Han[1]

1 Jurisdiction

1.1 People's Court in the People's Republic of China

The People's Republic of China (PRC) adopts one uniform legal system across its mainland (excluding Hong Kong and Macao special administrative regions). Within the one legal system, there are 31 administrative jurisdictions with over 3,500 courts spreading across different regions in the mainland. The courts in the PRC are called the People's Courts.

The jurisdiction of the People's Court is determined in two ways. First, the People's Court's jurisdiction is determined by its administrative territory. A court, except the Supreme People's Court, will only have jurisdiction over cases that are closely connected to its geographical administrative territories. Second, the People's Court's jurisdiction is determined by its supervising superiority. The People's Courts operate a four-tier system, which contains the Basic People's Courts, the Intermediate People's Courts, the High People's Courts and the Supreme People's Court. Civil and commercial litigation usually starts from the Basic or Intermediate People's Courts, depending on the amount involved in the dispute and whether they have foreign-related elements. If the dispute is foreign-related, the claim should normally be filed before an Intermediate People's Court. Very few claims will start at the High People's Court or the Supreme People's Court at the first instance; this will only happen when the disputes in question are of an extremely complicated nature or have a serious bearing on foreign relations between the PRC and other national states.

Hong Kong and Macao, being special administrative regions of the PRC, retain their own respective legal systems that are, respectively, influenced by the English and Portuguese legal systems due to historical reasons. They have their own judiciary body that is not subject to the PRC People's Courts

1 Solicitor, qualified in England & Wales and the People's Republic of China, Norton Rose Fulbright LLP; PhD (University of Southampton).

system. They also have their own respective Court of Final Appeal that can give final judgment on appeal cases.

1.2 Territorial jurisdiction

Territorial jurisdiction is the most common way by which a People's Court founds its jurisdiction. Factors including domicile, place of business, place of alleged injury or conduct, location of property and consent of the parties will be taken into account. A claimant must have certain connections with a local court due to the above factors in order to bring a case in that court.

The People's Court may exercise jurisdiction over a defendant who is domiciled, resides or conducts business within the court's administrative territory, regardless of the defendant's nationality. A civil claim generally shall be brought in the People's Court at the place of the defendant's domicile. If a defendant has both a domicile and a habitual residence, the court in the venue of the defendant's habitual residence will found jurisdiction. When there are several defendants who are domiciled or reside in two or more jurisdictional territories, the courts in those territories shall all have jurisdiction. In these circumstances, a claimant is allowed to choose any one of those competent courts to file the claim. If the claimant files a claim with two or more competent courts, the court first seized of the claim shall exercise jurisdiction.

For disputes arising out of insurance contracts, the court at the place of the defendant's domicile or habitual residence, or the court at the place where the subject matter insured is located shall found jurisdiction. For marine insurance cases, they are subject to the special jurisdiction of Maritime Courts in the PRC. There are 10 Maritime Courts in the PRC. They are located in Dalian, Qingdao, Tianjin, Shanghai, Nanjing, Wuhan, Xiamen, Guangzhou, Beihai and Haikou. Their jurisdictions are determined by their respective administrative geographical territory.

The Maritime Courts are equal to the Intermediate People's Courts in the PRC court system in terms of superiority. If the litigants are not satisfied with their first instance judgment from a Maritime Court, they may go on to the appellate court, which is normally the High People's Court, having jurisdiction over the territory where the Maritime Court is located, for an appeal. There is only one appeal in the PRC court system.

For maritime claims, the Maritime Court may found jurisdiction for granting interim measures when the subject matter of the interim measures is located in its jurisdiction, irrespective of parties' contractual agreement on jurisdiction or arbitration. Under the Maritime Special Procedure Law 1999, a ship can be arrested as security for a maritime claim. The arrest of a ship is regarded not as an action in rem, but as a procedure of preservation of a maritime claim. Similarly, a claimant may apply to arrest the cargo carried by a ship and her bunkers if the defendant owns the cargo or bunkers.

1.3 Consensual agreement on jurisdiction

Under PRC law, parties are allowed to choose jurisdiction through mutual agreement. Therefore, the People's Court's jurisdiction could also be established by consent of the parties, either before or after the dispute arises. Parties to a contract may choose to subject any disputes between them to the jurisdiction of the People's Court at the place of the defendant's domicile or habitual residence, where the contract is performed or concluded, or where the subject matter of the claim is located.

For foreign-related civil and commercial cases, such choice is subject to four conditions: (1) the agreement must be made in writing; (2) the court chosen must have actual connections with the dispute; (3) the dispute must involve foreign contracts or foreign property rights; and (4) the choice of jurisdiction shall not contradict any mandatory provisions on the People's Court's exclusive jurisdiction.[2]

As for exclusive jurisdiction, the civil procedure law of the PRC expressly excludes foreign courts from exercising jurisdiction over certain civil actions over which the People's Court shall have exclusive jurisdiction. The civil procedure law explicitly provides that the PRC People's Courts shall have exclusive jurisdiction over disputes concerning the performance of contracts of Chinese-foreign equity joint ventures, Chinese-foreign contractual joint ventures, or Chinese-foreign cooperative exploration and development of natural resources within the PRC.

In addition, certain actions shall be under the exclusive jurisdiction of a particular People's Court: (1) for claims arising out of a dispute over real estate, the People's Court of the place where the real estate is located shall have jurisdiction; (2) for claims arising out of a dispute over harbour operations, the People's Court of the place where the harbour is situated shall have jurisdiction; and (3) for claims arising out of a dispute over inheritance and succession, the People's Court of the place where the decedent was domiciled upon his death, or where the main estate is located, shall have jurisdiction.[3]

As to a non-exclusive jurisdiction clause, the Supreme People's Court held that such a clause does not exclude jurisdiction of a country that has jurisdiction over the disputes. For example, if the contract has a non-exclusive jurisdiction clause in favour of English courts, the PRC courts can still exercise jurisdiction provided that the disputes also fall within the PRC People's Court's jurisdiction under PRC law.

Under PRC law, the defendant's failure to object to jurisdiction will be deemed as consent to jurisdiction. It is therefore imperative that foreign

2 Article 34, Civil Procedure Law of PRC 2012; after the 2012 amendment of the Chinese Civil Procedure Law, these conditions are applicable for both foreign-related and domestic civil and commercial cases.

3 Article 33, Civil Procedure Law of PRC 2012.

defendants file a timely objection to the People's Court if they wish to have the case heard in another jurisdiction.

1.4 Forum non conveniens

The People's Courts also recognise the doctrine of *forum non conveniens*. On 17 April 2000, the Supreme People's Court issued a 'Notice on Several Questions in Adjudication and Enforcement concerning Civil and Commercial Cases with Foreign Elements', which provides that if the parties to a civil litigation are all non-Chinese and the disputes have no practical connection with China, a People's Court may advise the parties to choose alternative courts in other countries, as litigation in the People's Court would be unpractical in terms of the determination of evidence and enforcement of judgments.

On 26 December 2005, the Supreme People's Court further issued a memorandum of guidance on Trial of Foreign-Related Commercial and Maritime Cases. In the memorandum, the Supreme People's Court set out the following conditions for the courts to consider when applying the doctrine of *forum non conveniens*: (1) the defendant makes application to apply the doctrine of *forum non conveniens* or object the PRC court's jurisdiction; (2) the PRC court hearing the case has proper jurisdiction; (3) the parties have made no choice of jurisdiction in favour of the PRC courts; (4) the disputes do not fall within the exclusive jurisdiction of the PRC courts; (5) the disputes do not concern any PRC citizen, corporate entity or organisation; (6) the crux of the factual matrix surrounding the disputes does not arise in the PRC; and (7) it is more convenient for a foreign court that also has jurisdiction to exercise jurisdiction.

The doctrine prevents parties from commencing litigation in the PRC court for pure forum shopping reasons. It is almost certain that if a Chinese party is involved in the disputes, the PRC court will not readily give up its jurisdiction and the doctrine of *forum non conveniens* will not be applicable. The memorandum also made it clear that the fact that parallel proceedings have been issued in a foreign court does not prevent PRC courts from exercising jurisdiction even if the foreign court has already made a judgment, unless such judgment has been recognised and enforced in the PRC.

1.5 Service of process

Another factor affecting the PRC courts' jurisdiction over foreign defendants is service of process. Service of process in the PRC is deemed as a judicial conduct, and therefore only the court can serve process. The civil procedure law of the PRC provides six methods of service by the People's Court: (1) service upon the defendant in person; (2) service at the defendant's residence; (3) entrusted service through the court of the place where the defendant resides; (4) service by post; (5) service forwarded to the defendant by the defendant's employer; and (6) service by public notice.[4]

If the defendant resides outside of China, the extraterritorial service shall be made through: (1) the methods as provided for by international treaties to which both the PRC and the foreign country concerned are a signatory; (2) the methods permitted by bilateral agreements for judicial assistance between the PRC and the foreign country; (3) diplomatic channels; (4) service on the representative office or agent of the foreign entity in the PRC; (5) service by post, provided that the country where the foreign party resides permits service by post; (6) service by fax or email, provided that receipt thereof which can be confirmed; or (7) service by public notice if none of the preceding methods can be used.[5]

2 Applicable law

In the PRC, the rules on conflict of laws are codified in the Law on the Application of Laws to Foreign-Related Civil Relationships 2010 (the Code). The term 'foreign-related civil relationships' is defined by the Supreme People's Court in Interpretation I on the Law on the Application of Laws to Foreign-Related Civil Relationships (2012). It provides that the following matters will be deemed foreign-related matters:

(1) one or both parties are foreign natural persons, stateless persons or foreign legal persons;
(2) one or both parties' habitual residence is outside the PRC;
(3) the subject matter is located in a foreign territory; and
(4) the legal facts which give rise to, modify or extinguish private rights and civil obligations arising abroad.[6]

The Code is not a comprehensive codification of all the conflict of laws rules. Civil relationship matters prescribed by the Code include civil subjects: marriage and family, succession, property, obligations and intellectual property. Provisions on conflict of laws in other Codes such as the General Principles of Civil Law, Contract Law and Maritime Law are still effective and will prevail, as long as they are not contradictory to the Code.

The Supreme People's Court, in Interpretation I on the Law on the Application of Laws to Foreign-Related Civil Relationships (2012), directed that the Code also apply to Hong Kong or Macau-related civil relationships.

4 Articles 85, 86 and 88, Civil Procedure Law of PRC 2012.
5 Article 267, Civil Procedure Law of PRC 2012.
6 Article 1, Interpretation I on the Law on the Application of Laws to Foreign-Related Civil Relationships 2012.

2.1 General principles

The Code recognises party autonomy on the choice of law in foreign-related civil relationships. It provides that parties may, in accordance with laws, expressly select the laws that are to govern their foreign-related civil relationships. The law chosen by the parties does not need to have any actual connection with the legal relationship between the parties.

The choice of law must be 'in accordance with the provisions of the laws' and the choice of law must be made 'expressly'. Absent express choice of law, the PRC courts will also respect the parties' agreement on the law at the time of dispute. Party autonomy on the choice of law applies not only in contractual relationships, but also in certain tort, property and intellectual property relationships.

The express choice of law must not contradict the mandatory provisions of PRC law. These mandatory provisions are mainly related to Sino-foreign natural resources exploration joint-venture contracts and foreign investment contracts whereby foreign entities are buying Chinese assets from non-foreign-invested companies through joint ventures, purchase of shares or equities, or transfer of shares within the territory of the PRC.

In addition, the PRC laws and regulations in the following areas cannot be evaded by express choice of law: (1) employees' rights; (2) food or public health and safety; (3) environment safety; (4) foreign exchange; and (5) antitrust or anti-monopoly.[7] The PRC laws and regulations concerning these areas are deemed mandatory and shall prevail in all circumstances.

2.2 'Closest connection' test

The Code recognises the doctrine of 'closest connection' that is familiar to practitioners from common law jurisdictions. In the absence of any express choice of governing law, the laws of the place that has the closest connection to the foreign-related civil relationship in question will apply. In this regard, the PRC courts adopt the notion of characteristic performance.

Prior to the promulgation of the Code, on 23 July 2007, the PRC Supreme People's Court issued Provisions on Several Questions Relating to the Trial of Foreign-Related Civil or Commercial Contractual Disputes, which sets out a list of presumptions for determining the closest connection in different types of contracts. For insurance contracts, the law of the insurance underwriter's domicile shall apply. The laws applicable do not include conflict law or procedural law.

The PRC court may determine the contents of foreign law through: (1) the parties to the litigation; (2) the central authority of the contracting

7 Article 10, Interpretation I on the Law on the Application of Laws to Foreign-Related Civil Relationships 2012.

country under the bilateral agreement of judicial assistance between the PRC and the foreign country; (3) the Chinese embassy or consulate in the foreign country; (4) the foreign country's embassy or consulate in the PRC; or (5) Chinese or foreign legal experts.

If, however, the foreign law cannot be determined through the above means, PRC law shall be applied. Any failure to object to the applicable law before the end of the hearing at the trial will be deemed as an implied agreement to the choice of applicable law.

2.3 Detailed rules

2.3.1 Contracts

Subject to the mandatory laws, the Code provides that parties may agree to select the laws applicable to their contract. If the parties have not made such a choice, either the laws of the place where the party whose performance of the obligations most manifests the character of the contract is normally resident, or other laws that have the closest connection with the contract in question, will apply.

2.3.2 Consumer contracts

For consumer contracts, the laws of the place where the consumer is normally resident will apply. If the consumer opts for application of the laws of the place where the goods or services are provided or if the business operator does not engage in the relevant business activities in the place where the consumer is normally resident, the laws of the place where the goods and services are provided apply.

2.3.3 Employment contracts

The laws of the place where the employee works apply to the employment contract. If the place where the employee works is difficult to determine, the laws of the place where the main business of the employer is located apply. With respect to a placement arrangement, the laws of the place from where the placement worker was sent may be applied. This gives the placement workers the freedom to choose the law that is more favourable to them and enjoy the benefits under that law.

2.3.4 Tort

The Code has made major changes to the previous position with respect to tort law. In the past, the position adopted by the PRC courts was that the laws of the place where the tortious acts take place apply; this includes the law of the place where such tortious acts were committed and the laws of the place where the consequences of such tortious acts arise.

The new rules are more sophisticated. The primary position is that the laws of the place where the tortious act was committed will apply. However, if the parties are normally resident in the same place, then the laws of the place where they are normally resident will apply. Despite these provisions, if, after the occurrence of the tortious act, the parties agree on the choice of the applicable laws, such laws should be applied in accordance with their agreement. Nonetheless, if a right of personality, such as the right to one's name, right to one's image, right to one's reputation or right to privacy is infringed online or otherwise, the laws of the place where the party whose rights have been infringed is normally resident will apply, and there is no room for party autonomy in the selection of the applicable law.

2.3.5 Product liability

The laws of the place where the injured party is normally resident will apply to product liability claims. If the injured party opts for the application of laws of the place where the tortfeasor's main business is located or of the place where the damage occurred, or if the tortfeasor does not engage in relevant business activities in the place where the injured party is normally resident, the laws of the place where the tortfeasor's main business is located or of the place where the damage occurred will apply.

2.3.6 Unjust enrichment and negotiorum gestio

As to unjust enrichment and *negotiorum gestio*, the Code allows the parties to agree on the applicable law. If the parties have not made such a choice, the laws of the place where the parties are both normally resident will apply. If the parties are not normally resident in the same place, the laws of the place where the unjustified enrichment or *negotiorum gestio* took place will apply.

2.3.7 Arbitration agreement

The Code also enshrines the important rule that parties may agree to choose the laws applicable to an arbitration agreement. If parties did not specify the governing law of the arbitration agreement, the applicable law shall be the law of the seat of the arbitration. If the arbitration agreement did not specify the seat of the arbitration, the People's Court will apply Chinese law.

3 Dispute resolution

3.1 Litigation

To start litigation in the PRC, litigants need to provide their lawyers with several documents for submission to the relevant court hearing the dispute. Assuming the litigant is a foreign company, these documents are a Power of Attorney, a Certificate of Identity of Legal Representative and a copy of the Certificate of Incorporation of the company. Under PRC law, the term 'Legal Representative' specifically refers to the person who represents the corporate entity to fulfil its functions as a legal person and it is usually the director or manager who can sign legal documents on behalf of the company. These documents need to be notarised by the local notary public at the claimant's domicile, attested by the Ministry of Foreign Affairs or its equivalent at the claimant's domicile and then legalised by the PRC embassy/consulate in that country.

3.1.1 Issuing the proceedings

The Statement of Claim should be in the Chinese language. It can be signed/endorsed by the instructed PRC local lawyer on behalf of the foreign litigants as their attorney if the Power of Attorney is granted and submitted to the court.

The defendant shall submit to the court their Statement of Defence within 15 days (in the case of PRC domestic defendants)[8] or 30 days (in the case of foreign defendants)[9] after being served the Statement of Claim.

Assuming the defendant is a foreign entity, it also needs to submit its Power of Attorney, Certificate of Identity of Legal Representative and a copy of the Certificate of Incorporation, all of which should be notarised by the local notary public in the defendant's domicile and legalised in the PRC embassy/consulate in that country, to enter the proceedings.

3.1.2 Disclosure

Under PRC law, there are no rules of disclosure of documents in the civil proceedings. Parties are not required to disclose to each other or to the court every piece of relevant evidence that is in their possession. Instead, the basic rule is that the party who alleges should provide evidence to substantiate its allegations. In this regard, prior to the Civil Procedure Law 2012, the People's Supreme Court issued Rules on Evidence in Civil Proceedings (2001), which set out detailed rules on evidential matters.

8 Article 125, Civil Procedure Law of PRC 2012.
9 Article 268, Civil Procedure Law of PRC 2012.

Under the Evidential Rules (2001), after the People's Court accepts and registers the claim, they will issue notices to both the claimants and the defendants to impose a deadline (normally for a period of no less than 30 days unless parties have agreed to a shorter period) for them to submit evidence and supporting documents. If the deadline is difficult to meet, the parties can apply to the court for an extension, which is subject to the court's discretion. Parties can also reach an agreement among themselves on the deadline for submission of evidence, subject to the approval of the court. After the expiry of the deadline of submission of evidence, the court will arrange for parties to exchange evidence and attend an evidentiary hearing before the trial of the substantive issues. Normally, no new evidence will be allowed after that stage.

Under PRC law, the People's Courts have the power to order specific disclosure and inspection of documents in possession of the litigants or non-parties to the proceedings upon application by the litigants. If the parties concerned refuse to cooperate with the court to disclose the same, they may face sanctions such as detainment of up to 15 days or pecuniary fines or even criminal charges if they deliberately destroy crucial evidence or threaten the witness with violence not to provide evidence. In addition, the failure or refusal to provide the evidence may lead the court to give the benefit of doubt to the other party who can prove the existence of the evidence but having been denied access to them for no justifiable reasons if the evidence to be disclosed is against the party who holds them.

The concept of privileged documents does not exist in the PRC civil proceedings. The only relevant rule on this is that any comprising admission of facts made by parties during the proceedings with a view to reaching an amicable settlement under the mediation of the court cannot be used in the subsequent proceedings as evidence against the party who made the admission.

3.1.3 Expert witness

An expert witness is generally allowed in the PRC civil proceedings. Parties can nominate one or two experts to give their expert opinion before the court. However, the application to call expert witnesses is subject to the court's discretion. Further, the application must be made at least 10 days prior to the expiry of the time limit for disclosure of evidence. Overseas witnesses are also allowed and they can give evidence by way of written statements, video or audio tapes, or via video links to the court at hearings if conditions permit. In addition, the courts also have power to appoint a special institution or appraiser or surveyor to assist the courts on specific issues in addition to, or in place of, party-appointed experts.

3.1.4 Right to appeal

A decision by a local court is appealed to an Intermediate People's Court, which in turn is appealed to the Higher Court; a Higher Court's decision is appealed to the Supreme People's Court. Although the court at the next higher level than the trial court will hear the appeal, the Statement of Appeal should be submitted to the original trial People's Court for service on the respondent. The respondent shall submit its Submission of Reply within 15 days in the case of PRC domestic litigants or 30 days in the case of foreign litigants after receipt of the service. Once the Submission of Reply is received, the original trial court shall relay the same with the Statement of Appeal and the previous files of the case to the appellate court for its further action.

There is no restriction on the rights to appeal in terms of the grounds on which the appeal is made. However, the appellate court will in principle decide the appeal on the following grounds: (1) whether the facts are accurately established; (2) the law is correctly applied; or (3) the procedure is properly followed.[10] If the judgment is found to be in error, the appellate court will either amend the decision or return the case to the first instance court for a rehearing as it deems appropriate. In the event that the case was sent to the first instance court for a rehearing, the fresh judgment issued by the court after the rehearing can also be appealed.

A judgment made by the appellate court is final and effective on the date when it is delivered, and no further appeal is allowed. In the case that a final judgment was in error, a retrial may be applied for by the litigants to the next higher court (which should be at least an Intermediate People's Court) than the court delivering the final judgment through the adjudication supervision proceedings within six months after the effective date of the final judgment. However, during the period of the retrial, enforcement of the final judgment will not be interrupted.

3.1.5 Costs and interest

The losing party bears the court fees but does not typically owe the winning party its expenses and legal fees unless this is otherwise stipulated prior to commencement of the trial.

There are no specific laws or regulations in the PRC that mandate the award of interest on amounts found to be payable. Should a claimant not specifically seek in his claim interest on the amount he is claiming, the People's Court will generally not of its own volition award interest in its judgment. Accordingly, when bringing his claim in the first instance, a claimant should specifically claim interest and include details of when such interest should begin to accrue and the applicable interest rate and so on. The PRC court will then exercise its discretion as to whether to award interest.

10 Article 170, Civil Procedure Law of PRC 2012.

Given that the award of interest is entirely at the discretion of the court, it is difficult to second-guess its method of calculation of interest. The point in time from when interest starts to run is usually the disputed issue. The court may, at its discretion, decide that interest should start running either from the date when the disputed sum is payable or from the date when the disputed sum is ascertained. Likewise, the point in time at which such interest terminates is also at the discretion of the courts, and it may likely be either the day on which the judgment is satisfied or a particular end date fixed by the courts such as the date when the judgment becomes effective.

As regards the interest rate likely to be adopted by the People's Court (assuming that it has allowed the claim for interest), there are normally two different types of interest rate adopted by the PRC courts. One is the interest rate for deposits published by the People's Bank of China (PBoC) while the other is the interest rate for loans published by the PBoC. However, it would again be entirely within the discretion of the court which interest rate to apply.

3.1.6 Time limitation

Under PRC law, the time limit for commencement of civil proceedings is normally two years starting from the time when the claimant knew or should have known its rights were infringed. However, there are also shorter or longer time limitation periods under PRC law that may apply to different categories of claims. For instance, for personal injury and product liability claims, the time limit is one year, and for claims for compensation for oil pollution damage from ships, the time limit is three years, starting from the day on which the pollution damage occurred. The time limit can normally only be prevented from running by way of commencement of litigation or arbitration. The Supreme People's Court has held that time limitation cannot be extended or shortened by agreement between the parties.

As regards insurance claims, the time limit for commencement of claims against the insurer under non-life insurance is two years, and under life insurance is five years. However, there seems to be a slight difference between marine insurance claims and non-marine insurance claims as to when the time starts to run. As for marine insurance claims, the time starts to run from the date of occurrence of the insured accident, whereas for non-marine claims the time starts to run from the date when the insured knew or should have known of the occurrence of the insured accident.

As regards subrogated claims, the Supreme People's Court recently issued Interpretations on Insurance Law II (2013), which provides that the time limit starts to run from the time when the insurers paid the insurance indemnification to the assured. Under PRC law, subrogated claims must be brought in the name of the insurers, rather than in the name of the assured.[11] Upon payment of the insurance indemnification, the right of claim against the third party who caused the loss is automatically assigned to the insurer by operation of law. No letter of subrogation is needed for the assured to authorise the insurer to use its name to issue the proceedings against the third party.

3.1.7 Time for judgment

Under PRC law, for domestic disputes, the Court of First Instance shall conclude the case within 6 to 12 months after the claim has been started. However, in special circumstances, it may take longer for the court to consider and adjudicate the case. If so, the Court of First Instance must report to the court at the next higher level for approval on having more time to conclude the case. For appeal cases, the appellate court shall adjudicate the case within three months, but it can be extended subject to approval of the president of the appellate court.

As for commercial cases involving foreign elements, there is no mandatory prescribed time frame within which the court is required to deliver a judgment. However, there may be internal administrative rules within the local courts at different localities pursuant to which the judges are required to adjudicate the cases within a certain time frame.

3.2 Arbitration

The principal legislation governing the arbitration procedure in the PRC is the Arbitration Law 1995, which applies to all arbitration proceedings conducted in the PRC, whether domestic or foreign-related. This law contains various provisions on the general procedure of arbitrations, including the commencement of arbitration, the appointment of the Arbitral Tribunal, filing of statements of claim, the availability of interim measures, the conduct of the hearing and evidential matters. These provisions are supplemented by the more detailed arbitration rules of the arbitration commissions at different localities.

Under Arbitration Law 1995, the default number of arbitrators is three. Arbitration cases are usually heard by a panel made up of three arbitrators, with one arbitrator as chair. Each party is given the right to select an arbitrator of their own choice. However, the third arbitrator shall be jointly agreed and appointed by both parties or selected by the arbitral institution upon the parties' request.

Arbitration should be commenced according to the same time limits provided in the PRC Civil Procedure Rules. Hearings are typically

11 Article 16, Interpretations on Insurance Law II 2013.

completed within one or two days, which also reduces the legal fees and costs. There are no compulsory rules of disclosure of documents and it is a matter of agreement by the parties with the approval of the Tribunal.

3.2.1 Arbitration agreement

Pursuant to the Arbitration Law 1995, an effective arbitration clause should contain the following items:

(1) the intention of the parties to submit their disputes to arbitration;
(2) the scope of matters to be arbitrated; and
(3) the name of the chosen arbitral institution.

Pursuant to the Arbitration Law 1995, an arbitration agreement will be void if:

(1) the agreed matters for arbitration fall outside the scope of arbitrable matters as specified by law;
(2) a party to the arbitration agreement has no capacity for civil acts or has limited capacity for civil acts (which limit has been exceeded); or
(3) a party coerced the other party into concluding the arbitration agreement.

By way of guidance, China International Economic and Trade Arbitration Commission (CIETAC) – the most eminent PRC arbitral institution – has recommended the following model clause for parties to adopt in their contracts:

> Model Arbitration Clause (1)
>
> Any dispute arising from or in connection with this Contract shall be submitted to China International Economic and Trade Arbitration Commission (CIETAC) for arbitration which shall be conducted in accordance with the CIETAC's arbitration rules in effect at the time of applying for arbitration. The arbitral award is final and binding upon both parties.
>
> Model Arbitration Clause (2)
>
> Any dispute arising from or in connection with this Contract shall be submitted to China International Economic and Trade Arbitration Commission (CIETAC)__________Sub-Commission (Arbitration Center) for arbitration which shall be conducted in accordance with the CIETAC's arbitration rules in effect at the time of applying for arbitration. The arbitral award is final and binding upon both parties.

The parties may also stipulate the following matters in the arbitration clause: the place of arbitration and/or hearing; the language of arbitration; the number of arbitrators; the nationality of arbitrators; the method of selection of arbitrators; the applicable law of the contract; and/or the application of general procedure or summary procedure.

Under the Arbitration Law 1995, an arbitration agreement is independent from the main contract. Any amendments to or termination of the main contract does not affect the validity of the arbitration agreement.

3.2.2 Ad hoc arbitration and arbitration centres

Unlike other jurisdictions, *ad hoc* arbitration is not recognised under PRC law. All arbitrations seated in the PRC shall be submitted to an arbitral institution established in accordance with the relevant PRC laws.

The parties must therefore specify the name and place of the arbitral institution in their arbitration clause. In the absence of such specification, the arbitration agreement may be declared to be void. Accordingly, it is not sufficient only to provide for a certain set of institutional arbitration rules in the agreement. The arbitration agreement also has to clearly state the name of the arbitral institution that is to handle the dispute.

The leading Chinese arbitration institution is CIETAC. CIETAC has its own set of rules for the conduct of arbitrations under its auspices. CIETAC is now also promoting itself under the name of the Court of China Chamber of International Commerce. The current CIETAC rules were last updated in 2012.

Apart from CIETAC, the Shanghai International Economy and Trade Arbitration Commission (also known as the Shanghai International Arbitration Centre; previously known as the China International Economic and Trade Arbitration Commission Shanghai Commission, hereinafter referred to as 'SHIAC') is also well recognised. SHIAC recently set up a Shanghai Free Trade Zone Arbitration Court to facilitate foreign businesses that have disputes in the Shanghai Free Trade Zone, which was established in September 2013.

For maritime arbitrations, the most influential and well-recognised arbitral institution in the PRC is China Maritime Arbitration Commission (CMAC). CMAC only hears arbitration for maritime-related disputes including marine insurance disputes.

Under Arbitration Law 1995, the arbitration commission may rule on the validity of the arbitration agreement if the parties agree, failing which, such power is vested in the People's Court. Any disputes as to the validity of the arbitration agreement in foreign-related contracts shall be submitted to the Intermediate People's Court for a decision. If the Intermediate People's Court holds that the arbitration clause is not valid, such a decision shall be reported to the People's Court at the next higher level until it reaches the Supreme People's Court for a final decision.

3.2.3 Choice of arbitrators

Under PRC law, arbitrators have to satisfy certain minimum requirements regarding their qualifications and experience and have to be on the panel of arbitrators of the respective arbitration commissions.

The Arbitration Law 1995 is silent as to whether the parties are entitled to agree on the nationalities or other attributes of arbitrators to be appointed. Where the arbitration is being conducted under the auspices of CIETAC, the general view is that parties are free to agree on the nationalities of arbitrators, provided that they are listed on the CIETAC Panel of Arbitrators. If parties wish to choose arbitrators outside the CIETAC list, they must obtain prior approval from CIETAC.

A recent development is that the Shanghai Free Trade Zone Arbitration Rules (2014) allow parties to appoint arbitrators outside the SHIAC's registered list of arbitrators. Compared to other PRC arbitration institution rules, under the Shanghai Free Trade Zone Arbitration Rules (2014), parties are free to choose arbitrators of any nationality outside the SHIAC's list without the need of approval by SHIAC.

The chairman of the arbitration commission shall make a decision where the parties fail to decide upon the composition of the Arbitral Tribunal or fail to choose an arbitrator within the prescribed time limit.

3.2.4 Interim measures

A claimant may apply to the Arbitral Tribunal for interim measures. Such measures include application for preservation of evidence in the event that such evidence may be destroyed if no such immediate protective measures were taken or preservation of assets in the event that such assets may be removed by the party to avoid future liability. For asset preservation, the applicant shall provide counter-security in case his application is proven to be wrongful and causing damage to the innocent party at a later stage.

Upon receipt of such applications, the Arbitral Tribunal will then submit the same to the relevant People's Court at the place where the evidence or assets are located for their enforcement. The People's Court will only grant interim measures for arbitration seated in the PRC. If the seat of the arbitration is outside of the PRC, the People's Court will not intervene and will not grant interim measures to facilitate the arbitration commenced at non-PRC arbitration institutions. The only exception is that for maritime arbitration, the PRC Maritime Courts will grant interim measures such as arrest of ship, cargo or bunkers, preservation of evidence or injunction, upon parties' application regardless of the existence of any arbitration agreement or choice of jurisdiction clause.

3.2.5 Disclosure

There is no provision in the Arbitration Law 1995 or the CIETAC rules dealing with the issue of disclosure. In practice, the Arbitration Tribunal may, either by its own volition or at the request of a party, require the other party to produce evidence in support of its claim. Under the CIETAC arbitration rules, where the Tribunal wishes to consult an expert or appoint an appraiser, the Arbitration Tribunal may order the parties to submit to the expert or appraiser any relevant materials, documents, or properties and goods for check-up, inspection and appraisal.

There is no provision in the Arbitration Law 1995 or any other legislation allowing the courts to intervene in matters of disclosure. However, the courts may set aside an award in a domestic arbitration if a party has withheld evidence sufficient to affect the impartiality of the arbitration or if the arbitration award is based on forged evidence. If the Arbitral Tribunal considers that it needs to consult an expert or appoint an appraiser, the expert or appraiser may be required to attend the hearing and may be questioned or be required to explain his report.

3.2.6 The award

Under the Arbitration Law 1995, an arbitration award must comply with the following requirements:

(1) The award shall be made in accordance with the opinion of the majority of the arbitrators. Where the Arbitral Tribunal cannot reach a majority opinion, the award shall be made in accordance with the opinion of the presiding arbitrator.
(2) The Arbitration Tribunal must state in the arbitration award the claims, the facts of the dispute, the reasons on which the award is based, the result of the award, the allocation of the arbitration costs, the date on which and the place at which the award is made. The facts of the dispute and the reasons may be omitted if parties so require.
(3) The award must be signed by the arbitrators. Arbitrators who dissent may choose whether to sign the award or not.
(4) The arbitration award should be sealed by the relevant arbitration commission.

Pursuant to the CIETAC Rules, the Tribunal can also issue partial awards in relation to their findings on certain issues or parts of the claim before the final award is made.

3.2.7 Right to set aside

The Arbitration Law 1995 does not allow any appeal of an arbitration award. However, if a party is not satisfied with an award, he may apply to set it aside on the grounds specified by the law.

The Arbitration Law 1995 draws a distinction between domestic awards and foreign-related awards. The grounds for setting aside domestic awards and foreign-related awards are slightly different.

Under the PRC arbitration law, the grounds for setting aside domestic awards are:

(1) there is no arbitration agreement;
(2) matters decided in the award exceed the scope of the arbitration agreement or are beyond the authority of the arbitration commission;
(3) the formation of the Arbitration Tribunal or the arbitration procedure did not conform to statutory requirements;
(4) evidence on which the award is based was forged;
(5) the other party withheld evidence sufficient to affect the fairness of the award;
(6) during the course of the proceedings, one or more of the arbitrators demanded or accepted bribes, practised graft or made an award that perverted the law; or
(7) the award would be against the public interest.

Under the Arbitration Law 1995 and the Civil Procedure Law 2012, the grounds for setting aside foreign-related arbitral awards are:

(1) the parties have neither included an arbitration clause in their contract nor subsequently concluded a written arbitration agreement;
(2) the party against whom the application is made was not notified to appoint an arbitrator or to take part in the arbitration proceedings, or the said party was unable to present his case due to reasons for which he is not responsible;
(3) the formation of the Arbitration Tribunal or the arbitration procedure was not in conformity with the arbitration rules;
(4) the matters decided in the award exceed the scope of the arbitration agreement or are beyond the authority of the arbitration institution; or
(5) the award would be against public interest.

In summary, the People's Court will only examine the procedural issues involved in the foreign-related arbitral award when considering the setting aside applications, whereas for domestic awards the People's Court is also entitled to reopen the substantive issues in the awards when considering such an application.

The application to set aside an arbitration award shall be made to the Intermediate People's Court at the place where the arbitration commission is situated. Pursuant to the Arbitration Law 1995, upon receipt of an application to set aside an award, the People's Court may (if it considers necessary) notify the Arbitral Tribunal to re-arbitrate the dispute. In that case, the setting aside proceedings shall be stayed. If the Arbitration

Tribunal refuses to re-arbitrate the case, the court shall then proceed with the application to set aside the award.

Under the Arbitration Law 1995, the time limit for an application to set aside an arbitral award is six months after receipt of the award. This time limit applies to both domestic and foreign-related arbitration awards.

3.2.8 Foreign arbitration awards

The PRC is a signatory State to the New York Convention on the Recognition and Enforcement of Foreign Arbitral Awards 1958. The Convention came into force in the PRC on 22 April 1987. The accession was subject to both 'commerciality' and 'reciprocity' reservations. Therefore, foreign commercial arbitration awards can be enforced in the PRC on a reciprocal basis.

The process of enforcement of a foreign award is subject to a strict review and supervision system in the PRC, which is designed to prevent local courts from refusing enforcement without justifiable reasons. The PRC Supreme People's Court requires that a decision to refuse enforcement of a foreign arbitration award must be reported to and approved by the Supreme People's Court. Pursuant to this notice, if the first instance People's Court decides not to enforce a foreign award, it must refer the decision to the relevant High People's Court above it, who must also refer any decision to the Supreme People's Court for approval if a decision of refusal to enforce the award is made. Without the consent from the Supreme People's Court, no lower court is entitled to refuse enforcement of a foreign award.

An arbitration award issued by an Arbitral Tribunal seated in Hong Kong or Macao will be regarded as a foreign award. There are respective special arrangements between the PRC and Hong Kong and Macao on the recognition and enforcement of each other's arbitration awards. Most recently, in December 2009, the Supreme People's Court issued a guidance note on issues of recognition and enforcement of Hong Kong arbitral awards in mainland China. In the guidance note, it was also made clear that *ad hoc* arbitration awards issued in Hong Kong are enforceable in mainland China subject to conditions similar to Article V of the New York Convention, which were set out in the mutual agreement between the PRC and Hong Kong.

As for interim awards issued by a foreign Arbitral Tribunal, the position is less clear whether such awards will be recognised and enforced by the People's Court. The main reason why the People's Court may refuse to enforce such awards is that an interim award is not a final binding award and the People's Court may deem it as falling outside the scope of the 1958 New York Convention.

3.3 Mediation

It is common that the PRC courts invite the litigants to reach amicable settlement before a judgment is issued by way of mediation assisted by the

People's Court. If the parties agree and a settlement agreement is reached, the People's Court will issue a mediation memorandum that is signed by all parties and sealed by the court. A court's mediation memorandum is as valid as a judgment. However, mediation is not a necessary procedure and the parties are not obliged to accept the mediation offered by the court.

Similarly, the PRC Arbitration Tribunals may also invite the parties to settle their dispute by way of mediation under the Tribunal's assistance. However, parties are not obliged to resolve their dispute by mediation first before an arbitration award is given. If parties agree and a mediation agreement is reached, the Tribunal shall issue a mediation memorandum or arbitration award in accordance with the parties' agreement. The mediation memorandum and arbitral award have equal effects.

In addition, the China Council for the Promotion of International Trade (CCPIT) has also established a Mediation Centre. Upon the approval of the State Council, CCPIT started operating under the name of China Chamber of International Commerce (CCOIC) as its alternative name. It has been the first and the largest professional mediation organisation in China. CCPIT/CCOIC Mediation Centre has established 42 sub-centres in China and has been cooperating with its counterparts from over 10 countries in co-mediation operations and cooperation agreements, forming a mediation network covering China and reaching out to the world. In November 1994, CCOIC joined the International Chamber of Commerce (ICC) as a representative of the PRC business community and set up the ICC China National Committee (ICC China). The current applicable mediation rules were last updated in 2012.

The Mediation Centre has recommended the following mediation model clause for parties to adopt in their contracts:

> Any dispute arising from or in connection with this Contract shall be submitted to Mediation Centre of China Council for the Promotion of International Trade/China Chamber of International Commerce for mediation which shall be conducted in accordance with the Centre's Mediation Rules in effect at the time of applying for mediation. In case an amicable settlement agreement has been reached, the parties shall abide by the settlement agreement.

As regards the selection of the mediators, pursuant to the Mediation Rules, each party shall nominate one mediator from the list provided by the Mediation Centre unless it has been otherwise agreed. The mediators on the list are selected by the Mediation Centre from among PRC and foreign experts with professional knowledge or practical experience in the commercial, maritime and legal fields.

In practice, the majority of insurance disputes in the PRC are resolved by either litigation or arbitration. The use of mediation is not fully developed and not well recognised yet.

Part II

Specific forms of insurance

7 Liability insurance

Dr Tao Yu[1]

1 Fundamental theories of liability insurance

1.1 Liability insurance: a relationship among three parties

Liability insurance is an agreement under which an insurer promises to pay on behalf of an insured to a third party any sum, up to the policy limit and subject to the policy terms, that the insured is legally liable to pay to the third party as a result of the insured's tortious conduct. Based on this definition, liability insurance involves three parties, an insurer, an insured and a third party, and there are three kinds of relationships among them.

The first and core relationship is one between an insurer and an insured, based on the liability insurance contract, in which the insured promises to pay the premium on time and subject to all the terms of the contract in return for payment by the insurer when the insured is legally liable to the third party. In other words, liability insurers are not responsible for the loss of the insured himself, but for the liability the insured has assumed according to tort law.

The second fundamental relationship is the one between an insured and a third party who is caused loss by the insured, based on tort law. The reason why the insured is required to bear legal liability is because it has caused the property damage or physical injury of the third party and should pay damages according to tort law. This relationship is the trigger that activates the enforcement of the insurer's payment obligations. The third party may claim compensation from the liability insurer within the boundary of the liability insurance contract, and even bring an action against the insurer if it refuses to pay.

The third and last relationship is the one between an insurer and a third party who has suffered loss caused by the insured. The particularity of this relationship lies in the fact that, even without a contract between the insurer and the third party, without the insurer's tortious act against the third party,

1 Dr Tao Yu, PhD in Economics, University of International Business and Economics, Beijing.

the third party may claim compensation directly from the insurer and even bring an action against the insurance company when the insured's liability attaches. It is public policy that requires this particularity, and it is supported by liability insurance law in many countries.

1.2 History of liability insurance

Compared to countries in Europe and North America, China has developed liability insurance in a relatively short period of time. Before 1949, there were only a few kinds of liability insurance, such as lift liability insurance and travellers liability insurance. In the early 1950s, China had sold motor liability insurance, aircraft liability insurance and protection and indemnity insurance. But at that time, it was commonly believed that the negative effects of liability insurance were much greater than the positive, so that liability insurance was in fact banned for a long time until 1979.

In recent years, with the gradual maturation of the market economy and the rapid development of the legal system in China, the notion of the importance of liability hazards began to take root in people's minds, and liability insurance business in the domestic market has developed by leaps and bounds. According to statistics from the China Insurance Regulatory Commission, from 2001 to the end of April 2003, there were 253 kinds of liability insurance products filed with the CIRC. The scope of those products covered very broad areas involving various fields of society. The main classes were general liability insurance, motor liability insurance, employer's liability insurance, product liability insurance and professional liability insurance. In 2008, the total liability insurance premium income was RMB 8.17 billion (excluding motor liability insurance); the premium income from general liability insurance, employer's liability insurance, product liability insurance and professional liability insurance is, respectively, RMB 3.92 billion, RMB 1.89 billion, RMB 1 billion and RMB 0.92 billion.[2] In 2010, the total amount reached RMB 11.58 billion (excluding automobile liability insurance).[3]

But during this period, many problems have occurred in the Chinese liability insurance market, which have become the focus of fierce public debates, such as one insurer offering cover for drunk driving and one lawyer's charge that insurers were profiteering from compulsory motor liability insurance. These debates reflected the public attitude towards liability insurance and their basic understanding of this special product.

2 '2008 the Summary of Chinese insurance market', *2009 Yearbook of China's Insurance*, 2009.

3 '2010 Chinese insurance market operation analysis', *2011 Yearbook of China's Insurance*, 2011, p 20.

1.3 Liability risks

Liability hazards covered by third-party insurance are different from the natural hazards covered by first-party insurance, the key of which lies in the fact that liability hazards are the creation of the legal system rather than those of nature. The insured's house is burned by fire, a vessel is damaged by collision, crops are destroyed in a thunderstorm; all of these property losses are caused by natural hazards. So long as the accidents have happened and the damage occurred, the first-party insurance will provide the basis for compensation. But with liability hazards, even if the insured caused the damage, if the insured is not liable according to the law, the third-party insurance does not respond. It is because liability hazard comes from the provisions of the law. This kind of hazard is therefore subject to the legislator and judiciary. Compared to natural hazards, liability hazards are man-made, a purely artificial creation of the law. Even if one person causes another personal or property damage, if there is no law of tort, such damage will be borne by the victims themselves, and, as a result, there will be no liability hazards and liability insurance. Therefore, the enactment and revision of relevant laws and regulations will certainly influence the existence and development of liability insurance.

Another prominent difference of liability hazards is the extent of the insured cover. While the insured may reasonably estimate the extent of the maximum potential loss for first-party cover, the potential exposure to third parties is more difficult to assess.[4] When it comes to general property insurance, the value of the property insured defines the amount of maximum loss, but there is no such limit in the liability cover before the loss occurs. For example, a vehicle may cause a traffic accident that leads to some minor property damage or indeed a tragedy of heavy casualties. The damages may differ greatly between these two results. Even with the same number of casualties, the amount of damages, especially in terms of loss of wages, will have a great difference between a multinational enterprise executive and a retired worker. In short, one of the most important features of liability insurance is the inability to fully and precisely measure potential losses. Moreover, with the development and application of advanced technology and the aggregation of human beings, tortious events may lead to extremely high payouts, especially mass events, which may soon deplete billions of dollars. For example, BP has promised to pay USD 1 billion as an advance payment for restoring natural resources damaged by the April 2010 explosion of the Macondo oil rig that caused the Gulf of Mexico oil spill, which has been called the worst environmental disaster in the country's

4 D. Derrington and R. S. Ashton, *The Law of Liability Insurance*, 2nd edn, 2005, LexisNexis Australia, p 2.

history.[5] This advance payment is only a part of the whole compensation package.

Liability insurance covers liability hazards, the essence of which is the legal liability an insured may assume to a third party according to the law. Legal liability is adverse consequences borne by the actor for the breach of legal duty, contractual obligations or for the improper exercise of legal rights. The potential legal liabilities an insured may assume are varied, but not all of them could become the objective hazards a liability policy may cover.

First, liability insurance can only cover civil liability. Legal liability has multiple classification criteria, one of which is used to divide it into criminal liability, administrative liability and civil liability. While liability insurance insures civil liability, criminal liability and administrative liability cannot be the risk covered. This is because both criminal and administrative responsibility aims to make a negative evaluation of the illegal behaviour (i.e. the criminal and administrative offence) to punish the person who commits it, and to warn others not to engage in such behaviour. This kind of responsibility only has the function of punishment and warning, not that of compensation. If these responsibilities could be transferred to others through the insurance system, the systemic purpose of their function would be defeated. Therefore, these two responsibilities cannot be the subject matter insured by liability insurance. As to civil liability, the main function is to compensate the third-party victim who suffered loss as a result of the illegal behaviour, and to put him or her back in the position occupied before the loss occurred. The function to punish is secondary. The protection of the interests of the victim are more and more valued when the civil action is brought against the tortfeasor, and although liability insurance may weaken civil liability's function of punishing the tortfeasor and warning others against committing such illegal behaviours, it does enhance the function of protecting the victims. Thus, after considering the trade-off between the positive effect and the negative, it is accepted by the society that liability insurance protects victims against civil liability arising out of the insured's illegal conduct. In short, the legal liability covered by the liability insurance is only civil liability, but not criminal or administrative liability.

Second, liability insurance only covers liability in tort: 'It is fundamental to the concept of liability insurance that the liability which is covered is not the insured's liability for a breach of contract generally nor his or her liability to perform his or her contractual duties'.[6] In the United States, many precedents exclude breach of contract from liability insurance coverage, and

5 J. Pope, 'Gulf of Mexico oil spill damage money should be spent with public input, advocacy groups say', available at: www.nola.com/news/gulf-oil-spill/index.ssf/2011/11/environmental_and_community_gr.html (accessed 30 October 2011).

6 D. Derrington and R. S. Ashton, *The Law of Liability Insurance*, 2nd edn, 2005, LexisNexis Australia, p 2.

scholars generally believe that the risk insured by liability insurance should be the responsibility borne by the insured for the personal injury or property loss caused by his tortious conduct.[7] Chinese scholars have no objection to the point that liability insurances cover civil liability, but, for the proposition that liability insurances only cover tortious liability, they have failed to reach a unanimous opinion. There are many scholars in Taiwan province who believe that, in addition to tortious liability, liability insurance also insures someone's responsibility against a breach of contract.[8]

One of the reasons why some scholars believe that liability insurance may cover liability arising out of breach of contract is because they fail to comprehend the difference between liability insurance and credit insurance. It is credit insurance that covers some liabilities for breach of contract while liability insurance only covers tortious liability. These two liabilities cannot replace each other as the risk underwritten by the insurers even if they are both part of civil liability. They are different risks and have different characteristics, one of which is the factor affecting the probability of occurrence of the risk. As for individual risk, the occurrence of the breach of contract and the credibility of the Contracting Party are interrelated; the more credible the Contracting Party is, the lower the probability the occurrence of breach of contract. As for the risk in general, the probability of occurrence of breach of contract is negatively affected by the business cycle, thus the probability will be very high when the world is in economic crisis. But the risk arising out of tortious conduct is so different in that its probability is affected mostly by other factors, such as the danger and frequency of the activity and the standard of care of the parties. As a result, the two kinds of insurance products for these two liabilities entail a very different underwriting approach.

The main reason why a contractual liability cannot be a risk covered by liability insurance is, this author believes, that it is too uncertain to be an insurable risk for insurance products. Unlike tortious liability, contractual liability is difficult to determine solely based on the provisions of law since the terms of the contract itself represent the main standard to be used as a judgment base. The same act of a Contracting Party may be alternatively a breach of contract and a non-breach of contract as the terms of the contract vary. Even the risk assumed by credit insurance is limited to failure to pay, which is easily defined but is only one of the contractual liabilities.

There are two further issues deserving of attention: one is contractual liability covered by liability insurance under a hold harmless agreement, and the other is the concurrence of tortious liability and liability for breach of contract.

7 K. S. Abraham, *Insurance Law and Regulation*, 1990, The Foundation Press, pp 483–504.
8 See Liang Yuxian, *On Insurance Law*, 2004, Beijing: Renmin University Press, p 207; Yuan Zongwei, *Insurance*, 1981, Beijing: Hezuo Jingji Yuekan Press, p 355; Gui Yu, *Insurance Law*, 1984, Beijing: Sanmin Shuju, p 330.

1.4 Hold harmless agreement

Generally, a liability insurance policy will contain an exclusion clause excluding contractual liability. But the exclusion may not apply if the liability does exist in the absence of the contract. A hold harmless agreement is a legally binding contract designed to transfer one Contracting Party's legal liability to the other. Under this agreement, one party agrees not to sue the other party for some kinds of expenses, losses or damage that may result from a transaction or an operation. For example, suppose Company A, a toy manufacturer, has signed a hold harmless agreement with Company B, a retailer, in which Company A agrees to hold Company B harmless from any claims brought by a third-party victim relating to the manufacturing of the toy. If a mother purchases a defective toy from Company B and subsequently her child is injured, the mother may sue Company B, which could seek recourse from Company A. Under the terms of the hold harmless agreement, Company A would be responsible for paying expenses associated with the claims, including legal fees. The contractual liability under the hold harmless agreement is therefore the tortious liability assumed by the insured through such an agreement, rather than the liability for breach of contract.

1.5 Concurrence of tortious liability and liability for breach of contract

Some scholars have argued that some professional liability insurance covers contractual liabilities, since the professionals or their firms normally have a contractual relationship with their clients, but that is a misunderstanding based on the concurrence of tortious and contractual liability. In some situations, a breach of contract can simultaneously amount to the violation of an interest protected by tort law, and this is the concurrence of tortious and contractual liability. For example, a medical liability policy for a hospital provides protection for the insured against its liability to patients, and a patient is injured in surgery conducted by the insured's doctor who fails to follow generally accepted medical professional standards. The patient can bring an action against the hospital for damages under two legal theories: one is breach of medical contract, and the other is negligence. In such a case, the insurer cannot reject the claim just because the insured has a contractual relationship with the third-party victim, but the risk really covered by the liability insurance is the tortious one since the insuring agreement, in such a medical liability policy, usually states that the insurer shall pay 'damages because of injury to which this [insurance] applies caused by a medical incident'[9] in the United States, or 'damages because of personal injury caused by professional negligence'[10] in China.

9 Insurance Services Office, 'Physicians, surgeons and dentists professional liability insurance (claims made)' (ED. 03 81).

10 Article 3, PICC Medical Liability Insurance Clauses, 2011.

2 Present regulatory structure

China's legal system applicable to liability insurance is formed by the Insurance Act and relevant provisions of other laws and regulations. The provisions directly governing liability insurance in the Insurance Act of the People's Republic of China (the 'Insurance Act')[11] are those of Article 65 and Article 66. Article 65 is the essential provision, setting the foundation and a starting point for China's legal system of liability insurance. Article 66 is supplementary, addressing cover for litigation expenses. In addition to these two sections, other provisions applicable to liability insurance can be found in the Insurance Act, in particular in Chapter 1, 'General Principles', where section 1 is entitled 'General Rules'; also in Chapter 2, 'Insurance Contract', section 3 is entitled 'Property Insurance'. There are also relevant provisions in the 'Contracts Act of the People's Republic of China'.

Until now, the Insurance Act has experienced two major amendments: the first came into effect on 1 January 2003. Its purpose was to coordinate the law with WTO rules relative to the insurance industry in order to implement China's commitments for accessing the WTO. The second was effective on 1 October 2009, and its purpose was to offer better protection for Chinese insureds and enhance the Chinese Insurance Regulatory Commission (CIRC)'s supervision of insurers. During these two revisions, the provisions about liability insurance were further enriched, especially in the 2009 revision, which perfected the core provision governing liability insurance by adding a third party's right of direct action against the insurer in some situations and setting forth the conditions precedent to an insured's claiming under the insurance. These new changes are embodied in the newly revised Article 65 of the Insurance Act. This chapter will present a detailed analysis of Articles 65 and 66.[12]

2.1 Subject matter insured by liability insurance

The Insurance Act specifies in paragraph 4 of Article 65: 'Liability insurance means the type of insurance where the subject matter insured is the insured's liability to compensate a third party in accordance with the law'. This provision not only provides a legal definition of liability insurance, but also indicates that liability hazard is the type of risk underwritten by liability insurance. Compared with Article 12[13] of the Insurance Act governing the

11 See Appendix I.

12 For the wording of Articles 65 and 66, refer to Appendix I.

13 Article 12: 'When entering into an insurance contract, the assured under personal insurance shall have an insurable interest in the insured person.'
'The insured in property insurance shall have an insurable interest in the subject matter when an insured event occurs.'
'Personal insurance refers to the type of insurance where the life or body of human beings is the subject matter insured.'

risk underwritten by life insurance and property insurance, it may be observed that liability insurance differs greatly compared to property insurance and life insurance in terms of the risk underwritten. The former provides protection against the risk of liability hazard assumed by the insured and the latter against personal injury or property damage caused to the insured itself, which is a natural hazard.

Some will consider liability hazard and natural hazard too distinct to be confused. Unfortunately, in reality, it is not so. There is significant misunderstanding in the interpretation and application of paragraph 4 of Article 65 in Chinese judicial practice. The following cases may illustrate this misunderstanding.

At the beginning of 2010, Mr Li was driving his SUV on the road and saw a few pieces of coal lying on the road. He stopped the SUV and tried to pick up the coal from the road when his car had already passed the coal. Unfortunately, due to a sudden slip of the vehicle, Li was knocked dead on the spot. Thereafter, Li's family claimed under the motor liability insurance, the insured under which was the deceased. The insurer refused to pay on the ground that Mr Li, the owner of the SUV, was not a 'third party', according to the terms of the motor liability insurance contract. Li's relatives sued the insurance company. The court held that the insurer should pay the claim of Mr Li's relatives because Mr Li was the 'third party' under the motor liability policy. It was held that whether the deceased was a 'third party' or a 'passenger' should be judged on the standard of whether the victim is in the car or outside the car at the particular time when the accident happened. If the victim was in the car when the accident happened, he or she was a 'passenger'. But if the victim was outside the car, he or she was a 'third party'. The identity of the third party will therefore change depending on the scenario of the case. Since Mr Li was outside the car when the accident happened, he was a third party covered by the motor liability insurance.[14]

Although the court attempted a sensible analysis of the concept of 'third party', respectfully, it is submitted that it made a mistake. This is because a basic concept was neglected, namely that the risk underwritten by the liability insurer is a liability hazard, not a natural hazard. Thus, the damage to be compensated by a liability insurance policy is not the injury of the

'Property insurance refers to the type of insurance where property and the interests therein are the subject-matter insured.'
'An insured is a party whose property, life or body is covered by an insurance contract and who is entitled to claim under the insurance money. An assured may be the insured.'
'Insurable interest refers to a lawful interest which the assured or the insured has in respect of the subject matter insured.'

14 Rao Junhua and Pan Weina, 'Slip of auto killed the driver, liability insurance offer protection', available at: news.qq.com/a/20110216/001075.htm (accessed 31 October 2011).

insured itself, which is a risk insured by life insurance, but the liability of the insured. Regardless of whether Mr Li was in the car or outside the car, he could not assume legal responsibility for the consequences of his own death, including civil liability. Since there is no legal liability of Mr Li caused by his own death, why was the liability insurer of Mr Li obliged to pay the claim? Only if Mr Li had a life insurance policy, should his life insurer pay for his death. The key problem is a lack of real understanding of the risk insured by liability insurance. Unfortunately, this case is not unique; similar cases holding the liability insurer liable to a victim who is also an insured have occurred more than once, and the reason is always that the victim is transformed into a 'third party' under liability insurance because the victim is outside the vehicle at the time when the accident happened, thus the insurer needs to pay the claim. The case below[15] is more complicated and authoritative than Mr Li's case, since it may have involved other kinds of liability insurance and has been published in the 'Selection of Cases of People's Court', and may therefore have some effect as precedent.

The plaintiff Wen Jiajun purchased a motor insurance policy from the defendant insurer, including liability insurance with a limit of RMB 500,000 and the expiration date 7 January 2007. On 6 October 2006, a driver, Wu Xiaoming, hired by the plaintiff was driving the insured vehicle. When the vehicle arrived at He-Hui Highway, the driver parked the car on the highway and got out. Just at that time, he was hit by a truck driven by Zhu Haiping, which caused a traffic accident resulting in slight damage to two other cars and the death of Wu Xiaoming. After the accident, the public security authority assigned the responsibility to the parties involved, in which Wu Xiaoming bore the main responsibility and Zhu Haiping bore minor responsibility. At trial, it was held that Wu Xiaoming was 70 per cent responsible and Zhu Haiping 30 per cent responsible. The plaintiff, Wen Jiajun, bore part of the medical expenses during efforts to save Wu Xiaoming's life and, following the death of Wu Xiaoming, reached a compensation agreement with his family. After paying his share, the plaintiff claimed under the liability insurance, but the claim was rejected by the defendant insurer. Wen Jiajun sued the insurer. It was held that when the accident happened, the driver of the insured car, Wu Xiaoming, had already stopped the driving activity and got out of the car. It was considered more reasonable to recognise the identity of Wu Xiaoming, when hit by the truck, as a third party rather than the driver of the insured car. Therefore, the insurer, according to the terms of the compulsory liability insurance contract, bore the liability for compensation to the plaintiff.

15 *Wen Jiajun v China United Property Insurance Company Limited.* Meizhou Branch, Meizhou Municipality Intermediate People's Court (2008) Mei Zhong Fa Min San Zhong Zi No. 23, 18 November 2008.

This ruling was the same as the previous one, both of which made the basic mistake that the court only paid attention to the third-party identity of the victim, neglecting the basic principle that the risk insured by liability insurance is liability hazard, violating paragraph 4 of Article 65 in the Insurance Act. But in this case, the plaintiff might have other kinds of liability insurance to cover his loss. If he had purchased a driver on board liability policy, which covers the insured's liability to the injury of the employee driver caused by the accident, he might claim under his driver on board liability policy.

In judicial practice, cases involving the 'transformation from a passenger or a driver into a third party' theory is not uncommon. From 2004 up to now, such cases have occurred every year. The reasoning of the courts is basically twofold: one limb involves recognition of the unenforceability of the exclusion clause that excludes the insured, the lawful driver with his permission or the passenger from the coverage according to Article 17 of the Insurance Act, which results from the insurer's failure to make a warning and to specify the exclusion to the insured; the other limb involves the affirmation of the 'third-party' identity, which is based on the relative position of the victim to that of the vehicle. Following this logic, if the victim is outside the car when the accident happens, then he or she will be a third party under the protection of the motor liability insurance.

In fact, there is yet another class of cases involving the 'transformation from a passenger or a driver into a third party' theory. In such cases, the third-party victim is transformed from a passenger who is out of the car when he or she gets hurt. In one case,[16] on 1 June 2010, the plaintiff Yao Wei was driving his tractor on the road with his wife Sun Mei besides him. Unfortunately, the road was so rough that Sun Mei fell off the tractor on to the road, and then Sun Mei was crushed to death by the running tractor. The local public security authority produced an accident report, but did not analyse the accident and assign responsibility. Yao Wei had purchased, before the accident, a compulsory motor liability insurance whose policy period was from 13 February 2010 to 12 February 2011. Yao Wei claimed from the liability insurer but the claim was rejected. He and his child brought an action against the insurer.

There is no doubt that passenger on board liability insurance may cover any occupant of a vehicle other than the person operating it. But even if the insured purchased such a policy before the accident, the insurer may still refuse to pay because one of the exclusions under a passenger on board liability policy is the personal injury of a passenger who is not on board the vehicle. So when a passenger is outside the vehicle, no matter if voluntarily or pushed by an external force, and is injured by that vehicle, there will be

16 Tao Jiaping, 'How to indentify "the third party" under the compulsory auto liability insurance', Rule of Law in Jianghuai, No. 24, 2010 (case recorded in this article).

no liability insurance cover without the transformation theory. Under such circumstances, this theory does fill the cover gap without violating the basic principle of liability insurance and paragraph 4 of Article 65.

To sum up, existing cases applying the transformation theory can be divided into three groups: the first is where the insured injured himself or herself in the accident, and the basic scenario is the fact that the insured carelessly hurt himself or herself with the insured vehicle when the insured is outside the vehicle, such as the case of Mr Li's death caused by the slip of his SUV. In such cases, since the insured cannot bear legal responsibility for his or her own injury caused by his or her own fault, the liability hazard is missing in such cases. Thus, the application of the transformation theory will violate the basic principle of liability insurance and paragraph 4 of Article 65. For this reason, the application of the transformation theory shall not be allowed in such cases. The second group of cases is that in which a driver who is outside of the insured vehicle at the time of the accident is injured by that vehicle. The basic scenario is the fact that the insured vehicle's driver hired by the insured is injured by his or her own negligence when he or she is outside the vehicle, as in the Wen Jiajun case. In such cases, if the owner of the vehicle has purchased a driver on board liability policy, the relevant expenses will be covered by that policy. It is obvious that the transformation theory has always been applied in motor liability insurance, and the target group to be covered by this kind of insurance is not any person injured in the auto accident. The policy excepts from its scope the insured, the insured's driver and any passengers, because their risk can be addressed more suitably by other insurance products. Compulsory motor liability insurance, with its nature of public service, will not be overstretched and premium levels can be kept in an affordable range only if its coverage can be limited to a reasonable scope. This precludes the application of the transformation theory. The third group of cases is that in which a passenger who is outside of the insured vehicle at the time of the accident is injured by that vehicle. The basic scenario is the fact that a passenger who is, whether voluntarily or by external force, outside of the insured vehicle as a result of some emergency or accidental unforeseeable reason and is injured by that insured vehicle, such as the Yao Wei case. In such cases, there is a liability insurance gap since this kind of injury is excluded by the passenger liability insurance policy, and the transformation theory can fill that gap without breaking the basic principle of liability insurance that the hazard insured by liability insurance must be a liability hazard and the relevant provision of the Insurance Act. In the author's opinion, the transformation theory is of some use in such cases if the passenger on board liability insurance does not cover such injury of the passenger. And whether or not such injury is covered by passenger on board liability insurance depends on the court's interpretation of the exclusion clause relating to it.

The transformation theory is a creation by judges, designed, it appears, to fill some gaps in currently available motor insurance products. The original intention is good, but there may be some confusion or complications caused by this theory. In the author's opinion, the best way to solve this problem is to revise the present motor insurance policies, at least the family motor policies, making them more reasonable and complete, so that they cover, within one comprehensive policy, not only the insured's liability to the real third party in the motor liability coverage, but also the personal injuries or the property losses of the insured, his driver and other passengers on board in the other coverage. Until such time as policy terms are revised, the transformation theory may fill the gap.

2.2 Pay to the insured versus pay to the third party

Liability insurance has been characterised as providing an indemnity against liability to pay damages, as opposed to indemnity insurance, which indemnifies against actual loss and is called an indemnity contract.[17]

The relevant provision in the Insurance Act is paragraph 3 of Article 65. This provision clearly conveys the proposition that the insured will be compensated by the liability insurer only when he or she sustains actual loss. Based on a literal interpretation of this provision, it seems that we can reach a conclusion that China's liability insurance contract is an indemnity contract as mentioned above. The key difference between an indemnity contract and a liability one is that the indemnity contract will pay the insurance indemnity to the insured only when he or she suffers actual loss, while a liability contract will pay losses within the cover as soon as the insured's legal liability attaches. The phrase that 'the insurer shall not make the indemnity payment to the insured' in the provision seems to indicate that the liability insurer will only pay when the insured sustains the actual loss by discharging its liability. This is consistent with the indemnity contract's feature that unless the insured has suffered actual loss, there can be no compensation.

However, the reality is not quite so simple. In view of the final paragraph of Article 65, it is apparent that China's liability insurance contract is actually a liability contract instead of an indemnity contract. First, paragraph 4 of Article 65 specifies that the risk insured by liability insurance is 'an insured's legal liability to pay damages to a third party'. The literal meaning of 'legal liability' is different from the actual loss sustained by the insured as a result of discharging legal liability. The phrase 'the legal liability to pay' may be interpreted as the liability assumed in accordance with the law, which means that once the liability attaches, the insurer's responsibility to pay is enforceable whether or not the insured has discharged his liability. Therefore, paragraph 4 of Article 65 contradicts the actual loss requirement

17 E. M. Holmes, 'Holmes' Appleman on insurance', 2nd edn, 2000, Lexis Publishing, p 15.

imposed by the indemnity contract, and accords with the liability incurred requirement imposed by the liability contract. And so China's liability insurance contract should be regarded as a liability contract according to Article 65.

Second, it follows from paragraph 2 of Article 65 that the insured may directly request the insurer to indemnify the third party when his responsibility to the third party is fixed. If the insured delays, the third party may have the right to bring an action against the insurer. Since the insurer may be requested by the insured or the third party to pay directly to the third party, the insured clearly has not yet paid the third party and therefore has not sustained any actual loss. If the insured had already paid the third party, the request would instead have concerned the insurer's payment to the insured rather than to the third party. Therefore, based on paragraph 2 of Article 65, China's liability insurance contract should be classed as a liability contract.

Third, paragraph 3 of Article 65 does not prevent the insurer from directly paying the third party before the insured discharges its liability for damages. This provision empowers the liability insurer to refuse to pay the insured before he performs his legal obligation to pay damages to the third party.

Given that China's liability insurance contract is accordingly most naturally categorised as a liability contract, what were the legislator's intentions behind paragraph 3 of Article 65? On the surface, this provision is the measure adopted for solving a real problem, which became apparent before the 2009 revision of the Insurance Act, but in fact it originated from the mismatch of China's liability insurance framework and the misunderstanding of the indemnity principle by some relevant persons. At that time, there were some cases involving the payment mechanism of the liability insurance framework. The facts were as follows: when the insured's liability to the third party attached, the insured collected the indemnity from the insurer before paying damages to the third-party victim. After the liability insurer's payment to the insured, some of the insureds spent the money for other purposes rather than reimbursing the third-party victim, and then claimed inability to discharge the judgments against them. The consequence was that the third-party victim who really needed the insurance monies did not receive the due compensation, while the insured who caused the loss of the third-party victim earned unjustified enrichment.

In 1995, at the birth of the earliest Insurance Act, the subject matter insured was set out as 'an insured's legal liability to pay damages to a third party', which made a liability contract of a liability insurance contract. But in actual claims management, the practice became that the insured claimed directly from the insurer. Although the earliest Insurance Act stipulated that 'An insurer may, in accordance with the provisions of law or the terms of an insurance contract, directly pay insurance benefits to a third party', the third-party victim could only collect money from the insured when the insurer did not initially pay to the third party. Therefore, before the 2009 revision, when an insured claimed directly from the insurer, his obligation to pay damages might or might not be discharged. Once the insured obtained the indemnity before he paid the third-party victim, he might transfer it to the third-party victim as a lawful citizen should, or withhold it without paying the third party, which gave him the unjustified enrichment. The latter would inevitably result in a dispute and lead to social problems.

The root of the problem lies in the mismatch of the claims payment mechanism and the nature of a liability contract. When a liability insurance contract is a liability contract, the liability insurer should ideally be obliged to pay the third-party victim directly on behalf of the insured, since the occurrence triggering the liability contract is the attachment of legal responsibility to the insured and direct payment to the third party can avoid misappropriation by the intermediary, the insured, as well as conform to the nature of the contract. In addition, compensation for the liability of the insured goes directly to the ultimate beneficiaries without the risk of being withheld by the insured.

But when a liability insurance contract is an indemnity one, the only workable option is that the insured must claim directly from the insurer, having already discharged his obligation to the third party. The insurer should then have the right to verify that the insured has performed his obligation to the third party. If the insured sustains an actual loss, he may recover from the insurer; if he does not, he may not be reimbursed.

Having discussed the form of the liability contract, we now turn to the mixed payment mechanism. 'Mixed payment mechanism' refers to the current mechanism whereby the insurer pays the indemnity to the insured and may pay directly to the third party only when specified in the law or the insurance contract. Before the 2009 revision, there was no provision in the Insurance Act specifying actual loss as a precondition for payment to the insured. If the insurer was concerned that payment to the insured might lead to misappropriation of the funds rather than payment to the third-party victim, the insurer had no legal basis for stopping the payment until the insured had paid the damages to the third party. When a third-party victim obtained a court judgment against the insured, the insured's liability had crystallised even if the judgment debt had not yet been discharged. According to the law, at this moment the insurer should perform his obligation to pay the insured upon request, since the risk insured by China's liability insurance contract is 'an insured's legal liability to pay damages to a third party', which had already been satisfied in such a situation. It was therefore difficult for the insurer to reject the claim. An insurer might have attempted to defend the claim arguing the indemnity principle, but it would have been doubtful that the court would be willing to entertain this argument.

In order to resolve this problem, the 2009 amendments to the Insurance Act added a new paragraph 3 to Article 65, requiring the insured to fulfil the obligation to compensate the third-party victim before earning the right to recover from the insurer, thus resolving the conflict between the nature of the liability insurance contract and its payment mechanism and avoiding the occurrence of the problem mentioned above. Under this provision, if the insurer reimburses the insured before the insured compensates the third-party victim, resulting in the third-party victim's inability to recover the loss, the third-party victim may initiate legal proceedings against the insurer for his loss.[18]

In fact, the most effective option is still the insurer's direct payment to the third-party victim when the insured's liability has attached. Once the insured's legal liability is determined, the insurer shall on behalf of the insured pay directly to the third party, which not only eliminates the possibility of misappropriation of funds by the insured, but also saves social resources by reducing social cost spent on double formalities for transferring the insurance payment from an insurer to a third party.

The first three paragraphs of Article 65 of the Insurance Act actually set forth the basic structure of China's liability insurance payment mechanism, and make clear the precondition of the third party's directly bringing an action against the insurer. It follows from paragraph 1 of Article 65 that a liability insurer needs a legal or contractual basis to pay the third party directly.

The term used in paragraph 1 of Article 65 is 'may' (*keyi*), and, according to the provision, the insurer 'may' directly compensate the third party. The term 'may' is a word for conferring a right upon someone, which normally means that the insurer has the right to choose whether or not to pay directly to the third party. But if the relevant provision in a law is a mandatory one or the relevant terms in a contract use the word 'must' or 'shall', the insurer will have the duty to directly pay to the third party and loses the option. Some scholars have stated that it is not appropriate to use the word 'may' in this provision, with which the author also agrees. In conjunction with the other paragraphs of Article 65, the legislative meaning of this paragraph should be that insurers 'shall' directly pay to the third party only when the law or the insurance contract stipulates. The word 'may' contradicts mandatory stipulations requesting the liability insurer to pay directly to the third party in a law or an insurance contract.

The most important such provision is Article 76 of the Road Traffic Safety Act of the People's Republic of China (the 'Road Traffic Safety Act'), which stipulates:

> where a motor vehicle causes personal injury or death or any property loss in a traffic accident, the insurance company shall pay indemnity within the policy limit of the compulsory liability insurance. The part

18 Liu Janxun, *Resolutions to the Classical and Difficult Cases of Insurance Law*, 2010, Law Press, p 399.

in excess of the liability limit shall be indemnified according to the following provisions.

This paragraph is very clear: where a motor vehicle causes personal injury or property damage in a traffic accident, the liability insurer shall pay directly to the third party within the policy limit of the compulsory liability insurance. In other words, when the vehicle causing damage in an accident has the protection of a compulsory liability insurance policy, the primary obligor in such an accident is not the driver insured or the owner of the vehicle, but the compulsory liability insurer. The first part of Article 76 stipulates that there are two layers of liability concerning the auto accident, the first layer of liability to be borne by the liability insurer within the policy limit and the second layer of liability, 'the part in excess of the policy limit', to be borne according to the following paragraph of Article 76.

The insurer's direct payment to the third-party victim may be based on the terms of the contract as well as the provisions of the law. Terms providing for direct payment to the third party can be incorporated into the contract during the negotiating process. Since most insurance contracts are based on standard terms, the incorporation of the relevant provisions depends on the will of the insurers. The question is whether the liability insurers have an incentive to incorporate such a provision into the contract. In the author's view, they do not. The insurer's direct payment to the third party, in fact, accelerates the rate of payment, objectively reducing the time period the insurer controls the funds in question, which is also the time period the insurers earn interest upon the funds. Without such a contract term, the insurer need not pay the insured until judgment debt is satisfied. If the insured does not pay the third party because of inability or unwillingness to pay, the insurer may refuse to pay the insured according to paragraph 3 of Article 65. Of course, the insured may request the insurer to pay directly to the third party, where there is consensus between the insured and the third-party victim. If it is not the case, the third party will have to wait until the insured satisfies the requirement of 'delay making such request' in paragraph 2 of Article 65 before he can bring an action against the insurer. In addition, such a provision in a liability insurance contract may be the legal basis for a third party to directly sue the insurers, which is not their wish.

2.3 Third party's right of direct action

In many countries, the legal framework for liability insurance may under certain conditions confer a right of direct action against the insurer upon the injured third party, a mechanism that did not exist at the birth of liability insurance. At the early stages of the development of liability cover, the third-party victim could not bring a direct action against the insurer because liability insurance was in the form of a pure indemnity contract with no purpose other than protecting the insured's assets. As an indemnity contract, the insurer would compensate the insured only when he suffered an actual loss as a result of discharging the liability imposed by law. When an insured had not yet paid a third party for the damage caused by him, he suffered no actual loss and, thus, he would not recover from the insurer. In the liability insurance relationship among the three parties, the insured can make a claim against the insurer because of the contractual relationship between them, and the third-party victim can sue the insured for damages based on the insured's tortious acts against the third-party victim. Historically, the third-party victim's direct action against the insurer was barred since there is no privity of contract between the third-party victim and the insurer and no tortious conduct by the insurer towards the third party. Moreover, a typical liability insurance contract, at that time, normally contained a provision barring the third party's direct action against the insurer.

With the further development of liability insurance, the public, courts and the legislatures became increasingly aware of the importance of liability insurance as a means of providing protection for third-party victims and of the weakening of this protection when the liability insurance contract was in the form of an indemnity contract, as well as the indemnity contract's inherent unfairness to the third party and the insured. Therefore, courts and legislatures tended to require the insurer to adopt the form of the liability contract, whereby the insured's claim accrued when his liability attached. Courts thus empowered third-party claimants to directly sue the insurer, recognising the claimant as the beneficiary to the contract, and legislatures passed statutes requiring that every liability policy contain a provision setting forth the third party's right of direct action against the insurer.

Allowing third-party direct actions against the insurer has both advantages and disadvantages. If the third-party victim cannot obtain the right of direct action, the only way he can recover his loss is to sue the insured claiming damages. Not only may this prolong the time before the third party benefits from the insurance, but he may not obtain damages because of the insured's unwillingness or inability to pay. But the right of direct action against the insurer also has its disadvantages. As Keeton said:

> One well known manifestation of this view has been the rule that it is prejudicial for a statement to be made within the hearing of a jury to the effect that 'a defendant has insurance' or that 'a party's liability will be covered by insurance'. The rationales for such a rule are that knowledge of a defendant's insurance (1) would cause the jury either to render judgments against the insured more readily than if they thought that the insured would not be personally liable, or (2) might induce a jury to award an injured plaintiff compensation beyond that which is warranted by the circumstances.[19]

19 R. E. Keeton and A. I. Widiss, *Insurance Law: A Guide to Fundamental Principle, Legal Doctrines, and Commercial Practices, Practitioner's Edition*, 1988, West Publishing Co., p 1097.

Although China's trials have no jury, the judge's knowledge of the liability insurance will still play an important role in finding the insured liable or liable for more damages than appropriate. Furthermore, allowing direct action against an insurer also has entails possibility that 'the determination of the liability (which involves questions of tort law) might be confused by issues in regard to the liability of the insurance company (which is primarily predicated on a contractual relationship between the insurer and the insured)'.[20] Therefore, the arrangement of the third party's right to bring a direct action against the insurer needs to strike a balance among the conflicting interests.

China's legal system of liability insurance allows the victim, after satisfying some preconditions, to directly sue the insurer, as a result of four provisions: the first is Article 65 of the Insurance Act, which is applicable to liability insurance products outside the regulation of special laws; the second is Article 76 of the Road Traffic Safety Act, which is applicable to compulsory motor liability insurance; the third is Article 168[21] of the Civil Aviation Act of the People's Republic of China, which is applicable to aviation liability insurance; the fourth is Article 97[22] of the Special Maritime Procedure Law of the People's Republic of China, which is applicable to vessel-induced oil pollution liability insurance. The third and fourth are both special legislation with narrow application and will not be discussed in this chapter.[23]

20 Ibid. See further section 4 below.

21 Article 168: 'The victim of the injury or damage can take legal action directly against the insurer or guarantor only in the following circumstances, but this does not preclude the right per se of taking direct legal action in accordance with the legal stipulations in the insurance or guarantee contract:
(1) The insurance or guarantee continues to be effective as stipulated in (1) and (2) of Article 167.
(2) The operator has gone bankrupt.
Except within the domain of the right of contest stipulated in the first paragraph of Article 167, the insurer or guarantor should not contest against the legal action taken by the victim directly against them in accordance with provisions in this chapter on ground of the loss of effectiveness of the insurance or guarantee or the end of retroactivity.'

22 Article 97: 'With respect to a claim for indemnity against oil pollution damage caused by a ship, the person suffering for the damage may make the claim to the shipowner causing the oil pollution damage, or directly make the claim to the insurer bearing the liability for oil pollution damage of the shipowner or to other person providing financial suretyship. Where the insurer bearing the liability for oil pollution damage of the shipowner or the other person providing financial suretyship against whom an action is filed, he is entitled to require the shipowner causing the oil pollution damage to participate in the proceedings.'

23 See further Chapters 5 and 13 of this work.

2.3.1 Article 65 of the Insurance Act

From paragraph 2 of Article 65 of the Insurance Act, it follows that there are two preconditions the third-party victim will have to meet before he can directly bring an action against the insurer: first, that 'the liability of the insured for damages to the third party has been fixed', and second, that the insured delays the request to the insurer of direct payment to the third party.

The relevant provisions in the Insurance Act have built up a payment mechanism in which the insured's claim to the insurer is the main approach and the third party's direct recovery from the insurer is supplementary. Under such a mechanism, following the insured event, the third-party victim must first contact the insured who caused the accident. If the insured's liability to the third party is fixed through a settlement or a judgment and the insured pays for it, then the insured may recover from the insurer. If the insured does not want to pay after his liability is fixed, he may request the insurer to pay the third party directly. Even in such a situation, the third party may not bring a direct action against the insurer unless the insured delays making such request. Then the meanings of 'liability is fixed' and 'delay making such request' become the key to the third party's right of direct action. Therefore, we need to ask what the implications of these two phrases are.

The liability of the insured for damages to the third party has been fixed. It is not unique to China that the establishment of the insured's liability is the precondition for the third party to have the right of direct action against the liability insurer. This condition also appears in many statutes in other countries. For example, the Third Parties (Rights Against Insurers) Act 1930 of the UK also requires the determination of liability and quantum against the insured by way of judgment, arbitration award or settlement prior to a third party being able to claim against the insurer. In the United States, common law does not allow any direct action against the insurer, but some states have already passed statutes, known as direct action statutes, providing that every liability policy issued or delivered in the State shall contain a provision allowing the third party's direct action against the insurer under certain circumstances:

> The creation of direct-action statutes in the various U.S. jurisdictions and territories allows injured parties to bring claims directly against the insurers instead of tortfeasors causing damage or injury. When reviewing the language of the statutes and the jurisprudence covering the purpose of direct-action statutes, it is clear that the Legislation was generally designed to protect tort victims and allow the public access to insurance coverage regardless of the solvency of the tortfeasor.[24]

24 M. Mese, K. Miller Hawthorne D'Armond McCowan and Jarman, LLP, 'Direct-action statutes', *CGL Reporter*, 2003(15), pp 520–529.

Most such statutes require that the liability of the insured be finally determined through a final judgment against the tortfeasor or a written agreement between the insured, the third-party victim and the insurer before the third-party victim may bring an action.[25]A few statutes limit the right of direct action to a certain area, such as motor liability insurance. In Taiwan, the corresponding provision in its Insurance Act is paragraph 2 of Article 94, which specifies that 'when the liability of the insured for damages to the third party has been fixed, the third party may directly claim the damages with the insurer within the policy limit'. It is very likely that China's legislator referred to this Article when drafting paragraph 2 of Article 65 in the Insurance Act.

There is no doubt that once the third party obtains judgment against the insured in tort litigation, the liability of the insured to the third party, whether the establishment of the liability or the amount of the damages, should be regarded as 'fixed', since a final judgment given by an authoritative judicial body should determine the liability and quantum. Postulating a final judgment as a precondition for the victim's direct action against the insurer can outweigh the disadvantages mentioned above for allowing direct actions. First, since the judgment is determined, any confusion caused by combining the tort action and the insurance claim action together is eliminated. Second, since the liability itself and the amount involved have already been recognised by law, any risk of prejudice by the jury or the judge against the insurer is avoided. By the same token, an arbitration award obtained by a third-party claimant should have the same effect as a final judgment.

Settlements reached between the insured and the third party merit analysis in further detail. Normally, due to the influence of the quantum of damages on the legitimate interests of the liability insurer, the insurer will take part in settlement negotiations. As mentioned above, in the United States, a settlement can satisfy the precondition of the insured's bringing a direct action against the third party, establishing the insured's liability to the third party. That settlement is a written agreement between three parties, namely the insured, the third-party victim and the insurer. The situation in China is somewhat different in that the insurer usually does not participate in settlement negotiations. In the United States, the insurer has the duty to defend and the duty to settle. The latter seems more important in that the vast majority of all insurance claims are settled and the early settlement of claims can not only obviate defence costs, but also reduce the amount the liability insurer needs to pay. Liability insurers in the United States are therefore active in negotiating the settlement. In China, liability insurers usually do not participate in the settlement since they do not have the duty to defend and the duty to settle, and the defence costs and damages are

25 E. M. Holmes, 'Holmes' Appleman on insurance', 2nd edn, 2000, Lexis Publishing, p 48.

small compared to in the US. Although a liability insurance contract always contains a provision to the effect that without prior written approval of the insurer, the insured may not settle with the third-party victim, this provision is more likely to be used by the insurer to deny liability for the claim if a settlement is reached without its participation, an argument normally rejected by the court.

In China, in the author's opinion, when the settlement is essentially consistent with the law in terms of both the scope of the liability and the amount of the damages, it will be regarded as conforming to the requirement of 'the liability . . . is fixed', for the following reasons. First, a final judgment given by the court and a settlement reached between the insured and the third party are legally recognised approaches to determine the insured's tortious responsibility to the third-party victim. Given that the tortious responsibility is a kind of civil liability, which can be fixed by the free will of the parties concerned, the settlement reached by the insured and the third party is in accordance with the law as long as the will of the parties is true and lawful. But the amount agreed by the parties should be within the limits of the law because the settlement reached by the parties can affect the liability insurer. As stated by a judge who has written two books on insurance law and cases:

> An insured and a third-party victim may, in conformity with the law, negotiate the amount of damages and reach a settlement. An insurer shall pay indemnity in light of the amount agreed in the settlement, unless the amount agreed substantially exceed the standard for damages stipulated by relevant judicial explanations.[26]
>
> Under the liability insurance, the scope and the standard of the insured's responsibility to the third party for damages to be reimbursed by the insurer should be in accordance with the law, and should not be agreed at will by the insured and the third party beyond the standard set by the law.[27]

Second, some liability insurance contracts contain provisions specifically acknowledging the enforceability of mediated settlements, affirmed by the court. For example, a provision in medical liability insurance specifies:

> all sums of damages assumed by the insurer for each patient shall be subject to the amount of the damages settled by the patient or his close relatives, the insured and the insurer, or to which the insured shall be

26 Liu Jianxun, *Resolutions to the New Difficult Cases of Insurance Law*, 2007, Law Press, p 38 (the author is citing a judicial explanation, meaning the legal basis on which the parties concerned negotiate the amount of the damages).

27 Ibid.

> obligated to pay as a result of the settlement mediated by the court, the arbitration committee or the administrative department of public health, or of the decision, the award or the judgment made by them, but the sum shall not exceed the limit of medical liability stated in the schedule of the policy as applicable to each individual.[28]

This provision has expressly confirmed the validity of mediated settlements, affirmed by the court. The cases discussed below, *Langzhong Zhongshan Hospital v PICC Property and Casualty Company Limited Langzhong Branch*[29] and *PICC Property and Casualty Company Limited Anshun Xixiu Branch v Anshun Xixiu District People's Hospital*,[30] reflect the courts' attitude towards the recognition of the mediated settlement, especially when the mediator is a court or a government agency.

The author believes that the participation of insurers in the conclusion of settlement agreements has a positive social effect, which is not only conducive to the protection of insurers' legitimate rights and interests, but also helpful in assisting the third party to recover the loss without delay and saving litigation costs for society through timely acknowledgment of the enforceability of the settlement agreement and avoiding unnecessary litigation. But in reality, insurers rarely participate in such settlement, perhaps to preserve their rights to overturn an unsatisfactory settlement.

Delay by the insured in requesting payment to the third party. This requirement generally has no correspondent in the provisions setting forth the preconditions for the third party's right of direct action against the liability insurer in other countries. However, it is said that the requirement is similar to the provision about subrogation of creditors in China's contract law. Since there is no provision in the Insurance Act interpreting this requirement, it has been compared with subrogation in contract law. But actually these two are so different that the analogy may be misleading.

Subrogation simply means substitution of one person for another; one person is allowed to stand in the shoes of another and assert that person's rights against the defendant.[31] In the field of subrogation of creditors, it means that when a debtor delays exercising its creditor's right against the third party, prejudicing the rights of the creditor, the creditor may exercise the rights of the debtor under its own name. This right originated from the

28 PICC(2002)51 'Insurance Clauses'.

29 *Langzhong Zhongshan Hospital v PICC Property and Casualty Company Limited Langzhong Branch, Sichuan Province Langzhong Municipality Intermediate People's Court*, (2009) Lang Min Chu Zi No. 2512, 3 December 2009.

30 *PICC Property and Casualty Company Limited Anshun Xixiu Branch v Anshun Xixiu District People's Hospital*, (2009) An Shi Min Er Zhong Zi No. 19, Guizhou Province Anshun Municipality Intermediate People's Court, 17 November 2009. (In this case, the judgment of first instance was based on this clause, which was sustained by the court of second instance.)

31 D. B. Dobbs, *Law of Remedies*, 2nd edn, 1993, West Publishing Co., p 404.

French Civil Code of 1804. The corresponding provision in Article 73 of China's Contract Law specifies:

> If a debtor delays exercising its matured creditor's rights, to the detriment of the creditor, the creditor may apply to a people's court to be subrogated to the creditor's rights against the debtor and exercise them under its own name, except for such rights as belong exclusively to the debtor. The scope for exercising the subrogation is limited to the creditor's rights enjoyed by the creditor. The expenses of the creditor's exercising its subrogation shall be borne by the debtor.

The meaning of this is that if C is the creditor of A, and A is the creditor of B, and A delays exercising its matured creditor's rights against B, to the detriment of C, C may apply to a People's Court, under C's own name, to exercise A's rights and require B to return money to A, except A's exclusive rights such as pension and insurance indemnity.

In practice, it is not appropriate to use this form of subrogation to elucidate issues of the insured's right of direct action against the insurer, because it is too complicated and prolonged for the third-party victim. In view of the fact that liability insurance contracts in China are in the form of liability contracts, so that once the insured's liability to the third-party victim attaches the insurer bears the responsibility to pay the indemnity, the liability insurer is the actual debtor. The most efficient way of compensating the third-party victim is not by subrogation, but by letting the insurer pay the third party on behalf of the insured.

We can nevertheless refer to creditor's subrogation for the meaning of the word 'delay'. Since both provisions use this word in the context of requesting an obligor to a contract to pay a matured debt, we can borrow from the approach of creditor's subrogation. 'Delay' in exercising the right means that the debtor objectively does not request the third party to pay within a reasonable time. It involves objective action and the debtor's subjective mind should not be considered. In the field of liability insurance, the phrase 'delay making such request' may mean that the insured neither pays the third-party victim directly in accordance with the settlement, the arbitral award or the judgment, nor requests the insurer to directly pay the third-party victim within a reasonable time, regardless of whether the insured is at fault. What is reasonable time still needs to be clarified since it may mean the period set by the settlement, the arbitral award or the judgment, or a reasonable period thereafter for an insured to make such request.

2.3.2 Article 76 of the Road Traffic Safety Law

There is a distinct difference between compulsory motor liability insurance and most other liability insurance. In compulsory motor liability insurance, whether or not the third party can directly bring an action against the insurer is controversial both in legal theory and in judicial practice, but most judgments allow the third party to list the compulsory motor liability insurer as a joint defendant in a motor accident litigation against the insured. In this area, the rule in Article 65 of the Insurance Act, with its two preconditions for the third party's claim against the insurer, is replaced by Article 76 of China's Road Traffic Safety Law.

There are several reasons why a third-party victim may bring a direct claim against a compulsory motor liability insurer and list it as a joint defendant with the insured. First, Article 76 in China's Road Traffic Safety Law makes an insurer a primary obligor for compensating third-party victims. It stipulates:

> Where a motor vehicle causes personal injury or death or any property loss in a traffic accident, the insurance company shall pay indemnity within the policy limit of the compulsory liability insurance. The part in excess of the liability limit shall be indemnified according to the following provisions.

Accordingly, a compulsory motor liability insurer is not a legal person who bears the responsibility of payment to the insured based on the terms of the insurance contract, but an obligor who directly compensates a third-party victim within the policy limit in accordance with the law. This obligor is a primary one according to the law while the insured who causes the accident is the secondary one as long as he purchases a compulsory motor liability policy. In the context of other liability insurance, the insurer is the secondary obligor in that the insured should compensate the third party first and then claim from the insurer, or the insured must request the insurer to pay to the third party when his liability is fixed; but in the context of compulsory motor liability insurance, the insurer is the primary obligor in that it must pay the third party before the insured's payment, without anyone's request. Therefore, it is lawful for a third-party victim to directly file a motor accident claim against both the insurer and the insured since the insurer is the primary obligor for compensating the third party's loss if he wins the litigation.

Second, the theoretical basis of joining the insurer and the insured as defendants is that the object of action is identical subject to the relevant provision of the law. When a third party initiates litigation following a traffic accident, the issue to be tried is whether the insured should be liable to the third-party victim. If he is liable, his insurer will have to pay within the policy limit to the third party, and then the insured itself will pay the rest of the damages; if he is not, neither the insured nor the insurer will have responsibility to pay. As a result, the insured and the insurer have a common object of action.

Third, since the judgment of the motor accident litigation directly affects not only the lawful rights and interests of a third-party victim and an insured, but also that of a compulsory motor liability insurer, if the insurer did not participate in the litigation, how could the insurer safeguard its lawful rights and interests? The insurer being the defendant to the claim benefits not only the third party, but also the insurer itself.

Finally, listing a relevant compulsory motor liability insurer as a joint defendant to a motor accident claim is supported by most courts in China. In 2007, the Higher People's Court of Beijing Municipality discussed this issue in a seminar, recorded in a legal document, namely the 'Minutes of the Higher People's Court of Beijing Municipality's seminar on legal issues concerning damage resulting from road traffic accidents', stating that:

> according to the provision of Article 76 in China's Road Traffic Safety Law, the insurance company assumes the mandatory liability of indemnity within the compulsory motor liability policy limit. As for the question whether the insurance company should be listed as a third person or a joint defendant, it is still theoretically controversial. In order to ensure the uniformity of law enforcement among the courts in our city, the leading opinion of the persons attending this seminar is as follows: where a motor vehicle causes personal injury in a traffic accident, the victim should file an action against the party of the motor vehicle causing such injury and the insurance company offering the compulsory motor liability insurance covering the motor vehicle, and list them as joint defendants. If the victim only brings an action against the party of the motor vehicle causing such injury and the party of the motor vehicle applies to add the insurance company as joint defendant, the court should do so. If the victim does not list the insurance company as joint defendant when filing a claim, the court should clearly explain this to him. Having received the explanation, if the victim applies to add the insurance company as joint defendant, the court should do so; if the victim insists on not suing the insurance company, and the party of the motor vehicle causing such injury does not request to add the insurance company either, then the insurance company need not be added in the lawsuit.

Another supportive judicial explanation is the 'Provisions of No. 1 Civil Tribunal of the Higher People's Court of Zhejiang Province on a Trail of Cases concerning Disputes over Compensation for Traffic Accident Damage (for Trial Implementation)' effected on 1 July 2010. According to the relevant provisions, a liability insurer shall be a joint defendant in an underlying action unless the third-party victim is unwilling to add the insurer as the joint defendant after the court has explained clearly to him the relevant legal consequences and the insurer refuses to apply to be the defendant.

Since the third party may bring a direct action against the insurer according to the relevant provision of the Road Traffic Safety Law, are there any conflicts between this provision and the provisions of the Insurance Act setting forth the preconditions of direct actions against the insurer? The author believes that the answer is no, because the relationship between these two provisions is that between general law and special law. Article 76 of the Road Traffic Safety Law is special law, which only applies to the compulsory motor liability coverage, while Article 65 in the Insurance Act is general law, applicable to all liability insurance products except those regulated by special law, including compulsory motor liability coverage. Therefore, the third party under most types of liability insurance cover, including voluntary motor liability insurance, can directly sue the insurer on condition of having satisfied the two preconditions stipulated in Article 65. However, it has been pointed out that there is no clear indication of the person entitled to the direct insurance payment under Article 76 and it may be the insured instead of the third party. The author believes that this contention is untenable, since the relevant provision in the Insurance Act provides for the duty of the liability insurer to indemnify the insured, and there is no need to provide for this again in the Road Traffic Safety Law. The strongest argument is that the latter part of Article 76 is about the question of how to allocate the part of the loss of the third-party victim that is not covered by the compulsory motor liability insurance. The former part of the Article thus deals with the first part of the third-party victim's loss, and if the person entitled to the insurer's direct payment dictated by the former part of the Article were not the third-party victim, the Article could not have formed a complete logical structure.

Some scholars believe that a third-party victim may not bring a direct action against a liability insurer even within the field of the compulsory motor liability insurance according to the provision of Article 28 of the Regulation on Compulsory Traffic Accident Liability Insurance for Motor Vehicles, specifying that 'where an insured motor vehicle is involved in a road traffic accident, the insured shall file a claim with the insurance company', indicating that only an insured has the right to claim from the insurer, combining with Article 30[32]to mean that only the insured has the right to directly file an action against the insurer whereas the third party does not. However, these scholars seem to forget one basic rule of statutory interpretation, that is, a provision shall be construed within the legal context. In other words, the interpretation of a provision shall be subject to the limits imposed by the hierarchy of legal authority. In this context, these Articles of the Regulation should be construed subject to Article 76 of the Road Traffic Safety Law, leading to the correct interpretation that an insured has the right to claim directly from the insurer, but a third party will have the right to sue the insurer if neither the insurer nor the insured compensates

32 Article 30: 'Where a dispute arises between the insured and the insurance company over the indemnification, they may apply for arbitration or bring a claim to the people's court in accordance with the law.'

his losses, since the insurer is the primary obligor under Article 76. There is no provision in this Regulation that expressly bars the third party's direct action against the insurer. On the contrary, Article 31 of the Regulation clearly states that the insurer may pay to the insured or the third party. The author would reconcile the provision in Article 28 that only an insured has the right to claim from the insurer with the third party's right to claim directly as follows. First, the insured is in possession of the insurance policy and more conveniently placed than the third party to claim; second, the insured and the third party are entitled to directly sue the insurer under a different statute; and third, the Road Traffic Safety Law is superior law to the Regulation, and thus even if there were some provisions in the Regulation in conflict with Article 76, the latter should prevail pursuant to the basic rule of statutory interpretation.

In short, in a road traffic accident case, when the motor vehicle causing the damage is covered by a compulsory motor liability insurance policy, the third-party victim can bring a direct action against the insurer and list it as a joint defendant with the insured. This follows from the law and is supported by most of the courts in China.

2.4 Liability insurance for litigation expenses

In the United States, the liability insurance policy's insuring agreement contains two promises: (1) a promise to pay damages on behalf of the insured; and (2) a promise to defend the insured against claims brought by the third party seeking damages under the policy. In China, insurance law requires liability insurers to pay damages, but imposes no duty to defend the insured. Chinese law only requires liability insurers to pay litigation expenses incurred by the insured, subject to stipulation in the insurance contract. A liability insurance policy may also reserve the insurer's right to participate in an action brought against the insured.

In Europe, insurers offer legal expenses insurance (LEI), also known as legal protection insurance (LPI). LEI is a type of insurance policy sold to both individual and business customers, covering the potential costs and fees of legal action brought by third parties against the policyholder. By purchasing this insurance product, policyholders may have affordable protection for the legal fees charged and expenses incurred by hiring legal representation. In the UK, Germany, Belgium and Sweden, a relatively large proportion of the population have access to such insurance.[33] There are two main forms of such insurance, before-the-event and after-the-event. Most legal expenses insurance policies are before-the-event, while both types are common in some jurisdictions, notably the United Kingdom.

33 'The market for "BTE" legal expenses insurance', prepared on behalf of the Ministry of Justice, July 2007, p 8.

In China, Article 66 of the Insurance Act provides for legal expenses insurance subject to contrary policy stipulation. This statutory cover for the cost of arbitration or legal action and other necessary and reasonable expenses (hereinafter collectively referred to as litigation expenses) resembles the legal expenses insurance available in Europe in terms of the scope of coverage, but is similar to the duty to defend in the United States in terms of the form of cover. As for the scope, this cover is only responsible for reimbursing litigation expenses incurred by the insured and does not require the insurer to defend the insured, much like LEI. As for the form, the cover extends the original protection for legal liability and is not singled out as an independent policy for sale, which is similar to the duty to defend.

Article 66 permits contractual exclusion, and the compulsory motor liability insurance cover – the most important class of liability insurance products in China – does so through clause 10 of the 'Compulsory Auto Mobile Traffic Accident Liability Insurance Clauses', providing that 'the compulsory motor liability insurance does not cover the following losses and expenses: . . . (iv) the cost of arbitration or legal action and other relevant expenses'. As a result, no compulsory motor liability cover reimburses litigation expenses incurred by the insured. The rationale is that the main purpose of compulsory motor liability insurance is to protect the interest of third-party victims by compensating their losses suffered in the traffic accident. The limited funding available should be spent on compensating their personal injuries and property losses instead of litigation expenses.

If there is no such clause in the liability policy, the insurance should cover litigation expenses incurred by the insured, and some professional liability insurance contracts contain a clause expressly covering litigation expenses under certain conditions. However, there is another noteworthy trend. A few years ago, few insurers inserted such a clause in liability policies, thus the court would normally hold that the insurer should bear litigation expenses, while in recent years more and more insurers have inserted clauses excluding liability for litigation expenses.[34] Although such a clause in the policy may eliminate the insurer's responsibility for expenses according to Article 66, if the insurer requests the insured not to settle with the third-party victim in light of a clause in the contract stating that the insured should not promise to compensate the third-party victim without the insurer's permission, the insurer should nevertheless bear the litigation expenses even if Article 66 is excluded,[35] since those expenses were incurred upon the insurer's requirement.

The Insurance Act does not contain any definition of 'the cost of such arbitration or legal action and other necessary and reasonable expenses paid

34 Liu Janxun, *Resolutions to the Classical and Difficult Cases of Insurance Law*, 2010, Law Press, p 455.

35 Ibid.

by the insured' assumed by the insurers, potentially leading to further disputes.

3 Notification of claim

> The primary purpose of a notice requirement in an insurance policy is to afford the insurer a reasonable opportunity to protect its right. Prompt notice to the insurer maximises an insurer's opportunity to acquire information about the circumstances of a loss (usually by way of a timely investigation when witnesses are most likely to be available and while their memories of the events are generally the most accurate, as well as when there is usually the best opportunity to examine, record and preserve any physical evidence), which may be important both (1) to the insurer's determinations in regard to whether a loss is covered and (2) to the preparation of a defence to claims by a third party against the insured who is covered by a liability insurance policy.[36]

The requirement of prompt notice of a claim sometimes also protects the interest of the insured. For example, early notice may facilitate settlement, reducing the cost of litigation and eliminating the risk damages awarded by a judge or jury exceeding the policy limits and remaining an obligation of the insured. Another benefit of timely notice of a claim is that early investigation increases the probability that fraudulent claims will be detected, which is fully consistent with the best interests of the insured and insurer generally, the public, and mostly the insured.[37]

In China's liability insurance contracts, the notice requirement is one of the essential terms. The provision generally requires the insured to provide the insurer with written notice of loss upon receipt of information, or to forward to the insurer the relevant documents pertaining to a claim against him. If the insured fails to carry out such notice requirement as provided in the contract, the insurer may accordingly deny cover. But in judicial practice, even if the insured fails to satisfy the notice requirement, his claim against the insurer will usually not be affected.

In the case of *Bengbu Municipality Enterprises Occupational Disease Research Institute Haitian Hospital v PICC Property and Casualty Company Limited Guzhen Branch*,[38] the respondent, Haitian Hospital, had signed a medical

36 R E. Keeton and A. I. Widiss, *Insurance Law: A Guide to Fundamental Principle, Legal Doctrines, and Commercial Practices, Practitioner's Edition*, 1988, West Publishing Co., p 753.

37 Ibid.

38 *Bengbu Municipality Enterprises Occupational Disease Research Institute Haitian Hospital v PICC Property and Casualty Company Limited Guzhen Branch, Anhui Province Bengbu Municipality Intermediate People's Court* (2007) Beng Min Er Zhong Zi No. 132, 28 January 2008.

liability insurance contract with the appellant, PICC. The contract stated that the policy limit applicable to each person was RMB 300,000, within which the limit applicable to damages for mental suffering was RMB 90,000 and for legal expenses RMB 30,000. Clause 14 in the contract specified that 'in case the insured knows that a legal action, an administrative sanction or an arbitration may be filed against him, or receives the summons or other legal documents, the insured shall immediately give written notice to the insurer'. On 4 July 2006, a doctor in the hospital performed surgery on Shen Xiuyun, which caused her death. The Bengbu Municipality Medical Association evaluated the incident, determining that the accident was a grade I medical accident, which should be the insured's full responsibility. The relatives of the deceased sued the hospital on 11 April 2007. On 15 May, the hospital informed PICC about the date and place of the court hearing. But PICC did not present itself in the court. Finally, the court of first instance ordered Haitian Hospital to compensate the relatives of Shen Xiuyun for all losses, which it did. When PICC refused to reimburse the insured, the hospital brought an action against PICC.

PICC argued that the hospital had not given timely notice as required by the policy after the medical accident occurred, and that it had not given timely notice of the action against it by the relatives of Shen Xiuyun, causing an augmentation of damages for the medical accident because PICC had had no opportunity to prepare the defence, causing the court to err in ruling against the hospital. Further, PICC argued that the hospital neither informed the insurer nor took steps to appeal once the court ruled against it, which resulted in the order becoming final and binding. Therefore, it contended that PICC should not bear any part of the damages beyond the amount the court should have held.

The court of first instance held that the hospital had adequately performed its notification duties. The court of second instance affirmed the decision of the court below. The judgment was based on the Insurance Act prior to the 2009 revision, but the reasoning still holds sway. In this case, the insurer did not participate in the underlying action upon receiving the notice from the insured, which might have been assessed under the waiver theory in a US case, thus the insurer was not blameless, while in the next case the insurer is totally innocent.

In the case of *Langzhong Zhongshan Hospital v PICC Property and Casualty Insurance Company Limited Langzhong Branch*,[39] the insured, upon receiving the notice of claim from the third-party victim, reached a settlement with the third-party victim under the mediation of the court without notifying the insurer. The insurer denied cover on the ground that 'the

39 *Langzhong Zhongshan Hospital v PICC Property and Casualty Company Limited Langzhong Branch, Sichuan Province Langzhong Municipality Intermediate People's Court*, (2009) Lang Min Chu Zi No 2512, 3 December 2009.

plaintiff reached a settlement with the patient without the privity of our company and thus our company is not bound by the settlement'. There were two clauses in the insurance contract supporting the insurer's assertion: clause 14, 'In case the insured knows that a legal action, an administrative sanction or an arbitration may be filed against him, or receives a summons or other legal documents, the insured shall immediately give written notice to the insurer', and clause 16, 'If the applicant for insurance or the insured does not perform a duty provided for by clause 10 to clause 15, the insurer will have the right to relieve itself of liability for indemnification, or terminate the insurance contract as of the date of delivery of the termination notice to the insured'. However, the court did not accept the insurer's contention, ruling that the insurer should bear the responsibility to the insured for damages under the settlement, reasoning that clause 19 under the contract specified:

> all sums of damages assumed by the insurer for each patient shall be subject to the amount of damages settled by the patient or his close relatives, the insured and the insurer, or to which the insured shall be obligated to pay as a result of the settlement mediated by the court, the arbitration committee or the administrative department of public health, or of the decision, the award or the judgment made by them, but the sum shall not exceed the limit of medical liability stated in the schedule of the policy as applicable to each individual.

Clause 19 is a provision that most medical liability insurance contracts will contain. Interpreted literally, this clause sets out the standard of compensation for the insured and is not designed to relieve the insured of his duty to notify. However, in liability insurance cases involving the notice requirement, the court usually rejects the insurer's assertion that the insured's failure to comply with the notice requirement would deprive him of the right to insurance cover.

In addition to the notice requirement stipulated in the contract, China's Insurance Act also contains a corresponding provision. Although Article 21 is not well adapted to liability insurance, it may be applied by analogy.

According to Article 21, the insured's failure to notify does not necessarily result in a loss of cover. Conditions must be satisfied before the court dismisses the claim. First, the insured's failure to notify must have a subjective element, namely intent or gross negligence. If the insured is aware of the occurrence of the insured event and does not notify the insurer about it without good reason, it is possible to infer that the insured acted with intent or gross negligence. Second, the behaviour of the insured should objectively result in 'making it difficult to ascertain the nature, cause, extent of the loss, etc. of the incident covered by insurance', similar to the requirement of prejudice to insurer's interest in the US. Third, even if the behaviour of the insured causes uncertainty as to the nature, cause, extent of the loss, etc., the insurer must still indemnify the insured as long as 'the insurer knew or should have known of the incident in a timely manner through other channels'. This requirement can prevent the insurer from using the fault of the insured to forfeit the indemnity because the insurer shall adopt corresponding measures to protect its interests when it knew or should have known the relevant information, which is the very purpose of the notice requirement. Finally, even if all the conditions have been satisfied, the insurer should only reject the part of the insurance claim that is difficult to ascertain, and cannot deny the benefit of the insurance as a whole.

The insured's duty to notify per Article 21 superficially appears to be beneficial to the protection of the interests of the insurer, but in fact the real object being protected by this provision is the insured. Even in the absence of this provision, the insurer could still protect itself by inserting a notice clause into the contract, which might be so strict that even a tiny breach of the notification requirement could lead to loss of cover. But Article 21 eliminates this possibility by conferring on the insured a right to claim invalidation of the clause in an insurance policy when it is stricter than Article 21. The legal basis of this claim is Article 19 in the Insurance Act, which provides that any clause in an insurance contract will be void that uses the insurer's standard terms to exclude the legal rights of the policyholder, insured or beneficiary, or exempts the insurer from its legal obligations or aggravates the liability of the applicant for insurance or insured.

In conclusion, the author believes that even if the insured does not perform the duty of notification or does not do so in a timely manner, the insured will not lose any part of his cover unless there is evidence that the insurer's interests are prejudiced by the insured's failure to comply with the notification requirement in the insurance contract.

4 Intentional damage exclusion clause

An intentional damage exclusion clause in a liability insurance policy is an exclusion clause precluding cover for legal liability assumed by an insured to a third party for damage intentionally caused by the insured. The reason for including such a clause in the contract is twofold: one is that the insurance products cover only fortuitous losses, not loss or damage instigated by the insured; the other is that public policy should not allow tortfeasors to transfer liability for their intentionally caused harm to the insurers. However, liability insurance is usually the principal, or sometimes the only, source of compensation for an innocent victim of the insured's actions. That being the case, the public policy of ensuring appropriate compensation to innocent victims is sometimes in conflict with that of preventing an insurer from offering insurance to cover losses intentionally caused by the insured. Accordingly, the legislator and the courts will face a dilemma how to balance these two public policies.

4.1 Statutory provisions

The relevant provision is paragraph 2 of Article 27 of the Insurance Act.[40] According to that provision, the insurer has the right to refuse to pay where the loss-causing incident was brought about intentionally by the insured even in the absence of an intentional exclusion clause in the contract. In the Article, the phrase 'intentionally causes the occurrence of an incident covered by insurance' requires further analysis, especially the word 'intentionally' and the phrase 'an incident covered by insurance'. Paragraph 7 of Article 16 defines the phrase, specifying that 'an insured event refers to an event falling within the scope of cover agreed in the insurance contract'. The Insurance Act does not define the word 'intentionally', but we may construe it using the plain meaning rule, under which a word will be given its ordinary dictionary meaning. In Cihai (an Encyclopedia of the Chinese Language), 'intentionally' means 'deliberately; volitionally, do it with knowledge that it should not be done', and in the Modern Chinese Dictionary, it means 'volitionally'. Therefore, the phrase 'intentionally causes the occurrence of an incident covered by insurance' means that someone volitionally causes an event falling within the scope of the coverage under an insurance contract. In other words, in order to satisfy the exclusion requirement, the insured should volitionally cause an event falling within the scope of the cover under an insurance contract, not merely consciously do something that unfortunately produces loss or damage within the cover, which should not happen in normal circumstances. For example, in the *Caspersen*[41] case, the court finally upheld the claim against the insurer by a hatcheck girl who was pushed by the insured causing personal injuries, where the jury specifically found that the insured did not intend to injure the hatcheck girl, but just wanted to re-enter the coatcheck room. Thus, the excluded act may not be an impulsive, albeit intentional, act resulting in an unintended injury. In short, the exclusion stipulated in the Insurance Act requires that not only the means is intentional, but also the result must be some kind of damage or loss within the cover of the liability insurance policy.

Furthermore, when the insured does not desire the harm but knows with substantial certainty that it would occur as a result of his action, his act meets the requirement of 'indirect intention' in the legal theory of tort law and criminal law, which may entitle the insurer to reject the claim since the insured's act does 'intentionally' cause damage, while the insurer may compensate the insured or the third party according to paragraph 2 of Article 27 if the word 'intentionally' is construed with the plain meaning rule because the insured does not volitionally pursue the harm resulted from his action, but merely does not care about it.

40 See Appendix I.
41 *Caspersen v Webber* (1973) 298 Minn 93, 213 NW2d 327.

There is still one provision requiring attention, namely Article 22 of the Regulation on Compulsory Traffic Accident Liability Insurance for Motor Vehicles, according to which:

> In any of the following circumstances, an insurance company shall advance the emergency treatment expenses within the limit of liability for the compulsory traffic accident liability insurance for motor vehicles, and is entitled to recover such expenses from the party liable for the accident: . . . (3) the insured deliberately causes a road traffic accident. Where a road traffic accident occurs and results in property losses to the victim in any of the circumstances as provided for in the preceding paragraph, the insurance company shall bear no liability for making indemnity payments.

It means that the liability of the compulsory motor liability insurer for compensating the third-party victim when the traffic accident is caused intentionally by the insured is limited to payment of medical fees for saving the victim's life, which can be reimbursed by the insured. This Article seems to contradict paragraph 2 of Article 27 of the Insurance Act but actually does not, since paragraph 2 of Article 186 stipulates that 'in regard to compulsory insurance, if laws and administrative regulations provide otherwise, such provisions shall prevail'.

4.2 Terms of the contract

The wording of the intentional damage exclusion clause in liability contracts in China has a glaring deficiency in that it always states that the liability insurer should not be responsible for the damage, losses or fees caused by the following reason, including 'the insured's intentional act'[42] or for 'losses caused by the insured's intentional act'.[43] Construing the phrase 'intentional act' with its literal meaning may lead to an absurd interpretation of the whole clause because 'intentional act' means an act deliberately done by someone. For example, in the field of driving, 'intentional act' means all the driving action deliberately done by the drivers, including those deliberately done by drivers against the law, resulting in unintended losses, such as speeding, red-light running, etc., and if the losses caused by those acts were out of the scope of the motor policy, then there would be almost no compensation for third-party victims because those drivers do 'intentionally' act in that way for their own convenience or other reasons even if they do not intend

42 PICC (for record-keeping) [2009] No. 304 Public Liability Insurance Clauses (version 1999), etc.

43 China United Property Insurance Company Limited Automobile Liability Insurance Clauses Clause 7 Paragraph 6.

to cause loss or harm. In other words, they intend the means but not the results, which are still an 'intentional act' under the scope of the exclusion clause. Accordingly, when a trial involves such a clause, it may be either void pursuant to Article 19[44] of the Insurance Act for exempting the insurer from its legal obligations under the policy, or interpreted in favour of the insured and beneficiary according to Article 30[45] because it may have two or more different interpretations. Therefore, the intentional damage exclusion clause that is widely used in China's liability policy is arguably inappropriate and needs to be revised and perfected.

5 Relationship between underlying action and insurance action

Although the underlying tort action and the following insurance claim action involve the same facts, they may produce different results since the former is based on tort law and the latter on contract law and insurance law.

We have already discussed that liability insurers in China are under no obligation to defend their insured, while the relevant clause in the contract only confers the right upon insurers to participate in the underlying action and defend the insured or to participate in the settlement. In China's insurance practice, many insurers choose not to participate in the underlying litigation or in the settlement, but if the result is not satisfying they may contest it in the insurance claim action brought by the insured. However, the underlying action or the settlement is arguably critical for the insurer since in most situations the liability and the damages dictated by the ruling or the settlement determine the amount payable by the liability insurer, or at least affect that amount. Therefore, an important legal issue arises (i.e. whether the legal and factual matters determined by the underlying action or the settlement can be applied to the insurance claim action brought by the insured against the insurer, and, if the answer is positive, can these matters be changed in the insurance action?). The simple answer to the first question is yes; according to law and judicial practice, the determination of legal and factual matters in the underlying action or the settlement can certainly be transferred to the insurance claim brought by the insured against

44 Article 19: 'Where an insurance contract is concluded by way of standard forms provided by the insurer, the following terms shall be of no effect:
(1) terms that exclude the obligations of the insurer or increase the obligations of the assured or the insured; and
(2) terms that deprive the assured, insured or beneficiary of their legal rights.'

45 Article 30: 'With respect to an insurance contract entered into by adopting the standard clauses provided by the insurer, where a dispute between the insurer and the assured, the insured or the beneficiary arises from the understanding of a standard clause, the clause shall be interpreted in accordance with common sense. Where a standard clause has two or more interpretations, the people's court or arbitration institution shall interpret such a clause in favour of the insured and the beneficiary.'

the insurer. The case of *Haitian Hospital v PICC Guzhen Branch* mentioned in connection with the issue of notification requirement above is illustrative also on this issue.

The Court of First Instance held that, in regard to the claim submitted by the claimant, Haitian Hospital, against the defendant, PICC, seeking indemnification by the insurer for the damages determined in the underlying action, the defendant's contention was untenable that the insured should itself bear the part of the damages following from the court's mistaken application of the law. The court based its decision on the principle of *res judicata* and need for legal certainty and the finality of judgments. The court's decision was upheld by the Court of Second Instance.

There is no doubt that China's courts believe that matters determined by a legally effective judgment rendered by the People's Court trying the underlying case can be directly applied to the following liability insurance claim action, unless the insurer has successfully obtained some legal remedy against the judgment.

Leaving aside the application of the principle of *res judicata* and the availability of procedural remedies, the same facts may occasionally lead to different judgments in the underlying action and the following insurance action. Governing law may result in different interpretations of the same facts. In the underlying action brought by the third-party victim against the insured, the issues involved concern tort law, while in the insurance action brought by the insured against the insurer it usually involves contract law and insurance law. Therefore, an insured may assume liability to the third-party victim in accordance with tort law, and then fail to recover from the insurer in accordance with insurance law and contract law. The following case[46] illustrates this point.

In this case, the Shanghai Bar Association took out a Lawyers Professional Liability Insurance Contract with Ping An Property & Casualty Insurance Company of China, Ltd Shanghai Branch (hereinafter referred to as Ping An Company), covering the professional liability of all licensed lawyers registered in the Shanghai Bar Association. The contract stipulated that the insureds were all law firms who were members of the Shanghai Bar Association. The policy period was from 18 February 2004 to 18 February 2005, the retroactive date was 18 February 1998, and one of its exclusions was that the insurer would not be responsible for the economic losses of the client caused by a lawyer who privately accepted client business without the permission of the insured.

Jingye Law Firm was a registered member of the Shanghai Bar Association and an insured under the liability insurance contract. In September

46 *Shanghai Hongqiao Parking Company Limited v Ping An Property & Casualty Insurance Company of China, Ltd Shanghai Branch, Shanghai Municipality Second Intermediate People's Court*, (2007) Hu Er Zhong Min San (Shang) Zhong Zi No.195, 12 September 2007.

2002, Shanghai Hongqiao Parking Company Limited (hereinafter referred to as Hongqiao Company) signed a service contract with Zhuwei, a licensed lawyer of Jingye Law Firm, to bring an action over the matter of housing business affairs. Having receiving the fee and the relevant documents, Zhuwei failed to bring the action within the relevant time bar, thus causing loss for the Hongqiao Company. The company sued Zhuwei and Jingye Law Firm asking for compensation. The court gave judgment for the Hongqiao Company.

After the compulsory enforcement of the judgment, Jingye Law Firm filed an insurance claim with the Ping An Company to recover its losses, which was rejected on the ground that Zhuwei had accepted the case without the permission of the insured, thus bringing it within the scope of the exclusion clause and outside the scope of the liability of the insurer. Jingye Law sued the Ping An Company.

The Court of First Instance gave judgment in favour of Jingye Law Firm, holding that the matter could have been raised in the litigation between Hongqiao Parking and Jingye. Upon the insurer's appeal, the Court of Second Instance treated the matter as subject to the insurance policy and found that Zhuwei had indeed signed a lawyer service contract with Hongqiao Parking in the name of Jingye Law Firm without its consent. Indeed, he had not forwarded the fee paid by the client to the law firm, but had kept it for himself.

It also found that the main reason that Jingye Law Firm should assume the responsibility to the Hongqiao Company for Zhuwei's conduct was because Zhuwei signed the contract with Hongqiao Company in the name of Jingye Law Firm and the Hongqiao Company had justification to believe that Zhuwei was acting on behalf of Jingye Law Firm. In the underlying action, the judge had not made any finding as to whether Zhuwei had privately accepted the business, but had based his ruling on the theory of apparent authority. However, in the insurance action, the judge held that the case concerned a dispute involving an insurance claim, and should therefore be subject to the terms of the contract. According to the exclusion clause in the contract, Ping An Company had no liability to compensate the insured, Jingye Law Firm.

In this case, the Court of First Instance confused the insured's liability to the third party with the insurer's liability to the insured, thus making the wrong decision. But the Court of Second Instance correctly differentiated between these two legal relationships, understanding that these two liabilities were based on two different laws. The underlying action was based on the theory of apparent authority, while the insurance action was based on the exclusion clause of the insurance contract. Although the facts were the same, they lead to different legal consequences in the underlying action and the insurance claim action.

8 IP insurance in the Chinese legal climate

Dr Hua Li (Lena Todd)[1]

1 Greater awareness of intellectual property (IP) protection and risk of potential infringement

With the speedy growth of the economy in the past 30 years, Chinese companies have become more and more aware of the importance of IP protection, a growing awareness of intangible assets. They actively register their IP rights in China and the world. Statistics show that the State Intellectual Property Office granted 1.26 million patent applications in 2012, up 31.25 per cent from a year earlier. The number of trademark registration applications reached 1.42 million in 2012, a sharp rise from the 19,000 applications submitted in 1983, when the country's trademark law took effect. More than 845,000 publications were registered in China for copyright protection in 2013, up about 23 per cent year on year. The World Intellectual Property Organization said that China topped the world rankings for patent applications in 2013.[2]

Government policy also strengthens the importance of IP in the economy. China currently has four parliamentary IP laws and 19 regulations related to intellectual property rights protection, covering patents, trademarks, copyright and technical fields.[3] The government has passed several regulations to promote and improve patent quality to, and provide many policy benefits to IP companies.[4]

Facing the pressure of deteriorating environmental pollution, the Chinese government is attempting to transform its economic growth from rapid GDP driving to more care of the environment and sustainable economic growth with strong indigenous innovation capacity. The government has allocated

1 Hua Li, PhD, freelance researcher in IP law and Chinese litigation. Lihua94@gmail.com.
2 See: www.wipo.int/pressroom/en/articles/2013/article_0020.html (accessed 22 May 2014).
3 See the IP legislations and interpretations at: www.chinacourt.org/law.shtml (accessed 22 May 2014).
4 See 'New policies to favour hi-tech industry', available at: http://chinadaily.com.cn/china/index.html (accessed 22 May 2014).

special fiscal funding and has set a goal of making substantial progress in the creation, application, protection and management of IP by 2020.[5]

The Central government has encouraged banks to set up branches specialising in financial services for small and medium-sized enterprises, in particular expanding credit services for small technology enterprises by giving incentives to credit authorisers and applying tax exemptions. There is an IP evaluation agency in every province, which aims to pledge financing of IP by evaluating, registering and securing intellectual property rights. According to statistics, from 2008 to 2012, more than 1,869 trademarks were pledged against total lending of RMB 66.46 billion, RMB 21.46 billion of which were secured in 2012 alone. At the same time, in 2012, more than 146 copyrights covering 773 software products and works were authorised and lending of RMB 2.751 billion was pledged.[6]

Local governments also passed an attractive policy to encourage innovation and IP protection. The latest report from Shanghai's IP office shows that 357 local companies received nearly RMB 800 million in loans using patents and trademarks as collateral.[7] Medium-sized cities such as Nantong and Changzhou amended their Patent Subsidising Policy, so that a patent filed under the Patent Cooperation Treaty (PCT)[8] will be eligible for more subsidies than before. A company may be awarded with RMB 6,000 for a domestic patent application once it is approved. International patent filings will be subsidised with RMB 30,000. In addition, companies that manage their intellectual property rights successfully, and obtain patent advantages in business, will be commended with RMB 10,000–50,000.[9]

The sub-branch of the Bank of Communications in the city of Haimen introduced a financing pilot programme for small and medium-sized enterprises to secure assets-collateralised financing by pledging their intangible IP.[10] The Chanchen district of Foshan City, Guangzhou

5 See 'China's IP regime', available at: www.chinaipr.gov.cn/channel/policyindex.shtml (accessed 22 May 2014). In 2010, the OECD published its review of innovation for China on the expenditure of research and development for China, the world's third largest R&D performer. See: www.oecd-library.org (accessed 22 May 2014).

6 See 'How to register a pledged IP contract' and 'China further extends the scale of IP pledge financing', available at: www.chinaipr.gov.cn/policyarticle/policy/statistics/201304/1745671_1.html (accessed 22 May 2014).

7 See: http://service.shanghai.gov.cn/newdtbs/ComploxItems/InvestorComplox_224_236.html (accessed 22 May 2014).

8 Patent Cooperation Treaty 1970, as amended. China joined the PCT in 1993, which let patent applicants in China seek patent protection for an invention simultaneously in other countries by filing a single 'international' patent application, instead of filing several separate national or regional patent applications. See 'Provisions concerning the implementation of the Patent Cooperation Treaty in China', available at: http://english.sipo.gov.cn/laws/regulations (accessed 22 May 2014).

9 See: www.chinaipr.gov.cn/list/news/local/1/newscateinfo.html (accessed 22 May 2014).

10 See: www.china-insurance.com/baixing/newslist_news.asp?id=88631 (accessed 22 May 2014).

province, paid back to the insured companies in 2012 a total of RMB 1.44 million for infringement investigations of patent rights.[11]

Thus, Chinese companies are beginning to actively manage and exploit their IP rights to be converted into competitive products and services, to realise value from them. IP insurance itself also strengthens and ensures wider public access to IP, and the wider diffusion of key technologies, by identifying the right and helping prevent infringements. It is noticeable that more companies develop an IP strategy, to enter the world market using IP as an important medium. More than 600 Chinese manufacturers exhibited at the Las Vegas Consumer Electronics Show in 2012, and according to the Chinese Trade Office, more than 90 per cent of them have established US offices to protect their IP interests.[12] Since 2005, the EU has set up an IP working group with the Chinese government to provide funds and a framework to help European small and medium-sized businesses protect and enforce their intellectual property rights in China, and for Chinese companies and industry to understand trade-related technical issues in the EU.[13]

Most big Chinese companies including Lenovo Group Ltd, ZTE Corp. and Haier Group, Huawei, and the Bank of China have established European headquarters in France, Germany, the UK and other European countries. In particular, many small and medium-sized companies with IP sectors entering the media, technology, construction and car industries have also invested in Europe. According to figures presented at the 16th EU-China Summit in November 2013, the European Union and China are two of the biggest traders in the world. China is now the EU's second largest trading partner behind the United States and the EU is China's biggest trading partner.[14]

Naturally, the more exploited a right, the greater the added value it will produce, the more markets it will enter and the more issues related to IP rights will occur. Especially for IP as intangible property, the risk in using it is significant. Because of its intangible nature, infringement in respect of unauthorised use of intellectual property rights by a third party is very common indeed, by way of passing off and unfair competition. The pursuit of legal proceedings relating to an act of passing off or unfair competition committed by another party is also common in respect of intellectual property.

11 See: www.fszlbx.cn (accessed 22 May 2014).

12 See: www.chinaexhibition.com/china_trade_shows_list_by_industries.html (accessed 22 May 2014).

13 European Commission, 'Bilateral interactions with China', available at: http://trade.ec.europa.eu/doclib/docs/2013/april/tradoc_150992.pdf (accessed 22 May 2014).

14 See: http://ec.europa.eu/trade/policy/countries-and-regions/countries/china/ (accessed 22 May 2014).

IP owners find that their patents and rights are being used by others, and at the same time they are facing actions from third parties for IP infringement when they attend international exhibitions or shows, or sell goods outside China. One example is that in early 2003, Huawei, a leading telecom company, was sued by another world leading networking manufacturer, Cisco Systems, for infringing its patents and illegally copying source code used in its routers and switches. The case was settled with Huawei voluntarily withdrawing the products from the market.

2 Insurance helps IP protection and innovation

IP insurance is introduced to decrease the above risk and uncertainty around IP exploitation. The designed purpose is for IP companies to enter into a contract with an insurance company that will pay the specific loss to the IP companies, when the insured risk happens, so the IP owners or users can continue their business. Basically, IP insurance is treated like normal property insurance against any risk happening in exploiting IP. IP insurance may cover legal costs in investigation, litigation, other expenses and damages, and even business losses. In turn, it plays a role as a deterrent to potential infringers. Insured IP is not merely intangible property, it is a practical, warranted asset for a company in which to invest, that may be pledged in business transactions and that may make the business more attractive to potential investors. IP insurance can reassure funding from individuals, financial institutions and venture capitalists in respect of exploitation activity or research and development (R&D) contracts.[15]

China's first insurance product for copyright trading was unveiled in Beijing in 2006, jointly developed by Cinda Property & Casualty Insurance Ltd and the Beijing Oriental Yonghe International Copyright Trade Centre. The insurance was designed for copyright transactions. Under this insurance contract, if policyholders were defrauded by a fake copyright and then had claims filed against them by copyright owners, the insurance firm would offer a fixed royalty to them for the loss due to copyright infringement, as well as legal fees. Internet service companies including Sina, Youku and Ku6 were among the first to take out policies. Leading copyright users such as Huayi Brothers Media, copyright owner of a series of well-known Chinese movies, also use copyright insurance.[16]

15 See International Chamber of Commerce (ICC) and World Intellectual Property Organization (WIPO), 'Making intellectual property work for business', available at: www.wipo.int/export/sites/www/freepublications/en/intproperty/956/wipo_pub_956.pdf (accessed 22 May 2014).

16 See 'China's insurance industry faces six big challenges', available at: www.china-insurance.com/ (accessed 22 May 2014).

Pilot cities to carry out insurance innovation work were designated in 2007.[17] The main focus of insurance of IP in China is currently on patents. Insurance companies have mostly provided patent infringement insurance covering pursuit of infringers, pursuit of a Contracting Party for breach of a licensed agreement, and pursuit of a third-party action. Others also cover defence of infringement, defence of breach of agreement, defence of third-party action including legal fees, court fees, and investigation fees and other direct losses. The sub-branch of Life Insurance of China in the city of Handan has offered patent infringement insurance covering case investigation and legal fees of about RMB 20,000 in a year. The premium ranges from RMB 2,000 to RMB 5,000.[18]

Not all policies will be suitable for all companies. Companies can choose a suitable insurance policy to cover their specific need and liability based on their size, business activity and geographical location. Most insurance covers the costs of being sued or pursuing an infringer, or legal fees. Until now, no company offers IP insurance covering IP enforcement, or revenue warranties, or outcome quality guarantees. In China, most insurance is now taken on 'opinion-only' terms; there is no policy to insure against losing the case and having to pay the legal costs and compensation of the other party. There are many causes and market factors that may affect an insurance policy.[19] This chapter explores IP cases to analyse the effect that the Chinese IP litigation has had on the insurance companies and clients in drafting the insurance policy to cover damage or profit.

IP litigation in China makes it risky for insurance companies to offer such cover, because they simply cannot, based on past cases, predict in which situation a litigant has a good chance of winning. In the following, the author will seek to analyse why IP litigation may block an insurance company from offering such a policy.

3 IP litigation is an arbitrary exercise of discretion rather than rule-based

Chinese judges are not required in trial, before making decisions, to inform the parties what criteria or view they would adopt towards a specific issue, or to tell the parties which factors are relevant or irrelevant, based on the balance of probability. They can arbitrarily, without giving notice or

17 See: www.chinaipr.gov.cn/list/news/local/1/newscateinfo.html (accessed 22 May 2014).

18 See: http://hebei.hebnews.cn/2013-07/09/content_3345193.htm (accessed on 22 May 2014).

19 See Xue Qi, Shuangli Shen and Mingqiang Li, 'Preliminary studies of intellectual property insurance', *Insurance Studies*, 2006, vol. 7, 28. See also D. Syrowik, 'Insurance coverage for software-related patent and other intellectual property disputes', 1996, *Michigan Bar Journal*.

consulting both sides, make adjudication beyond the argued issues, or while ignoring some facts in the proceedings.

Because of the significant costs in money and time and the uncertainty of result, IP litigation should naturally be a measure of last resort for IP parties, but the number of IP disputes steadily rises each year in Chinese courts. In 2011, local courts at all levels across the country received 59,612 new IP-related civil cases and concluded the trials of 58,201 cases, up by 38.86 per cent and 39.51 per cent, respectively, from the previous year; a total of 1,137 cases of unfair competition were filed with courts.[20] The number of intellectual property rights cases marked a 42 per cent rise year on year, exceeding 50,000 for the first time. Rising numbers of IP cases reflect booming IP economic activities, but also remind us to look at what guidance the IP litigation in China has given to economic activity.

Let us start from some recently occurring trademark cases to analyse judicial opinion in China. There has been a significant amount of litigation about what the obligations are for online service providers when a claim is that a seller is trying to pass off counterfeit goods as originals on the internet.

Taobao.com is the biggest e-commerce website in China; it is mainly engaged in platform providing rather than doing the business itself. Therefore, all the products sold on it belong to third parties. Taobao, like eBay, Amazon and other online service providers, provides a 'take-down' notice that a trademark owner or product provider can submit if they find an infringement or a counterfeit item being sold on its auction site by an unauthorised third party.

Under section 57 of the Chinese Trademark Law, as well as Article 50(2) of the implementing rules, if an internet user commits infringement through an internet service, the victim of the tort shall be entitled to notify the internet service provider to take such necessary measures as deletion, blocking or disconnection. If, after being notified, the internet service provider fails to take necessary measures in a timely manner, it shall be jointly and severally liable for any additional harm together with the internet user. Essentially, the Trademark Law requires online companies and service providers, just as they would with on-street shops, to take necessary steps to monitor the activities of their internet users.[21] The difficulty lies in how to evaluate whether the ISP (internet service provider) has taken necessary measures to block online IP infringement.

In *Yinian Fashion Ltd v Duguo Fan and Taobao.com*[22] (case one), the claimant argued that clothes with cartoon bears, sold by the defendant on

20 See SPC spokesman Sun Jungong's speech at a press conference held by the SPC in the city of Suzhou in east China's Jiangsu province, available at: www.fszlbx.cn (accessed 22 May 2014).

21 See Chapter 7 of Chinese Trademark Law of China 2013.

22 The Judgment No. 52 (2011) Yangminsan (zhi) Chuzi, available at: www.china.com.cn/guoqing/zwxx/2012-03/23/content_24970937.htm. 衣念(上海)时装贸易有限公司诉浙江淘宝网络有限公司、杜国发侵害商标权纠纷

Taobao.com, were very similar to its clothes and infringed its registered trademark. The claimant requested Taobao to delete the infringing advertisement on the website made by the defendant. Taobao deleted the infringing information after the claimant's seventh warning notice. The claimant sought damages for joint liability for its losses. Yangpu District Court of Shanghai upheld the claimant's claim, and the final judgment held that Taobao should have deleted the infringing ads promptly and that it should pay joint duty for the consequential losses of the claimant of about RMB 10,000. But the decision had ignored one fact, which Taobao advanced in its defence, as to why it took nearly one month to delete the ads; some infringing products were illustrated with a poor-quality picture, and time was needed, they argued, to communicate and to confirm that the described goods were indeed those claimed by the trademark owner.[23] Without reasoning as to what was wrong with Taobao's conduct, or what Taobao should have done, it was an arbitrary exercise to say that Taobao should have deleted the infringing advertisements promptly.

In *Fangnaier Guangzhou v Liu and Taobao.com*[24] (case two), the plaintiff claimed that the clothes sold on Taobao.com were fake Fangnaier, and that its brand name, 'TEENIEWEENIE, E-LAND', was infringed by the defendant and Taobao. After receiving the complaint, Taobao deleted the advertisement, but a week later similar pictures were to be found on its website. The plaintiff argued that Taobao should shut down the account to stop the infringement once finding the continued infringement after the first information deletion. Taobao had fuelled the infringement and this constituted an aid in infringement. But No 3 Wuhan Court held that Taobao had quickly deleted the infringing advertisement and that no further loss or damage was caused to the plaintiff, so there was no infringement.

In *Beijing Financing Adviser Ltd v Channa and Taobao.com*[25] (case three), the defendant sold pirated e-books of a share-dealing training course, edited by the claimant company on Taobao.com. Haidian District Court held that Taobao was jointly liable with the defendant for the claimant's damage, but Taobao defended on the basis that it had quickly deleted the infringing web link after receiving the complaints from the plaintiff, and Taobao had no duty and ability to check that the e-books sold by the defendant were the same as the claimant's, especially given that there were many similar advertisements on its website. But the Beijing court stressed that the claimant

23 Quote from the defendant part in the final judgment.

24 Available at: www.hubeigy.chinacourt.org/public/detail.php?id=21325 (accessed 25 May 2014). (广州芳奈儿诉淘宝网、武汉四皇冠淘宝店商标侵权纠纷.)

25 The Judgment No 1614 (2010) Haiminchuzi, available at: www.china.com.cn/guoqing/zwxx/2012-03/23/content_24970937.htm (accessed 25 May 2014). 知钱（北京 ）理财顾问有限公司诉 王超，浙江淘宝 网络 有限公司侵犯 著作权纠纷案 .

had done a great deal of work and investment into this book, and Taobao had only deleted the infringing link after several notices. The deletion had not been quick enough and they should therefore pay RMB 20,000 to the plaintiff.

It is difficult to discern a consistent rule behind these cases. There was no clarified rule or reasoning to let us understand what a Chinese judge would rely on to decide whether an internet service company had been aware of the illicit nature of specific information, and nevertheless did not remove links to it. What is then the starting ground and base to test whether an e-commerce business, such as Taobao, has taken necessary measures, in a timely manner, in a specific case, to ensure that it has done its part efficiently?

These three decisions all stressed the importance of prompt deletion or removal of the illegal activities after receiving a general complaint, or after becoming aware of a genuine infringement. But the situations in the three cases were quite different. In case one, the image presented by the claimant was too blurred for Taobao to identify the infringing goods. Case two concerned continuous material misrepresentation of an infringing activity. In case three, there were many such advertisements for sale without a franchised licence. The distribution of an e-book is not like the sale of physical goods, where a brand owner cannot restrict downstream resale of its goods once an initial authorised sale is made. Instead, for a copyrighted e-book, the copyright owner has exclusive rights for distribution of copies. Without showing an authorisation licence, all resale is illegal. Under section 48 of the Copyright Act, the online distributor is liable for secondary infringement based on what it knew, or should have known, of the infringement. It is therefore not necessarily the case that timely deletion is really the main factor for the Chinese judges who made these decisions. But the judgments in all these cases used the same ground (timely deletion of infringing ads) to support or disprove Taobao's conduct. None of them can persuade us to agree with such adjudication, based on one week being prompt and one month not quick enough. Without justifying that there is more than one cause of delay of deletion, we just cannot arrive at a 'more likely than not' proof standard, like the Chinese judge did.

Judicial decisions usually serve as a model in shaping the code of conduct, especially in emerging industries such as the internet business. The digital age has created substantial new opportunities for creative content, and substantial challenges for trademark law and copyright law. Chinese courts do not need to follow or distinguish what rules and experience have built up in the specific field, not to mention following, referencing or deviating from these decided rules. Even basic rules may frequently be disregarded without good reason. Such uncertainty and inconsistency in the application of codified law becomes a deterrent rather than a promoter for IP insurance policy.

In *Starbucks Corporation and United Starbucks Coffee Shanghai Co. Ltd v Shanghai Starbuck Co. Ltd*[26] both sides engaged in a soft drinking coffee service. The claimants first registered the 'STARBUCKS' trademark in the US in 1985, and later the 'STARBUCKS' trademark series were registered in more than 120 countries and gained prestige around the world. The 'STARBUCKS' trademark was registered on the Chinese Mainland in 1996, but its Chinese word mark '星巴克', was first registered in Chinese Taiwan in February 1999 and was recognised as a 'well-known' mark. In December 1999, the '星巴克' trademark was approved for registration in China by Starbucks Corporation under Class 42. It developed business by franchising and advertising use of the '星巴克' trademark in the Chinese-speaking regions, and was familiar to the public of the mainland in large cities such as Beijing, Shanghai and Shenzhen.

The claimants (Starbucks) claimed that the defendants' usage of '星巴克' either as a coffee cup logo or as the shortened enterprise name in business activities constituted trademark infringement and unfair competition. They further argued that the 'STARBUCKS' (Class 42) and '星巴克' (Class 42) trademarks should be treated as well-known trademarks and enjoy a higher protection than a normal trademark, due to the international prestige of the 'STARBUCKS' trademark series. Further, the claimants' advertising and use of the '星巴克' trademark in the Chinese-speaking regions was earlier than the defendant's right to its enterprise name, and thus the claimants were entitled to prior rights. The trademark series of 'STARBUCKS' as an entirety should not be split by time and territory from mainland China to Taiwan and Hong Kong.[27]

The defendant, Shanghai Starbuck, was pre-approved and set up in October 1999 and began a coffee business in March 2000 mainly in the Shanghai market. The defendants argued that in terms of the time of authorisation its right to the enterprise name was prior to the claimants' trademark rights. The registered '星巴克' trademark and the registered 'STARBUCKS' trademark should be independent from each other in different registration areas, and the reputation established in another area was irrelevant to the present case. It was unfair to use its reputation in another market as a standard to prove its well-known reputation in the Chinese market. According to the Implementation Measures for the Registration and Administration of Enterprise Names, an enterprise is entitled, as of the date of establishment, to enjoy the rights to the name, using it in its business activity within its scope.[28]

26 (2004) Hu'erzhongminwu (Zhi) Chuzi No. 1 (first trial). (2006) Hugaominsan (Zhi) Zhongzi No. 32 (final judgment). 上海统一星巴克咖啡有限公司诉上海星巴克咖啡馆有限公司 (2006) 沪高民三（知）终字第32号.

27 Reference to the statement of facts from the claimant.

28 Starbucks Corporation, see the statement from the defendant.

The trial court and the High Court both held that Starbucks Corporation had been the first to use the characters '星巴克' in Chinese Taiwan on 1 February 1999, and that the defendant, Shanghai Starbucks, should have been fully aware of the fact that the 'STARBUCKS' and '星巴克' trademarks enjoyed a strong reputation in the same industry in the world. It was difficult to believe that the defendant's use of the Chinese characters '星巴克' for 'Starbucks' was merely due to a coincidence of originality.

The courts held that Shanghai Starbuck had subjective malice in registering the Chinese characters '星巴克' as the trade name for its enterprise. Shanghai Starbuck's conduct fell under section (5) of the Trademark Law (i.e. 'causing other damage to another's right to the exclusive use of the registered trademark'),[29] violated the principles of fairness, honesty and good faith for civil activities and infringed Starbucks Corporation's right to the exclusive use of 'STARBUCKS' and '星巴克'. The defendant's business name registration had obvious malice, and caused the public to misidentify or misunderstand the trademark registrant and the enterprise name owner, and constituted unfair competition against Starbucks Corporation.[30]

From the findings of fact and the reasoning regarding the reputation earned by the claimant, it is clear that the Shanghai courts considered a mark's reputation based not only on the local market, but also on the whole of the Chinese-speaking market, as well as the international market. From this judgment, we may also infer a rule that rushing registration of a Chinese mark translated from a well-known brand name will be regarded as a malicious registration, and therefore is invalid.

But in the following cases, where the same issues arose as to how to evaluate a company reputation and how to identify a Chinese word mark translated from a well-known world brand name, Beijing courts have not shown any concern for consistency with the above case of *Starbucks Corporation v Shanghai Starbuck*. It is noteworthy that the judgment in the case of 'STARBUCKS' and '星巴克' was included in the Supreme Court Annual Report of complex and typical IPR protection as a good example of Chinese progress in IPR protection.[31]

In *Pfizer Products v Lian Huan Medicine, Wireman Company and Others*,[32] the claimants sought to split the argument around a registered shape mark into two cases to resolve the overlapping claims.

29 Article 52(5), Trademark Law of China 2001; this article is revised by Article 57 of the Trademark Law of China 2013.

30 See the identified and confirmed facts in the judgment.

31 See Annual Legal Report from the Supreme Court of China, 2008–2011, available at: www.court.gov.cn (accessed 22 May 2014).

32 (2007) Higher Court of Beijing, Gaominzhongzi No. 1684, 1687, 辉瑞产品有限公司 v. 广州威尔曼药业, 江苏联环药业, 北京健康新概念大药房. (2007) 高民终字第 1684 号. (2007) 高民终字第 1687 号.

The background was that the plaintiffs registered a shape trademark with an English brand name 'Viagra' on a drug for erectile dysfunction in China, and sold their products in the Chinese market with an unregistered Chinese trademark, '伟哥' or '万艾可'. In 2005, they found that the defendants produced the same shape drug with Chinese words '伟哥'. The claimants sued the defendants for infringing the registered trademark rights on its three-dimensional blue rhombus-shaped trademark, claiming that the first defendant (Lian Huan Medicine) and the second defendant (Wireman Company) had illegally produced the same shape of products, and that the third defendant (Xing Gainian Pharmacy) had illegally sold such infringing products. The two claimants claimed in another separate case that the defendants' acts also constituted unfair competition and infringement of its unregistered well-known Chinese trademark '伟哥'. Its Chinese word mark, '伟哥', was first introduced and advertised in Taiwan and Hong Kong and was recognised as a 'well-known' trademark. The defendant maliciously tried to register it and used it on the same shape product as the claimant's, which caused confusion to the customers and damaged its good reputation in the same kind of drug market. The claimants sought an order requiring the three defendants to stop producing or selling the illegal product, to destroy all products in stock and the production model, and to pay damages of RMB 50,000.

The claimants (Pfizer) filed two separate cases successively in 2005[33] against the three defendants for registered trademark infringement in Judgment No. 11350 and unregistered trademark infringement and unfair-competition in Judgment No. 11351. Their argument was that in 2003, they had obtained a three-dimensional blue rhombus-shaped registered trademark, with the brand name 'Viagra', as a pharmaceutical product in category 5. In 2005, they found that the third defendant had sold a drug in the form of a pill of the same shape and colour, produced by the first defendant (Lian Huan), while the brand name 'Weige 伟哥' and '(™)' sign on the drug package and on the pill were licensed by the second defendant (Wireman). The claimants also found their three-dimensional blue rhombus-shaped trademark, together with the sign 'Weige 伟哥' and '(™)', occurring prominently on the second defendant's website and advertising brochure. The claimant provided seven newspaper articles and documentary evidence of drug sales in foreign and Chinese markets to prove that their unregistered Chinese trademark '伟哥' and the brand name 'Viagra', along with the special registered three-dimensional blue rhombus-

33 For the first trial judgments, see *Pfizer Products Inc. & Pfizer Pharmaceutical Chemistry v WireMan Pharmaceutical Chemistry, Xinggai Nian Pharmacy, and Lian Huan Pharmaceutical Chemistry* (2005) No. 11350, No. 11351, the first trial judgment of the First Intermediate Civil Court of Beijing. 辉瑞产品有限公司 v. 广州威尔曼药业, 江苏联环药业, 北京健康新概念大药房. 北京市第一中级人民法院民事判决书 (2005)一中民初字 第 11350号. 一中民初字第11351号.

shaped trademark, had been well known in China, Hong Kong and Taiwan.[34]

The key defendants (Lian Huan and Wireman) contended that the claimant's three-dimensional trademark had no distinctive character, and the registered mark should be revoked because of lack of distinctive character.[35] They had applied to the Administrative Bureau for revocation of the registration and applied to the court for a stay, pending the revocation result. They also argued that Judgment No. 11351 was a repetition of Judgment No. 11350, concerning the same period undertakings between the same litigants. The defendants argued that filing this case broke the principle of *lis pendens* and the principle of 'one loss one remedy' (against repetitive litigation). They requested the striking out of this repeat litigation. In the hearing of Judgment No. 11351, the defendants especially stressed a public notice in a newspaper from Pfizer's lawyer, which declared that 'Viagra' was the registered trademark, and that its Chinese name was also once used, '万艾可', owned by Pfizer Products Inc. The second defendant contended that in 1998 he had applied to the Registrar for the trademark 'Weige 伟哥' in medicine, and that in 2002 its application had entered into opposition procedure pending final declaration. Therefore, they were legally using their mark pending registration as 'Weige 伟哥 and (™)'. The third defendant (Xinggai Nian) contended that it had no duty to pay any damages to the claimants. He argued that he bought it from a proper high street shop and that the shop receipt should prove that he did not know they were an infringing medicine.[36]

In the first proceedings, leading to Judgment No. 11351, the judge at first instance supported the claimant and gave compensation for the effects of the infringement in the amount of RMB 30,000. He also issued an injunction against the three defendants, requiring them to stop producing and selling infringing products.[37] In Judgment No. 11351, the First Instance Court held that the defendants had infringed the claimant's unregistered mark and that their actions amounted to unfair competition, on the basis that 'Viagra' and 'three-dimensional blue rhombus-shaped trademark' were well known, and that the defendant's use caused confusion among consumers, leading to their failure to recognise the original genuine drugs of the claimant. But in Judgment No. 11350, the same court with a different

34 Reference to the statement of facts from the plaintiff in the first litigation No. 11351 and No. 11541 (second trial judgment).

35 The first defendant provided several other medicine products from other factories with a similar three-dimensional shape to prove that the plaintiff's registration lacked distinctiveness.

36 See the statement of facts from the defendants in the first trial No. 11351, and No. 11541 (second trial judgment).

37 See *Pfizer Products Inc. & Pfizer Pharmaceutical Chemistry* (2005) Yizhongminchizi No. 11351.

judge took the view that the defendants did not infringe the claimant's rights to a registered or unregistered mark and that their actions were not unfair competition. Both cases were appealed to the Higher Court, which approved in Judgment No. 11350, but reversed the first instance Judgment No. 11351.

Comparing these judgments, in the first instance Judgment No. 11351, the judge did not mention the evidence handed in by the defendant and a warning notice to the public against fake 'Viagra' in newspapers from Pfizer's lawyer. But in Judgment No. 11350, the same court clearly used this lawyer's notice as the main evidence to support its decision on the issue of the Chinese word '伟哥', or '艾哥尔' as the translation of 'Viagra'.

The Higher Court of Beijing also reversed Judgment No. 11541 and affirmed the other first instance judgments on the following grounds. First, registration rights were separate in each independent legal area. The success of the registration of 'Weige 伟哥' in Taiwan and Hong Kong did not guarantee its recognition in the mainland of China, because each company was a separate independent entity in each of these regions. Second, it held that 'Viagra' was an English word mark and it had been translated by the media into several Chinese words: '偉哥', '威哥尔', '伟哥' and '艾哥尔'. There was no direct existing recognition between 'Viagra' and '伟哥'. The official anti-forgery action was intended to protect genuine 'Viagra' products in the Chinese market, not to prove its Chinese name, especially as the claimant had confirmed its Chinese name through its lawyer's notice in a newspaper. The defendant's actions did not amount to unfair competition because the defendant's product package, the blue shape drug pill also had clear marks 'Weige 伟哥' and '(™)' on the surface, and could not be confused by customers with the claimant's blue shape and 'Viagra' mark.[38]

On appeal, the respondent argued that the First Instance Court had not sufficiently considered whether its mark was a well-known unregistered trademark in China. The court did not properly consider its goodwill abroad and did not consider its registration in Hong Kong and Taiwan, nor the arguments that the defendant's action amounted to malicious registration and bad faith in business against competition law in 'a manner contrary to honest commercial practices' and against prior use.[39]

As to the failure to make a decision regarding whether the claimant's mark was well known or not, the Higher Court of Beijing held that the claimant did not formally use the Chinese mark '伟哥' in its products except in media articles, and was unable to provide any evidence to prove that the mark '伟哥' was a well-known trademark abroad. Indeed, it is difficult to see how a Chinese character mark could become well known in other countries. It is unpersuasive to interpret separately the claimants' business reputation

38 See the final judgment, No. 1687 and 1684.
39 See the fact statements from the plaintiff in Judgment No. 11541.

and consumers' confusion on 'Viagra' in the Chinese market and abroad. Based on 'Viagra' sales abroad and in China, its specific shape and colour, the official administrative anti-faking action in China and the warning notice to the public against the faked drug etc., there was a strong implication that the defendants would try their best to copy the claimant's drug to create a direct association that their drug had the same quality as 'Viagra' for erectile dysfunction. The defendants' action was highly likely to cause confusion among consumers about the originality of the genuine drug, and further presented a high risk to public safety.

The reasoning in the present case is in opposition to the judicial recognition and interpretation of the Shanghai Higher Court in 'STARBUCKS' and '星巴克'. Without referring to precedent or inferring any confirmed rules and authority, Beijing courts declared that the business reputation should be limited to its registered area; the hurried registration of a Chinese word mark, translated from another company's globally well-known brand name, was legal and not malicious, unless the Chinese name was also used and well-known abroad.[40]

The prior decision in *Starbucks* covers the same ground as in *Pfizer*. The only difference from Starbucks is how to evaluate the argument that Pfizer had also used '万艾可', not just '伟哥', as its Chinese translation name in business promotion. The Beijing first instance and appeals courts did not answer this question in their judgments, but based their decisions on a different line of reasoning. The courts in China have done little to compel themselves to apply substantial IPR law coherently and consistently. Here also is reflected the design of the Chinese court system, which is not geared towards maintaining a coherent application of law.[41]

Without a precedent rule to ensure consistency in the application of the law, Chinese legal decisions not only cause chaos and give rise to conflicting outcomes resulting from similar cases, but have also lost a chance to gradually develop and enrich the understanding of the statute law on a case-by-case basis as in the UK. For example, a good foundation for answering questions of similarity and confusion in a trademark is provided by section

40 See the final judgment, No. 1687 and 1684.

41 In the UK, the first instance court deals with the exposition of both facts and law, while the appellate court focuses its discussion and analysis of the relevant law based on the findings by the first instance judge. In China, the roles of First Instance and Appellate Courts are repetitive and overlap; both not only find facts, but also offer statements of applicable law. There is no clear distinction between the First Instance Court and the Appellate Court; indeed, the appeal proceedings often take the form of a complete rehearing. This produces an obvious result: findings of fact are not detailed enough at first instance, and interpretation and reasoning of law is no deeper, wider nor necessarily consistent in the Appellate Court. Reading judgments from Chinese Appellate Courts, one can easily find new facts and findings, accepted upon appeal, which were not even mentioned at first instance.

52 of the Trademarks Act itself and by Article 11 of the Supreme Court Judicial Interpretation,[42] but after reading the judgments on trademark infringement and passing off, it is still unclear what would constitute an infringement through the use of a similar trademark in China. Existing judgments do not permit safe conclusions to be made on the interrelationship between the facts of an individual case and the applicable law. The judgments reiterate the provision as follows: 'the defendant uses similar marks on similar goods; such use would cause general consumers to make wrong associations or misunderstanding, consequently bringing harm to the plaintiff's right to exclusively use the trademark'.[43]

4 Application of IP law is by declaration rather than by clarification

Chinese courts do not arrange a case management stage for litigants and lawyers to argue about or check the applicable law and its applicable conditions. This gives the impression that Chinese IP law must have been structured to cover every detail and to be context-sensitive, with each section pointing to a specific condition, and that therefore there is no need for Chinese courts to undertake any discussion or examination. But when reading the argued issue and the reasoning of behind the application of the law in individual cases, the impression is often that the legislation lacks clarity, especially on the process of interpretation and coherent consideration of relevant factors involved.

In *Blue Lotus Culture Company v Blue Lotus Food Company*,[44] the claimant brought an action against the defendant for trademark infringement and unfair competition in 2006. The claimant's case was that in 2002, he had registered 'Blue Lotus' as a trademark in pub service. The defendant maliciously used the trademark in his shop window and the business logo,

42 'Similar goods' under the Chinese Trademark Law 2013 means goods that have identical functions, uses, production entities, sales channels, target consumers, etc., or goods that would normally be considered to have a certain connection and thus easily cause confusion. 'Similar services' means services whose purpose, content, methods of provision, target users, etc. are identical or services that would normally be considered to have a certain connection and thus easily cause confusion.
'Similar goods and services' means that a certain connection exists between the goods and services that could easily cause confusion.

43 See the conflicting judgments in the following cases: *Blue Lotus Culture Company v Blue Lotus Food Company*; *Lacoste Ltd v Crocodile Internation PTE Ltd*; *The Forge Plant of Jiahe County v Huaguang Machinery Ltd*; *Li Huiyan v Wanjiang Co. of Dalian*; *Weiyada Pen of Ningbo v Chenguang Stationery*; *Qingdao Hisense Electronic Co. v Qingdao Hisense Computer Co. (2007)*; *Neimengu Mengniu Diary Group Co. v Neimengu Wine Co.*; and *Dellinternational Ltd v DELL International English of Beijing*.

44 *Blue Lotus Culture Company v Blue Lotus Food Company* (2006) Yizhongminchuzi No. 11273, decided by the No. 1 Intermediate People's Court of Beijing. 北京蓝莲花文化艺术有限责任公司 诉北京兰莲花坊餐饮有限公司.

which caused confusion among consumers as to whether they belonged to the same company. The defendant applied to the court to strike out the claimant's claim on grounds of legal finality and issue estoppel. He contended that in 2003 he had registered 'Blue Lotus' as part of his company name and had a legal right to use this mark; in particular, in 2004, the court had tried the dispute regarding 'Blue Lotus' between them, and the defendant had paid RMB 20,000 to the claimant according to the final judgment, on ground of misuse of 'Blue Lotus' in its business service. Therefore, according to the doctrine of legal finality, one issue could not be tried twice, enabling the claimant to get damages twice for one loss, so the court should strike out the claimant's second suit about the same issue.[45]

After setting out the definition of 'same issue', that 'the same claimant brings more than one suit subsequently against the same defendant, about the same facts with the same grounds', the judge refused the defendant's contention and held that the judgment in 2004 had only confirmed that a trademark infringement existed in the service brochures and menu, and did not judge whether there was infringement in respect of the business logo, shop windows and awning. In particular, he held that the 2004 judgment had not resolved the confusion caused by the defendant's misuse of its company name 'Blue Lotus'. Therefore, the judgment could not have binding effect on the second set of proceedings, and there was no *res judicata* to bar the issue in the second suit, because they pertained to different issues with different facts (regarding the logo, the windows and the yellow book). In the second litigation in 2006, the judge held that the claimant had obtained his trademark right prior to the defendant's company name right, and that the defendant had prominently used the similar part in his company name in service and caused confusion among customers, thereby breaking competition law rules. In the end, the judge in the second litigation issued an injunction prohibiting the defendant from using 'Blue Lotus' as a company name and in all business advertisements, whether in a menu or logo.[46] The defendant paid the litigation costs and damages twice (respectively, RMB 20,000 and RMB 50,000) for the same loss (passing off and trademark infringement).

In neither judgment is it explained whether the defendant used the claimant's mark simultaneously or subsequently in service brochures, menu, business logo, shop windows or awning before or after 2004 (the first litigation). It is difficult to see how the judge in the second proceedings could have imagined that the effect of trademark confusion or infringement was only caused by the logo and window display, without considering the factors of the menu and brochure. It is also difficult to imagine how the

45 Reference to the statement of facts from the claimant and the defendant.

46 See the identified and confirmed facts by the trial judge, and the applied statutes and legal issues addressed by the Trial and Appellate Court.

compensation could have been calculated in the first litigation without consideration of all relevant business circumstances, including damages in respect of the window display. Could it really be that Chinese judges regard business reputation and goodwill separately from the logo and other physical aspects of the above activity? Could the injunction judgment in the first suit have only barred the defendant from using 'Blue Lotus' in some but not all aspects of its business promotion in food service?

After reading this judgment, one has to wonder whether some Chinese judges recognise legal finality at all. To say the least, even if the judge regarded the service brochures and menu, business logo, shop windows and awning as newly occurring acts after the first trial, on subsequent grounds for passing off, he should first examine whether the subsequent evidence existed at the earlier stage or had been discovered after the first proceedings. If the subsequent evidence had been available during the first proceedings, and the claimant deliberately separated the infringing acts into two cases, the second proceedings should be barred by *res judicata*, because they are in fact the same cause of action.

In a similar situation, the need for legal finality was given proper consideration in *Huangxin v Shanghai Agva Culture Company and Fortune Supermarket*.[47] In this case, the claimant sued the defendants for infringement of the trademark 'Agva', registered in 2005 for electronics, in category 20. It was argued that the first defendant had used the claimant's trademark on a similar product, and that the second defendant had sold the infringing product in a main street shop. He sought an injunction preventing further infringement, and damages of RMB 50,000 from both defendants. The first defendant contended that he had obtained licence rights from a third party (Jingshen Leather Factory), and used its trademark, registered in 1999 in category 18. The defendant applied for revocation of the claimant's trademark on grounds of invalidity, but failed. The judge held that the first defendant had infringed the claimant's trademark rights and ordered payment of damages of RMB 10,000 to the claimant. In 2006, the same claimant sued the same two defendants again for trademark infringement in a local district court. He claimed that the second defendant should be jointly liable with the first defendant for infringement of his mark, damages being RMB 15,000.

In these second proceedings, the judge held that the disputed issues were identical to those in the first proceedings, and struck out his claims based on *res judicata* and issue estoppel.[48]

47 *Huangxin v Shanghai Agva Culture Company and Fortune Supermarket* (2005) Erzhongminchuzi No. 11073, decided by No. 2 Intermediate People's Court of Beijing (2005). 黄欣诉被告上海艾歌华文化用品公司. (2005) 二中民初字第11073号.

48 *Huangxin v Shanghai Agva Culture Company and Fortune Supermarket* (2006) Chaominchuzi No. 6708, decided by People's Court of Chaoyang District, Beijing.

There is no doubt that the facts of the second litigation were the same as the first. The claimant should not have been permitted to initiate the second proceedings, harassing the defendant and wasting legal resources. But Chinese courts are not obliged to inform the parties to a case of their understanding of the IP law issues involved in the case or to distinguish other cases on their facts, which creates an assumption that Chinese judges might have the same or similar views on how to apply the law in different cases. But when we put together all these similar argued issues and compare the judicial decisions, the impression is overwhelming that Chinese judges must have had dissimilar views towards the applied law to reach such different conclusions. If they had the same or similar views toward *res judicata* and issue estoppel, the conclusions reached on the matters at issue would have been different.

5 IP insurance reform of adjudication

Litigations such as these convey the impression that the deeper pocket or the party with powerful backing will be poised to win. Legal proceedings should result in the final determination of disputes, not only in terms of natural justice and transparent procedure, but also the acceptance of the public and its belief in the rule of law. Chinese IP litigation has not arrived at such a level as to earn the public's trust. The general public, as well as the parties to individual disputes alike, still frequently feel judicial discretion to be biased, arbitrary, inconsistent and partly closed and isolated, and are unable to guide their business and practice accordingly. Such judicial risks for IP insurance are even worse than disputes over car accidents, which are to some extent controlled by random events. Judicial risk in China is man-made and controlled by arbitrary power, which makes it impossible for insurance participants to establish a solid reference to fix premiums. IP litigation in China makes it risky for insurance companies to offer cover, simply because they cannot, based on the framework of past cases, predict whether a party has a good chance of winning. If the arbitrary discretion makes it impossible for insurance underwriters to predict compensation based on the likely outcome of the proceedings, how can the parties determine a fair premium to invest and fund in advance? In the end, legal enforcement of private rights and contracts is becoming an increasingly relevant sticking point in the Chinese insurance market.

Reading Chinese judgments on IP matters, we strongly feel that Chinese judgments are far behind the development of its economy and the complexity of its society. Judicial opinion still relies heavily on an authoritative power to declare wrong or right, infringement or non-infringement. Adjudication by such methods becomes increasingly inadequate to meet the challenges and complexities of a multifaceted society. The only certain method for a litigant to win a case is to influence those with power over the judiciary. For insurance to be a valid and productive method for mitigating intellectual property risks in China, it would be essential to ensure that some basic judicial standards are uniformly adhered to: transparent process (fairly examining the issues raised), coherent reasoning (analysing the argued points equally comprehensively in the judicial decision) and consistent application of law (respecting and following precedent and rule of law at national level). Chinese economic development and social complexity, of which insurance is an essential part, now require that the risks of litigation become less a question of a gamble and more a question of risk management. As part of that process, China needs to consider reforming its judicial system.

9 Legislative and regulatory methodology and approaches

Developing catastrophe insurance in China

Johanna Hjalmarsson and Mateusz Bek[1]

1 Introduction

Many geographical areas are subject to catastrophic events such as floods or earthquakes regularly devastating the lives of large number of consumers. The availability of insurance in some form or other helps people get their lives back on track after a catastrophic event and protects their property from dilapidation or destruction. Where the risks are widespread and pervasive, there is a social risk in that many people may find themselves homeless or living in a dangerously unstable home. All societies must find a way to address such risks, and where the insurance industry is not in a place to provide sufficient cover, ultimately the State is the insurer of last resort. States are increasingly seeking to prepare for this task by creating or making possible favourable conditions for the private insurance industry to help absorb some of the risk. This paper considers recent developments in China and discusses some options available.

Natural disasters may have a devastating impact upon society. Sadly, human misery caused by destruction of housing and local infrastructure by a hazard often cannot be completely avoided. Possession of a consumer

1 Informa Senior Research Fellow in Maritime and Commercial Law and Senior Research Assistant, Institute of Maritime Law, Southampton Law School, University of Southampton. The authors are grateful to James Dingjing Huang, Southampton Law School, for his assistance with Chinese source materials in 2014, and to Jenny Jingbo Zhang, Lecturer in Maritime and Commercial Law, Southampton Law School, University of Southampton, for her assistance with research in 2013. Remaining errors are attributable to the authors. Although the authors presented a study entitled 'Flood insurance – some thoughts for an emerging catastrophe insurance market' at the Chinese Insurance Law Conference, 22–23 April 2013 in London and Southampton, the following text is quite unrecognisable, not least because there has been rapid development in the intervening period. The conference was organised with the support of the Confucius Institute and the British Insurance Law Association. The Flood Insurance project was made possible by a much appreciated grant from Public Policy@Southampton and resulted notably in the report 'Future availability of flood insurance in the UK', available at: http://eprints.soton.ac.uk/354173/ (accessed 9 January 2014).

catastrophe insurance policy, as a means of mitigating the property losses or damage and loss of personal effects and goods, is becoming increasingly important. Worldwide, many consumers residing in areas of catastrophe risk are unaware of the role insurance may play in giving them peace of mind in the face of potential disasters, or may not have access to worthwhile insurance. The Chinese consumer insurance market is characterised by widespread consumer insurance in cities, but not to the same extent in more rural or semi-urbanised areas. In addition, household insurance is one of the seven types of insurance that proved unprofitable in 2012.[2]

The main issue for Chinese disaster insurance is earthquake insurance because it is normally excluded by most available insurance products, while floods, storms and typhoons are covered by existing available insurance products. Catastrophe insurance remains fairly incipient in China but in the trail of a number of recent natural disasters including floods, earthquakes and tsunamis, there is growing realisation that widespread protection is needed for both industry and population to quickly recover from incidents and events, and that the contribution of the private sector is vital to achieve this purpose. This realisation appears to be present at the highest level – the Third Plenum Communique of August 2013[3] has been interpreted as meaning that insurance companies can play a greater role in disaster management and relief.[4] A further policy document following on from the Third Plenum Communique is entitled 'Decision of the Central Committee of the Communist Party of China on Some Major Issues concerning Comprehensively Deepening the Reform'. In Chapter III, entitled 'Accelerating the Improvement of the Modern Market System', this document expressly mentions that a catastrophe insurance system should be established in China (Part III (12)):[5]

> **12. Improving the financial market.** We will open the financial industry wider, and allow qualified non-governmental capital to set up, in accordance with law, financial institutions such as small or medium-sized banks on the precondition that this comes under stronger oversight. We will push ahead with reform of policy financial institutions. We will improve the multi-layer capital market system, promote reform toward a registration-based stock-issuing system, promote equity financing through diverse channels, develop and regulate the bond

2 See *China Insurance Year Book 2013*, National Edition, p 15.

3 The translation used for this article is available at: http://chinacopyrightandmedia.wordpress.com/2013/11/12/communique-of-the-3rd-plenum-of-the-18th-party-congress/ (accessed 10 June 2014).

4 See: www.scmp.com/business/china-business/article/1372667/catastrophe-insurance-scheme-way-huge-risks-may-deter (accessed 10 June 2014).

5 An imperfect English translation of the document is available at: www.china.org.cn/china/third_plenary_session/2013-11/16/content_30620736.htm (accessed 10 June 2014).

> market, and increase the proportion of direct financing. *We will improve the compensation mechanism for the insurance industry, and establish an insurance system for catastrophe risks.* We will develop inclusive finance. We will encourage financial innovations, and enrich the financial market with more levels and more products.
>
> (emphasis added)[6]

The background to these developments in policy at the highest level is the recent major earthquakes and the current situation where disasters such as flood and drought have caused significant loss for agriculture and farming in Northeast China.

2 The example of agricultural insurance in China

While individual consumer losses are a highly undesirable problem, especially in the context of large-scale disasters, and uninsured consumers are a burden for the government to bear, the effects on agriculture of natural disasters are not limited regionally or even nationally, but may have extensive repercussions in the form of famine and social upheaval, as well as on the economy generally. While support for consumer insurance is therefore only at a pilot stage, agricultural catastrophe insurance has enjoyed the attention of the China Insurance Regulatory Commission (CIRC) for some time, with the People's Insurance Company of China (PICC) providing agriculture insurance since the early 1980s. This mostly unprofitable product line was scaled down ahead of the privatisation of the PICC in 2003, but with considerable policy support, pilot projects commenced in 2002.[7] Apart from making agricultural insurance a policy priority and increasing its visibility, more concrete measures have been taken at the level of local government, using a wide range of models described as follows:

> There is the joint model in which the government and insurance companies assume the risk together, the agency model in which the government assumes the risk while insurance companies operate as the agent and the insurer model in which insurance companies operate with policy support.[8]

6 See: www.china.org.cn/china/third_plenary_session/2014-01/16/content_31212602_3.htm (accessed 10 June 2014).

7 A history of agricultural insurance in China back to the 1930s may be found at Zhou Yanli, 'An introduction to the development and regulation of agricultural insurance in China', *The Geneva Papers*, 2009, 34, pp 78–84, available at: www.genevaassociation.org/media/247644/ga2009_gp34(1)_zhou.pdf (accessed 10 June 2014).

8 Ibid., p 82.

As from 2007, there is also financial support at the central level.[9] Up to 80 per cent of premiums have been subsidised by the government to support mostly unprofitable products, making it the world's second largest market for agricultural insurance.[10] Premium income from agricultural insurance was over RMB 24 billion in 2012, with a year-on-year growth of 38.25 per cent. The premium income of agricultural insurance stands for 4.51 per cent of property insurance business and 4.35 per cent of property insurance companies' business.[11] As for indemnity payments, in 2012, they stood at over RMB 13 billion, with a year-on-year growth of 60.61 per cent.[12] In 2012, the total amount of the sum insured of agricultural insurance was over RMB 900 billion, with a year-on-year growth of 38.06 per cent; 183 million smallholder households were underwritten, with a year-on-year growth of 8.3 per cent; and 970 million mu[13] of main crops were underwritten, with a year-on-year growth of 20.59 per cent, which amounts to 40.2 per cent of the area under crops nationwide.[14]

However, compensation to farmers is said not yet to be adequate.[15] The introduction has been heavily subsidised and characterised by a mixture of voluntary and compulsory insurance, and a range of risk models in relation to crops.[16] Following the pilot projects, a number of firms are now being licensed in this area of business,[17] and a regulatory framework has been enacted. The Agricultural Insurance Regulation 2013 now provides that the State Council should establish a risk-sharing system for agricultural insurance, underwriting catastrophic disasters. Local governments are also encouraged to develop such systems.

There are obstacles inhibiting the effectiveness of agricultural insurance in China. While the idea of a premium subsidy derived from the government sounds plausible, it causes problems. For instance, as the local authorities are required to match Central government's input in certain circumstances, they may be reluctant to promote agricultural insurance. There has also been research leading to the conclusion that a lack of trust in government-

9 Ibid.

10 Charles Stutley, *Agricultural Insurance in Asia and the Pacific Region*, RAP Publication 2011/12, Food and Agriculture Organization of the United Nations, Regional Office for Asia and the Pacific, Bangkok 2011 ('FAO Report'), p 139, available at: www.fao.org/docrep/015/i2344e/i2344e00.pdf (accessed 9 June 2014).

11 See *China Insurance Year Book 2013*, National Edition, p 13.

12 Ibid.

13 A unit of area in China: 1 mu equals 666.67 square metres.

14 See *China Insurance Year Book of 2013*, National Edition, p 13.

15 See: www.globaltimes.cn/content/746075.shtml (accessed 10 June 2014).

16 See, generally, FAO Report.

17 It appears that at least 10 firms were licensed for such business in the second quarter of 2013 alone: www.postonline.co.uk/post/news/2311109/circ-approves-agricultural-insurance (accessed 9 June 2014).

sponsored insurance products acts as a barrier for farmers' willingness to participate in insurance programmes.[18]

3 Consumer catastrophe insurance: predicting the future

Against the background of developments in agricultural insurance in the period since it was declared a priority and in light of the policy declaration regarding the priority status of insurance against catastrophe risks, we may now expect similar policy developments in the general catastrophe insurance field, in particular the consumer sector. The expansion should be expected to be methodical, if not slow, to be based on experiences from pilot projects with some, albeit limited, input of international expertise and to be backed up by regulatory and supervisory support, finance at the local or regional level and ultimately also centralised funding. Given China's political development over the last several decades, it is perhaps not surprising that the political model that seems to have been preferred in relation to support for agricultural insurance has been the public private partnership over pure market solutions with some regulatory support, and that there is a compulsory element to some forms of agricultural insurance.[19]

Two pilot projects initiated in 2013 are particularly interesting as they are highly likely to be followed by many more, in various forms: Yunnan is piloting earthquake insurance and the city of Shenzhen is set to pilot comprehensive disaster insurance, not limited to earthquakes. The China Insurance Regulatory Commission (CIRC) is supportive of these initiatives, which are undertaken by working groups backed by the regional authorities. The CIRC's support is arguably essential for the success of these schemes – it appears to have had some influence on agricultural insurance in participating in research, encouraging specialised products, backstopping the reliability of the products on offer by supervisory means and regulating premiums and claims settlement.[20] The view of the CIRC in relation to agricultural insurance was that:

> within the vast territory of China, there are a great variety of crops and livestock, different agricultural structures as well as different levels of agricultural and social-economic development, because of these differences, the establishment of an agricultural insurance system should be carried out step by step based on the experiences from the pilot projects.[21]

18 H. Cai *et al.*, 'The effect of microinsurance on economic activities: evidence from a randomized field experiment', available at: www.sas.upenn.edu/~hfang/publication/sow/restat-revise-5.pdf (accessed 11 June 2014).
19 FAO Report, pp 29–30.
20 Zhou Yanli, p 83.
21 Ibid., p 84.

If the experience of agriculture is of any guidance, the CIRC will prefer to carry forward experiences from the pilot projects into workable models, rather than seek to learn from the experiences of other countries. It does appear that although China is not looking abroad for models, it will continue to welcome foreign capital into the resulting scheme, and it intends to legislate to provide stability in support of the private-sector involvement.[22]

4 Legislation

The authors would thus expect China to legislate in support of the catastrophe scheme to be introduced – both based on the history of agriculture insurance where the Agriculture Insurance Regulation 2013 was preceded by extensive pilot projects, achievement of a degree of market capacity and licensing of companies to carry out this form of business, and on the fact that international investors in a market require legislation for their peace of mind and stability. What, then, should be the contents of such legislation? The authors would make the following observations, drawing in particular on three examples of solutions devised elsewhere to offer a few thoughts on their applicability to the Chinese situation. The first is the Flood Re model recently proposed in the UK with the aim of resolving the issue of availability and affordability of flood insurance in that country. The second is New Zealand's scheme of statutory consumer insurance against natural disasters. Last but not least is the Turkish Catastrophe Insurance Pool. The reflective process is geared towards discussing the legislative needs transpiring from the models and that may be foreseen to apply also to the Chinese market, a market characterised by reasonably good penetration of business insurance, but where consumer insurance is mainly taken out by high-income families in cities. Penetration in rural areas of China is poor. Existing risks include a wide variety of natural disaster risks including floods, storms, earthquakes, tsunamis and debris flow.

5 The setting up of a scheme

In contrast to China, the market in the United Kingdom is extremely well developed with high rates of penetration and fairly well-known and assessed risks. The problem here is not how to conquer new markets, but how to maintain the stability of the current, arguably unsustainable market situation. Developments in catastrophe insurance in the UK are so recent that it is worth first providing a brief key to the state of play.

22 *India Times*: http://articles.economictimes.indiatimes.com/2014-03-11/news/48118104_1_catastrophe-insurance-insurance-market-china-insurance-regulatory-commission (accessed 10 June 2014).

The risk of flooding due to heavy rain and insufficient structural protection has already caused widespread heavy losses. According to governmental data, in England alone, more than 5.2 million properties are at risk of flooding – that is nearly one in six. It is further estimated that between 200,000 and 500,000 households in the UK are at *significant* risk of flooding.[23] Should investment in flood protection be kept at the current level, an additional 280,000 properties will be at such a risk by 2035.[24]

On 27 June 2013, the government and the insurance industry agreed a Memorandum of Understanding (MOU) on how to develop a scheme, known as Flood Re. The scheme is designed to ensure that flood insurance remains widely available and affordable.[25] From the outset of negotiations, which took place during a period of heavy recession in the UK, it was made clear by the government that no financial backing whatsoever would be made available for the scheme, but that it would support the scheme in other ways. As part of such backing, the Water Act 2014 was enacted, Part 4 of which lays the foundations for the Secretary of State to make detailed provisions as to the structure and working of the scheme including a compulsory obligation for insurers in the relevant market segment to participate. It is planned to be up and running summer 2015. For the time being, the members of the Association of British Insurers, a body representing the UK insurance industry, will voluntarily continue to meet their commitment to keep offering flood cover to existing customers in accordance with the Statement of Principles.[26]

The Flood Re model is loosely based on Pool Re, a reinsurance scheme for terrorism risks formed in 1993 in response to the threat posed by the Irish Republican Army (IRA) and other terrorist activity. According to the MOU and the Water Act 2014, Flood Re will be a not-for-profit entity, owned and managed by the insurance industry itself, with the aim of providing affordable flood cover for every household at high flood risk for a period of 25 years. It is believed that during this period, a smooth transition

23 See supplementary written evidence submitted by Association of British Insurers (ABI) (WB 22), available at: www.publications.parliament.uk/pa/cm201314/cmpublic/water/memo/wb22.htm (accessed 10 June 2014).

24 See 'Managing flood and coastal erosion risks in England: 1 April 2012 to 31 March 2013. Report by the Environment Agency, 11', available at: http://a0768b4a8a31e106d8b0-50dc802554eb38a24458b98ff72d550b.r19.cf3.rackcdn.com/LIT_8443_200ddd.pdf (accessed 10 June 2014).

25 For the text of the MOU, see: https://consult.defra.gov.uk/flooding/floodinsurance/supporting_documents/20130626%20Flood%20Insurance%20MOU%20June%202013%20unprotected.pdf (accessed 5 February 2014). See also: www.abi.org.uk/News/News-releases/2013/06/ABI-and-Government-agree-Memorandum-of-Understanding-on-scheme-to-safeguard-UK-flood-insurance (accessed 10 June 2014).

26 For a detailed treatment of the Statement of Principles, see *Future Availability of Flood Insurance in the UK*, pp 9–13.

to risk-reflective premiums will take place,[27] hence gradually diminishing the need for any sort of legislative interference with the private market. Although the statute makes it clear that the provisions relating to Flood Re will be repealed after 25 years, it is not yet certain whether Flood Re will simply cease to exist at the end of the period, or whether it will then transition into a market participant on commercial terms. There are obvious problems with either solution. There are incentives for the industry to maintain it as a not-for-profit entity, but it has been made clear that at the end of the 25-year term, no further government support will be available. Therefore, such an evolution will only be possible with an improvement in flood management, increasing spending on flood protection[28] and effective implementation of the National Planning Policy Framework.[29] The government has also committed itself to compel any insurer offering home insurance to participate in Flood Re by means of the 'flood insurance obligations' provisions.[30] The obligations will not enter into force at the same time as the rest of the Act, but will be triggered by the responsible minister if there is a need – either because Flood Re fails to resolve the problem, or because new entrants to the insurance market, who are not committed to the solution thus devised in cooperation with the current market participants begin to offer home policies without flood cover included, thus competing with other market participants on advantageous terms.[31]

Flood insurance, as a part of a comprehensive household policy, will be provided by the scheme to each property in the UK having a technical flood risk premium greater than the relevant 'eligibility threshold'. Other properties would continue to be covered by the industry in the commercial market. Flood Re will be funded by an annual charge totalling GBP 180 million, which will notionally equate to GBP 10.50 in respect of each household provided with combined home insurance by the relevant insurer. It will thus constitute a formalisation of existing practice whereby the 500,000 properties at significant risk of flooding are currently cross-subsidised by a levy on top of the premium on every other household

27 Water Act 2014, sections 64(2)(b) and 83(1).

28 See, generally, 'Standard Note SN/SC/5755. Flood defence spending in England (14 January 2013)', available at: www.google.co.uk/url?sa=t&rct=j&q=&esrc=s&source=web&cd=4&cad=rja&ved=0CEkQFjAD&url=http%3A%2F%2Fwww.parliament.uk%2Fbriefing-papers%2Fsn05755.pdf&ei=eyvyUvioCdGS7AaCvoDIBg&usg=AFQjCNGcZecuBtZvlWDPKQzbV8DCLi89Rg&sig2=dHOfsYIF_XqQwrzn2wUGrw&bvm=bv.60799247,d.ZGU (accessed 10 June 2014).

29 See *National Planning Policy Framework* (Department for Communities and Local Government, March 2012), [17], [94], [99]–[104], [143], [156], [162], [166] and [192], available at: www.gov.uk/government/uploads/system/uploads/attachment_data/file/6077/2116950.pdf (accessed 10 June 2014).

30 Water Act 2014, section 70.

31 It is thought that the scheme will require approval from the EU, an obstacle that is unlikely to materialise in China.

insurance policy. The aggregate annual liability of Flood Re will be capped at a monetary level equivalent to a 1:200 year loss scenario (in accordance with current actuarial modelling, GBP 2.4–2.5 billion). It is not yet clear what would happen should the cap be exceeded.

Lessons to be learnt from the setting up of Flood Re must naturally wait until the scheme is fully functional. However, at this stage, it may be said that the heavy involvement of the industry – the scheme has been negotiated in detail between the Association of British Insurers and the government and continues to be a collaborative effort – means that it is likely to avoid some elementary problems from the outset. For instance, the industry is clear that it must take responsibility for and fund the project. The legislative support needed is already in place and ready to be triggered, leaving the insurance market in no doubt of the government's willingness to support the scheme. Any clashes with EU competition law can be addressed at an early stage and jointly by the government and the industry.

On the other hand, as is so often the case in contract negotiations, the parties may be avoiding discussion of critical issues in the hopes of establishing sufficient consensus. The regulatory ambivalence inherent in the constitution of the scheme is explained below. The consensus approach may also be the explanation for the fact that the end stage of Flood Re has not yet been clarified – will it be run down, will it persist as a non-profit insurer or will it be privatised and turned into a profit-based reinsurer? The Y2K problem that so engulfed the world for a few short seconds was reportedly the result of programmers not being able to think beyond their own internally predicted lifespan. Perhaps similar short-termism problems will arise here.

6 Achieving penetration

The next question is how to ensure widespread take-up of the various schemes proposed. New Zealand, a country plagued by frequent earthquakes, operates a government-managed pool, the Earthquake Commission (EQC), based on statutory provision whereby earthquake cover is 'deemed' to be included in any policy covering fire insurance.[32] The cover is considered not to give rise to a contractual relationship between the Earthquake Commission and the private property owner.[33] The scheme

32 See the New Zealand Earthquake Commission Act 1993.

33 See *Earthquake Commission v Disputes Tribunal* (1996) 10 PRNZ 317, where the insured was denied *locus standi* in the Disputes Tribunal because their claim did not arise in contract and was thus outside of the Tribunal's jurisdiction. See also *Coughlan v Earthquake Commission* [2007] NZHC 178, where it was held that the EQC is not covered by the Insurance Law Reform Act 1977 and therefore not barred from imposing a time limit upon a claim under the EQC Act 1993. The EQC Act 1993 itself nevertheless contains numerous references to a contract of insurance in relation to the arrangement therein established.

deals only with private property, excluding commercial property from cover. The premium income of the pool is calculated as a percentage of the total premium paid. The pool obtains its reinsurance in the global market and benefits from a governmental guarantee for which it pays an annual fee.

The New Zealand EQC Act 1993 provides an example of how catastrophe insurance might be provided to consumers who would otherwise be left either uninsured or exposed to an unaffordable premium. It is also an example of how risks can be spread in an uncomplicated manner to a large section of the population by deeming insurance to be in place when a widespread form of cover such as fire insurance is taken out. The success of this scheme depended largely on the market penetration of fire insurance. At the time of the enactment of the legislation, 97 per cent of households were insured under policies covering fire damage. By contrast, China is still very much an emerging consumer insurance market. Tying statutory natural catastrophe insurance to private market policies covering a particular form of damage would not achieve the same result as in the case of New Zealand, until some form of home cover is more widespread. This will be a different picture in the many sub-segments of the Chinese market and there may well be particular markets where penetration is already sufficient, for instance in the very large cities.

Generally, the penetration rate for household insurance in China is extremely low. It was recently estimated to be roughly at 1 per cent. Therefore, adopting a model similar to that introduced in New Zealand, based on tying natural catastrophe cover to existing comprehensive household insurance policies, would be unlikely to achieve the aim of providing a universal solution to the problem outlined above. On the other hand, it is not inconceivable that the availability of such a product together with appropriate marketing thereof would positively influence the take up of standard property insurance.

7 Premium calculation

Food for thought on premium calculation is provided by the Turkish example, also designed to deal with earthquakes. The Turkish Catastrophe Insurance Pool (TCIP)[34] provides an example of catastrophe insurance that is compulsory for every registered homeowner. Having carried out a consultation, the government concluded that the TCIP should be a not-for-profit public entity, providing compulsory insurance for all registered urban dwellings; should have sufficient capacity to materially limit the government's fiscal exposure to catastrophe risk; should be designed to build a national catastrophe fund over time, capable of paying all but the most catastrophic insured losses; and should encourage mitigation through

34 For further information, see the TCIP website: www.tcip.gov.tr/ (accessed 11 June 2014).

risk-based premium rates. The system is designed to rely on the distribution and claims settlement capabilities of the Turkish private insurance market.[35] Under TCIP, cover is provided to every dwelling irrespective of whether it is located in an urban or a rural area. Such economic inequality as might exist[36] is addressed by differentiating the rate of premium according to the perceived level of household income and location, and imposing a cross-subsidy mechanism or providing financial aid to those not able to afford the cover.

Imposing a flat rate of premium for the catastrophe insurance cover provided may well prove counterproductive. Setting the premium at a low level, allowing households with little income to benefit from the scheme, means that it will take longer to build up a fund capable of meeting claims arising out of either a disaster occurring within a short period of time from the inception of the system or a large catastrophe. Conversely, setting the premium at too high a level would pose a risk of a large portion of the public not being able to afford the cover. Rather than attempting to strike a balance, it would be more sensible to differentiate the premium charged for the policy on the basis of both household income and the risk zone in which the property concerned is located. The differentiation may be gradually reduced and any sort of subsidy diminished in value. However, if there is a perception of social inequality and injustice in society, differentiated premiums may lead to unnecessary tensions between the subsidising and subsidised segments of the population.

In order to ensure fiscal stability, it might be advised to stipulate a cap on the amount payable per each disaster occurring. Should the insurance industry consider the magnitude of the catastrophe to be such as to trigger claims the quantum of which is likely to exceed the specified limit, it would be obligated to notify both the body responsible for the administration of the system and the government. Upon such a notification, a decision could be made to halt the settlement of any claim submitted in relation to the damage caused thereby. In the event that the losses rightly claimed actually exceed the capped amount, the policyholders would be paid on a pro rata basis.

8 Enforcement by incentive

Rendering insurance compulsory would not necessarily ensure its success, unless a proper enforcement mechanism is also introduced at the same time.

35 See, generally, E. Gurenko, R. Lester, O. Mahul and S. Oguz Gonulal, *Earthquake Insurance in Turkey. History of the Turkish Catastrophe Insurance Pool*, 2006, The World Bank.

36 For an analysis of income inequality in China, see J. Knight, 'Inequality in China: an overview' (2014) 29(1) *The World Bank Research Observer 1*. See also 'Inequality: recent trends in China and experience in the OECD area' in *China in Focus: Lessons and Challenges*, 2012, Paris: OECD.

TCIP may offer some examples of useful legal measures promoting take-up of disaster insurance. The Turkish government rejected the idea implemented in New Zealand, namely combining natural catastrophe insurance with fire insurance policies. It was thought that selling them as a package would make catastrophe cover subject to considerably higher affordability constraints. By selling it separately from comprehensive household insurance, the growth of catastrophe insurance coverage in Turkey is no longer limited by the general growth of property insurance penetration. The problem encountered by TCIP was that a nationwide pool operated in a two-stage model with the countryside operating according to one model and the city according to another, was that insurance was not sufficiently widespread to 'deem' earthquake to be included with any useful effect. The scheme is compulsory,[37] but actual compulsion is unlikely to work. Although compulsion or 'deeming' is not a feature of the scheme, homeowners are required to present a valid earthquake insurance policy if they wish to register their land or seal any real estate transaction. Moreover, homeowners have to present their insurance policy to open accounts for water, natural gas, electricity and telecommunications services. To further increase take-up using a market-based incentive, premiums are varied according to the earthquake zone and type of building insured, still leaving a certain amount of cross-subsidy for the greatest risks. The scope of the scheme is purposely narrow, leaving out contents insurance and related losses, which are left to the market to provide. The scheme hereby seeks to keep premium costs low.

To achieve these ancillary enforcement mechanisms, concerted policy and measures are required. Past measures taken by other bodies for their own policies will need to be assessed for their compatibility with the new policy. In 1998, the People's Bank of China[38] issued the Residential Mortgage Regulation, section 25 of which provides that before the mortgage contract is concluded, the mortgagor is required to obtain household insurance or to delegate to the mortgagee to obtain such insurance. In compliance with this provision, banks have tied the sale of insurance to the mortgage loan (e.g. a bank will require a mortgagor to buy a specific household insurance, failing which the loan will not be permitted or the mortgagor will be subject to a relatively higher interest). Therefore, in 2006, the China Banking Regulatory Commission (CBRC) issued a notice that forbade banks from stipulating with mandatory effect that residential mortgage insurance must be acquired. In January 2012, the CBRC issued another notice on rectifying irregular behaviours of banks.[39] Paragraph 1(5) of the 2012 notice provides that banks shall not tie loans or any other financing service to financial

37 On compulsory insurance, see further below.
38 The Chinese Central Bank.
39 Yin Jian Ban Fa No. 3, 2012. This notice is available in Chinese on the CBRC's website.

products such as insurance, wealth management products and funds. Most of those household insurance products do not cover earthquakes and sometimes earthquakes are written as an additional risk. However, it might be beneficial to review these notices to establish to what extent, if any, they interfere with the widespread take-up of disaster insurance.

9 Compulsory insurance

There are two reasons to make insurance compulsory in some segments, one economic and one social. If insurers are expected to cross-subsidise policies, legislation will be needed, even if the market does not have objections to the model. A cross subsidy will operate as a transfer of premiums payable from low-risk policyholders to high-risk policyholders. If some insurers are at liberty to offer insurance that does not cross-subsidise the higher risks, they can offer insurance exclusively to low-risk insureds and may remove the most profitable market segment from under the feet of insurers who do operate the cross-subsidy.

It may be necessary to stipulate in some markets that insurance is to be compulsory, to ensure that cover take-up is given sufficient extension. For instance in a rural earthquake zone, there may be householders who opt out of insurance and prefer to take their chances and rebuild their home in case of an earthquake, but then prove incapable of doing so when the risk materialises. Equally, in an urban area, a newly formed company may decide against insuring its assets as a transitional measure to build up the business, which may then be destroyed by an earthquake instead of having a chance to rebuild. Similarly, as a result of the cross-subsidy, low-risk householders may traverse the breaking point where the additional cost of the insurance makes it no longer worthwhile and they will prefer to opt out of the cover. To ensure that this better class of risk remains in the pool and continues to contribute premium income, legislation or regulation making insurance compulsory in some areas and for some segments of business may be necessary. Whether such legislation or regulation is national, with implementation locally by decree, or local or regional in nature, will have to be a matter for the legal system to decide based on social needs, economic calculations and the variety of statute-type instruments constitutionally available.

10 Public-private partnerships and the law

The UK government and its industry partners developing Flood Re have shown some ambivalence as to whether the fund should be regarded primarily as a public or private body. The setting up of a national, regional or local fund is an option that will doubtless be employed in some market segments in China, where heavy government involvement is required for the market to function at an appropriate level. Particular legal concerns arise in relation to such funds and there are regulatory issues of principle to be decided. Identifiable tensions arise between public governance and private contractual relationships, some of which may affect the viability of the scheme, especially if they cause bureaucracy or unnecessary costs causing the commercial market to withdraw from the segment. In the UK, Flood Re is currently planned to be set up by the insurance industry as a private operator subject to the rules of the Financial Conduct Authority on customer treatment and the rules of the Prudential Regulation Authority on keeping reserves to cover liabilities; however, because of its compulsory nature, some of its income will be viewed by Parliament as tax, and therefore subject to rules governing public spending and ultimately to the authority of Parliament. This double governance is bound to exact a heavy toll in terms of compliance.

Thus, it should be carefully considered which regulator is to govern the fund to be set up in each case. An insurance body operating on commercial terms would be expected to submit to financial services regulation as described in another chapter in this book.[40] If so, it might prove difficult to convince some parts of the public sector or the population that the fund is a private-sector-type operator and that its funding is restricted to responding to policies issued, and not available for alternative purposes, however important. Public perception of such a body would have to be carefully managed, especially if the premium income were somehow regulated or made compulsory by statute.

On the other hand, if a potential fund is to be an exclusively government-funded body, with its revenue resulting from taxes or otherwise from the public budget, it might be that it *should* be subject to political influence. If so, the public-sector governance framework will apply and it may then prove difficult or burdensome for the CIRC regulatory framework also to apply. These problems are in no way unique to China – the complexity of funding of catastrophic risks with the involvement of government is universally enhanced by the fact that public financing and budgeting are governed by rules and good practice, as well as the pressures of the electorate and the political establishment with ideas for how the funds should be used. It would not be the first time if political forces were tempted to withdraw money from the fund administered by the pool for the purpose of financing part of the public budget deficit or to subsidise other government-supported programmes.[41] In Turkey, Catastrophe Insurance Law No. 6305 provides for an exhaustive list of purposes for which the revenue of the TCIP may be used to prevent such occurrences.[42]

40 See Fu, Chapter 2 of this work.

41 In 1990, the New Zealand government reallocated NZD 239 million from the Earthquake and War Damage Fund, as it then was, to other uses.

42 The corresponding provision in the New Zealand legislation is similar: Earthquake Commission Act 1993 section 15.

The importance of these issues is that commercial market participants will require guarantees both that there is sufficient funding available in the market, also from government sources, to meet the liabilities in question, but they will also need reassurance that they are not participating in a scheme where funds will later be diverted to other purposes – for instance, an arrangement to cover floods in one area should not be diverted to address problems following an earthquake in another, however heartrending the scenes of devastation and however heavy the political pressure. Ultimately, any decisions in this regard should be taken at the outset and not put off in the hopes of a later resolution, and should be preceded by careful assessment and dictated by sustainability, transparency and democracy.

11 Conclusions

The models presented here demonstrate some of the challenges encountered in developing an efficient natural disaster cover. Such cover is essential to the survival of a society affected by large-scale natural disasters. The government will inevitably be the insurer of last resort for rescue and clean-up operations and to ensure that the population is catered for in terms of emergency and long-term accommodation. In the event of a major natural disaster, it is impossible to accomplish all this within the confines of an ordinary annual budget and a long-term savings operation must be mounted and the power of the private insurance market harnessed.

The New Zealand model, in spite of its virtues, is probably fatally unsuitable for markets with very low insurance penetration, but in a country of China's size and variety could usefully be considered regionally, for larger cities at risk where market penetration is satisfactory. The Turkish model provides a better fit for much of the Chinese market, but offers the challenge of creating public awareness of the scheme and not least trust therein so that potential insureds take out insurance in the first place and the funds can begin to accumulate. It will also require firm regulatory support, both in terms of statute and supervision, to attract foreign investors into the insurance market.

The current evidence is that the CIRC is encouraging regional and local schemes for disaster insurance. This is highly apposite. On the one hand, China's sheer size and the multitude of potential forms of disaster and the variety of insurance markets represent a unique stabilising factor and an opportunity to spread risks from each incident to non-affected insureds in locations remote from the disaster zone; but more importantly, the lack of insurance penetration in nearly all markets means risks cannot be properly spread, so that adverse selection and lack of uptake are very real obstacles to a successful scheme. Further, while nothing could be easier than to compel or deem insurance to have been made, the newness of the insurance solution to this particular problem and the resulting challenge of building confidence in insurance means that take-up of insurance may be slower than is required to build a successful scheme. That said, the potential Chinese insurance market is immense and all that is required is for pockets of insurance solutions to begin to develop, and for these to be sustainably supported by government stipulation, regulation and financial means, for a proper, liquid market that is attractive to international finance to develop in the intermediate term.

Part III

Marine insurance

10 An introduction to the law and practice of marine insurance in China

Professor Pengnan Wang[1]

1 The sources of marine insurance law in China

1.1 The law of marine insurance contracts in China: Chapter 12 of the Chinese Maritime Code

The Chinese Maritime Code, as the first commercial code in the New China, came into effect on 1 July 1993. Chapter 12 of the Chinese Maritime Code contains provisions on the contract of marine insurance.[2] There are 41 Articles from Article 216 through Article 256, which are divided into six sections as shown below:

(1) Section 1: Basic Principles
(2) Section 2: Conclusion, Termination and Assignment of Contract
(3) Section 3: Obligations of the Insured
(4) Section 4: Liability of the Insurer
(5) Section 5: Loss of or Damage to the Subject Matter Insured and Abandonment
(6) Section 6: Payment of the Indemnity

On 13 November 2006, the Supreme People's Court of the People's Republic of China issued the first judicial interpretation on the law of marine insurance entitled Provisions of the Supreme People's Court on the Hearing of Cases of Marine Insurance Disputes, which came into effect on 1 January 2007. The Supreme People's Court of China is currently preparing the second judicial interpretation on the law of marine insurance, having considered the numerous appeal and petition cases of marine insurance disputes in recent years.

1 Senior Partner, Wang Pengnan & Co., Dalian, P. R. China, www.wpnlawyer.com.
2 See Appendix II.

1.2 General insurance law in China

The first Insurance Act of China was promulgated in 1995; thereafter there have been two amendments to it, and the present Insurance Act was amended on 28 February 2009, and came into effect on 1 October 2009. The Insurance Act governs both personal insurance and property insurance, and also governs regulatory matters in relation to commercial insurance companies, insurance agencies and brokers.

The Supreme People's Court of China issued the first judicial interpretation on the Insurance Act in 2009,[3] which mainly clarified in which cases the new Insurance Act 2009 should be applied.

The second judicial interpretation was issued by the Supreme Court on 6 May 2013, and came into effect on 8 June 2013.[4]

Many Higher People's Courts, including Shanghai Higher Court, Guangdong Province Higher Court, Zhejiang Province Higher Court and Shandong Province Higher Court, issued their own guidelines on the hearing of insurance cases before the second judicial interpretation was issued.

Judicial interpretations issued by the Supreme People's Court of PR China are a source of law. The above mentioned guidelines made by Higher Courts or any other courts (including the Supreme Court) are not law, but actually bind the lower courts within the jurisdiction; for example, Guangzhou Maritime Court is bound by the guidelines made by Guangdong Province Higher People's Court, but Dalian Maritime Court is not obliged to follow them.

1.3 Summary: the sources of marine insurance law in China

According to Article 1 of the Provisions of the Supreme People's Court on the Hearing of Cases of Marine Insurance Disputes in 2006:

> to hear the case of a marine insurance dispute, the provisions of the Maritime Code should be applied; where the Maritime Code does not have provisions, the related provisions of the Insurance Act should be applied; where neither the Maritime Code nor the Insurance Act contain provisions, the Contracts Act and other related laws should be applied.

Therefore, in accordance with Chinese law, a contract of marine insurance will be governed by the Maritime Code 1992, then the Insurance Act 2009, the Contracts Act 1999 and other existing civil laws in China.

3 Interpretation I of the Supreme People's Court on Several Issues concerning the Application of the Insurance Act of the People's Republic of China (Interpretation I).

4 Interpretation II of the Supreme People's Court on Several Issues concerning the Application of the Insurance Act of the People's Republic of China (Interpretation II).

2 Main features of marine insurance law in China

In many aspects, the Chinese Maritime Code is the same as or similar to corresponding provisions set out by the Marine Insurance Act 1906. In the following, the author will highlight certain rules that are different from English law.

2.1 Valued marine policies

The Chinese Maritime Code follows the international practice and the Marine Insurance Act in providing that a marine policy may be a valued one. Where the policy is valued, the agreed value is, as between the insurer and the assured, conclusive of the insurable value of the subject matter intended to be insured. In practice, the agreed value usually exceeds the actual value, sometimes significantly so. This benefits both parties.

If the policy is unvalued as in the case of all non-marine insurance, the assured is placed back in the financial position occupied as at the time of inception of risk, which is the basic principle of indemnity. However, it is strange that the Chinese Maritime Code also stipulates that the insurable value of the ship, marine cargo, ocean freight and other marine subject matter, if not agreed between the insurer and assured in the policy, should be its actual value when the insurance liability commences.

In the context of marine insurance, the measure of indemnity never seeks to compensate the assured for the actual loss sustained, whether or not the marine insurance policy is valued.

2.2 Duty of pre-contractual disclosure

The core of existing law is set out in Articles 222 and 223 of the Chinese Maritime Code. Unlike what applies in the context of non-marine insurance, the assured's duty of disclosure in the context of marine insurance is not limited to the inquiries raised by the insurer before the contract is concluded. The assured's duty is to make a fair presentation of the risk; the test is to be applied from the perspective of the insurer.

In the case of dishonest non-disclosure, the insurer may avoid the policy and retain the premium; in the case of innocent or negligent non-disclosure, the insurer is also entitled to discharge the contract or demand a higher premium, but the insurer may not refuse any claim arising before the termination of the contract, provided that the non-disclosure did not have an impact on the occurrence of the claim. There have been a few cases in which insurance companies in China successfully refused claims on the grounds of the assured's obvious non-disclosure.

2.3 Warranties

Warranties as stipulated in MIA 1906 section 33, if provided in a marine policy, will be effective according to Article 235 of the Chinese Maritime

Code, but current Chinese law does not provide any further stipulation on the definition of warranty, nor on the remedy in the event of breach. It leaves the policy terms and conditions to make everything clear, so that the term 'warranty' itself has no legal meaning under the current law in China.

2.4 Sue and labour

The insurer should pay sue and labour expenses in addition to the indemnity. Sue and labour is subject to underinsurance. The particular expenses incurred for acting on the specific instructions of the insurer are of sue and labour. Sue and labour also includes reasonable expenses for survey and assessment of the value for the purpose of ascertaining the nature and extent of the peril insured against.

The insurer should pay sue and labour even if there is no such provision in the policy. Furthermore, maritime courts in China often extend the scope of sue and labour. However, in more than one leading judgment delivered by the Supreme Court, legal costs including court fees and lawyers' fees incurred for the protection of the insurer's subrogation have been held not to be sue and labour expenses. It is submitted that the assured is not obliged to take any positive legal action to protect the insurer's subrogation before the insurance indemnity is paid, though the insurer is entitled to make corresponding deduction from the insurance indemnity where the assured positively gives up its claim against a third person before the insurance indemnity is paid.

2.5 Subrogation

According to the Chinese Maritime Code and the Special Maritime Procedure Law 1999, the insurer should claim and may sue a liable third party in its own name from the time the insurance indemnity is paid to the assured.[5] At the same time, the assured loses the right to claim against the third party.

An arbitration agreement between the assured and the third party may not bind the insurer when the insurer exercises its right of subrogation, which has become an independent cause of action in China according to present leading cases and judicial interpretation delivered by the Supreme Court of China.

Foreign insurance companies should be very careful about time bars, which may not be extended by any agreement out of court under the existing law in China, but might be recounted from the time when the insurance indemnity is paid to the assured according to the recent judicial interpretation of the Insurance Act 2009 by the Supreme Court of China.[6]

5 Article 252, Chinese Maritime Code; Article 94, Special Maritime Procedure Law.
6 Article 16 of the Interpretation II.

3 The impact of general insurance law upon marine insurance law

3.1 The principle of insurable interest

The Chinese Maritime Code does not require the insured to possess an insurable interest. The Insurance Act 2009 introduced a requirement that a claimant must possess an insurable interest in the subject matter of a property insurance policy at the time of loss (instead of at the time of the contract being made, as is the case with life insurance).

The Insurance Act 2009 also provides a definition of insurable interest: an insurable interest refers to a lawful interest that the proposer or the insured has in respect of the subject matter insured.[7] It is welcome that Chinese courts tend to relax the requirement of a lawful interest in the insured subject matter if one reviews the guidelines provided by a few Higher Courts in China. For example, economic interest and commercial expediency are actually accepted as legal interests. However, there still exist many uncertainties in cases such as the seller's legal interest after the goods are loaded on board the carrying vessel, and the cargo assured's legal interest regarding a certain per cent of profit on goods (a PPI insurance) in a marine cargo policy without a clear increased value clause as in ICC clauses.

3.2 The insurer's duty to explain the exclusion clauses in a standard insurance contract

The Insurance Act 2009 requires an insurer to 'make specific and clear explanations' on the exclusion/exemption provisions in a standard insurance contract when the contract is concluded.[8] Otherwise, the exclusion/exemption provisions in the contract do not bind the assured.

The above duty has become the most serious headache when an insurer defends on grounds of the exclusion/exemption clause(s) because the insurer has to prove that he has made specific and clear explanations on the exclusion/exemption clause(s) to the assured. Furthermore, the Chinese courts tend to adopt an expansive interpretation of the scope of the exclusion/exemption clause(s). The composite result means that, in many cases, an insurer may not be able to invoke any clauses at all in relation to the exclusion, exemption and the franchise in a contract of insurance.

Following over 17 years of heated debate of the duty upon insurers under the first Insurance Act 1995 to explain exclusion clauses, Chinese courts now tend to accept that a special note of the exclusion/exemption clause on the insurance proposal form signed by the proposer itself conclusively

7 Paragraph 6 of Article 12 of the Insurance Act 2009.
8 Article 17, Insurance Act 2009.

demonstrates that the insurer has explained it to the assured, that the warranty clauses and conditions precedent for any claim do not belong to the exclusion/exemption provisions and that any special agreements including the deductible or franchise are not subject to the explanation provision.

However, in almost every insurance case the assured will be inclined to argue that it did not receive any specific and clear explanation of the exclusion/exemption clause from the insurer. It is submitted that in a contract of marine insurance, the insurer is not obliged to explain the exclusion/exemption clauses in a standard marine insurance form, because the assured is a businessman, and the standard forms have been used for many years, so the assured should have understood all provisions in the standard forms. But presently the maritime courts in China only relax the requirement of 'specific and clear explanations' to some extent.

3.3 The court's discretion to explain a standard insurance contract in favour of the assured

The Insurance Act 1995 introduced the *contra proferentem* rule in China,[9] and it has been used abusively by Chinese courts because the insurance companies have deep pockets and many PICC P&C standard property insurance conditions – including the marine insurance forms – provide quite limited and unfair covers in order to limit the insurers' exposure to risks, including moral hazards in some aspects.

The later Contracts Act 1999 extends the application of the same rule of interpretation to all contracts, but fortunately the Contracts Act additionally stipulates how to understand the meaning of a term in a standard contract in order to avoid the abusive use of this rule. Under common law, as far as is known to the author, this rule is ancillary and is rarely used by courts, but in China it is a very popular rule in explaining a standard insurance contract by Chinese courts. This means that Chinese insurance companies should be much more careful in drafting insurance conditions and terms.

3.4 Delay in payment of premium

The Insurance Act does not provide for any remedy where the premium is not paid in full or on time, but the guidelines issued by Higher Courts have in fact made new law in this respect within the corresponding geographical jurisdiction of the Higher Court. The related provisions stated in the guidelines are different from the Judicial Interpretation [Provisions] on the Hearing of Cases of Marine Insurance Disputes, which was promulgated

9 This rule is now provided by Article 30 of the Insurance Act 2009.

by the Supreme People's Court in 2006. According to the Judicial Interpretation, the insurer under a marine insurance policy may not cancel or terminate the contract where the marine policy has been issued, or after the insurer's liability has attached in case the assured does not pay the full premium in time as agreed.

3.5 Delay in payment of insurance indemnity or claims

According to the Insurance Act, within 60 days after receiving the claim documents, the insurer should effect payment of at least part of the claims, which can be ascertained where the other part of claims cannot be ascertained.[10] The Insurance Act also stipulates that an insurer should complete the assessment of insurance cover after receiving the complete claims documents, inform the assured of the insurer's decision whether or not to pay the indemnity, and should effect payment of claims within 10 days after reaching a claims settlement agreement with the assured, failing which the insurer should pay damages for late payment of claims that have been suffered by the assured in addition to the insurance indemnity claim itself and the statutory interest thereof.[11] This is very different from the present English law. Once an assured has provided the insurer with the complete claims documents, the insurer is obliged to settle the claim almost immediately.

These provisions are very important for a marine assured because marine insurance claims are often very large but cannot be fully ascertained quickly. However, unfortunately the Insurance Act does not provide for the remedy of the assured if the insurer fails to abide by it. Ultimately, the payment of insurance claims (whether in part or in full) in time depends on the credit of an insurer. The ample competition and the product-line-style claims management result in comparatively quick payments being the rule in the motor insurance sector in China, but the delays in the payment of much more complicated marine insurance claims may be the root of great frustration for the assured.

3.6 Substantially increased or reduced risks

The Maritime Code and main PICC P&C marine insurance conditions do not touch upon the issue of increased or reduced risks after a contract of marine insurance is concluded. The Insurance Act fills in the gap to some extent; subject to provisions of a contract of insurance to the contrary, a substantial increase or reduction of risks of a subject matter will result in the adjustment of the premium; furthermore, where the risks increase

10 Article 25, Insurance Act 2009.
11 Article 23, Insurance Act 2009.

substantially, the insurer may terminate the contract if the contract of insurance allows the insurer to do so.[12]

However, insofar as is known to the author, premium adjustment or termination of contract has not yet taken place in the marine insurance market in China – although the author would not like to guarantee that this will not be attempted by someone, some day.

3.7 Fraudulent insurance claims

According to the Insurance Act, in the case that: (1) there is no accident at all; or (2) the accident is deliberately caused by the assured, the insurer has the right to terminate the contract, to take back the indemnity paid, to claim for expenses incurred and to retain the premiums.[13] But it is not clear whether the insurer may forfeit any normal insurance claim arising before the date of fraud.

However, if the losses claimed and their causation are partly untrue or exaggerated by the assured, the insurer is only entitled to refuse payment of the untrue or exaggerated part of the claim. It is submitted that where an assured has been guilty of a fraudulent claim and the majority thereof of its causation is false or forged the assured may forfeit the whole claim to which the fraud relates. The borderline remains a grey area in the law.

Article 242 of the Chinese Maritime Code only makes it clear that the insurer shall not be liable for loss caused by any intentional act of the assured. It is submitted that general average and sue and labour should be excepted from the scope of this rule.

3.8 Direct actions against a liability insurer

A third party may sue the liability insurer directly under the Insurance Act 2009.[14] But the China P&I Club, as a non-commercial insurance company, is not subject to the Insurance Act 2009, so it should not be directly sued by a third party in accordance with the Insurance Act. It has not yet been finally established whether a foreign mutual insurance association would be similarly excluded.

3.9 Reinsurance

In the Insurance Act, there are only two Articles in relation to reinsurance in Chinese law, which define the concept of reinsurance and make it clear that a contract of reinsurance is independent of the original insurance contract.

12 Articles 52 and 53, Insurance Act 2009.
13 Article 27, Insurance Act 2009
14 Article 65, Insurance Act 2009.

In the present insurance markets in China, a strange placement arrangement is popular: a sole underwriter is stated in the policy, but in fact the underwriter co-insures the subject matter with other insurance companies, of which sometimes the assured is aware, but sometimes not. It is hard to identify its legal nature for it is neither reinsurance nor co-insurance.

3.10 Concluding remarks

It is important to identify the legal nature of a contract of insurance: marine or non-marine, because a contract of marine insurance means the application of many peculiar concepts, rules and principles such as constructive total loss, a much stricter duty of disclosure by the assured, valued policy, salvage, general average and lost or not lost rule etc., which are not applicable to a contract of non-marine insurance. We have encountered difficulties in determining the nature of harbour equipment insurance and group personal accident liability insurance for crew members by ship operators.

Caution is warranted in the application of the provisions of the Insurance Act in marine insurance disputes, considering the fact that marine insurance is purely commercial, and should be in line with international practice in many cases.

4 The main features of marine insurance clauses in China

4.1 The brief history of PICC P&C Hull Clauses

4.1.1 Before 1972

The People's Insurance Co. Ltd, known as PICC, was established on 20 October 1949. COSCO was established on 27 April 1961 to operate its own ocean fleets. PICC insured COSCO ships with institute hull clauses until 1972.

4.1.2 First PICC Hull Clauses 1/1/72

In 1972, PICC started using its own hull clauses. It was quite simplified, compared with ITCH 1970.

4.1.3 PICC Hull Clauses 1/1/86

The 1972 clauses were printed (but not amended) each year thereafter until they were amended on 1 January 1986 by reference to the new ITCH 1/10/83.

4.1.4 PICC P&C Hull Clauses 2009

After several mergers and reorganisations, PICC Property & Casualty Co. Ltd was established in July 2003 to continue the marine insurance business of the former PICC. Before the amended Insurance Act of China came into effect on 1 October 2009, every insurance company including PICC P&C codified all its insurance clauses including hull insurance conditions (if any), and reported them for record to the China Insurance Regulatory Commission (CIRC).

Compared with PICC Hull Clauses 1/1/86, PICC P&C Hull Clauses 2009 only contains minor amendments. Currently, other Chinese insurance companies actually use the same hull insurance clauses as PICC P&C Hull Clauses 2009, though each Chinese insurance company endorses its own name on its hull policies and clauses.

Therefore, it seems that it is the market, not any government authority or any marine or property insurance institute, that 'selects' the customary and common use of PICC P&C hull insurance conditions, though competition among Chinese insurance companies is intense. The big players include PICC P&C, China Pacific Property & Casualty Insurance Co. Ltd (CPIC), Ping An Property & Casualty Insurance Co. Ltd of China (Ping An) and China Continent Property & Casualty Insurance Co. Ltd (a subsidiary of China Re), and PICC P&C still has a more than 50 per cent marine insurance market share in China.

4.2 The main features of PICC P&C Hull Clauses 2009, compared with ITCH 1/10/83

(1) There is 4/4 ship collision and FFO liability cover.
(2) Furthermore, collision may be indirect; no actual contact is required.
(3) There is no disbursements warranty.
(4) Increased value cover is popular, and shipowners are free to write a low insured value and insured amount, so that a CTL is relatively easily triggered.
(5) The ISM Code has not yet been incorporated – hull insurers still rely on the traditional ship unseaworthiness exclusion clause in addition to the ship class warranty clause.
(6) Lack of its own necessary standard additional clauses such as:
    (i) GA absorption;
    (ii) recommissioning;
    (iii) leading underwriters, but as mentioned above, undisclosed co-insurance is popular in China;
    (iv) leased equipment; and
    (v) provision of security etc.
(7) It is common to incorporate some standard market institute clauses such as:
    (i) institute warranties; and

(ii) radioactive contamination and chemical/biological/electromagnetic weapons/cyber-attack exclusions.

4.3 Emerging trends in Chinese hull insurance market

4.3.1 Fleet insurance organised by the head office of a corporate group

Local and specialised shipping companies belonging to a group may not themselves select the insurer or co-insurers, but may select a leading underwriter among the co-insurers appointed by the head office of the group. The individual shares among co-insurers are also fixed between the insurers and the head office of the group.

4.3.2 Use of ITCH 1/10/83 in fleet insurance

From 2012, Sinotrans and the leading underwriters including CPIC, PICC P&C, Ping An and China-Re started using ITCH 1/10/83 instead of PICC P&C Hull Clauses 2009, and each individual shipping company in the Sinotrans group may select its own leading underwriter. Such an arrangement continues for the year of 2013. English law and practice still apply, but the jurisdiction is changed to the maritime courts of PR China.

4.4 A brief history of the PICC marine cargo clauses

New China had its own ocean marine cargo insurance clauses in 1963, which were amended in 1972, 1981 and 2009. The amendments in 2009 were quite limited. The PICC marine cargo insurance clauses 1/1/1981, referring to the Institute Cargo Clauses 1/6/1963, still represent the prevalent ocean marine cargo insurance clauses in Chinese insurance markets.

4.5 The main features of PICC P&C Marine Cargo Clauses 2009

(1) The revolution of the Institute Cargo Clauses A, B and C 1/1/1982 did not affect the Chinese insurance markets. The present PICC P&C Marine Cargo Clauses 2009 still use the traditional terms regarding the classification of covers: Free from Particular Average (FPA), With Average (WA) and All Risks. The insured-friendly improvements in the ABC clauses, such as the general cover of entry of seawater, are not employed by the PICC P&C Marine Cargo Clauses 2009.

(2) Piracy is still considered a war risk under PICC P&C Marine Cargo Clauses 2009.

(3) There are 11 kinds of standard 'ordinary' additional covers that may be selected by an insured where the main cover is FPA or WA. There are also five kinds of standard 'special' additional covers that may be used where the main cover is 'All Risks'.

(4) Trading clauses are available only in relation to frozen products and wood oil in bulk.
(5) The warehouse-to-warehouse clause is too 'simplified', which results in it being difficult to explain.
(6) The popular use of Institute Cargo Clauses ABC 1982 or 2009.

Since the cargo insurance conditions are determined by the sales contract, and the Institute Cargo Clauses including its trading clauses are widely accepted in international commodity transactions, the use of Institute Cargo Clauses ABC is popular among marine cargo policies issued by Chinese insurance companies.

The Maritime Courts of PR China often face the challenge of interpreting the Institute Cargo Clauses in accordance with English law and practice.

4.6 Remarks

At present, PICC P&C is reluctant to consider the amendment of its marine insurance conditions, though the covers and ancillary terms on both hull and cargo provided by PICC P&C are apparently insufficient.

Shanghai Institute of Marine Insurance (SIMI) established on 26 December 2013 will replace PICC P&C to draft and amend marine insurance clauses to be used in the Chinese market, and is currently drafting marine liability insurance terms in addition to considering the amendment of PICC P&C hull clauses 2009.

11 Law and practice of civil liability insurance for ship-source oil pollution damage in China

Professor Lixin Han[1] *and Ke Wei*[2]

1 Introduction

China has successively joined the Civil Liability Convention 1969 (CLC 1969), the Civil Liability Convention 1992 (CLC 1992) and the Bunker Convention 2001 to deal with compensation for ship-source oil pollution damage. Relevant domestic laws and regulations have been enacted to implement provisions of conventions, such as the Marine Environmental Protection Law of the PRC, Regulations on Administration of Prevention and Control of Ship-source Pollution to the Marine Environment and Measures for the Implementation of Civil Liability Insurance for Vessel-Induced Oil Pollution Damage of the PRC (the 'Measures'). These laws and regulations have explicitly regulated the scope of vessels insured for oil pollution, the insured amount, insurance institutions, the issuing of oil pollution certificates and so on. In the practice of insurance for oil pollution, underwriters of civil liability insurance for oil pollution damage include mutual insurance institutions (P&I Clubs) and commercial insurance companies. Civil liability insurance for ocean-going ship-source oil pollution damage is usually included in the policy of protection and indemnity insurance for ships, and in this policy the amount of compensation limit is set higher than the requirements of CLC 1992 or the Measures; as concerns civil liability insurance for oil pollution damage from coastal and inland ships, it is underwritten by commercial insurance companies similarly to ocean-going vessels, or covered by separately purchased civil liability insurance for ship-source oil or bunker oil pollution damage.

The project entitled Demonstration Project of Blanket Civil Liability Insurance for Coastal Ship-source Oil Pollution Damage, 2013–2014 was officially launched in Beijing on 1 January 2013 by the Ministry of

1 Doctor and Professor of the Institute of International Maritime Law, Doctoral Supervisor, Vice Dean of Law School, Dalian Maritime University; Arbitrator of CMAC & CIETAC.

2 Shipping Risk Team, International Department of PICC Dalian Branch; LL.M., Dalian Maritime University.

Transport of the PRC and the China Insurance Regulatory Commission, and signifies a step forward for civil liability insurance for ship source oil pollution damage in China.

2 Legislative status of civil liability insurance for ship-source oil pollution damage in China

2.1 International conventions on oil pollution joined by China and their implementation

2.1.1 CLC 1969

In terms of marine historical development, civil liability insurance for ship source oil pollution damage in China has gradually developed as a result of the process of joining the International Convention on Civil Liability for Oil Pollution Damage, 1969 (the 'CLC 1969') and meeting the requirements of the convention.[3] This convention came into force on 19 June 1975. In addition, the Chinese government acceded to CLC 1969 and requested Chinese ships carrying oil to buy civil liability insurance for vessel-induced oil pollution damage in order that such ships should get a convenient passage in territorial waters of every Contracting State. Upon the request of China Ocean Shipping (Group) Company ('COSCO'), with reference to the context of the risks of civil liability for oil pollution covered by foreign P&I Clubs, the People's Insurance Company of China (PICC) drafted the 'Oil Pollution and Other Protection and Indemnity Insurance Clauses' on 1 January 1976, covering the few oil tankers that were undertaking international maritime transportation at that time. Meanwhile, COSCO applied for a guarantee from the City Bank through American Family Insurance staked by American Insurance Group. At that time, the insurance policy against oil pollution and other protection and indemnity insurance was just a nominal policy, which made it easier for Contracting States to check that, in fact, shipowners were bearing their own risks.[4]

CLC 1969 came into force for China on 29 April 1980, and the Ministry of Transport of the PRC presently issued an instrument to demand that Chinese ships carrying more than 2,000 tons of oil in bulk as cargo and undertaking international routes must have oil pollution insurance, and that the China Maritime Safety Administration (China MSA) should issue or renew the Certificate of Insurance or Other Financial Security in Respect

3 Ministry of Transport, [Jiao Chuan Jian] No. 995(1976), issued by the Ship Superintendent Agency of the Ministry of Transport on 25 August 1976.

4 Haiming Wang, *Hull Insurance Theory, Practice and Business Management*, Dalian Maritime University Press, 1st edn, January 2006, p 331.

of Civil Liability for Oil Pollution Damage (the 'Certificate')[5] for them in accordance with the provisions of the convention.[6] Soon afterwards, in the Notice on the Implementation of the International Convention on Civil Liability for Oil Pollution Damage 1969, the Ministry of Transport emphasised again that Chinese ships carrying more than 2,000 tons of oil in bulk as cargo and undertaking international routes must comply with the provisions of CLC 1969. As concerns Chinese ships carrying more than 2,000 tons of oil in bulk as cargo but engaging in domestic routes, the Ministry of Transport could issue the Certificate for them if they were insured ships; otherwise, shipowners should apply for the Credit Certificate of Insurance in Respect of Civil Liability for Oil Pollution Damage from the MSA located in the ship's port of registry. Since 1 October 1980, ships without these above-mentioned Certificates cannot engage in the transport of oil cargoes. Foreign ships carrying over 2,000 tons of oil in bulk as cargo that are registered in Contracting States can be approved for entering the territorial waters of China with the Certificate issued by the competent authorities. The ships carrying over 2,000 tons of oil in bulk as cargo that are registered in non-Contracting States can be approved for entering the territorial waters of China only with the Certificate of Civil Liability for Oil Pollution Damage authorised by the China MSA and the competent authority of that State.[7]

2.1.2 CLC 1992

Along with the International Convention on Civil Liability for Oil Pollution Damage 1992 (CLC 1992) coming into force for China on 5 January 2000, the China MSA promulgated the Notice on the Implementation of the International Convention on Civil Liability for Oil Pollution Damage 1992 for Chinese Tankers Undertaking International Routes, which requires that any ships carrying more than 2,000 tons of persistent oil in bulk as cargo and registered in China (including barges and oil capsules and so on) could be approved for engaging in the transport of oil cargoes after obtaining the Certificate from the China MSA in accordance with CLC 1992. The Certificates originally issued in accordance with CLC 1969 were abolished when CLC 1992 came into force.

5 In shipping practice, such a Certificate is usually called a Blue Card.
6 Ministry of Transport, *The Notice of Acceptance of the International Convention on Civil Liability for Oil Pollution Damage* [Jiaogangjianzi No. 334 (1980)] issued by the former body of China MSA of the Ministry of Transport.
7 Ministry of Transport, the Notice on the Implementation of the International Convention on Civil Liability for Oil Pollution Damage, 1969 [Jiaogangjianzi No. 1600 (1980)].

2.1.3 International Convention on Civil Liability for Bunker Oil Pollution Damage 2001

The Bunker Convention 2001 came into force on 21 November 2008. On 23 December 2008, that is, before it came into force for China on 3 March 2009, China MSA had already promulgated the Notice on the Implementation of the International Convention on Civil Liability for Bunker Oil Pollution Damage 2001, which requires that Chinese ships over 1,000 gross tonnage undertaking international routes and coastal routes must obtain insurance or other financial security and the Certificate of Insurance or Other Financial Security in Respect of Civil Liability for Bunker Oil Pollution Damage; foreign ships over 1,000 gross tonnage could be approved for entering Chinese ports after holding such a Certificate issued by a Contracting State's competent authority or its authorised agency.

2.2 National legislation on compulsory insurance for ship-source oil pollution damage

2.2.1 Marine Environmental Protection Law

Article 66 of the Marine Environmental Protection Law of the PRC, revised in 1999 (the 'Marine Environmental Protection Law'), provides that:

> The State shall make perfect and put into practice a responsibility system of civil liability compensation for vessel-induced oil pollution, and shall establish ship's oil pollution insurance, oil pollution compensation fund system in accordance with the principles of owners of the ship and the cargoes jointly undertaking liabilities for vessel-induced oil pollution compensations. Specific measures for the implementation of ship's oil pollution insurance and compensation fund system for oil pollution damage shall be formulated by the State Council.[8]

Given that the Marine Environmental Protection Law belongs to the body of administrative law, the above Article could be regarded as an authorisation to the State Council for 'making perfect and putting into practice' the compensation system for vessel-induced oil pollution damage, which means that the State Council has the power to enact specific and relevant measures.

2.2.2 Regulations on prevention of pollution

The revised Regulations on Administration of Prevention and Control of

8 Article 66, Marine Environmental Protection Law 1999 (official translation).

Ship's Pollution to the Marine Environment 2009 (the 'Regulations on Prevention of Pollution') came into force on 1 March 2010, and the Regulations on Administration of Prevention of Ship-source Pollution in the Waters of the PRC 1983 were simultaneously abolished. Chapter 7, entitled 'Compensation for Damage of Ship-source Pollution Accidents', of the Regulations on Prevention of Pollution expressly stipulates the basis of liability and limits of liability of ship-source oil pollution accidents, civil liability insurance for ship source oil pollution damage and a compen-sation fund for oil pollution damage. For example, Article 53 of these Regulations provides that for ships navigating within the territorial sea of the PRC, the owners shall buy civil liability insurance against vessel-induced oil pollution damage or obtain corresponding financial security in accordance with the provisions of the competent authorities of transport under the State Council. However, ships of less than 1,000 gross tonnage carrying non-oil substances are exempt therefrom.

The amount of the civil liability insurance for vessel-induced oil pollution damage or the obtained corresponding financial security by shipowners shall be not less than the compensation amount of oil pollution damage that follows from the Chinese Maritime Code and the international conventions that the People's Republic of China has concluded or acceded to.

The maritime administrative organisation of China determines and promulgates the commercial insurance institutions and the mutual insurance institutions undertaking insurance in respect of civil liability for ship-source oil pollution damage upon taking advice from the insurance regulatory authority of the State Council.

Article 54 of the Regulations on Prevention of Pollution provides that the owners of Chinese ships possessing insurance against civil liability for ship source oil pollution damage or corresponding financial security shall, by submitting the nationality certificate for the ship, the insurance policy against civil liability for ship-source oil pollution damage or corresponding financial security document, apply for the Certificate of Insurance or Other Financial Security in Respect of Civil Liability for Oil Pollution Damage from the maritime administrative organisation located in the ship's port of registry.[9]

9 Article 54 of the Regulations on Prevention of Pollution provides that: 'In respect of a vessel with Chinese nationality which has been covered by the civil liability insurance of vessel-induced oil pollution damage or the relevant financial securities in accordance with Article 53 of the Regulations, the owner shall apply for the civil liability insurance certificate or the financial security certificate from the Maritime Administration at the port of registry of the vessel with presentation of the Certificate of Nationality, the insurance policy of vessel-induced oil pollution damage or the evidence of financial security.'

2.2.3 Measures for the implementation of civil liability insurance for vessel-induced oil pollution damage of the PRC

The Measures enacted by the Ministry of Transport according to the Marine Environmental Protection Law, the CMC and the Regulations on Prevention of Pollution came into force on 1 October 2010. They systematically stipulate criteria for all kinds of ships that should possess civil liability insurance against vessel-induced oil pollution damage and their insured amounts. The procedure of applying for authorisation of insurance agencies to undertake coverage of civil liability for ship source oil pollution damage and the procedure of applying for the Certificate according to the authority of the Regulations on Prevention of Pollution are also regulated by the Measures.

2.2.3.1 SCOPE OF APPLICATION OF THE MEASURES

Paragraph 1 of Article 2 of the Measures provides that for ships carrying oil substances and ships of more than 1,000 gross tonnage carrying non-oil substances that navigate within the territorial sea of the PRC, the owners shall buy civil liability insurance for vessel-induced oil pollution damage or obtain corresponding financial security in accordance with the Measures. The Measures were revised by the Ministry of Transport in August 2013.

2.2.3.2 THE CIVIL LIABILITY INSURANCE AMOUNT FOR SHIP-SOURCE OIL POLLUTION DAMAGE AND THE INSURANCE CERTIFICATE

For a ship carrying persistent oil substances in bulk, the insurance limit should be no less than the following minimum amounts:

(a) 4,510,000 SDR for a ship of less than 5,000 gross tonnage;
(b) For a ship of more than 5,000 gross tonnage, 631 SDR for each additional gross tonnage in addition to the above-mentioned amount; however, the aggregate amount shall not in any event exceed 89,770,000 SDR.

The insurance agency shall issue the Certificate for such ships.

For a ship carrying non-persistent oil substances in bulk or a ship of more than 1,000 gross tonnage carrying non-oil substances, the insurance limit should be no less than the following:

(a) 275,000 SDR for a ship with a gross tonnage ranging from 20 to 21 tons;
(b) for a ship with a gross tonnage ranging from 20 to 300 tons, 500 SDR for each additional gross tonnage in addition to the amount mentioned in subparagraph (a);
(c) 167,000 SDR for a ship with a gross tonnage ranging from 300 to 500 tons;

(d) for a ship with a gross tonnage ranging from 501 to 30,000 tons, 167 SDR for each additional gross tonnage in addition to the amount mentioned in subparagraph (c);
(e) for a ship with a gross tonnage ranging from 30,001 to 70,000 tons, 125 SDR for each additional gross tonnage in addition to the amount mentioned in subparagraph (d);
(f) for a ship with a gross tonnage over 70,001 tons, 83 SDR for each additional gross tonnage in addition to the amount mentioned in subparagraph (e).

For a ship of more than 1,000 gross tonnage carrying non-persistent oil substances, the insurance agency shall issue the Certificate of Insurance or Other Financial Security in Respect of Civil Liability for Bunker Oil Pollution Damage and the Certificate of Insurance or Other Financial Security in Respect of Civil Liability for Non-Persistent Oil Pollution Damage. For a ship of less than 1,000 gross tonnage carrying non-persistent oil substances, the insurance agency shall issue the Certificate of Insurance or Other Financial Security in Respect of Civil Liability for Non-Persistent Oil Pollution Damage.

For a ship of more than 1,000 gross tonnage carrying non-oil substances, the insurance agency shall issue the Certificate of Insurance or Other Financial Security in Respect of Civil Liability for Bunker Oil Pollution Damage.

For a ship engaging in the transport of goods between the ports of the PRC or engaging in coastal operation, the limit of the insurance or other financial security in respect of civil liability for oil pollution damage shall be calculated by 50 per cent of the limits in paragraph B (above).

Comparing the provisions of the Measures with those of CLC 1992, the latter merely requires a ship carrying more than 2,000 tons of persistent oil in bulk as cargo to have compulsory insurance. The scope of ships with compulsory insurance required in the former is definitely larger than the latter. In addition, the insured amount of ships carrying persistent oil in bulk as cargo is the same as the limits in the Protocol of 2000 amending CLC 1992,[10] demonstrating that the Chinese government has attached great importance to the need for protecting the victims of oil pollution damage and the marine environment.

2.2.3.3 QUALIFICATION OF INSURANCE INSTITUTIONS

According to Article 8 of the Measures 2010, ships flying the Chinese flag are required to apply for and hold a civil liability insurance certificate for

10 The Amendments to the 1992 Protocol of the International Convention on Civil Liability for Oil Pollution Damage (CLC) 2000.

vessel-induced oil pollution damage from insurance institutions, which are permitted and announced by the China MSA, or maintain a letter of guarantee, letter of credit or other financial security issued by insurance institutions or other domestic financial institutions such as banks approved and announced by the China MSA. The provisions relating to qualification of insurance institutions in the Measures 2010 are as follows.

Article 9, Mutual Insurance Institutions Undertaking Civil Liability Insurance for Vessel-Induced Oil Pollution Damage, shall comply with the following requirements:

(a) Register in the territory of China, or have a representative office or an agency in the territory of China.
(b) Net fund of last year shall exceed 100 million dollars or net fund per ton shall exceed 3 dollars.
(c) Insurance clauses shall be in accordance with laws, administrative regulations, rules of China, and international conventions joined or ratified by China.

Article 10, the Commercial Insurance Institutions Undertaking Civil Liability Insurance for Vessel-Induced Oil Pollution Damage, shall comply with the following requirements:

(a) Be established with the approval of China Insurance Regulatory Commission, hold a Licence for Operating Insurance Business, and be registered in the administrative departments for industry and commerce and possess a business licence.
(b) Net assets of the previous year shall exceed RMB 700 million.
(c) Solvency of the previous year shall be more than 100 per cent.
(d) Insurance clauses should accord with laws, administrative regulations, rules of China, and international conventions joined or ratified by the PRC.

After auditing and confirming the insurance institutions that meet the requirements of the Measures, the China MSA will announce the results to the public before 30 November every year. According to the Notice Announcing the List of Civil Liability Insurance Agencies for Vessel-Induced Oil Pollution Damage for Chinese Vessels in 2013, issued on 5 December 2012, there were 26 insurance institutions eligible to provide civil liability insurance for oil pollution damage for Chinese vessels.[11] Compared with the list for the previous year, there were three more institutions than in 2012.

11 China MSA, [Haichuanbo No. 828(2012)], available at: www.msa.gov.cn/Notice/Notice/307b281a-8a4f-4eea-a91f-58da69c25a9d.html (accessed 16 May 2014).

However, it is noteworthy that the current Measures, as revised by the Ministry of Transport in August 2013, have removed the aforesaid requirements of authorisation for insurance institutions.[12] The new Article 8 of the Measures 2013 provides as follows:

> The owners of vessels flying the Chinese flag shall acquire civil liability insurance for vessel-induced oil pollution damage from commercial insurance institutions legally established within the territory of China, or mutual insurance institutions legally established within the territory of China or having a representative office or agency within the territory of China, or shall obtain letters of guarantee, letters of credit or other financial guarantee issued by the aforesaid insurance institutions and domestic banks.
>
> The owners of vessels flying the Chinese flag shall acquire civil liability insurance for vessel-induced oil pollution damage or obtain financial guarantee from insurance institutions with compensation capabilities, and the insurance institutions shall produce the relevant documents proving their compensation capabilities to the owners of vessels flying the Chinese flag.

3 The market status of civil liability insurance for oil pollution damage in China

Before the Measures came into effect in 2010, there were no relevant laws and regulations regulating civil liability insurance for the risk of ship-source oil pollution damage, and a protection and indemnity policy for ships usually covers the risk of oil pollution damage. It is therefore difficult to distinguish the market of civil liability insurance for oil pollution damage for Chinese ships from other forms of insurance.

Historically, civil liability insurance for oil pollution damage has been underwritten mainly in the form of mutual insurance. However, there is a legal barrier for mutual insurance in the Chinese market. Mutual insurance associations (P&I Clubs) in China are registered with the Ministry of Civil Affairs and are therefore regarded as corporations aggregate.[13] The administration and regulation of a corporation aggregate are different from those of insurance companies (which are classified as enterprise legal persons). As a result, mutual insurance in China may not be conducted following the

12 The aforesaid Articles 9 and 10 of the former Measures (2010) have been deleted after the revision.

13 According to the General Principles of Civil Law of China 1986, legal persons are divided into enterprise legal persons and non-enterprise legal persons. A corporation aggregate is a non-enterprise legal person. See Chapter 3, General Principles of Civil Law of China 1986.

principles and concepts of (commercial) insurance and the China Insurance Regulatory Commission is not a valid regulatory body for mutual insurance. In addition, although it is common that foreign P&I Clubs undertake mutual insurance in China, such practice is in lack of supervision because there is no designated regulatory body competent for this type of insurance business.

In the current market of protection and indemnity insurance, the situation is that China Shipowners Mutual Assurance Association (CSMAA), PICC P&C and other commercial insurance companies, as well as foreign P&I Clubs, compete in the market each according to their own business goals.

CSMAA is an association giving priority to developing the main ocean-going fleet, with focus on coastal and inland ships as its second priority. In fact, to some extent, CSMAA is unwilling to accept insurance of coastal and inland ships that have a low safety factor. The coastal and inland ships covered by CSMAA are mainly old ones that were transferred from the ocean fleet that originally belonged to China Shipping. The insurance products of CSMAA include P&I insurance, hull insurance, defence risk, war risk, strikes risk, etc. But CSMAA maintains high standards and members must notably join the International Association of Classification Societies and maintain the class of their ships, and most coastal and inland ships cannot therefore meet the requirements of membership. Also, CSMAA has little interest in underwriting independent civil liability insurance for ship-source oil pollution damage.

PICC P&C and other domestic commercial insurance companies focus mainly on insurance for coastal and inland ships, with insurance for ocean-going ships as a supplement. The business model for protection and indemnity insurance business employed by domestic commercial insurance companies is that they obtain proportional reinsurance cover from foreign P&I Clubs, or purchase excess of loss reinsurance alone. The operational model of PICC P&C is: (a) Mutual insurance business for ocean-going vessels of PICC P&C is reinsured through the West of England Insurance Service (Luxembourg) S.A. by means of proportional reinsurance. The West of England underwrites a 70 per cent share and PICC P&C underwrites the remaining 30 per cent share. In practice, PICC P&C sets its deductible at a low rate in its mutual insurance in order to compete with foreign P&I Clubs including the West of England. Therefore, the amount that exceeds PICC's deductible but is lower than West of England's deductible is undertaken by PICC; other indemnity payments are shared by PICC and West England in proportion according to the contract of reinsurance. (b) For coastal and inland ships, it arranges excess of loss reinsurance from foreign P&I Clubs. According to the PICC P&C's shipping department, due to the poor effectiveness of the law in relation to claims for oil pollution damage, the P&I insurance of coastal and inland ships have a low risk profile, so that there is no need to reinsure. PICC P&C has published Clauses of Additional Insurance for Coastal and Inland Ship's Oil Pollution Liability, and has offered insurance for oil pollution damage to shipowners since 2000.

At present, such clauses have become the primary contents of the Clauses of Civil Liability Insurance for Coastal and Inland Ship-source Bunker Oil Pollution. Other insurance companies also have similar clauses, such as Clauses of Civil Liability Insurance for Ship-source Oil Pollution Damage made by Ping An Property & Casualty Insurance Company of China Ltd, which covers insurance for ship-source oil or bunker oil pollution damage. Each of the insurance companies conveys an impression that such insurance business carries good profits and a desire to expand the scale of business.

Foreign P&I Clubs have successfully developed their business relying on their professional service and well-deserved reputation. The insurance products provided by them are flexible and comprehensive, and they cover civil liability insurance for oil pollution in their P&I insurance and charterer's liability insurance. But foreign P&I Clubs have high requirements for member ships that are difficult for most Chinese coastal and inland ships to fulfil.

In conclusion, the subjects of civil liability insurance for ship-source oil pollution in China include mutual insurance institutions (P&I Clubs) and commercial insurance companies. The civil liability insurance of ocean-going vessels is mostly contained in the ship's protection and indemnity policy, and in this policy the limit of compensation is set higher than the requirements of CLC 1992 or the Measures. Civil liability insurance of coastal and inland ships may be underwritten by commercial insurance companies, in a manner similar to ocean-going vessels, or covered by separately purchased civil liability insurance for ship source oil or bunker oil pollution damage. In the market of civil liability insurance for coastal and inland ship-source oil pollution, PICC P&C holds an approximate 55 per cent market share.

4 Latest development of civil liability insurance for coastal ship-source oil pollution damage: the demonstration project of blanket insurance

4.1 Fundamental contents of the demonstration project of blanket insurance

The demonstration project of blanket insurance (hereinafter referred to as the Project) was jointly promoted by the Ministry of Transport and the China Insurance Regulatory Commission on 27 December 2012 was officially launched in Beijing on 1 January 2013, and marks a new step forward for civil liability insurance for ship-source oil pollution damage in China. The Project is entitled Demonstration Project of Blanket Insurance for Coastal Ship-source Civil Liability for Oil Pollution Damage 2013–2014. The ships covered by this Project are Chinese coastal ships that should be insured subject to the requirement of the Measures and other relevant documents, including newly built ships with temporary nationality for the sea trial. Under the Project Framework Agreement, the China Maritime

Safety Administration is Party A, each individual insurance company is Party B and Beijing Century Insurance Brokers Ltd is Party C. These three parties have jointly signed the agreement to implement the Project. The proportion of each insurance company's co-insurance share is shown in Table 11.1.

Table 11.1 Proportion of co-insurance share

Insurance company	*Co-insurance share (%)*
PICC P&C	37.5
Ping An Property & Casualty Insurance Company of China Ltd	28
CPIC	14
CCIC	10
Sunshine Insurance Group Corporation Ltd	8.5
China Life Insurance Company Ltd	2

The Project is rigorously organised; the management system is made up of a joint working group, a routine work execution group, a claims service group, a provincial level claims service group and a service centre. It has designated responsible officers and their contact information from the central to local levels. The joint working group is mainly responsible for coordination of the main operation mechanism and significant items; the routine work execution group is mainly in charge of implementing significant decisions of the Project and coordination of routine work; the claims service group is mainly responsible for coordination of accident claims; the provincial level claims service group is mainly responsible for reporting accident scene survey work carried out in the province's sea area; and the service centre is in charge of offering services to policyholders and the insured (e.g. handling insurance, certificates and claims).

It is said that all MSAs directly under China MSA have received an internal document, to the effect that the Blue Cards issued by insurance companies not included in the Project should be approved and conferred relevant Certificates by MSA. In fact, this Project is only an optional new channel for the insured to obtain civil liability insurance for ship-source oil pollution damage. Although the aim of this Project is not to unify the market of civil liability insurance of coastal ship-source oil pollution damage, it nevertheless represents the policy orientation of the Chinese government on the issues of civil liability insurance for vessel-induced oil pollution damage.

4.2 Purpose of the demonstration project of blanket insurance

The newly launched demonstration project aims to build up a 'co-insurance' system for nationwide civil liability insurance for coastal ship-source oil pollution damage capable of unifying insurance and claims handling arrangements for the purpose of promoting the stabilisation and development of the insurance market for coastal ship source oil pollution damage. The competition is quite fierce in the insurance market, although the insurance companies' proportion of marine insurance business has shrunk greatly due to the global economic downturn. If cut-throat competition takes place in the market of civil liability insurance for coastal ship-source oil pollution damage, China's domestic corporations will be the final victims. The Project is designed to promote the stability of the insurance market, strengthen the claims paying ability for coastal ship-source oil pollution damage, and increase the efficiency of surveys and payment of claims after pollution incidents, which can ensure compensation for the victims in time and help them resume production and life.

4.3 Problems existing in the demonstration project of blanket insurance

Civil liability insurance for ship source oil pollution damage in China has made unprecedented progress. There are now three ways to buy insurance of this kind: (1) shipowners buy protection and indemnity insurance to cover oil pollution damage, and provide an insurance amount equal to or higher than the legal limits; (2) shipowners buy civil liability insurance for ship-source oil or bunker oil pollution damage directly from insurance companies; and (3) shipowners buy civil liability insurance for ship-source oil or bunker oil pollution damage directly from the Project.

This shows that the Project just offers one more channel to insure for oil pollution. But industry insiders are caustic about the Project; even some officers of the MSA indicate that the Project would not develop prosperously. In the authors' opinion, the problems of the Project are as follows:

(1) The foothold of intervention of the State administrative power is that oil pollution will damage the environmental rights and interests so there should be intervention by public authorities. However, civil liability insurance for vessel-induced oil pollution damage belongs to the commercial sphere; market subjects can compete fairly in this field, which is in accordance with the requirement of establishing a socialist market economy. Intervention of public authorities violates the principle of fair competition applied in the commercial insurance market.
(2) In the marine insurance business, hull insurance and protection and indemnity insurance are by now well-established ways for the owners of ocean-going ships to prevent and control risks. After the entry into force of CLC 1969, CLC 1992 and Bunker Convention 2001, every P&I Club covers civil liability for oil pollution damage among the protection and indemnity risks and provides insurance in an amount higher than what is required by the related international conventions.

In recent years, even coastal shipowners are inclined to buy protection and indemnity insurance in order to get more comprehensive protection. So it is hard for the Project to reach the expected effect.

(3) It is apparent that this Project does not reflect upon the peculiar business pattern of domestic insurance companies. City-level companies have their finances independently accounted and need to consider their combined cost and profit margin. After the launch of the Project, the business of civil liability insurance for ship-source oil pollution damage will be distributed both among the head insurance companies and within their own branch companies. It is a serious problem left to the joint working group and the head insurance companies' competent departments how to allocate the proportion of coinsurance among head companies and within their own branch companies. This must ultimately have an influence on the market of civil liability insurance for ship-source oil pollution damage in China.

5 Conclusion

In conclusion, the Chinese government takes the performance of international conventions acceded to by her seriously, with particular attention paid to the establishment and improvement of the legal system for the protection of the marine environment. The China Insurance Regulatory Commission, the Ministry of Transport, the Ministry of Finance and some other ministries and commissions attach importance to the establishment of an indemnity mechanism with respect to oil pollution damage. Such an indemnity mechanism has been established whose pillars are the civil liability insurance system and the compensation fund system[14] for ship-source oil pollution damage. The legislation pertaining to civil liability insurance for ship-source oil pollution damage is basically formed and the insurance market for ship-source oil pollution damage is developing well. With the support of the Chinese government and joint efforts by shipowners and insurance companies, we believe that the future of civil liability insurance for ship-source oil pollution damage in China will be bright.

14 Ministry of Transport and Ministry of Finance jointly issued *Administrative Measures of Collection and Usage of Compensation Fund for Ships' Oil Pollution Damage* on 11 May 2012, which came into force on 1 July 2012.

12 Cargo insurance documents in letters of credit

Jingbo Zhang[1]

1 Introductory background

1.1 Cargo insurance in international trade

Cargo insurance has played a vital role in international trade since the development of carriage of goods by sea in the early nineteenth century. A key feature of the contract for international sale of goods is that the risk passes on or as from the shipment and the seller is not responsible for the loss at sea.[2] If anything goes wrong after the risk has passed, the buyer who has no physical control over the goods but has paid for them will rely heavily on the carriage contract and the insurance contract to compensate its loss. It is also well recognised that the international sale of goods is essentially a documentary sale (i.e. the seller symbolically delivers the documents representing the goods to the buyer and gets payment even before the goods have physically arrived at the destination). Since the bundle of documents passed by the seller is going to provide the security guarantee to the buyer, the buyer is confident to pay for the documents and expect the contractual cargo or at least reimbursement if the cargo has been lost or damaged. Under c.i.f. and c.i.p. terms,[3] the seller is not only obliged to insure the consignment as agreed in the sale contract, but also to tender the proper insurance documents to the buyer, so that the buyer will be able to recover the amount of its loss from the underwriters.

1 BA, LLB, LLM, Lecturer in Commercial and Maritime Law at School of Law, University of Southampton. Member of Southampton Institute of Maritime Law.

2 The principle applies to sales in non-arrival terms, including terms involving carriage of goods by sea such as f.o.b. (free on board) and c.i.f. (cost, freight and insurance), and also terms used for multimodal transport, such as c.i.p. (cost insurance paid to . . .).

3 C.i.f. terms are used for carriage of goods by sea; however, c.i.p. terms are often used for multimodal/containerised shipment. In this chapter, the author will mainly focus on c.i.f. terms and use it as a default example.

1.2 Letters of credit and insurance documents

The letter of credit, as a primary instrument of payment in international trade transactions, has been described as the 'life-blood of international commerce'.[4] The buyer, as requested by the seller in the sale contract, normally finds an issuing bank to open a letter of credit according to the sale contract terms. The letter of credit stands for an unconditional payment promise made by the issuing bank to the beneficiary (normally the seller), which offers a secure way for the seller to get the payment. Once the letter of credit is opened, it will be independent from the sale contract and the payment will be unaffected by any defences arising from the underlying sale contract. The bank has to pay for the documents as long as the documents constitute a complying presentation. Conversely, the bank is only entitled to pay the seller when the documents are compliant with letter of credit requirements. Therefore, before the bank decides to honour or negotiate the documents, it will scrutinise the documents carefully. Without doubt, the insurance document, as one of the most important documents in c.i.f. and c.i.p. sales, will inevitably be required by the letter of credit and examined by the bank.

1.3 Legal framework for letters of credit

With increasing importance taken by letters of credit in international trade, the International Chamber of Commerce (ICC)[5] has spared no effort to summarise and unify international practices and usages in relation to letters of credit transactions since 1920. Although these ICC products are not mandatory regulations, they have been widely used in about 95 per cent of letter of credit transactions. The most recently published version, Uniform Customs and Practice for Documentary Credits Publication in 2008 (UCP600),[6] along with its supplementary International Standard Banking Practice for the Examination of Documents under UCP600 Publication No. 745 in 2013 (ISBP745),[7] have provided a new comprehensive framework for documentary examinations in letters of credit. In particular, the UCP600 Article 28 and ISBP745 section K have expressly dealt with the requirements for examining insurance documents in accordance with market expectations.

4 *Harbottle (RD) (Mercantile) Ltd v National Westminster Bank Ltd* [1978] Q.B.146 at p 155, per Kerr J.

5 To avoid confusion, the International Chamber of Commerce is referred to in this chapter as ICC, and the Institute Cargo Clauses will be referred to as ICC with the addition of (A), (B) or (C), as appropriate in the context.

6 ICC Publication No. 600, also referred to as UCP600.

7 ICC Publication No. 745, also referred to as ISBP745.

It is clear that the applicability of UCP is not in the nature of a legal or regulatory measure. As UCP itself states, the Rules apply to any documentary credit when the credit expressly indicates that it is subject to these rules. Where it does, the Rules will bind all parties unless expressly modified or excluded by the credit.[8] In the UK, the UCP will not have the force of law unless the parties have expressly incorporated it into their contract. As a common law jurisdiction country, the English courts have established and developed case law to regulate letters of credit that do not incorporate the UCP. These cases have reflected the expectations of English courts in judging acceptable insurance documents in letters of credit transactions, as well as in international trade, although some of them were decided very differently from the UCP position.

Comparatively, China, as a civil law jurisdiction country, has neither enacted any statutes nor adopted any unified judicial interpretations concerning letters of credit transactions for more than 20 years after the Chinese economic reform in 1978.[9] With the significant economic growth and the pressure resulting from a large number of letter of credit disputes, the Fourth Civil Division of the Supreme People's Court, which hears numerous foreign-related commercial cases, has taken the initiative of drafting a set of Chinese Letter of Credit Rules: the Provisions on Several Issues concerning the Trial of Disputes over Letters of Credit (the 'LC Judicial Interpretations'). The LC Judicial Interpretations became effective on 1 January 2006 and as the first Chinese statute on letter of credit, it has uniquely provided a legal basis for letter of credit business in China. The Judicial Interpretations is in maximum conformity with the international standard banking practices, especially UCP. In Article 2, it states that in the adjudication of letter of credit related cases before a Chinese court, where the parties have agreed on the application of any international customs, such agreement shall be enforced. Absent such agreement, the UCP and other relevant standards as formulated by the International Chamber of Commerce shall be applicable.[10] It is evident that the UCP is used as a set of default rules in the Chinese courts, even without express or implied agreement from parties.

8 UCP600 Article 1; UCP500 Article 1.

9 Unlike the UK, court judgments and arbitral awards are not considered as legal sources, as China adheres to the civil law system, but they may be quite persuasive when no specific rule in relation to the disputable issue of concern can be referred to.

10 The LC Judicial Interpretations Article 2 has laid down a general rule for LC disputes, while in its Article 6, the standards of documentary examinations are especially concerned. The Supreme Court insists on the same principle, namely, absent an agreement from parties, the UCP and other relevant ICC standards should apply.

1.4 Influence from the law of marine insurance

Whether the tendered insurance documents can be accepted under a letter of credit transaction depends not only on the law of documentary credit, but is also restricted by insurance law and practice. Even more, the position of insurance law, especially marine insurance law, which had a significant impact on international sale of goods carried by sea, would inevitably influence UCP revisions on insurance sections and judgments concerning the examination of insurance documents in letter of credit cases:

> Insurance law has, from the earliest times, consisted, on the one hand, of positive law, that is statutes, codes or common law, and, on the other hand, standard insurance terms agreed between the parties which supplement or supersede that law.[11]

The UK has the most influential legislation in the field of marine insurance – the Marine Insurance Act 1906 (MIA 1906) and the most widely used cargo insurance standard forms in the world – the Institute Cargo Clauses (ICC) A, B and C.[12]

Having realised the important and unique characteristics of marine insurance, the Chinese legislator enacted the Maritime Code with an insertion of Chapter 12, 'Contract of Marine Insurance', in 1993.[13] In the Chinese cargo insurance market, both the Institute Cargo Clauses and the China Insurance Clauses are used. The China Insurance Clauses, based on the Institute Cargo Clauses 1963, were drafted by the People's Insurance Company of China for the purpose of expanding the Chinese cargo insurance market. The China Insurance Clauses (PICC Clauses), most recently revised in 2009, are categorised into four groups based on the nature of carriage. Among them, the Ocean Marine Cargo Clauses is the form used for international shipping practice and will be examined later.

1.5 Objectives of this chapter

This chapter aims to examine and reveal the requirements for cargo insurance documents under letter of credit transactions in two countries, namely the UK and China. Since Article 2 of the Chinese LC Judicial

11 John Dunt, *International Cargo Insurance* (Informa Law from Routledge 2012) paragraph 15.18.

12 The most recent revision of the Institute Cargo Clauses was in 2009.

13 See Appendix II in this work. The Chinese Insurance Act, which governs general insurance contracts, was legislated in 1995 and recently revised in 2009. The Maritime Code takes precedence over the Insurance Act in relation to marine insurance, and according to the Insurance Act Article 184, it only steps in if no specific rule from the Maritime Code can be referred to.

Interpretations has established default application for the UCP even without agreement between the parties, it is submitted that, in usual circumstances and without an express exclusion from the parties, the Chinese courts would customarily follow the position of UCP600 to examine the compliance of insurance documents under a letter of credit.[14] However, it is likely that the recent appearance of ISBP745 (as a detailed supplement of UCP600 in documentary examinations) published in 2013 will bring some transitional adjustments for practitioners involved in LC transactions, as well as for the Chinese courts. Therefore, the author will first look at the provisions relating to insurance documents in the UCP600 and scrutinise the corresponding updates in the ISBP745.

With the UCP600 operating as a default rule under Chinese law, it will be of interest to examine the different positions between the UCP600 and the English common law in relation to the criteria for accepting insurance documents in LC. In this paper, the author will use the UCP600 insurance provisions as a chief source to analyse issues arising from day to day transactions, and accordingly compare them with the English common law position. Moreover, in each part, the author will observe the influence brought by the law of marine insurance on documentary credit transactions and endeavour to uncover the existing loopholes in cargo insurance documents examinations.

2 Form of insurance document

By virtue of MIA 1906 section 21, a contract of marine insurance is deemed to be concluded when the proposal of the assured is accepted by the insurer, whether the policy will then be issued or not. Similarly, in the Chinese Maritime Code (CMC) Article 221, it is stipulated that a contract of marine insurance is concluded after the insured puts forward a proposal for insurance and the insurer accepts the proposal with the agreed terms and conditions of the insurance. Obviously, a policy is not a prerequisite to the validity of an insurance contract. Since the preparation of a policy of insurance takes some time, it is not always practicable to obtain actual policies of insurance. In order to facilitate business, certificates and open covers are therefore commonly used in the modern insurance market. The form of an insurance certificate is variable, but its essential feature is to certify that the goods in question have been insured under a referred policy. An open cover is taken out in cases where a party makes regular shipments in the course of his trade. Under an open cover, a certificate

14 The Chinese LC Judicial Interpretations was enacted in 2006, at a time when UCP500 was the current revision of the UCP. However, with the development of UCP600 since 2008, most LC transactions will now use UCP600 and presumably the Chinese courts will choose to follow modern international banking practice.

of insurance or a declaration will be issued in respect of each shipment insured.[15]

The UCP600 has followed the above insurance market practice in Article 28(a), which recognises that, subject to agreement otherwise in the LC, an insurance policy, an insurance certificate or a declaration under an open cover can all be an acceptable form in an LC presentation.[16] However, cover notes will not be accepted, as stated in Article 28(c). Moreover, the UCP600 Article 28(d) further provides that 'an insurance policy is acceptable in lieu of an insurance certificate or a declaration under an open cover'. However, it is not vice versa: namely, if a policy is called for, an insurance certificate or a declaration under an open cover cannot be substituted.[17] This arguably suggests that the UCP considers a policy to be conceptually distinct from any other insurance documents, in particular from a certificate.[18] In this part, the central question lies in what kinds of insurance document the bank is obliged to accept under an LC transaction. By answering this question, the author will review the distinctions between a policy and a certificate set up by the law, and then further point out whether the distinctions will cause difficulties in LC transactions.

2.1 Express requirements in LC should prevail

It is obvious that the express requirements in a letter of credit must be followed by a bank in the process of documentary examination. The reason is that the parties should get what they want by tailoring their contract. If a party has specified a policy in his contract, something that is not a policy but is *like* a policy is not good enough for him. 'He is entitled to have a document of the very kind which he has agreed to take, or at least one which does not differ from it in any material respect'.[19] According to the English case law, this statement of principle is just as applicable to a letter of credit as to a contract of sale.[20]

15 The assured must notify the insurer immediately upon learning that the cargo insured under the open cover has been shipped or has arrived. If no declaration of shipment has been made under the open cover, the presentation of this open cover policy would not be accepted in international trade. Cf. *South African Reserve Bank v Samuel Co. Ltd* (1931) 40 Lloyd's Rep 291, pp 298–299.

16 It is arguable that this is a non-exhaustive list and that further types of insurance document might be acceptable under UCP600.

17 The UCP600 Drafting Group, *Commentary on UCP600: Article by Article Analysis* (Publication No. 680, Paris 2007), p 131. The Commentary has further pointed out that 'whilst an insurance certificate or declaration under an open cover provides proof of insurance, in the case of a claim, if there is any discrepancy in the insurance cover between the policy and the certificate or declaration under the open cover, the insurance cover in the policy will prevail'.

18 M. Bridge (ed.), *Benjamin's Sale of Goods*, 8th edn, 2010, Sweet and Maxwell, paras 23–155.

19 *Wilson & Co. v Belgian Grain Co.* [1920] 2 KB 1, p 9 per Bailhache J.

20 *Donald H. Scott v Barclays Bank Ltd* [1923] 2 KB 1, p 11 per Bankes LJ.

Nevertheless, in the context of a c.i.f. contract, the English courts have held that even where the contract permitted other insurance documents than policies, the tendered document should 'provide as near as possible to the buyer the same protection and rights as he would get by a policy'.[21] It has been suggested that tender of an unsatisfactory certificate would be bad, even if the contract did permit tender of a certificate.[22] Although these were not cases concerning LC, they arguably reflected the desire of English courts in protecting the essential points under an insurance document (i.e. the assured's rights against the underwriter, with the extent of those rights ascertainable by reference to an identified or identifiable policy, or perhaps in some other way, such as by reference to terms known in the trade).[23]

Since the UCP is not a set of compulsory rules, the parties can expressly modify or exclude the UCP provisions in their LC.[24] In the Chinese LC Judicial Interpretations, Article 6 addresses this point. It states that where a dispute concerns the examination of documents presented under an LC, rules as agreed by the parties shall be applied. Moreover, if there is an overlap or inconsistency between an LC express requirement and a UCP provision, the former should prevail over the latter, which applies only by general incorporation. Consequently, if an LC specifically requires a policy, an insurance certificate would not be a proper tender, regardless of the fact that the UCP600 Article 28(a) has designated an insurance certificate as an acceptable form. However, no evident minimum requirements similar to those resulting from English cases can be found in the UCP or in the Chinese LC Judicial Interpretations. The UCP reiteratively emphasises that a bank will not examine the terms and conditions in an insurance document, let alone the rights of the assured contained in the presented document.

2.2 When LC is silent as to the forms of insurance documents

What is the default position if the letter of credit does not specify which form of insurance document should be tendered? If the UCP600 is going to apply, the bank will accept a range of insurance documents, such as an insurance policy, an insurance certificate or a declaration under an open cover. However, it is well known that a policy is distinguishable from other certificates, because a policy is a document that embodies a contract, while a certificate is a document issued by insurers or sometimes even by someone else, asserting the existence of a contract. For the different legal effects between a policy and a certificate, neither the Chinese Maritime Code nor

21 *Promos SA v European Grain & Shipping* [1975] 1 Lloyd's Rep 375, p 388.
22 *De Monchy v Phoenix Insurance Co. of Hartford* (1928) 33 Com. Cas. 197
23 Benjamin, para 19-048.
24 Article 2, UCP600.

the Insurance Act offers many clues.[25] Under English marine insurance law, a policy may be treated very differently from an insurance certificate or a declaration under an open cover. Therefore, what is the default situation if the UCP is not going to apply?

The early English cases have established that a policy of insurance is an essential document under c.i.f. contracts.[26] It is also well recognised that a document of insurance is not a good tender in England under an ordinary c.i.f. contract unless it is an actual policy, and unless it falls within the provisions of the Marine Insurance Act 1906. This point has been discussed by McCardie J. in the leading trade case, *Diamond Alkali v Bourgeois*,[27] in which he summarised three main reasons why tender of a certificate was insufficient compared with a policy. The first reason was that the person to whom such a tender was made would be unable to determine from the certificate what the full terms of the insurance were. The second deficiency was that such certificates were not transferable by endorsement under MIA 1906 section 50(3), which only mentioned the assignability of a policy. Third, the certificates would not comply with the formal requirements of MIA 1906 section 22, by which a contract of marine insurance would be inadmissible in evidence unless embodied in a policy. Thus, he concluded that a certificate of insurance fell within a different legal classification to that of a policy of insurance and would not offer the same legal protection to the holder.

The same issue was the subject of attention from the English court later in a pre-UCP documentary credit case, *Donald H. Scott v Barclays*,[28] in which a document was tendered by the seller to the bank to satisfy the LC requirement of an 'approved insurance policy'.[29] This certificate stated certain terms of the insurance, but for others it expressly referred the reader to the policy itself, and no one looking at the certificate alone could tell what the terms of the insurance were. Atkin LJ held that the presented document did not purport to be a policy at all, but only a certificate to prove that the policy had been issued, for the reason that it did not contain on its face the terms of the actual contract of insurance or the risks against which the insuring company purported to secure the assured. He further pointed out that:

25 CMC Article 232 only states under the provision of an open cover that 'where the content of the insurance certificates issued by the insurer separately differ from those of the open policy, the insurance certificates issued separately shall prevail'.

26 *Ireland v Livingston* L. R. 5 H. L. 395; *Hickox v Adam* (1876) 34 L. T. 404; *Johnson v Taylor Bros. & Co.* [1920] A. C. 144.

27 *Diamond Alkali Export Co. v Bourgeois* [1921] 3 KB 433, pp 456–457.

28 *Donald H. Scott v Barclays Bank Ltd* [1923] 2 KB 1.

29 Although in this case the LC expressly required an 'approved insurance policy', the court did not arbitrarily categorise the tendered document. Instead, the court endeavoured to analyse the difference between the tendered certificate and the required policy.

the bankers, who may have to rely upon the policy of insurance to cover them from loss in case they have no effectual recourse against the customer at whose request they have given the credit, have no means of discovering to what extent they are covered, and that is a perfectly valid objection to this document.[30]

From the above judgment, it is apparent that a valid policy must be one containing all the terms of insurance and the bank is entitled to reject an insurance document not containing the full terms on its face under an LC presentation. Nevertheless, the case has left two issues open. First, would an insurance certificate be good tender under an LC transaction as long as it evidences all the terms in the policy?[31] Second, is a bank entitled to accept nothing less than an insurance document that will comply with the MIA 1906 provisions relating to policies of marine insurance? Bankes LJ thought that it was not necessary to lay down any hard and fast rule, so he reserved his opinion upon the status of insurance certificates concerning the effect of MIA 1906, which was discussed by *Diamond Alkali* in the context of a c.i.f. contract.

2.3 Effect of MIA 1906 on LC

It is clear that under English law, a seller is, prima facie, bound to tender a policy of insurance, which contains the full terms of insurance, as well as gives the rights under MIA 1906 to a buyer under a sale contract. However, the case law leaves the conclusion open in the context of LC. The question is, will English marine insurance law have any impact on the interpretation of documents presented under LC and UCP600? The answer is arguably no, since the issue here is not about the needs of a buyer on c.i.f. or any other terms, but rather what is required by the terms of a credit. It is suggested that the concerns of insurance documents under a sale contract are irrelevant to the acceptability of a document under an LC. Existing case law reflects no more than a commercial expectation placed on the underlying contract, in which the buyer wishes to hold a reliable insurance document. By contrast, in the context of an LC, if the applicant wants a document that fits a particular need, it should specify so in the credit. Moreover, the status of a policy in marine insurance law is debatable and

30 *Donald H. Scott v Barclays Bank Ltd* [1923] 2 KB 1, p 17. The judge articulated concerns for the bank's security; however, in current practice, the bank may focus on efficacy rather than precaution of risk. This is reflected by the ISBP745 section K22 that banks need not examine general terms and conditions in an insurance document.

31 In *Donald H. Scott*, Bankes LJ and Scrutton LJ tended to think that whether the insurance document contained the full terms of the insurance contract was the decisive point for acceptance. However, by way of inference from Atkin LJ's words, he would not have validated the presented insurance document even if it contained full terms.

is subject to change under English law.[32] A document may be a policy even though it does not contain all the terms of the insurance, but incorporates by reference certain Institute Clauses.[33] Customary documents, such as the American certificates of insurance, might be permitted as a tender in lieu of policies.[34]

Under UCP600, the credit must specify the requirements of an acceptable insurance document, since the bank will accept any documents meeting with the credit requirements without regard to the individual terms and conditions.[35] There are no unified rules for what constitutes a 'policy'. The term 'policy' could be interpreted as being a document containing a full indication of contract terms, either by express statement or by incorporation of a well-known and accessible document, such as Institute Cargo Clauses, even though the bank may not be concerned with this point and may accept any such document as presented. It seems that the UCP600 is reluctant to explicitly respond to a piece of national legislation, even one as influential as the MIA 1906.[36] Imagining hypothetically that marine insurance law were to influence the interpretation of the transitional UCP, which concept of a policy should prevail? It is suggested that where by reason of the UCP600 Article 28(a), an open cover document is acceptable, it will not be defective simply because the document refers to the terms of the policy itself, which will be unknown to the bank and cannot be examined by the bank. Nonetheless, the document itself must comply with the LC requirements if there are any and pass the conditions set out in other UCP provisions.[37]

32 In English law, many of the 1906 Act's requirements relating to the contents of a policy have been repealed: those that remain are identification of the assured (section 23(1)), signature by or on behalf of the insurer (section 24(1)), and designation of the subject matter insured with reasonable certainty (section 26 (1)). However, the repeal is not replicated in other countries that have adopted legislation based on the English statute.

33 *Malmberg v H & J Evans* (1924) 30 Com. Cas. 107, p 112.

34 Note the difference in relation to American certificates of insurance that are 'accepted in this country as policies'; see *Wilson, Holgate v Belgian Grain and Produce* [1920] 2 KB 1 at 7. However, in *Donald H Scott Co. Ltd v Barclays Bank Ltd* [1923] 2 KB 1 at 17, Atkin LJ held that an American certificate could not be tendered in place of a policy under a banker's commercial credit.

35 UCP600 Article 28(g).

36 Taking assignment as an example, in the MIA1906 section 50(3), the only form for the purpose of assignment is the marine policy. The ISBP745 section K19, however, adopts a different method by stipulating that a contract of marine insurance can be assigned by endorsement without limiting the form of documents as the MIA 1906 does.

37 Such as UCP600 Article 14(d) – no data conflict with other documents and Article 14(f) – fulfil the function as an insurance document.

2.4 Prohibited forms

In the absence of express stipulation to the contrary in an LC, cover notes will not be acceptable.[38] A cover note is commonly issued by the broker as his own indication rather than with the authority of the insurer. It is clear that the buyer has a direct right of action on the policy against the underwriters; however, on a broker's cover note the assured has apparently no right of action against anybody, even where the cover note is indorsed. Moreover, as Bailhache J held, 'a right of action against a broker even if it exists is a very different right from that of an action against underwriters'.[39]

Nevertheless, where a broker acts as the agent of the insurer and holds such authority from the insurer, his position is different, since the UCP600 Article 28(a) allows an insurance document issued and signed by the underwriter's agent or proxy, as long as such signature can indicate their agency relations.[40] In addition, an insurance document may also be issued on an insurance broker's stationery, provided the insurance document has been signed by an underwriter or its agent.[41]

From the above analysis, it is clear that a cargo insurance policy will make for the best presentation in an LC transaction, since it comes within definite, established and statutory legal rights. Other forms, such as insurance certificates and declarations under an open cover, are frequently used and recognised in LC transactions. While Chinese law has not distinguished the different insurance forms involved in international trade to the level of detail of English law, an unquestionable point is that a broker's cover note will not be acceptable in an LC transaction without contrary statements.

3 Risk coverage

It is the traders' job to tailor their sale of goods contracts and to designate the risks to be covered by the insurance. When traders choose the LC as their payment method, they also need to specify their requirements in the LC for exchange of payment. UCP600 has intentionally left the risk coverage issue at the parties' option. Article 28(g) stipulates that a credit should state the type of insurance required and, if any, the additional risks

38 UCP600 Article 28(c) common law held the same position in international sale contracts (i.e. unacceptability of a broker's cover note), which was considered obiter in the early case: *Wilson, Holgate v Belgian Grain and Produce* [1920] 2 KB 1, p 9; *Promos SA v European Grain & Shipping* [1975] 1 Lloyd's Rep 375, p 388.

39 *Wilson, Holgate v Belgian Grain and Produce* [1920] 2 KB 1, p 9.

40 The requirement for a signature is new in the UCP600. It requires the agent's signature to indicate the insurer or the underwriter for whom the agent is acting. The key point is to identify the capacity and indicate the principal.

41 ISBP745 section K3.

to be covered. Clearly, if a particular coverage is required, the LC may need to require that the insurance document contains a specific inclusion clause.

3.1 'Usual' or 'customary' risks

It is common to see that an LC requires a cargo insurance document covering 'usual' or 'customary' risks. Under common law, absent specific stipulation, the risk terms in the presented insurance documents have to be those customary to the trade concerned. Although whether the risk coverage complies with the 'usual' and 'customary' requirements is a matter of fact, consideration is still given to certain elements, such as the character of the goods, the nature of the vessel and the route of the transit. As Atkin LJ held in *Donald H. Scott v Barclays Bank Ltd*,[42] the requirement of an 'approved insurance policy' should mean a policy to which no reasonable objection could be made by reasonable commercial men. For example, a policy to pay 'total loss by total loss of vessel only' was held inadequate in the New Zealand frozen meat trade in which it was customary to tender an 'all risks' insurance.[43] As a result, the buyer was entitled to claim damages for a partial loss of the consignment from the bank, which had paid for the 'unusual' insurance policy in the LC transaction.

Since the standards of 'usual' and 'customary' necessarily vary from case to case, the UCP has endeavoured to avoid the ambiguities and controversies brought by these terms. Article 28(g) of the UCP600 attempts to relieve a bank from considering the risk coverage, which states that 'an insurance document will be accepted without regard to any risks that are not covered if the credit uses imprecise terms such as "usual risks" or "customary risks"'. It can be inferred that total silence with respect to the risks covered under the UCP cannot import a requirement for being a 'usual' cover, as under common law.

3.2 All risks

The expression 'all risks' is often used in insurance cover, and its meaning has been argued in a number of decisions as a term of art. All risks cover was defined as follows by Lord Sumner in *British and Foreign Marine Insurance v Gaunt*:[44]

> There are, of course, limits to 'all risks'. They are risks and risks insured against. Accordingly the expression does not cover inherent vice or mere wear and tear . . . It covers a risk, not a certainty; it is something, which

42 [1923] 2 KB 1 p 17.
43 *Borthwick v Bank of New Zealand* (1900) 6 Com. Cas. 1.
44 [1921] 2 AC 41.

happens to the subject matter from without, not the natural behaviour of that subject matter, being what it is, in the circumstances under which it is carried.[45]

Under the Chinese PICC Ocean Marine Cargo Clauses, 'all risks' insurance covers all risks of loss or damage to the insured goods whether partial or total, arising from 'external causes' in the course of transit.[46] The Chinese courts have taken a broader interpretation of external causes than just recognising 11 types of risk illustrated in the clauses.[47] Similar to the English Institute Cargo Clauses, the PICC clauses have also expressly excluded the traditional limitations from the all risks cover.[48] Evidently, one cannot expect all risks insurance to cover every risk, especially for those that are both traditionally and customarily excluded.

Although the precise extent of 'all risks' cover remains an open question to traders, it has substantially been avoided by bankers in the UCP600. Article 28(h) stipulates that when a credit requires 'all risks' coverage, the insurance document need not have an all risks heading and it does not matter that certain risks are excluded, provided that the document contains an all risks notation or clause. An insurance document indicating that it covers Institute Cargo Clauses (A) satisfies a condition in a credit calling for an 'all risks' clause or notation.[49] So does an insurance document indicating that it covers the PICC 'All Risks' clauses.

Inherent in the UCP rule of 'all risks' is the assumption that an all risks cover does not require each and every possible risk to be covered under the policy. This is consistent with the position under common law and the insurance market. However, there must also be some limit to the risks that can be excluded. Does Article 28(h) mean that even if the insurance is in practice of little value because of extensive exclusions, the document will nevertheless be accepted by the bank? It has been suggested that the discretion should be left to the bank. If the cover provided is so cut down by the exclusions that it would clearly fall short of the cover to be reasonably expected for the transaction in question, it should be rejected.[50]

Nevertheless, such discretion will inevitably bring uncertainties to the LC system. In particular, it would affect the independence of the bank from the underlying contract. It is difficult to quantify the scope and number of

45 [1921] 2 AC 41, p 57.

46 PICC Ocean Marine Cargo Clauses 2009, clause I(3).

47 *Fenghai v PICC Hainan*, The Supreme People's Court Case No. (2003) Min Si Ti Zi 5; *Zheshen v Dazhong Insurance & Dazhong Insurance Suzhou*, Wuhan Maritime Court Case No. (2005) Wu Hai Fa Shang Zi 229.

48 See ICC (A) 2009, clause 4 and PICC Ocean Marine Cargo Clauses 2009, clause II.

49 ISBP745, section K18.

50 A. Malek and D. Quest (eds), *Jack: Documentary Credits*, 4th edn, 2009, Tottel Publishing, para 8.136.

exclusions an 'all risk' cover may contain before the exclusions negate the purported 'all risks' prefix of the cover altogether. By contrast, in respect of Article 28(h), all the bank needs to see is the existence of an 'all risk' notation or clause. If the buyer wishes to ensure that the goods are covered to his satisfaction, he must ensure that the credit contains the degree of specificity that would serve his purpose.

3.3 Exclusions

It has long been a principle of marine insurance, since enacted in the MIA 1906 section 55, that the insurer is not liable for any loss attributable to the wilful misconduct of the assured or for any loss proximately caused by delay, and that, unless the policy otherwise provides, the insurer is not liable for ordinary wear and tear, ordinary leakage and breakage, inherent vice or nature of the subject matter insured. Articles 242 and 243 of the Chinese Maritime Code set out four comparable exclusions, including 'intentional act of the assured', 'delay in the voyage', 'fair wear and tear, inherent vice or nature' and 'improper packing'.

Due to the numerous exclusion clauses currently appearing on insurance documents and in order to relieve the burden on the bank involved in the documentary examinations, UCP600 Article 28(i) states that an insurance document may contain reference to any exclusion clause. Obviously, this open Article was made to cater for any possible exclusion clauses. Nevertheless, questions may arise when reading this open exclusion Article together with Article 28(h), which states that an insurance document containing all risks notation will be accepted without regard to any risks stated to be excluded. Can any risks be excluded from the coverage, even if they effectively defeat the nature of the 'all risks' policy? The ICC Banking Commission has given a series of explanations in its official opinions. If a credit specifically requires 'Institute Cargo Clauses (A)', an insurance document stating 'Institute Cargo Clauses (A) excluding . . .' would be deemed to be discrepant under UCP. However, if the document contains reference to certain exclusions and these are not directly linked to a specific insurance clause, the document would not be discrepant.[51]

Once again, it is not for the bank to examine the document to see if it provides adequate protection for the trader or itself, and the bank is not liable if the goods suffer a loss that is not insured. Banks are only required to review the conditions of insurance as detailed on the face of the insurance document. The purpose of Article 28(h) and Article 28(i) is to discourage

51 G. Collyer and R. Katz (eds), *Unpublished Opinions of the ICC Banking Commission 1995–2004* (ICC Publishing No. 660, Paris 2005) R532; Gary Collyer and R. Katz (eds), *ICC Banking Commission Collected Opinions 2005–2008* (ICC Publication No. 697, 2009) R686, R634.

the practice of merely stating 'all risks' without specifying the risks to be covered. In effect, the outcome of the rule is a form of penalty for the careless party. Apparently, there is no minimum limit for the risk coverage in the UCP as under common law, nor usual or customary insurance requirements. Thus, the traders must include express and detailed requirements for risk cover when opening an LC.

4 Goods covered

At common law, the policy must insure the goods specified in the credit for the voyage contracted for[52] and insurance must be confined to goods sold.[53] Where the policy covers a greater quantity than that contracted for, the buyer may reject.[54] In order to protect the exclusive interests of the cargo owner, insurance documents must relate to the goods that have been shipped. The UCP does not make express provision in relation to this, but the requirement in Article 14(d) that the documents must not conflict with one another brings about this result. The description of the goods and the journey or voyage covered by an insurance document must be in no conflict with the transport document, the commercial invoice or other documents.[55] Moreover, insurance documents must relate to the goods that have been shipped, so as to unequivocally identify the goods under the LC.[56] Although there are no specific provisions for the subject matter covered by the insurance under the UCP insurance section, it is still restricted by the cross-examinations between the documents, and arguably the criteria remain the same as under common law.

5 Period of cover

5.1 Dates of cover

Insurance coverage should be effective from the date that the goods are entrusted to the carrier. In *Forestal Mimosa Ltd v Oriental Credit Ltd*, the judge held that the insurance documents were acceptable notwithstanding that the declarations of shipment were made two days later than the actual shipment date, presumably because the goods were effectively covered from the date of shipment.[57] The UCP600 Article 28(e) also reflects this position.

52 *Landauer v Craven and Speeding Bros* [1912] 2 KB 94, p 105.
53 *May and Hassell v Exportles of Moscow* (1940) 45 Com Cas 310.
54 *Hickox v Adams* (1876) 34 LT 404; *Manbre Saccharine v Corn Products* [1919] 1 KB 198.
55 UCP600 Article 14(e) and Article 18(c).
56 The linkage requirement is an ambiguous issue under UCP600; however, it was explained in *Banque de L'Indochine et de Suez SA v JH Rayner (Mincing Land) Ltd* [1983] QB 711.
57 [1986] 1 Lloyd's Rep 329, p 335.

It stipulates that 'the date of the insurance document must be no later than the date of shipment, unless it appears from the insurance document that the cover is effective from a date not later than the date of shipment'. The ICC Banking Commission further explained the situation in its official opinion, which held that an insurance document dated after the date of shipment would be acceptable if the insurance document indicated that cover had been effected from warehouse to warehouse.[58]

5.2 Entire transit cover

It is well established that the insurance must cover the whole transit contemplated and it must provide continuous cover from shipment to the c.i.f. destination specified in the contract.[59] In *Lindon v White*,[60] the tender of the insurance policy was held to be ineffective since it only referred to the port of arrival rather than to the buyer's warehouse as described in the contract. Clearly, the old standard sea cover cannot satisfy the market needs. It therefore becomes customary for a warehouse-to-warehouse clause to be inserted in Lloyd's policies. Clause 8 of the Institute Cargo Clauses 2009 is recognised as the transit clause, which provides that the insurance attaches from the time the subject matter insured is first moved in the warehouse or at the place of storage for the purpose of the immediate loading into or onto the carrying vehicle or other conveyance for the commencement of transit. Cover continues during the ordinary course of transit and terminates on completion of unloading from the carrying vehicle or other conveyance in or at the final warehouse or place of storage at the destination named in the contract of insurance.

Chinese law for its part does not set out any specific rule to regulate the duration of the insurance and Article 14 of the Insurance Act allows the parties to freely negotiate the contract in this respect. However, in the PICC Ocean Marine Cargo Clauses, section III clause 1 is known as the 'Warehouse-to-Warehouse Clause', which deals with goods that are in the 'ordinary course of transit'.[61] The wording of this clause is based on the transit clause under the Institute Cargo Clauses 1963 and it is still similar to the current Institute Cargo Clauses 2009.

The UCP600 reflects the English law and the current insurance market practice in Article 28(f)(iii), which states that 'the insurance document must

58 Gary Collyer and Ron Katz (eds), *ICC Banking Commission Collected Opinions 2009–2011* (ICC Publishing No. 732, Paris 2012) R766.

59 *Belgian Grain and Produce v Cox* (1919) 1 Ll. L. Rep 256.

60 [1975] 1 Lloyd's Rep 384

61 UCP600 does not address the situation when cargo is not in the 'ordinary course of transit'. The corresponding clauses for this situation can be found in Section III clause 2 of the PICC Ocean Marine Cargo Clauses and clauses 8.3 and 9 of the Institute Cargo Clauses.

indicate that risks are covered at least between the place of taking in charge or shipment and the place of discharge or final destination as stated in the credit'. It is a new Article introduced from paragraph 188 of the ISBP2003 and it provides no more guidance as to when these points are applicable: 'the better interpretation is that the coverage must correspond to the transport and cover the entire transport'.[62]

6 Currency and amount of insurance

6.1 Insurance currency

There is no decisive answer under common law as to whether the bank must accept an insurance document that is payable in a different currency compared with the currency in the LC. In *Donald H. Scott v Barclays*,[63] Bankes LJ refrained from giving any opinion whether a policy expressed in dollars was a good tender under an English letter of credit. In *Malmberg v HJ Evans*,[64] Bailhache J held that the fact that the policy was issued abroad should not make it objectionable. However, the question was left undecided by the Court of Appeal. The editors of Benjamin have suggested that the acceptance of an insurance policy issued by a foreign currency depended on whether such a policy was a 'usual' policy in international trade.[65] By contrast, the UCP situation is much clearer. UCP600 Article 28(f)(i) expressly requires that the insurance document must be in the same currency as the credit.

6.2 Insurance amount

The UCP600 Article 28(f)(i) clearly states that the insurance document must indicate the amount of the insurance coverage. In Article 28(f), the UCP600 further illustrates a set of methods to evaluate the required insurance amount. Article 28(f) stipulates that a requirement in the credit for insurance coverage to be for a percentage of the value of the goods, of the invoice value or similar is deemed to be the minimum amount of coverage required. If there is no indication in the credit of the insurance coverage required, the amount of insurance coverage must be at least 110 per cent of the CIF or CIP value of the goods. When the CIF or CIP value cannot be determined from the documents, the amount of insurance coverage must be calculated on the basis of the amount for the requested payment or the gross value of the goods as shown on the invoice, whichever is

62 James E. Byrne, *The Comparison of UCP600 & UCP500* (ICC 2007), p 217.
63 [1923] 2 KB 1, p 14.
64 (1924) 29 Comm. Cas. 235, p 238.
65 Benjamin, para 19-042.

greater. However, there is no maximum percentage of insurance coverage under UCP.[66]

The MIA 1906 ascertains the measurement for the insurable value of goods in its section 16(3), which provides that subject to any express provision or valuation in the policy, the insurable value should be the prime cost of the property insured, plus the expenses of and incidental to shipping and the charges of insurance upon the whole. Common law has adopted a similar approach to that of the UCP in setting up the minimum requirement. In *Johnson v Taylor Brothers*,[67] the court decided that in the absence of express stipulation as to the precise amount to the minimum cover required, the reasonable value of the goods must be insured.[68]

Concerning the maximum insurance amount, the positions in both common law and the Chinese Maritime Code are different from the UCP600. In *Banki Melli Iran v Barclays Bank (DCO)*,[69] it was admitted that the insurance policy was defective because it was for an amount in excess of that stated in the credit. In the CMC Article 220, it is stipulated that 'the insured amount shall be agreed upon between the insurer and the assured. The insured amount shall not exceed the insured value.[70] Where the insured amount exceeds the insured value, the portion in excess shall be null and void'.

As a result, under common law, the bank may be entitled to reject an insurance document that shows the insurance amount in excess of the value stated in the letter of credit. If the UCP600 applies, no such limit would be appropriate unless the credit is explicit in imposing a ceiling on the amount of cover. Nevertheless, if Chinese law applies, the position under UCP600 will arguably be qualified by the CMC as to the maximum insurance amount. Overinsurance probably will not affect a bank's decision to accept such an insurance document; however, the excess amount of insurance will be treated as null and void by the CMC.

6.3 Excess and franchise

A franchise is an amount or percentage stated in a policy that must be reached before any claim is payable. If it is reached, then the claim is payable

66 ISBP745, section K12.

67 [1920] AC 144, p 149.

68 MIA 1906 Article 16(3) sets up the measurement for the insurable value of goods. Subject to any express provision or valuation in the policy, the insurable value should be the prime cost of the property insured, plus the expenses of and incidental to shipping and the charges of insurance upon the whole.

69 [1951] 2 Lloyd's Rep 367, p 376.

70 The CMC Article 219 provides that the insurable value of the subject matter insured shall be agreed upon between the insurer and the assured. Where no insurable value has been agreed, it shall be the aggregate of the invoice value of the cargo, plus freight and insurance premium when the insurance liability commences.

in full.[71] An excess or deductible is similar to a franchise save that once the amount or percentage is reached, only the amount in excess of it is recoverable. In the UCP600 Article 28(j), it states that an insurance document may indicate that the cover is subject to a franchise or excess (deductible). The UCP does not require an insurance document to state 'irrespective of percentage', which are the words customarily used to indicate that there is to be no franchise provision. However, when a credit requires the insurance cover to be irrespective of percentage, the insurance document should not contain any clause stating that the insurance cover is subject to a franchise or an excess.[72] Nevertheless, the Article says nothing about the acceptable level of the excess when the credit itself is silent. It is doubtful whether a bank could reject a document that shows an unusually large excess or franchise, which may result in an unreasonably low indemnity for the assured.[73] Unfortunately, neither common law nor the Chinese statutes provide any specific guidance on this point.

7 Assured and assignment

Detailed discussions of the rules relating to assignment of marine policies and to insurable interest under Chinese law can be found in previous chapters of this book. Here, it is only necessary to briefly review the rules surrounding assignment and explore the connections with international sales of goods paid for by LCs. As a rule, 'a marine policy is assignable unless it contains terms expressly prohibiting assignment. It may be assigned either before or after loss'.[74] Common law has established that a marine policy can be assigned after loss,[75] even though at the time of the loss the assignee had no interest in the subject matter of the insurance.[76] Clearly, the assignability of marine policies is essential for the operation of the international sale of goods, and the assignability of a marine policy after the loss of the subject matter is in accordance with the characteristic of international chain sales. However, under English law, the assignment of the subject matter of the policy does not carry with it the policy itself, so that a separate and contemporaneous assignment of the policy is necessary.[77] A marine

71 In foreign insurance, 'franchise' may be used to mean what in English insurances is termed an 'excess' or a 'deductible'.

72 ISBP745, section K14.

73 Jack, para 8.145.

74 MIA 1906 section 50(1). The insurance policies are automatically assignable even if the policy or certificate is not made out to order.

75 *Lloyd v Fleming* (1872) LR 7 QR 299.

76 *J Aron & Co. v Miall* (1928) 98 LJKB 204. This means that a bank that has paid against documents can claim the insurance compensation as assignee, even though the goods were lost and it had no insurable interest when the goods were lost.

77 MIA 1906 section 51.

policy may be assigned by endorsement thereon or in other customary manner, without notice to the underwriters unless the policy otherwise provides.[78] It seems the law leaves it to the parties to freely choose their method of assignment, provided it is lawful.[79]

Under Chinese law, with a view to facilitating international sales, the CMC Article 229 also provides that a contract of marine insurance for the carriage of goods by sea may be assigned by the assured by endorsement or otherwise, and the rights and obligations under the contract are assigned accordingly. Nor does assignment of the insurance contract require the prior consent of the insurer or notification to the insurer. Moreover, with respect to cargo insurance, either marine or non-marine, the Chinese Insurance Act requires no notification in relation to assignment of the subject matter.[80] 'It is therefore concluded that sale or assignment of the subject matter insured under cargo insurance will automatically give rise to an assignment of the contract of insurance'.[81]

Concerning assignability of an insurance document under LCs, the UCP600 does not specify any requirements in itself; however, the new ISBP745 has been developed with the practical perspective in mind and supplementing the gap left by the UCP600. In the ISBP745 section K19, it is specified that an insurance document should be in the form required by the credit and, where necessary, be endorsed by the entity to whose order or in whose favour claims are payable. Nevertheless, the ISBP745 has changed the position in section K20, which stipulates that a credit should not require an insurance document to be issued 'to bearer' or 'to order'.[82] It further explains that when a credit requires an insurance document to be issued 'to order of (named entity)', the document need not indicate 'to order' provided that the named entity is shown as the insured party or claims are payable to it, and assignment by endorsement is not expressly prohibited. Clearly, the aim is for the ISBP to be in accordance with insurance practice and to discourage the use of credits, as well as insurance documents that do not indicate the name of an insured party.[83]

78 MIA 1906 section 50(3).

79 Mere delivery is not, however, a customary assignment. Cf. *Safadi v Western Assurance Co.* (1933) 46 Lloyd's Rep 140.

80 Insurance Law 2009, Article 49.

81 Dunt, para 13.19.

82 Previously, a document issued to bearer is acceptable where the credit requires an insurance document endorsed in blank, and vice versa. See ISBP No. 681 Article 179.

83 In MIA 1906 section 23(1), it stipulates that a marine policy must specify the name of the assured, or of some person who affects the insurance on his behalf. In the Chinese Insurance Act Article 18, it also states that an insurance contract shall contain the names and residences of the assured.

13 Insurer's limitation of liability for maritime claims

Dingjing Huang[1]

1 Introduction

As one of the features of the International Convention on Limitation of Liability for Maritime Claims 1976 (LLMC 1976) compared with its predecessor, LLMC 1976 includes liability insurers on the list of persons entitled to limit their liabilities. By virtue of Article 1(6) of LLMC 1976, a liability insurer shall be entitled to the benefits of this convention to the same extent as the assured himself. In addition, the UK passed its new Third Parties (Rights against Insurers) Act in March 2010. The 2010 Act is set to replace the Third Parties (Rights against Insurers) Act 1930, although a commencement date is yet to be appointed. In this context, the possible impact of the 2010 Act on the insurers' rights under the limitation regime needs to be examined. LLMC 1976 is followed by the Chinese Maritime Code, thus a similar position in respect of insurers' rights of limitation may be found under Chinese law.

This chapter will mainly discuss insurers' rights under LLMC 1976 and its equivalent national law in China. It will also examine if any changes will be brought by the Third Parties Act 2010. A comparative study will be made on English law and Chinese law regarding insurers' rights under the limitation regime. Moreover, reference will be made to other limitation systems besides the global limitation, including the International Convention on Civil Liability for Oil Pollution Damage 1969 (CLC 1969), the International Convention on Liability and Compensation for Damage in Connection with the Carriage of Hazardous and Noxious Substances by Sea 2010 (HNS Convention), the International Convention on Civil Liability for Bunker Oil Pollution Damage 2001 (Bunker Convention 2001), and the Athens Convention Relating to the Carriage of Passengers and their Luggage by Sea 1974, as amended by the 2002 protocol thereto (Athens Convention 2002).

1 Dingjing Huang, LLB, LLM, Part-Time Tutor in Law, PhD Candidate, Member of the Insurance Law Research Group, Southampton Law School, University of Southampton.

2 LLMC 1976 and LLMC 1996

The idea of shipowners' limitation of liability is a fruit of public policy aiming to encourage trade and to support the shipping industry. The concept of limitation of liability has been widely accepted among shipping nations and has achieved successful international harmonisation through international conventions. Among the limitation conventions, the Convention on Limitation of Liability for Maritime Claims 1976 and its 1996 protocol (LLMC 1996) are of the most importance worldwide. The LLMC convention covers most maritime claims relating to the operation of a vessel and therefore it is important to review the insurers' rights under this regime.

As one of the features brought by LLMC 1976, the 1976 Convention includes liability insurers into the list of persons entitled to limit their liabilities.[2] Article 1(6) of the LLMC 1976 provides as follows:

> 6. An insurer of liability for claims subject to limitation in accordance with the rules of this Convention shall be entitled to the benefits of this Convention to the same extent as the assured himself.

This Article is kept unrevised in LLMC 1996.

It is pointed out in the *travaux préparatoires* of the LLMC Convention 1976 and of LLMC 1996 (the *travaux préparatoires* of LLMC) that the purpose of such a provision is to prevent the result where the benefits of limitation can only be invoked by the shipowner, not by his liability insurer when the claimant proceeds against the insurer under a 'direct action' statute.[3] The underpinning consideration is that the shipowner's right would be interfered with if his insurer is not able to invoke limitation to the same extent as the shipowner himself because the insurer then must charge the premium on the basis of his 'excess liability' to the claimant. This premium must ultimately be paid by the shipowner.[4]

However, two questions would seem to arise from the provision of the above Article in the LLMC 1976. First, under what circumstances does the issue of insurer's limitation of liability arise? Second, to what extent would insurers be able to limit their liability under the LLMC: namely what is the meaning of the term 'to the same extent' in Article 1(6)?

With regard to the first question, it is submitted that the rights of the insurer with respect to the insured will be determined by the insurance

2 Note that it was CLC 1969 that for the first time included liability insurers under the limitation regime; however, CLC 1969 provides for compulsory insurance and the situation may therefore be different. The position of the CLC 1969 is reviewed in section 5.

3 CMI, *The travaux préparatoires of the LLMC Convention 1976 and of the Protocol of 1996*, p 56; according to the *travaux préparatoires*, such a result is arrived at in US courts.

4 CMI, *The travaux préparatoires of the LLMC Convention 1976 and of the Protocol of 1996*, p 56.

policy, and therefore the convention would only apply to an insurer when a direct action is brought against him by a third party.[5] However, it was not the intention of the draftsmen of LLMC 1976 that the Convention should stipulate in what circumstances a direct action may be brought against the insurer. It is pointed out in the *travaux préparatoires* of LLMC that the effect of Article 1(6) is to prevent that the right of global limitation is circumvented by giving the claimant the right of direct action against the insurer of the limited liability. It is further stated that 'the Draft Convention is not intended to interfere with direct action statutes as such'.[6] It follows that the issue of circumstances under which a direct action may be brought against the liability insurer is left to the domestic legislation of the member states. In the following, the position of English law and Chinese law in respect of direct actions against insurers will be discussed.

Concerning the second question, the intention of this provision appears to be to place the liability insurer in no worse position than the assured, insofar as limitation is concerned, where a direct action is brought against the insurer. In other words, the liability insurer should not be able to limit his liability in the situation where the assured is not entitled to limitation. However, there is no further provision in the LLMC 1976 or 1996 regarding the insurer's rights. It is submitted that the wording of Article 1(6) of LLMC 1976 is unclear in that, on the one hand, it suggests that the convention does not impose liability on the insurer; on the other hand, it does not expressly extend the cover available so as to provide full compensation for a claim where the right to limit is lost.[7] The term 'to the same extent' may also mean that the insurer should always be able to limit its liability to the extent that the shipowner is entitled to limit.

The draftsmen of LLMC 1976 left the Article as it was drafted because they found it difficult to achieve an agreement on whether the insurer should be entitled to limit its liability regardless of the shipowner's right to limit.[8] Thus, the answer to the second question should again be sought in national law.

To summarise, both LLMC 1976 and 1996 simply provide for the entitlement of insurers to limit their liability for maritime claims. In the absence of further provisions in the conventions, the real scope of insurers' right of limitation must be examined under the national law of each member state. What follows is a review of English law and Chinese law, respectively.

5 For further on direct actions by third parties under the law of China, see, generally, Tao Yu, Chapter 7 of this work.

6 CMI, *The travaux préparatoires of the LLMC Convention 1976 and of the Protocol of 1996*, p 56.

7 See B. W. B. Reynolds and M. N. Tsimplis, *Shipowners' Limitation of Liability*, 2012, London: Kluwer Law International, p 40.

8 CMI, *The travaux préparatoires of the LLMC Convention 1976 and of the Protocol of 1996*, p 57.

3 English law position

3.1 When will a third party be able to sue the liability insurer?

The UK is a member state of LLMC 1976 and therefore Article 1(6) of that convention has the force of law in the UK.[9] The main obstacle to a third party claiming rights under a contract is the concept of privity of contract. In the case of a contract of insurance, only the parties to the contract or an assignee have the ability to enforce the contract terms. Nevertheless, a direct action can be brought under certain circumstances by a third party against the insurer in the UK under the Third Parties (Rights against Insurers) Act 1930 (Third Parties Act 1930).

Section 1(1) of the Third Parties Act 1930 provides as follows:

> Where under any contract of insurance a person (hereinafter referred to as the insured) is insured against liabilities to third parties which he may incur, then—
>
> (a) in the event of the insured becoming bankrupt or making a composition or arrangement with his creditors; or
>
> (b) in the case of the insured being a company, in the event of a winding-up order being made, or a resolution for a voluntary winding-up being passed, with respect to the company, or of a receiver or manager of the company's business or undertaking being duly appointed, or of possession being taken, by or on behalf of the holders of any debentures secured by a floating charge, of any property comprised in or subject to the charge; if, either before or after that event, any such liability as aforesaid is incurred by the insured, his rights against the insurer under the contract in respect of the liability shall, notwithstanding anything in any Act or rule of law to the contrary, he transferred to and vest in the third party to whom the liability was so incurred.

Thus where the insured has failed to satisfy its creditors and has been wound up, the unsatisfied third parties under liability insurance may 'step into the shoes' of the assured and take over whatever rights the assured has against the insurer under the liability policy. The aim of the Third Parties Act 1930 is to protect insurance proceeds from the effects of the insured's insolvency. In the case of marine insurance, a liability insurer would be sued directly by a third party in the circumstances where the insured shipowner is insolvent or has been ordered to wind up. Due to the widespread usage

9 Section 185(1), Merchant Shipping Act 1995.

of 'one-ship companies', a claimant of a maritime accident may easily come to face the insolvency of the shipowning company. In this situation, the claimant may invoke the 1930 Act and claim directly against the insurer.

In addition, the Rome II Regulation also provides for direct actions against liability insurers. According to Article 18 of the Regulation, such claims may be brought if permitted either by the law applicable to the non-contractual obligation or by the law applicable to the insurance contract.[10] Although this provision allows direct actions against a liability insurer, such an action is subject to the applicable law for the cause of action. Thus this provision is of little substantive effect with regards to claims brought directly against the insurers, and the substantive right thereof is still governed by the national law of the Member States.

3.2 To what extent may an insurer limit its liability?

As mentioned earlier, Article 1(6) of LLMC 1976 provides that the liability insurer shall be entitled to the benefits of limitation 'to the same extent' as the insured. Meanwhile, section 1(4) of the 1930 Act provides that, where the right of the assured is transferred to a third party,[11] the insurer shall be under the same liability to the third party as he would have been under to the insured.[12] Therefore, it would appear that the insurer's liability towards a third party claimant shall be back to back with its liability to the insured. In this sense, the insurance contract may have an impact on the insurer's liability to the third party.

The rights of a third party under an insurance contract are considered in the joint decision in *The Fanti* and *The Padre Island*.[13] In this case, two appeals were heard together by the House of Lords. Both the owners of the vessel *Fanti* and the vessel *Padre Island* entered their ships in P&I Clubs for the purpose of insuring themselves against a wide range of risks not covered by an ordinary policy of marine insurance. In 1983, the vessel *Fanti* was sailing from Rostock in East Germany bound for Nigeria with a cargo of cement belonging to the claimants (namely the third party under the

10 Article 18, Regulation (EC) No. 864/2007 of the European Parliament and of the Council of 11 July 2007 on the law applicable to non-contractual obligations (Rome II):
'Direct action against the insurer of the person liable
The person having suffered damage may bring his or her claim directly against the insurer of the person liable to provide compensation if the law applicable to the non-contractual obligation or the law applicable to the insurance contract so provides.'

11 Section 1(1), Third Parties Act 1930.

12 Section 1(4), Third Parties Act 1930 provides that:
'Upon a transfer under subsection (1) or subsection (2) of this section, the insurer shall, subject to the provisions of section three of this Act, be under the same liability to the third party as he would have been under to the insured . . .'

13 [1990] 2 Lloyd's Rep 191.

insurance contract). On 28 March, it was discovered that the vessel's No. 3 deep tanks were flooded and that water was entering lower holds No. 2 and No. 4. A distress call was made and the vessel was escorted into Portuguese waters near Cascais by a salvage tug. Both ship and cargo were abandoned to the salvors.

Soon after the casualty, the claimant cargo owner started an action in respect of its loss against the owner of the *Fanti*. Judgment was entered in default of notice of intention to defend on 3 October 1983 for damages to be assessed. In due course, the damages were assessed but nothing was paid in or towards satisfaction of the judgment. On 30 July 1984, the shipowner was ordered to be wound up on the claimants' petition in the Companies Court of the Chancery Division. Under these circumstances, the claimants started arbitration proceedings against the P&I insurer on the basis of the Third Parties Act 1930.

Similarly, there was also a cargo claim arising out of the voyage of the *Padre Island*. The judgment against the shipowner was not satisfied and the shipowner was ordered to be wound up. Relying on the Third Parties Act 1930, the third party claimant brought an action against the P&I Club in respect of its loss of cargo.

In both cases, cargo claims were covered by the liability insurances provided by the P&I Clubs and a 'pay to be paid' provision was included in the rules of both clubs.

In *The Fanti*, section 4 of the rules of the P&I Club provided that the members shall:

> be protected and indemnified against all or any of the following claims and expenses which he shall have become liable to pay and *shall in fact have paid* for loss or damage caused to . . . property carried on board a ship entered in this class.
>
> (emphasis added)

In *The Padre Island*, under Rule 2 of its rules the club undertook to: 'Protect and indemnify members in respect of losses or claims which they as owners of the entered vessel shall have become liable to pay and *shall have in fact paid* . . .' (emphasis added).

The question before the House of Lords was whether or not the 'pay to be paid' clause in the insurance contract was applicable to the direct action brought by a third party against the insurer. The House reviewed the 'pay to be paid' clause together with the 1930 Third Parties Act.

Section 1(1) of the Third Parties Act 1930 provides that, where any of the specified events occurs, the insured's 'rights against the insurer under the contract in respect of the liability shall . . . be transferred to and vest in the third party'.[14] In addition, section 1(4) of the Act provides that: 'upon

14 Section 1(1), Third Parties Act 1930.

a transfer under subsection (1) . . . of this section, the insurer shall . . . be under the same liability to the third party as he would have been under to the insured'.

These two provisions set up the basic scope of the rights against insurers where a direct action is brought by a third party. In the view of the House of Lords, the above provisions indicate that the legislature never intended to put a third party in any better position as against an insurer than that of the insured himself. Therefore, the members had no accrued rights to be indemnified by the P&I Clubs since they had not satisfied the condition precedent of discharging the liabilities to the third parties themselves, and the third parties could not, as a result of the statutory transfer of rights, have transferred to them any better or larger rights than those that the members had previously possessed. Lord Brandon was of the view that:

> [T]he effect of these provisions is that, in a case where the insurer would have had a good defence to a claim made by the insured before the statutory transfer of his rights to the third party, the insurer will have precisely the same good defence to a claim made by the third party after such transfer.[15]

As an exception, section 1(3) of the 1930 Act provides, inter alia, that:

> In so far as any contract of insurance . . . in respect of any liability of the insured to third parties purports whether directly or indirectly to avoid the contract or to alter the rights of the parties . . . upon the happening to the insured of any of the events specified in paragraph (a) or paragraph (b) [winding up order] of sub-section (1) of this section . . . the contract shall be of no effect . . .

This provision is to invalidate terms in the insurance contract, which avoids the insurer's liability where the insured is insolvent. Nevertheless, it was held by the House of Lords that the 'pay to be paid' clauses contained in the contracts of insurance made between the members and the P&I Clubs did not fit into the description of section 1(3) in respect of avoiding the contracts or to alter the rights of the parties where the members being ordered to be wound up. Therefore, the 'pay to be paid' provisions were held to be valid.[16]

Based on the above reasoning, the House of Lords allowed the appeal from the P&I Clubs, holding that the claimant did not have the right to be indemnified by the association. The decision of *The Fanti* and *The Padre Island* confirmed that as a matter of English law it is well established that

15 [1990] 2 Lloyd's Rep 191, p 198.
16 Ibid., pp 197 and 203.

the 'pay to be paid' clause operates as a complete defence to a claim if the liability in question has not been discharged by the insured member, since such discharge is a condition precedent to the insured member being indemnified by the Club.[17]

The decision in *The Fanti* and *The Padre Island* further confirmed that any rights between the insurer and the third party are subject to the insurance contract. In this sense, the terms of the insurance contract would still apply even though the claim against the insurer is transferred to a third party; as a result, the insurer is protected by the terms of the insurance contract and the insurer may avoid payment under the policy where there is a breach of the insurance contract;[18] for example, the Marine Insurance Act 1906 provides, inter alia, that the insurer is not liable if the assured is in breach of an express or implied warranty in the policy, 'whether it be material to the risk or not'.[19]

A further question is whether Article 1(6) of the LLMC 1976 would affect the position of this decision. First of all, the right of limitation is a statutory privilege rather than a contractual right. Therefore, the decision of *The Fanti* and *Padre Island* is not directly related to the insurer's right of limitation. Therefore, the *The Fanti* and *Padre Island* decision seems not to resolve the question whether the rights and obligations between the insured shipowner and the third party are applicable identically between the insurer and the third party.

In a hypothetical case, where the cargo is lost due to the reckless act of the shipowner with knowledge that such damage would probably result, the shipowner is deprived of the right to limit liability against the cargo claimants and it has been argued that the insurer has then lost the right to limit liability as well because the insurer can only limit to the same extent as the shipowner.[20] Where the shipowner is still in business, the insurer will not face any direct actions brought by third parties and may rely on the provisions in the insurance contract. Where the shipowner is insolvent, the insurer may still use the insurance contract terms to shield himself according to the decision in *The Fanti* and *The Padre Island*. In addition, the act or omission of the shipowner may be regarded as wilful misconduct in terms of the Marine Insurance Act 1906 and the insurer would not be liable for the damages.[21]

17 *The Prestige* (No. 2) [2014] 1 Lloyd's Rep 309, p 315.

18 If such breach entitles the insurer to avoid the payment. See B. W. B. Reynolds and M. N. Tsimplis, *Shipowners' Limitation of Liability*, 2012, London: Kluwer Law International, p 38.

19 Section 33, Marine Insurance Act 1906.

20 See B. W. B. Reynolds and M. N. Tsimplis, *Shipowners' Limitation of Liability*, 2012, London: Kluwer Law International, p 39.

21 As was the result in the Canadian Supreme Court case *Peracomo Inc. v Telus Communications Co. ('The Realice')* 2014 SCC 29.

In this sense, Article 1(6) of the 1976 Convention should be considered together with Article 4 of the 1976 Convention and section 55 of the Marine Insurance Act 1906. Article 4 of the 1976 Convention provides that a person liable shall not be entitled to limit his liability if the loss resulted from his personal act or omission committed 'with the intent to cause such loss, or recklessly and with knowledge that such loss would probably result'.[22] By virtue of this provision, where the cargo is lost due to the reckless act of the shipowner with knowledge that such damage would probably result, the shipowner is deprived of the right to limit liability against the cargo claimants. Thus, it has been argued that the insurer would lose the right to limit liability as well because the insurer can only limit to the same extent as the shipowner.[23]

On the other hand, section 55(2) of the Marine Insurance Act 1906 provides, inter alia, that the insurer is not liable for any loss attributable to the *wilful misconduct of the assured*, but, unless the policy otherwise provides, he is liable for any loss proximately caused by a peril insured against, even though the loss would not have happened but for the misconduct or negligence of the master or crew. According to this provision, it is submitted that the conduct preventing the shipowner from limiting liability may also prevent him from successfully prosecuting a claim against his liability insurer. In such a case, where the shipowner is guilty of wilful misconduct, the insurer may have a defence under the insurance contract against a third party claimant; and at the same time, although the shipowner is not entitled to limit his liability under the limitation convention, the insurer does not have any liability. Even though the Marine Insurance Act 1906 does not expressly provide for the situation where the loss is caused by the insured's act or omission committed 'recklessly and with knowledge that such loss would probably result',[24] the insurer will often have a defence under the insurance policy for such a situation.[25]

In this sense, the Limitation Convention would appear to be applicable only where the insured shipowner does not lose his right of limitation under

22 Article 4, LLMC 1976.

23 B. W. B. Reynolds and M. N. Tsimplis, *Shipowners' Limitation of Liability*, 2012, London: Kluwer Law International, p 39.

24 It is submitted that the term 'willful misconduct' in section 55(2) of the Marine Insurance Act 1906 does include the insured's act or omission committed 'recklessly and with knowledge that such loss would probably result'; see R. Merkin, *Marine Insurance Legislation*, 5th edn, 2014, Informa Law, p 90.

25 For example, Rule 3(10) of the American Club provides that:

'(no right of recovery from the Association in respect of any loss, damage or expense a Member may have sustained, directly or indirectly, by reason of:) Claims arising in circumstances where there has been willful misconduct on the part of the Member, defined as an act intentionally done, or a deliberate omission, by the Member with knowledge that the performance or omission will probably result in injury, or an act done or omitted in such a way as to allow an inference of a reckless disregard of the probable consequences.'

English law, where the right of limitation is lost by the insured, the insurer may rely on the insurance contract or the Marine Insurance Act to avoid liability.

Nevertheless, as LLMC 1976 has the force of law in the United Kingdom, it is submitted that according to Article 1(6) of the Convention, the insurer may not be able to rely upon those provisions of the insurance contract or the Marine Insurance Act 1906, which have the effect of restricting his liability to the insured.[26] The term 'to the same extent' in Article 1(6) of LLMC 1976 may imply that where the insured shipowner's entitlement to limit is forfeited, his insurer shall not be entitled to limit and have to meet the claim of the third-party claimant in full. Following this view, the decision of *The Fanti* and *The Padre Island* appears to be affected. Moreover, such a position would impose a potential burden on insurers, which is against the intention behind LLMC 1976.[27] One suggested solution to the problem is to interpret section 1(1) of the Third Parties Act 1930 in favour of the insurer, in particular the following words:

> his (the insured) rights against the insurer under the contract in respect of the liability shall, notwithstanding anything in any Act or rule of law to the contrary, be transferred to and vest in the third party to whom the liability was so incurred.

The wording 'notwithstanding anything in any Act or rule of law to the contrary' may be construed so as to have the effect that transfer of the insured's rights to the third party is not impacted by Article 1(6) of LLMC 1976, and that LLMC 1976 only applies after the rights are determined under the Third Parties Act.[28] In this sense, the decision of *The Fanti* and *The Padre Island* should still be followed for the purpose of determination of the third party's rights and, as a result, the insurer may still rely on the terms of the insurance contract.[29]

3.3 Third Parties (Rights against Insurers) Act 2010 (Third Parties Act 2010)

The Third Parties Act 1930 is set to be repealed by the Third Parties (Rights against Insurers) Act 2010. The 2010 Act received royal assent on 25 March 2010 but is not yet in force. The 2010 Act makes a number of changes

26 P. Griggs, R. Williams and J. Farr, *Limitation of Liability for Maritime Claims*, 4th edn, 2005, Richmond LLP, p 15.

27 Ibid.

28 Ibid., p 16.

29 B. W. B. Reynolds and M. N. Tsimplis, *Shipowners' Limitation of Liability*, 2012, London: Kluwer Law International, pp 39 and 40.

compared to its predecessor, with the aim of making it easier and quicker for a third-party claimant to recover compensation from the insurer of an insolvent insured. Regarding the insurer's defences in a direct action brought by a third party, the general position of the 1930 Act, whereby the third party's claim against insurers is only as good as the insolvent insured's claim, is followed by the 2010 Act.[30]

However, three exceptions to the general rule are set out at section 9 of the 2010 Act. First, where the transferred rights are subject to some condition the insured has to fulfil, anything done by the third party that, if it had been done by the insured, would have fulfilled the condition, will be treated as if done by the insured;[31] second, transferred rights will not be subject to any condition that requires the insured to provide information or assistance to the insurer if the condition cannot be fulfilled because the insured no longer exists;[32] and third, the transferred rights are not subject to a condition requiring the prior discharge by the insured of the insured's liability to the third party.[33]

With regard to the third exception, the outcome of *The Fanti* and *The Padre Island* is challenged. In the case where the policy includes a 'pay to be paid' clause requiring the insolvent insured to have discharged its liability to the third-party claimant before being entitled to an indemnity from its insurers, such clauses will no longer be enforceable against the claimant. However, section 9(6) of the 2010 Act provides that, in the case of a marine insurance contract, this exception applies only to the extent that the liability of the insured is a liability in respect of death or personal injury.[34] Therefore, for a third party claiming against the insolvent shipowner's insurer for liability in respect of cargo damage or damage to the ship, the decision of *The Fanti* and *The Padre Island* remains applicable. Nevertheless, these exceptions apparently are not related to limitation of liability issues.

In addition, section 2(4) of the 2010 Act provides that: 'the insurer may rely on any defence on which the insured could rely if those proceedings were proceedings brought against the insured in respect of the insured's liability to P (the third party)'.

This provision expressly affirms the insurer's right to invoke limitation of liability as a defence. However, even if there were no such provision, the insurer would still be entitled to limit his liability relying on LLMC 1976.

30 Law Commission, Third Parties (Right against Insurers), available at: http://lawcommission.justice.gov.uk/areas/third-parties-rights-agaisnt-insurers.htm (accessed 26 May 2014).

31 Section 9(2), Third Parties Act 2010.

32 Section 9(3), Third Parties Act 2010.

33 Section 9(5), Third Parties Act 2010.

34 Section 9(6), Third Parties Act 2010.

To conclude, the new changes brought by the Third Parties Act 2010 will not affect the position of English law regarding insurers' right to limit liability for maritime claims.

4 Chinese law position

4.1 Under what circumstances would the issue of insurer's limitation of liability arise?

Although China is not a Contracting State of LLMC 1976, Chapter XI of the Chinese Maritime Code 1992, which provides the statutory regime for limitation of liability for maritime claims in China, demonstrates great reliance on LLMC 1976. Following that Convention, the Chinese Maritime Code also provides for the insurer's right to limit its liability with different wording. Article 206 of the Chinese Maritime Code provides that:

> Where the assured may limit his liability in accordance with the provisions of this Chapter (Chapter XI), the insurer liable for the maritime claims shall be entitled to the limitation of liability under this Chapter to the same extent as the assured.

However, there is nothing in the Chinese Maritime Code providing that an insurer may invoke the right of limitation. As the LLMC 1976 is followed in the Chinese Maritime Code, it would appear that the intention of including this Article in the Chinese Maritime Code is also to provide insurers with the right to limit where there is a direct action brought against the insurer by a third party.

The rights of a third party against an insurer are set out in Article 65 of the Chinese Insurance Act 2009, which provides that:

> The insurer may indemnify a third party directly for losses or damages caused by the insured under liability insurance in accordance with laws and provisions in the contract.
>
> Where the insured under liability insurance causes loss or damage to a third party and the indemnity liability for compensation to the third party is determined, the insurer shall, upon the request of the insured, make the indemnity payment directly to the third party. Where the insured is indolent in making such a request, the third party is entitled to claim directly against the insurer for the portion of indemnity entitled to.

Unlike the Third Parties Act 1930 under English law, a third party's right to claim against the liability insurer is not dependent on the insolvency of the insured but on the laches of the insured in performing its right. Paragraph 2 of Article 65 of the Insurance Act is a reflection of Article 73 of the Chinese Contract Law 1999, which provides that where a debtor does not promptly exercise his matured creditor's rights and thereby causes losses to the creditor, the creditor may apply to the court to subrogate the creditor's rights of the debtor and exercise those rights in the creditor's name.[35] It would appear that Article 65 of the Insurance Act extends the principle under Chinese contract law to non-contractual relationships.

Although the aforementioned Article in the Insurance Act provides for the possibility of a direct action against the insurer, this Article may not be applicable for an action brought by a third party against the P&I Clubs under Chinese law. According to Article 6 of the Chinese Insurance Act, insurance business in China can be carried out by insurance companies and other insurance institutions,[36] and Article 183 of the Insurance Act provides that the Act is only applicable to commercial insurance business carried out by such 'other insurance intuitions'.[37] Although a P&I Club fits in with the category of other insurance institution, mutual insurance business is, according to the traditional view of Chinese law, regarded as non-commercial insurance. In addition, unlike the Marine Insurance Act 1906, there is nothing in the Chinese Insurance Act or the Chinese Maritime Code providing for the applicable law of mutual insurance and P&I Clubs.[38] Therefore, a P&I Club seems to be out of the scope of the Chinese Insurance Act. Such a position would disappoint the third-party claimant in the situation where the insured shipowner is incapable of compensating the third party.[39] As P&I Clubs undertake a large number of liability insurances for shipowners, it is necessary to establish a clear regime under which third parties may bring direct action against P&I Clubs and requirements and under which any restrictions applicable to both parties are clarified.[40]

4.2 To what extent may an insurer limit its liability?

As mentioned above, the wording of Article 206 of the Chinese Maritime Code on insurer's right of limitation is different from Article 1(6) of LLMC 1976.

It would appear that the position of insurers under the Chinese Maritime Code is clearer than that under the LLMC 1976. By virtue of Article 206

35 Article 73, Chinese Contract Law 1999.

36 Article 6, Chinese Insurance Act 2009.

37 Article 183, Chinese Insurance Act 2009.

38 Section 85(4) of the Marine Insurance Act 1906 provides that: 'Subject to the exceptions mentioned in this section, the provisions of this Act apply to a mutual insurance.'

39 It is possible for the third party claimant to sue a P&I Club directly on the basis of contract law or to sue the club as a guarantor where the club provides a letter of indemnity. For more details, see Beiping Chu, 'On the direct action against the P&I Club in China', *Annual of China Maritime Law*, 2002, vol. 13, p 222.

40 See Chapter 5, section 6, 'Direct action against P&I Club'. See also Beiping Chu, 'On the direct action against the P&I Club in China', *Annual of China Maritime Law*, 2002, vol. 13, p 222.

of the Chinese Maritime Code, the insured shipowner's entitlement to limit its liability is a condition precedent to the insurer's right to limit. [41] Therefore, in circumstances where the insured loses its right to limit his liability according to Article 209 of the Chinese Maritime Code, the insurer would appear not to be entitled to invoke limitation of liability.

Article 209 of the Chinese Maritime Code is almost identical to Article 4 of LLMC 1976, which provides that:

> A person liable shall not be entitled to limit his liability in accordance with the provisions of this Chapter, if it is proved that the loss resulted from his act or omission done with the intent to cause such loss or recklessly and with knowledge that such loss would probably result.

The same question would arise as under English law. Where the right to limit is lost by the shipowner, will the insurer be able to rely on the insurance contract to avoid liability? Unfortunately, there is no provision in the Chinese Maritime Code or the Insurance Act providing for a similar position to the decision in *The Fanti* and *The Padre Island* or the Third Parties Acts 1930 and 2010. In this regard, reference may be made to Judicial Interpretation I of the Supreme Court on Certain Issues concerning the Application of the Contract Law.[42] Article 18 of this judicial interpretation provides that the defences to which the sub-debtor is entitled against the debtor may be invoked by the sub-debtor against the creditor where the creditor is subrogated into the right of the debtor. Following this provision, the insurer's defences against the insured shipowner under the insurance contract may be used against the third-party claimant. Therefore, the insurer may rely on the insurance contract terms to avoid liability in the case where the insured shipowner in not entitled to limit liability. Nevertheless, it is noteworthy that this provision in the judicial interpretation is made to interpret Article 73 of the Chinese Contract Law. It is therefore only applicable to contractual relationships, whereas the liability of the insured under liability insurance is very often non-contractual. Although the Insurance Act appears to extend the principle of Article 73, it does not necessarily follow that the judicial interpretation is also extended.

If Article 18 of Interpretation I on Contract Law were applicable, the insurer would be able to rely on the defences in the insurance contract or the Chinese Maritime Code. Article 242 of the Chinese Maritime Code provides that 'the insurer shall not be liable for the loss caused by the intentional act of the insured'. This provision is intended to be a counterparty of section 55(2) of the Marine Insurance Act 1906. However, instead of 'wilful misconduct', this Article uses the term 'intentional act'.

41 Article 206, Chinese Maritime Code.
42 See Chapter 5, section 6.2.

It is arguable that 'intentional act' does not cover the situation of recklessness, and that therefore there is potentially a gap between Article 242 and Article 209 of the Maritime Code, which will cause the insurer to have unlimited liability. The author would suggest that a broad interpretation be given to Article 242. Under criminal law, 'intent' may refer to both direct intent and oblique intent. Under the latter, the event is a natural consequence of a voluntary act and it is foreseen as such.[43] It would therefore appear that the concept of oblique intent is similar to the description of 'recklessly and with knowledge that such loss would probably result' under the limitation regime in the Chinese Maritime Code. Although resulting from a different legal context, reference may be made to this concept and the word 'intentional' in Article 242 may be given a broad interpretation including both 'direct intent' and 'oblique intent'. If such an interpretation is accepted, the liability insurer would enjoy better protection against a third-party claimant; otherwise, the insurer will not be able to avoid liability where the limitation is broken due to the shipowner's reckless act or omission.

5 Other limitation rules

5.1 International Convention on Civil Liability for Oil Pollution Damage (CLC 1969) and its 1992 Protocol (CLC 1992)

As mentioned in the *travaux préparatoires* to the LLMC 1976 and of the Protocol 1996, the idea of including liability insurers in the list of persons entitled to limit their liability originated from CLC 1969.[44] CLC 1969 provides for an 'absolute' right to limit for the insurer, namely, the insurer providing financial security for the pollution damage under the convention is entitled to limit his liability irrespective of the shipowner's right to limit.[45] Although CLC 1992 revised the conditions for when the shipowner would lose its right to limit liability, the provision regarding the insurer's right of limitation was kept. Both the UK and China are Contracting States of CLC 1992 and thus the above provision applies in both countries. It is noteworthy that the insurers referred to in the CLC conventions are those providing compulsory insurance. Such a position is helpful to encourage insurers to provide compulsory insurance service in a more efficient way.

43 Article 14, Criminal Law of China. Although oblique intention is not expressly provided in this Article, it is submitted that Article 14 covers both direct intention and oblique intention.

44 *The travaux préparatoires of the LLMC 1976 and of the Protocol 1996*, p 56.

45 Article VII(8), CLC 1969.

5.2 Hazardous and Noxious Substances Convention 2010 (HNS Convention 2010)

Following CLC 1992, HNS Convention 2010 also provides the insurer under the convention with the right of limitation independent of the insured shipowner's entitlement. Provisions regarding the insurer's right to limit and discharge of the shipowner's limitation are identical with those in CLC 1992. HNS Convention is not yet in force and neither China nor the UK is a Contracting State.

5.3 International Convention on Civil Liability for Bunker Oil Pollution Damage 2001 (Bunker Convention 2001)

The Bunker Convention 2001 contains a detailed provision in respect of insurers' protection under direct actions brought by third parties. According to Article 7(10) of the Convention, the insurer is entitled: (1) to invoke the shipowner's defences including limitation of liability under LLMC 1976 or other applicable national or international regime; (2) to limit its liability to an amount equal to the limits of liability under LLMC 1976 or other applicable national or international regime in the case where the shipowner is not entitled to limitation; and (3) to invoke the defence that the pollution damage resulted from the wilful misconduct of the shipowner, which may avoid the insurer's liabilities under the insurance contract.[46] With such a provision, the scope for compensation by an insurer to a third-party claimant under the Convention is reduced.

Both China and the UK are member states of the Bunker Convention 2001. The Convention came into force in the UK on 21 November 2008 and came into force in China on 9 March 2009.

5.4 Athens Convention Relating to the Carriage of Passengers and their Luggage by Sea (Athens Convention 2002)

The Athens Convention 2002 contains a provision similar to Article 7(10) of the Bunker Convention 2001. Article 4bis(10) of the Athens Convention provides that, in the case where a claim is made directly against the insurer or other person providing financial security, the amount set out in Article 4bis(1) applies as the limit of liability even if the carrier or the performing carrier is not entitled to limitation of liability; and the insurer or other person providing financial security may further invoke the defences that the carrier would have been entitled to invoke in accordance with this Convention and the insurer may invoke the defence that the damage resulted from the wilful misconduct of the assured.

46 Article 7(10), Bunker Convention 2001.

The Athens Convention 2002 came into force on 23 April 2014. The UK has implemented the Athens Convention by means of the Merchant Shipping (Carriage of Passengers by Sea) Regulations 2012. China is not a member state of the Athens Convention.

5.5 LLMC 1976 and other limitation rules

Comparing LLMC 1976 with the limitation regimes mentioned in the above section, the insurer's rights under LLMC 1976 is different from others in that LLMC 1976 does not provide the insurer with an independent right of limitation whereas, under other limitation regimes outlined in the above, the insurer's right of limitation is independent of the insured's act or omission. It is submitted that the approach of those limitation regimes as discussed in section 5 ought equally to be followed in the LLMC framework.[47] In fact, while drafting the LLMC 1976, such a point of view was proposed by an observer from BIMCO who contended that the LLMC 1976 should include the principle recognized in Article VII(8) of CLC 1969.[48] However, this suggestion was not supported by the committee. It was considered that the insurer would be protected by terms in the insurance contract. It is noteworthy that all those aforesaid limitation frameworks impose compulsory insurance on shipowners for specific maritime claims, and those conventions themselves contain provisions regarding direct action against the insurers providing compulsory insurance service. Therefore, those conventions need to provide a favourable system for insurers so that the shipowners under those conventions will be in a position to acquire compulsory insurance; otherwise, the insurer may ask for high rates of premium and, as a result, the shipping industry may have reservations about the desirability of Contracting States joining the conventions.

In terms of LLMC 1976, it provides limitation for general maritime claims, covering a larger scope in terms of types of claims than other limitation systems.[49] A direct action may only be brought against the insurer in limited situations provided in national laws and regulations. Therefore, a more general provision regarding insurer's limitation would permit member states (or a country adopting the LLMC limitation framework) to achieve a better balance between different parties (i.e. third party claimants, shipowners and insurers) by means of national legislation, notwithstanding that it may bring uncertainty.

47 Yuanjun Xia and Qun Li, 'Pattern choice of marine liability insurer's right to limit liability', *Journal of Ocean University of China (Social Sciences Edition)*, 2011 (6).

48 CMI, The *travaux préparatoires* of the LLMC Convention 1976 and of the Protocol of 1996, p 57.

49 Article 2, LLMC 1976; LLMC is normally regarded as a 'global limitation'.

6 Conclusion

Although insurer's limitation of liability for maritime claims is provided under both English law and Chinese law, the insurer may still face the risk of being exposed to unlimited liability.

Under English law, where the shipowner is entitled to limit, the insurer is also entitled to limit; where the shipowner loses his right to limit, the insurer may be liable for full compensation because of the term 'to the same extent' in LLMC 1976. However, it is arguable that the LLMC only comes into play after the liability is determined and the insurer may rely on the protections provided by the insurance contract and the Marine Insurance Act 1906.

In terms of Chinese law, the Chinese Maritime Code provides that the insurer's right to limit liability is subject to the insured shipowner's entitlement of limitation. In the event the shipowner is not entitled to limit, the law is unclear as to whether the insurer will be able to rely on the terms of the insurance contract or the provision of the Maritime Code. Even if the insurer may rely on the provision of the Maritime Code, the different scope of Article 206 and Article 242 may bring difficulty for the insurer.

In contrast with English law, Chinese law is far from clear in respect of direct actions against liability insurers, especially marine liability insurers operating as mutuals. The Chinese Insurance Act 2009 allows the third party to claim directly against the liability insurer, but the Act does not set out clear requirements and restrictions of such direct actions. In particular, it is unclear whether the rights and obligations between the insured and the insurer are applicable identically in a direct action brought by the third party. And more importantly, the position of P&I Clubs needs to be considered by the Chinese legislature.

14 Insurance contract law reform in England

Lessons for Chinese insurance law

Dr Meixian Song[1]

1 Introduction

The modern regime of English insurance law has been largely derived and developed from early marine insurance, which is the oldest form of insurance known to the common law jurisdictions. The business of marine insurance was firmly developed in England by as early as the sixteenth century. Given this development of the insurance market over a considerable period of time, substantial numbers of cases have inevitably accumulated and eventually established a set of systematic principles under English law. Based upon more than 150 years of judicial authority, the English Marine Insurance Act came into effect in 1906 to reflect the law in the form of statutes notably as a result of the remarkable work of Sir Mackenzie Chalmers. Consequently, English marine insurance law has over its long history developed to a high level and has exerted significant impact on both common law and civil law jurisdictions.

Recently, however, when the general insurance industry has seen rapid development and improvement with the long-term assistance of numerous institutions and associations, it is suggested that English insurance law seems to be somewhat out of date. In particular, the Marine Insurance Act 1906 is in part redundant, as well as incomplete. Therefore, aiming to balance the interests of the insured and insurer by law and to reflect the needs of modern insurance practice and make both sides aware of their rights and obligations, a review of insurance contract law was set up and promoted by the Law Commission for England and Wales and the Scottish Law Commission and has carried out significant work since 2006. It will probably last until the end of 2015. So far, three Consultation Papers have been published in July 2007, December 2011, and June 2012. In particular, the Consumer Insurance (Disclosure and Representation) Act 2012, which entered into force on 6 April 2013, is a noteworthy outcome of the reform

1 Lecturer in Maritime Law, University of Exeter, PhD (Southampton Law School), LLM (UCL), LLB of Dalian Maritime University (China).

project. On 28 January 2014, the Law Commission launched the first draft Bill of the Insurance Contracts Act 2014.

It is noteworthy that in the context of the Law Commission's project, no distinction has been drawn between marine and non-marine insurance. Some of the proposals in fact aim to rewrite elements of the law predating the 1906 Act. Accordingly, the reforms applicable to insurance contract law are likely to extend to the rules of marine insurance. Various important issues in respect of marine insurance have been considered and included under this scheme; for instance, insurable interest, broker's liability, warranties, etc. It is expected that these issues will be effectively reformed and new legislation implemented on the basis of a thorough review and investigation.

In comparison, Chinese law is, as is well known, a civil law system that is influenced by various other jurisdictions whether civil law or common law. Concerning maritime law and insurance contract law, a significant transplantation of English law can be perceived, especially the impact of the 1906 Act on Chinese marine insurance legislation and practice. China produced its first piece of comprehensive insurance legislation in 1995. Lately, substantial amendments have been made to the Insurance Act 2009. Meanwhile, the Chinese Maritime Code (CMC) contains specific rules regarding marine insurance in Chapter 12,[2] which prevails over the overlapping rules contained in the 2009 Act.[3]

Interestingly, major reforms of the new Chinese Act regarding insurance contract law embrace a number of the same questions as those considered in the context of the UK law reform project. Thus, this chapter will summarise and introduce the UK insurance contract law reform project, with regard particularly to marine insurance law. English law reform will be highlighted for the purpose of improving the legal regime applicable to the Chinese marine insurance market and effectively implement the general insurance law in the marine field.

2 History of English insurance law

The marine insurance policy is the oldest form of insurance policy under common law. It is normally recognised that the history of marine insurance starts from Lloyd's coffee house around the late eighteenth century. However, the concept of marine insurance can be traced back from as early as the sixteenth century, when the merchants alighted at Lombard Street London and established marine insurance business. In 1570, the centre

2 Articles 216–256 of the Chinese Maritime Code 1992.

3 Article 184 of the 2009 Act provides that the Chinese Maritime Code provisions in terms of marine insurance prevail over those therein, whereas, for the issues untouched in the CMC, the regulations in the Act shall be followed; where neither document provides legal ground, the contract law applies.

moved to the Royal Exchange on Cornhill and the Chamber of Assurances was chartered and operated as an underwriting centre and arbitration centre. Based upon the successful establishment and development, life insurance has been created and mutually influenced with the law of marine insurance. By the middle of the seventeenth century, marine and life insurance were well set up in England.

Unfortunately, in the Great Fire of London in 1666, the Royal Exchange was destroyed and the history of the insurance market stepped onto a new page, leading directly to its renowned present. Lloyd's was founded in 1688, beginning with 'insuring' a stolen watch, but remained focused on marine insurance from the outset. Subsequently, the Bubble Act facilitated the expansion of Lloyd's to be the centre of insurance, since the Act prohibited the formation of companies from underwriting insurance policies, unless chartered. Therefore, individuals who gathered at Lloyd's coffee house became an active group besides the statutory monopoly over insurance of two companies, the Royal Exchange Assurance Co. and the London Assurance Co. The old Lloyd's SG form was produced during this period in 1779, remaining valid until 1982. Meanwhile, the direct ancestor of Protection and Indemnity (P&I) Clubs, shipowners' mutual societies also provided assurance service. After the repeal of the Bubble Act in 1824, Lloyd's and the P&I Clubs naturally became the dominant member of the insurance market. Overall, the formation of Lloyd's is also regarded as the formative period of the English marine insurance market.[4]

The nineteenth century was a robust period for the insurance industry. Plenty of insurance companies were established and numerous forms of insurance policies were created besides marine, life and fire policies. Most importantly, substantial decisions were made and contributed to the 12-year great work of Sir Chalmers, the enactment of the English Marine Insurance Act 1906. In retrospect, the first statute in substantive marine insurance law was the Marine Insurance Act 1745, which was specifically concerned with the requirement of the insured's insurable interest in order to put an end to the wagering contract in the form of marine insurance. The 1745 Act remained in force until its incorporation into the Marine Insurance Act 1906. Subsequently, the Marine Insurance Act 1788 required the names of all parties interested in a marine policy to be inserted into the policy, which was repealed by the Marine Insurance Act 1906 insofar as it applied to marine insurance: it still operates as regards non-marine policies on goods. Finally, the Policies of Marine Insurance Act 1868 addressed the issue of the assignment of marine policies and has been reproduced in sections 50–51 of the Marine Insurance Act 1906.[5] In one word, the Marine

4 R. Merkin 'Australia: still a nation of chalmers?', *UQLJ*, 2011, 30(2), p 189.

5 See R. Merkin, *Marine Insurance Legislation*, 5th edn, 2014, London: Routledge, Chapter 1.

Insurance Act 1906 has covered a wide range of substantive matters from the cases and the former acts as a classic piece of statute under English common law.

Moreover, the Institute of London Underwriters formed in 1884 and established standard terms for various classes of marine insurance contracts, which are adopted in conjunction with the SG form.[6] For the last century, marine insurance cases were decided in reliance upon the 1906 Act and the agreements. The insurance market including marine insurance has been greatly promoted and improved, such that the standard clauses of marine policies have been modernised in replacement of the SG form in 1983. Nevertheless, insurance contract law, particularly the English Marine Insurance Act 1906, is confronted by challenges from modern practice in the twenty-first century.

3 The proposals of reforms on insurance contract law

Insurance contract law is set out in part in the Marine Insurance Act 1906. This Act incorporates general principles of insurance law and has been held to apply to all forms of insurance contracts, not simply to marine insurance. However, as the Act was not a civil law code designed to provide answers to future problems, but rather a summary of the existing rules and practice in 1906, it is well recognised that it has not kept pace with the times and can produce results that fail to meet the expectations of the market.[7] Moreover, in terms of the ongoing law reform project, it does not particularly distinguish marine insurance from other types so that any fundamental amendment on the principles of insurance contract law will affect the propositions in the law of marine insurance as well.

English Law Commission Consultation Paper No. 182 and Scottish Law Commission Discussion Paper No. 134[8] was released in July 2007, addressing the issues of pre-contract duty of disclosure/representations and warranties. The second consultation paper, the long-awaited English Law Consultation Paper No 201 and Scottish Law Commission Paper No 152,[9] was finally published on 20 December 2011. It addresses five issues: Issues Paper 4, Insurable Interest, January 2008; Issues Paper 6, Damages for Late Payment and the Insurer's Duty of Good Faith, March 2010; Issues Paper 7, The Insured's Post-Contract Duty of Good Faith, July 2010; Issues

6 R. Merkin, *Colinvaux & Merkin's Insurance Contract Law*, 2002, Sweet & Maxwell, vol. 2, p 20470.

7 R. Merkin 'Australia: still a nation of chalmers?', *UQLJ*, 2011, 30(2), p 189.

8 Available at: www.justice.gov.uk/lawcommission/docs/cp182_ICL_Misrep_Non-disclosure_Breach_of_Warranty.pdf (accessed 13 August 2014).

9 Available at: www.justice.gov.uk/lawcommission/docs/cp201_ICL_post_contract_duties.pdf (accessed 13 August 2014). Any references in this chapter to the 'consultation paper', without further specification, refer to this paper.

Paper 8, The Broker's Liability for Premiums, July 2010; and Issues Paper 9, The Requirement for a Formal Marine Policy, October 2010. The second consultation paper was followed by a third in June 2012, on the business insured's duty of disclosure and warranties. So far, the Consumer Insurance (Disclosure and Representation) Act 2012 came into force on 6 April 2013.

4 Pre-contract non-disclosure/misrepresentation/ warranties

This issue is the most crucial goal of this reform project. The first Consultation Paper, which is based upon Issues Papers 1, 2 and 3, discusses the scope and effect of the insured's duty of disclosure and representation and whether the remedy of avoidance of the insurance contract for insurers is too harsh for assureds. It is noteworthy that a distinction between consumer insurance and business contracts is drawn in the consultation paper. Consumer in this context is defined as 'any natural person acting for purposes outside his trade, business or profession',[10] whereas business assureds place covers for the contrary purpose and normally hold different positions in negotiation. Marine insurance is largely within the scale of business insurance, while a marine policy may fall into the group of consumer insurance due to the purpose of cover. Accordingly, marine (consumer) insurance contracts are now also subject to the Consumer Insurance (Disclosure and Representation) Act 2012 and further amendment on business insurance.

4.1 The insured's non-disclosure and misrepresentation

In respect of a contract of the utmost good faith, it is recognised that the Marine Insurance Act 1906 embodies a partial codification of the common law, which is applicable to other types of insurance.[11] Section 17 affirms the requirement of the utmost good faith and provides a remedy of avoidance of the policy in the case of violation. Sections 18 and 19 amplify the rules of disclosure and section 20 provides those of misrepresentation. Wide criticism of these provisions has triggered a proposal to reform this part of the law but has been too long in the making.[12] It is suggested that the current English law in respect of the utmost good faith is overly harsh mainly in two respects. On the one hand, the test of non-disclosure and misrepresentation is far from the expectations of the insurance market and

10 Ibid., cited from FCA (Financial Conduct Authority) glossary handbook.

11 *Pan Atlantic Insurance Co. Ltd v Pine Top Insurance Co. Ltd* [1995] AC 501, 508, per Lord Mustill.

12 Insurance Law, Non-Disclosure and Breach of Warranty (1980) Law Com No. 104, paragraph 1.21.

represents an imbalance between the interests of the insured and insurer. This long-established test makes no reference at all to the insured's objective intent (i.e. honesty, negligence or fraud). The materiality of the information and inducement into concluding a cover are the two common major elements to constitute both non-disclosure and misrepresentation. The test of materiality provided by sections 18(2) and 20(2) is known as the 'prudent insurer test' and is based upon the judgment of the insurer. Inducement is also a question in respect of the insurer's mind and decisions.[13] Both elements of the test take considerable account of the insurer's benefit, which no longer suits the current market.

On the other hand, the remedy available to the insured's breach is oversimplified and strict, which is evidently unjust to the insured under some circumstances. The remedy is provided by section 17 that 'A contract of marine insurance is a contract based upon the utmost good faith, and, if the utmost good faith be not observed by either party, the contract may be avoided by the other party'.

For over 30 years, self-regulation has played a considerable role in adapting to the needs of the modern market. However, it seems that this method cannot substitute the need for reform of the 1906 Act in this regard. In 1977, a statement of practice was issued by the industry bodies covering general insurance and life insurance, but later largely replaced by the FSA (Financial Services Authority) regulations and the FOS (Financial Ombudsman Service) guidance. It is recognised by the Law Commissions that these overlapping layers of regulation fail to substitute law reform.

Unlike consumer insurance, most marine insurance contracts should, as proposed by the Law Commissions, follow the rules governing business insurance. The insured must also in future volunteer information but subject to the standard of the knowledge and realisation of a reasonable insured instead of the test in favour of the insurers established by the 1906 Act and the cases thereupon. This proposition has been supported by the editors of the current edition of *Arnould*.[14] Moreover, regarding section 17, the assured should be protected by statutes from the avoidance of the contract where the information is provided honestly and with due diligence.

4.2 Breach of warranties

The concept of warranties in the context of marine insurance is different from the one in the common law. Warranties have the equivalent effect to the terms of condition, the breach of which will discharge the insurer from

13 A circumstance or representation is material 'which would influence the judgment of a prudent insurer in fixing the premium, or determining whether he will take the risk'.

14 J. Gilman *et al.*, *Arnould's Law of Marine Insurance and Average*, 18th edn, 2013, Sweet & Maxwell, p 585.

all further liability. Pursuant to section 33(1), warranty is defined as 'a warranty by which the assured undertakes that some particular thing shall or shall not be done, or that some condition shall be fulfilled, or whereby he affirms or negatives the existence of a particular state of facts'.

Two main problems exist in the English marine insurance law in relation to warranties. One is the confusing and complex wordings that may constitute a warranty; the other is the unreasonable remedy of the insurer's automatic discharge of liability upon breach. Whether a statement amounts to a warranty or condition precedent or an ordinary term is essentially a matter of construction.[15] As for the legal effect of breaching a warranty, the paper proposed, on the one hand, that a causal link between the breach and the loss should be required and established instead of an 'automatic' termination of the policy. On the other hand, it could be agreed that the insured's expectation should be taken into account and prevent termination when the insurer avails himself of the breach.

4.3 The role of intermediaries

It is ordinary practice in the insurance market that the assured purchase the cover through brokers who will advise the business or intermediaries who simply pass information to the insurers. Section 19 imposes on the agents the duty to disclose material information. Section 20(1) deems the misrepresentation made by the insured's agent to be the act of the assured; accordingly, the assured bears the liability of such representation. The Law Commissions have called for a clarification of the roles of agents, distinguishing the agents of the insurers from those of the policyholders. The test is suggested by the paper to be whether the agent has made an analysis of the market and business. The fault or wrongdoings of the insurer's agents should not affect the rights of the assured.

In the marine insurance market, the term 'agents' used in relation to the process of effecting a policy refers to brokers, and brokers are as a rule the agents of the assureds. However, intermediaries who merely sell a range of covers for the insurers may become involved in the chain of intermediaries, and their non-disclosure and misrepresentations will then not be subject to sections 19 and 20 and give rise to any negative consequence against the assureds. Additionally, it is noted by the Law Commissions that the remedies arising from section 19 in terms of agents' non-disclosure shall be explicitly provided; the draft Insurance Contracts Bill 2014 has shown an intent to repeal section 19. Instead, the agent should apply the same standard of care as the assured or the proposer of a policy in various specified situations in the Bill.

15 *HIH Casualty and General Insurance Ltd v New Hampshire Insurance Co.* [2001] 2 Lloyd's Rep 161.

4.4 Consumer Insurance (Disclosure and Representations) Act 2012

The Act was enacted on 9 March 2009 and applies to all 'consumer insurance contracts' entered into on or after 6 April 2013 (section 12(4)).

Section 2(5)(b) articulates that:

> the application of section 17 of the Marine Insurance Act 1906 (contracts of marine insurance are of utmost good faith), in relation to a contract of marine insurance which is a consumer insurance contract, is subject to the provisions of this Act.

The significant change, as echoed in the consultation paper, is that the Act abolishes the duty on the consumer to volunteer facts that would be material to the insurer, and merely requires the assured to take reasonable care not to make misrepresentation. The consumer is obliged to take reasonable care not to make misrepresentation (section 2(2)). A qualifying misrepresentation is classified as 'deliberate or reckless' and careless (section 5). Rules 2 to 9 of the Schedule 1 to the 2012 Act articulate the different effects of breaches under each categorisation:

(1) Where misrepresentations are deliberate or reckless, the insurer retains the entitlement to avoid the contract, refuse all claims and to retain any premium already paid, except where to do so would be 'unfair' to the consumer.
(2) Where consumers make careless misrepresentations, the circumstances are further differentiated into three kinds. Only in circumstances where the insurer would not have entered into the contract on any terms would the insurer be entitled to avoid the contract. In such circumstances the insurer would be obliged to return the premium paid. If the insurer would have entered into the contract but on different terms (other than those relating to premium) and so requires, then the contract is to be treated as if it had been entered into on those different terms. Alternatively, if the insurer would have entered into the contract but would have charged a higher premium, then the insurer may reduce the amount to be paid on a claim proportionally.

This Act is comparable to Article 16 of the Chinese Insurance Act 2009, which also takes account of the subjective mind of the assureds when they provide inaccurate yet material information. Where an assured is deliberately in breach, insurers are not liable for losses occurring before they terminate the contract and can also keep the premium.[16] Where an assured

16 Article 16, Chinese Insurance Act 2009.

acts with major negligence, insurers enjoy the same rights as in the previous situation, but the premium is refundable. Where an assured has provided the information with mere negligence or other circumstances, insurers are not entitled to terminate contracts, such that the validity of contracts and liabilities are not affected by such non-disclosure or misrepresentation.

It can be observed that English law may be stricter to assureds in the case of misrepresentation or non-disclosure, as major negligence in Chinese law may be equivalent to recklessness in English law and mere negligence may be interpreted as carelessness. However, it is a matter of definition and interpretation of the terms when applying these provisions in China.

5 The insured's post-contractual duties of good faith

This topic focuses essentially on fraudulent claims and the remedies available to insurers, which is deemed as the other side of the insurer's duty to pay for a valid claim on the basis of mutual duties of good faith instead of the old-fashioned unilateral utmost good faith in the Issue Papers 7. The insured's duty not to make a fraudulent claim is held to be a form of a continuing duty of utmost good faith.[17]

As mentioned in the previous part, section 17 of the 1906 Act gives rise to confusion, as it only specifies one remedy, namely avoidance of contract. English courts have long struggled with this provision and criticised its approach in *The Star Sea*.[18] In light of the demand for a more flexible and tailored regime of remedy, the consultation paper basically accepts the proposition in the issue paper and a more completed set of rules are amplified, notably recommending that the policyholder's whole claim can be forfeited if it is connected with fraud, as well as any subsequent claims in a case where insurers take immediate steps to terminate the policy for breach. In the Draft Insurance Contracts Bill 2014, clause 10 states that, in the case of fraudulent claims, the insurer has a right to choose whether to terminate the contract from the time of the fraudulent act, and that only claims relating to such fraud and from then on shall be affected.

Under Chinese law, Article 27 of the Insurance Act 2009 distinguishes three categories of fraud such that every category leads to a different legal remedy. Just as with breaches of pre-contractual duties of good faith, in Chinese law, insurers are not entitled to avoid the contract. Where fraudulent claims are made in the case that no casualty has ever occurred, insurers are allowed to terminate the contract and retain the premium. Where assureds deliberately cause losses or injuries, insurers are also entitled to terminate the contract and retain the premium, except that insurers shall return the premium of a life policy if the fraud is committed

17 *Black King Shipping Corporation v Massie (The Litsion Pride)* [1985] 1 Lloyd's Rep 437.
18 *Manifest Shipping Co. Ltd v Uni-Polaris Insurance Co. Ltd* [2001] UKLH 1.

after the assured has paid at least two years' payment of premium. Where assureds exaggerate the amount of a claim by fraudulent means, insurers are only discharged from liability for the exaggerated portion. Furthermore, assureds are obliged to return any sums paid and also are liable for any expenses accrued due to such payment to insurers under all aforementioned circumstances.

This Article is basically consistent with the Law Commissions' proposals; however, it remains unclear whether the contract is terminated automatically or by election by the insurers in Chinese law. Moreover, the issue of subsequent claims is not addressed in the provisions. The literal reading of the Article simply entitles the insurers to exercise a right to terminate the contract when the assured reports the fraudulent claims to them. It seems that insurers cannot exercise this right until they actually have notice of the fraud. If any subsequent claim is made before that, insurers are hardly able to rely on this Article, unless the subsequent claims are also fraudulent, in order to discharge their liabilities and forfeit the claims.

6 Damages for the insurer's late payment

Another topic is whether a policyholder should be entitled to damages arising from the insurer's refusal of a valid claim, or an unjustifiable significant delay. Under current English law, unlike Scots law and Chinese law, a policyholder is merely entitled to claim for the loss plus interest, but not any further loss such as a foreseeable financial loss. It is suggested that English insurance contract law is not in line with the principles of contract law.

This rule has been well illustrated in *Sprung v Royal Insurance (UK) Ltd*,[19] where the assured claimant had been forced out of business in a difficult condition owing to the insurer's rejecting the claim that was decided to be valid later. The Court of Appeal held that the assured was not entitled to claim the further loss for lost opportunity to sell his business. The Marine Insurance Act 1906 does not recognise any liability other than that set out in the Act itself.[20]

Numerous propositions have been presented in terms of justifying further damages for the insurer's late payment or arbitrary non-payment, including the insurer's breach of utmost good faith or an action in tort. The Law Commissions' overall conclusion in the Consultation Paper is to change the law and separate good faith from the duty to pay claims. Moreover, the cause of action in tort law is not plausible or practical for protecting the insurer from an extended and unpredictable liability.

19 [1999] 1 Lloyd's Rep IR 111; [1997] CLC 70.

20 *Ventouris v Mountain (The Italia Express)* [1992] 2 Lloyd's Rep 281.

Clause 12 of the draft Insurance Contracts Bill 2014 provides that 'It is an implied term of every contract of insurance that if the insured makes a claim under the contract, the insurer must pay any sums due in respect of the claim within a reasonable time'. This is in line with Article 23(1) of China's Insurance Act 2009. However, Chinese law further clarifies the length of 'reasonable time'. It provides that insurers shall fix the amount of indemnity without undue delay, in the case of complex scenarios and unless otherwise agreed, insurers shall extend the time up to 30 days. Once the agreement of indemnity is concluded, insurers shall pay within 10 days or in the agreed period. However, Chinese law does not prescribe specifically the legal consequence of late payment. Nevertheless, foreseeable losses arising from the late payment are recoverable in accordance with Chinese contract law principles.

7 Formal requirement of policy

Section 22 of the 1906 Act is concerned with the formal requirement for a policy. A policy is the only accepted form of evidence of a marine insurance contract; a rule not applicable to other types of insurance. The original justification of this provision is to chase the stamp duty imposed on marine insurance in accordance with the Stamp Act 1795, under which the policy was designated to be the legally stamped document. However, this stamp duty was abolished in 1970, while section 22 remained. In practice, at present the insurers barely take advantage of this provision in order to reject a claim, although section 22 fully supports and legalises this action. Therefore, it is proposed in the project that section 22 should be repealed.

In Chinese law, the conclusion of an insurance contract, whether marine or non-marine, is only subject to the mutual agreement of the parties, irrespective of the final issue of policy.[21] In particular with marine insurance contracts, the purpose of issuing a policy is primarily to record the specific terms and conditions.

In a practical setting,[22] at the outset the assured provides a proposal to his broker. Then the broker passes on the proposal to the insurer to review. Through the discussion between the broker and the insurer, the terms and conditions and premium are agreed in the form of a slip, which is a document produced by the broker to the insurer. Once the insurer initials the slip, that insurer is at that point in time legally bound by the insurance contract.[23] Finally, after the conclusion of the contract, the insurer issues a policy and promises to indemnify the assured in accordance with the terms for losses

21 Article 221, Chinese Maritime Code and Article 13, Chinese Insurance Act 2009.

22 See H. Bennett, *The Law of Marine Insurance*, 2nd edn, 2006, Oxford: Oxford University Press, Chapters 2 and 8.

23 *Ionides v Pacific Fire & Marine Insurance Co.* (1871) LR 6 QB 674.

arising out of the insured perils. Now that the stamp is no longer a valid legal requirement, it is doubted that no outstanding reason can reduce the evidential effect of the slip compared with the policy in terms of the existence of a contract, which is stated in section 89. So far, the requirement for a formal marine policy is no more than a matter of standard of proof at present. The essential issue that shall be considered and reviewed is whether it is a right and proper standard to deem a marine policy as the only admissible form of evidence.

Therefore, the consultation paper includes a few sections contained in the 1906 Act:

(1) A marine insurance contract may be enforced even if it is not embodied in a formal policy document, and the legislation should not require a marine insurance contract to be in any particular form. That in turn means that sections 22, 23 and 24 of the 1906 Act can be repealed.
(2) Section 89 in terms of the reference to the slip of the 1906 Act can also be repealed, the definitions of particular words and terms in the schedule can be retained, as they codify the common law and are found in other policies. Further, section 21 of the Act, which states that the contract is concluded when the proposal is accepted even if the policy is issued later and that reference may be made to the slip or cover note, should be amended merely to state that the contract is concluded when the proposal is accepted.
(3) Section 52 should be repealed, the term 'policy' should be either replaced by 'contract' or redefined as meaning 'contract', section 2(2) should either be repealed or restated to mean that where an insurance contract covers shipbuilding, a ship launch or 'any adventure analogous to a marine adventure', the parties may include an express term to designate the insurance as marine insurance for the purposes of the 1906 Act.
(4) The Law Commissions have left open to consultation whether the statement in section 50(3) that a marine policy can be assigned by indorsement or in other customary manner should be amended to state that a marine insurance contract may be assigned in any customary manner or as agreed between the parties to the transfer.

8 Insurable interest

Insurable interest is a fundamental concept in insurance law, and requires the assured to have a legal relationship with the subject matter insured and to suffer loss on the occurrence of an insured peril. This concept was introduced into insurance law mainly for avoiding wager/gaming, long regarded as an abuse of the regime of insurance both in the commercial sense and in public welfare terms. Gambling policy is a historical product deriving from the immature operation of insurance. Prior to the 1906 Act, the classic definition of insurable interest has been provided in the landmark case *Lucena v Craufurd*,[24] referring to 'a right in the property, or a right derivable out of some contract about the property, which in either case may be lost upon some contingency affecting the possession or enjoyment of the party'. The 1906 Act has followed this definition and states in its section 5(2) that:

> In particular a person is interested in a marine adventure where he stands in any legal or equitable relation to the adventure or to any insurable property at risk therein, in consequence of which he may benefit by the safety or due arrival of insurable property, or may be prejudiced by its loss, or by damage thereto, or by the detention thereof, or may incur liability in respect thereof.

Insurable interest is also a reflection of the doctrine of indemnity. The principle of indemnity basically applies to all contracts of insurance. Per Brett LJ, in *Castellain v Preston*,[25] the principle of indemnity is the foundation of every rule in indemnity insurance, such as a marine or fire policy. It entitles the assured to get a full indemnity against the loss that he suffered; however, the assured cannot retain compensation in excess of his loss that he suffered. In terms of insurable interest, if there is a legal link between the loss and the assured, there is no liability of indemnity recognised in the legal sense on the side of the insurer.

In light of the Gambling Act 2005, which came into force on 1 September 2007, and its repeal of section 18 of the Gaming Act 1845, indemnity insurance, which includes most forms of property and liability insurance other than marine, will not be rendered unenforceable due to the lack of an insurable interest. Marine insurance retains its own rules. Remaining unaffected by the Gambling Act 2005, pursuant to section 4(2) of the Marine Insurance Act 1906, an agreement made lacking insurable interest is a wagering contract, which according to section 4(1) is void. Therefore, it is suggested that the requirement of insurable interest becomes redundant in insurance contract law. The Law Commissions Issues Paper No. 4 published in 2008 addresses the question whether the law on insurable interest should be repealed and Consultation Paper 2011 showed a desire for retaining the concept. In respect of marine insurance, four issues are noteworthy: in summary, the time when insurable interest must attach; the suggestions on repealing the 1909 Act as to criminal penalties; the statutory requirement of identifying the party interested in the policy under section 23 of the 1906 Act; and the definitions of insurable interest provided by sections 7 through 14 of the 1906 Act.

24 (1806) 2 Bosanquet and Puller (New Reports) 269, 127 E.R. 630.
25 (1882–83) L.R. 11 Q.B.D. 380.

The 2011 consultation paper considers that the definition of insurable interest ought to be widened so as to cover a right in the property that is the subject matter of the insurance or a right arising out of a contract in respect of it. The specific examples of insurable interest in marine insurance, set out in sections 7–14 of the Marine Insurance Act 1906, should be left as they are. The Law Commissions were satisfied by evidence that these provisions work well. That is a rather odd conclusion, given that some of them are redundant, such as the references to bottomry and respondentia, and others have been overtaken by legislative developments (e.g. the rules on interest in part of an unascertained bulk), and the best that might be said of them is that they are harmless.[26] Nevertheless, it is still questioned whether the proposed definition is wide enough.

Second, pursuant to section 6(1) of the 1906 Act, the assured shall have an insurable interest at the time of the loss as had been affirmed by *The Moonacre*.[27] However, this stipulation is distinct from other types of insurance contract where the insurable interest must attach at the inception of the policy. Since the law on gaming contracts provides that a contract related to gambling shall not prevent its enforcement, the result is that such a policyholder no longer needs to show an insurable interest at any stage to prove that the contract is not a wager. It has been argued that the Gambling Act 2005 will change the position in marine insurance contracts, although divergent views have been raised.[28] It is concluded in the consultation paper that there should be a statutory basis for insurable interest in the form of a general requirement. In order to make a claim, the assured must show insurable interest at the time of the loss in terms of non-life insurance. Therefore, the provisions of the Marine Insurance Act will remain unchanged in this regard.

Another question is concerned with the stipulation of section 23, which requires the policy to specify the name of the assured or of the person who effects the insurance on his behalf. The Marine Insurance Act 1788 requires the names of those interested to be inserted into all policies on goods. It is strongly proposed that the failure to specify the name in the policy ought not to be available to the insurer to void the contract by law. A remedy is available where the name of the assured is material information that touches the issue of utmost good faith. Accordingly, the statutory regulation is no longer necessary and should be abolished.

Fourth, Consultation Paper 2011 suggests that section 1(1) of the Marine Insurance (Gambling Policies) Act 1909 should be repealed, which has been strongly proposed in the issues paper. The provision creates the criminal

26 R. Merkin, 'Reform of insurance law: the Law Commissions' consultation paper of December 2011', *Insurance Law Monthly*, vol. 24, no. 2.

27 *Sharp v Sphere Drake Insurance (The Moonacre)* [1992] 2 Lloyd's Rep 501.

28 R. Merkin, 'The repeal of the prohibition on gambling', *Insurance Law Monthly*, December 2005.

offence of effecting an insurance contract in the absence of an insurable interest. The criminal penalty has lost its necessity and function in light of the current market. Therefore, such a severe punishment in law should be repealed rather than remain in the dust.

Overall, the Law Commissions' queries in this regard reflect less severe attitudes towards gambling policy currently. The review on insurable interest in the law of marine insurance serves as a reminder that it may be the time to detach the stringent link between gambling contract and insurable interest in the modern context, rather than removing the concept and statutory rules entirely from the 1906 Act. The courts need to grapple with the new challenge to get rid of the historical and strict confinements of insurable interest; instead, the nature of insurable interest should always be regarded as the fundamental basis to apply in law.

The Chinese Maritime Code contains no provision concerning insurable interest in its marine insurance chapter. Article 48 of China's Insurance Law 2009 states that insurable interest is merely a condition precedent to the assured's right of making claims, which has nothing to do with the validity of the policy itself. Therefore, in Chinese law, both marine insurance and non-marine insurance contracts are unaffected by the lack of insurable interest. So far, this is in line with English law pertaining to indemnity insurance other than marine insurance law.

9 Conclusion

Notwithstanding striking differences of codifications between common law and civil law, the new Chinese Insurance Act has been brought out in 2009 and several issues have been provided the same as the aforementioned proposals in the UK. Nevertheless, the impact of the Insurance Act 2009 on the marine insurance cases gives rise to problems and inconsistencies.[29] It has been widely suggested that the CMC including the chapter on marine insurance necessitates thorough reform. On the one hand, the UK's law reform project provides substantial material and reference. On the other hand, in a broad sense, the process and experience of the British Law Commission's project may be valuable for carrying out Chinese marine insurance law reform in the future.

In light of the observation on the historic background of English marine insurance law and the process of this project, the following issues are noteworthy.

First of all, it is paramount and essential to have a good knowledge of the current marine insurance market, in particular with the negotiating

29 For the detailed analysis, see Yanbin Wang, 'Impacts of the revised insurance law on the current marine insurance contract law regime of China', *Annual of Chinese Maritime Law*, 2011, vol 22(1), pp 60–72.

positions of the insurers and the assureds. A thorough review and investigation shall be conducted in order to ascertain at what degree the law balances the benefit between the two parties. For instance, the tests of non-disclosure, misrepresentation and breach of warranties and the remedy regimes is shifting from the insurer-favoured to a balanced status by virtue of reforming the English Marine Insurance Act. Due to the different degrees of maturity of the insurance markets, the rules under English law are invariably not completely practical and reasonable in Chinese jurisdiction. Therefore, besides the just and fair principle in law, the Chinese marine insurance law reform shall reflect and adapt for the expectations and development of the industry.

Also, it should be noted that the English industry regulations and standard clauses play a very important role, supplementing the 1906 Act. The assistance and development of industry regulations and standard clauses shall not be overlooked in the process of reviewing the law. On the one hand, they provide the most valuable and accurate indicators to reflect the conditions and demand of the market. On the other hand, widely recognised rules in practice, despite the absence of statutory effect, will facilitate the implementation of the law and reduce the number of disputes arising from ambiguity or the lack of knowledge.

Although it seems unnecessary to bring out a separate and independent Act of marine insurance law such as the English 1906 Act, the function of statutes in Chinese law is significantly more than a snapshot of the present practice and judgments. Therefore, the marine insurance chapter in the Chinese Maritime Code represents a completed structure and comprehensive contents despite the remarkable work of the Insurance Act 2009.

On the other hand, the progress and reforms of Chinese insurance law should also remind the UK Law Commissions of a necessity to change or abandon the old-fashioned principles and rules in order to fit in a global trend, although the London market remains the most appealing market.

Translators' notes

A few words are necessary on the method of translation. The language of codified law requires a high degree of standardisation, which is not always possible or desirable in the target language. The main purpose of this translation is to employ English legal language insofar as possible, to allow the text to be easily absorbed by a reader with a background in English common law, and some choices are dictated by that overarching goal. That said, there are some distinctions and concepts that do not lend themselves to direct translation.

Thus, the terminology 'assured' and 'insured' are used in this translation to reflect a particular distinction in Chinese law relating primarily to life or person insurance. An 'assured' is always an initial party to the insurance contract, whereas the 'insured' may or may not be a Contracting Party, but is always the person to whose life or person life insurance pertains. Other translations use the term proposer, but the use of the term persists beyond the moment of contract formation, for which reason we have opted for 'assured' instead. Several provisions mention assured, insured and insurance beneficiary together. The beneficiary is the person designated to receive the indemnity, not necessarily a Contracting Party or the person whose life is insured under the policy.

While we have used the word 'Act', the preferred word in the UK for a piece of legislation, the nomenclature chosen for its subdivisions and individual provisions is that of EU law, with Chapters, Sections and Articles for individual provisions. It is thought that this nomenclature is consistent and sufficiently familiar to an English-trained lawyer or insurance professional.

Further, the original Chinese text distinguishes between the payments under indemnity and non-indemnity policies, using different terminology for each. This translation generally uses the single English term 'indemnity' for the payment under the insurance, whether indemnity or non-indemnity insurance is at issue, and 'compensation' when an additional term is needed.

Finally, the Act uses a single word, '解除', for when the policy is cancelled, whether this is prospectively (as with termination) or with retroactive effect (as with avoidance). Chinese contract law determines the remedy of the cancellation in each case. We have opted to use the word avoid, and forms thereof, where it appears that all effects of the contract are reversed, and termination (and forms thereof) where it appears that the contract is cancelled with prospective effect only.

There may be other controversial choices evident in the translation. We welcome observations and hope that this translation will be a useful tool in itself to stimulate research and discussion of Chinese insurance law.

Dingjing Huang, Haihua Song and Johanna Hjalmarsson

Appendix I
Insurance Act 2009

Order of the President of the People's Republic of China (No.11)

The Insurance Act of the People's Republic of China, as revised and adopted at the 7th session of the Standing Committee of the 11th National People's Congress of the People's Republic of China on 28 February 2009 is hereby promulgated, and shall come into force on 1 October 2009.

President of the People's Republic of China: Hu Jintao
28 February 2009

中华人民共和国保险法
(1995年6月30日第八届全国人民代表大会常务委员会第十四次会议通过　根据2002年10月28日第九届全国人民代表大会常务委员会第三十次会议《关于修改〈中华人民共和国保险法〉的决定》修正　2009年2月28日第十一届全国人民代表大会常务委员会第七次会议修订)
Insurance Act of the People's Republic of China, 2009
(Adopted at the 14th Session of the Standing Committee of the Chinese National People's Congress on 20 June 1995; revised according to the 'Decision concerning the Amendment to the Insurance Act of the People's Republic of China' at the 30th Session of the Standing Committee of Ninth National People's Congress on 28 October 2002; amended at the 7th Session of the Standing Committee of the 11th National People's Congress on 28 February 2009.)

第一章　总　　则
Chapter I: General Provisions

第一条　为了规范保险活动，保护保险活动当事人的合法权益，加强对保险业的监督管理，维护社会经济秩序和社会公共利益，促进保险事业的健康发展，制定本法。
Article 1
This Act is formulated for the purpose of regulating insurance activities, protecting the lawful rights and interests of the parties of insurance activities,

strengthening supervision and administration of the insurance industry, safeguarding social and economic order as well as social and public interest, and promoting the healthy development of the insurance industry.

第二条　本法所称保险，是指投保人根据合同约定，向保险人支付保险费，保险人对于合同约定的可能发生的事故因其发生所造成的财产损失承担赔偿保险金责任，或者当被保险人死亡、伤残、疾病或者达到合同约定的年龄、期限等条件时承担给付保险金责任的商业保险行为。

Article 2

'Insurance' in this Act refers to a commercial insurance transaction whereby an assured, in accordance with the terms and conditions of a contract, pays a premium to an insurer, and the insurer undertakes to indemnify the insured where property loss or damage is caused as a result of the occurrence of an insured event, or to pay an indemnity[1] upon the occurrence of death, injury, or illness of the insured or the attainment of a certain age, time limit or other requirements agreed upon in the contract.

第三条　在中华人民共和国境内从事保险活动，适用本法。

Article 3

This Act is applicable to the conduct of insurance activities within the territory of the People's Republic of China.

第四条　从事保险活动必须遵守法律、行政法规，尊重社会公德，不得损害社会公共利益。

Article 4

The conduct of insurance activities shall be in compliance with laws and administrative regulations, shall observe social ethics, and shall not harm social and public interests.

第五条　保险活动当事人行使权利、履行义务应当遵循诚实信用原则。

Article 5

Parties to insurance activities shall observe the principle of good faith in exercising their rights and fulfilling their obligations.

1 Translators' note: The original Chinese text distinguishes between the payments under indemnity and non-indemnity contracts. This translation generally uses the single English term 'indemnity' for the payment under the insurance, and 'compensation' when an additional term is needed.

第六条　保险业务由依照本法设立的保险公司以及法律、行政法规规定的其他保险组织经营，其他单位和个人不得经营保险业务。

Article 6

Insurance business shall be carried out by insurance companies incorporated in accordance with this Act and other insurance institutions prescribed by laws and administrative regulations; other entities or individuals shall not carry out insurance business.

第七条　在中华人民共和国境内的法人和其他组织需要办理境内保险的，应当向中华人民共和国境内的保险公司投保。

Article 7

Any legal persons or other associations within the territory of the People's Republic of China that need insurance covering risks within the country shall effect insurance with insurance companies within the territory of the People's Republic of China.

第八条　保险业和银行业、证券业、信托业实行分业经营、分业管理，保险公司与银行、证券、信托业务机构分别设立。国家另有规定的除外。

Article 8

Insurance business shall be carried out and administrated separately from banking, security and trust business; insurance companies shall be set up separately from banking, security and trust organisations, unless otherwise provided by the State.

第九条　国务院保险监督管理机构依法对保险业实施监督管理。

国务院保险监督管理机构根据履行职责的需要设立派出机构。派出机构按照国务院保险监督管理机构的授权履行监督管理职责。

Article 9

The insurance regulatory body under the State Council is responsible for the supervision and administration of the insurance industry in accordance with the law.

The insurance regulatory body under the State Council sets up local offices as needed for performing its responsibilities. The local offices shall perform their responsibilities of supervision and administration in accordance with the authorisation of the insurance regulatory body of the State Council.

第二章 保险合同
Chapter II: Insurance Contracts

第一节 一般规定
Section I: General Provisions

第十条 保险合同是投保人与保险人约定保险权利义务关系的协议。

投保人是指与保险人订立保险合同，并按照合同约定负有支付保险费义务的人。保险人是指与投保人订立保险合同，并按照合同约定承担赔偿或者给付保险金责任的保险公司。

Article 10

An insurance contract is an agreement whereby the assured and insurer agree upon their rights and obligations.[2]

An assured refers to a party who enters into an insurance contract with an insurer and who is obliged to pay the premium in accordance with the contract. An insurer refers to an insurance company which enters into an insurance contract with an assured and is obliged to pay an indemnity or compensation in accordance with the contract.

第十一条 订立保险合同，应当协商一致，遵循公平原则确定各方的权利和义务。除法律、行政法规规定必须保险的外，保险合同自愿订立。

Article 11

An insurance contract is entered into when consensus is reached and the rights and obligations of the parties shall be determined according to the principle of fairness. Insurance contract shall be concluded exercising free will, except for those insurances which are compulsory according to laws and administrative regulations.

第十二条 人身保险的投保人在保险合同订立时，对被保险人应当具有保险利益。

财产保险的被保险人在保险事故发生时，对保险标的应当具有保险利益。

人身保险是以人的寿命和身体为保险标的的保险。

财产保险是以财产及其有关利益为保险标的的保险。

被保险人是指其财产或者人身受保险合同保障，享有保险金请求权的人。投保人可以为被保险人。

保险利益是指投保人或者被保险人对保险标的具有的法律上承认的利益。

2 Translator's note: The terminology 'assured' and 'insured' are used in this translation to reflect a particular distinction in Chinese law. An 'assured' is always an initial party to the insurance contract, whereas the 'insured' may or may not be a Contracting Party, but is always the person to whose life or person life insurance pertains.

Article 12

When entering into an insurance contract, the assured under personal insurance shall have an insurable interest in the insured person.

The insured in property insurance shall have an insurable interest in the subject matter when an insured event occurs.

Personal insurance refers to the type of insurance where the life or body of human beings is the subject matter insured.

Property insurance refers to the type of insurance where property and the interests therein are the subject matter insured.

An insured is a party whose property, life or body is covered by an insurance contract and who is entitled to claim under the insurance. An assured may be the insured.

Insurable interest refers to a lawful interest which the assured or the insured has in respect of the subject matter insured.

第十三条　投保人提出保险要求，经保险人同意承保，保险合同成立。保险人应当及时向投保人签发保险单或者其他保险凭证。

保险单或者其他保险凭证应当载明当事人双方约定的合同内容。当事人也可以约定采用其他书面形式载明合同内容。

依法成立的保险合同，自成立时生效。投保人和保险人可以对合同的效力约定附条件或者附期限。

Article 13

An insurance contract is concluded where an assured makes an application and the insurer agrees to underwrite the risk. The insurer shall issue an insurance policy or other insurance certificate to the assured in a timely manner.

An insurance policy or other insurance certificate shall specify the terms of the contract as agreed between both parties. The parties may also agree to set out the contents of the contract in other written form.

A lawfully concluded insurance contract shall take effect upon its conclusion. The parties may also attach conditions or a time limit with regard to the effectiveness of the contract.

第十四条　保险合同成立后，投保人按照约定交付保险费，保险人按照约定的时间开始承担保险责任。

Article 14

Where an insurance contract is concluded, the assured shall pay the premiums as agreed and the insurer shall accept the insured risk from the agreed time.

第十五条 除本法另有规定或者保险合同另有约定外，保险合同成立后，投保人可以解除合同，保险人不得解除合同。

Article 15

Unless otherwise provided in this Act or the insurance contract, where an insurance contract is concluded, the assured may avoid[3] the contract whereas the insurer may not avoid the contract.

第十六条 订立保险合同，保险人就保险标的或者被保险人的有关情况提出询问的，投保人应当如实告知。

Article 16

When entering into an insurance contract, the assured shall make a truthful disclosure where the insurer inquires about the circumstances of the subject matter insured or the insured.

投保人故意或者因重大过失未履行前款规定的如实告知义务，足以影响保险人决定是否同意承保或者提高保险费率的，保险人有权解除合同。

If the assured fails to make such a disclosure as provided in the preceding paragraph intentionally or in gross negligence and such failure affects the decision of the insurer whether to underwrite or to increase the premium rate, the insurer shall have the right to avoid the contract.

前款规定的合同解除权，自保险人知道有解除事由之日起，超过三十日不行使而消灭。自合同成立之日起超过二年的，保险人不得解除合同；发生保险事故的，保险人应当承担赔偿或者给付保险金的责任。

The right of avoidance provided in the preceding paragraph shall lapse where the insurer does not exercise the right within 30 days after the insurer knows the cause of avoidance. After two years from the date of the conclusion of the contract, the insurer may not avoid the contract; where an insured event occurs, the insurer shall be liable for the indemnity payment or paying the insurance compensation.

投保人故意不履行如实告知义务的，保险人对于合同解除前发生的保险事故，不承担赔偿或者给付保险金的责任，并不退还保险费。

Where an assured intentionally fails to make a truthful disclosure, the insurer shall not be liable for the indemnity payments or compensation in respect of an insured event that occurred before the avoidance of the contract, and premiums already paid are not returnable.

3 Translators' note: Chinese legal terminology uses the same word, '解除', for avoidance and termination. Recognising that there is no term in English that encompasses both termination and avoidance, the translators have opted to generally use the word avoidance, except where termination is clearly the appropriate term.

投保人因重大过失未履行如实告知义务，对保险事故的发生有严重影响的，保险人对于合同解除前发生的保险事故，不承担赔偿或者给付保险金的责任，但应当退还保险费。
Where an assured in gross negligence fails to make truthful disclosure so as to contribute materially to the occurrence of an insured event, the insurer shall not be liable for the indemnity payments or insurance compensation in respect of an insured event that occurred before the recession of the contract, but the premiums already paid shall be returned.

保险人在合同订立时已经知道投保人未如实告知的情况的，保险人不得解除合同；发生保险事故的，保险人应当承担赔偿或者给付保险金的责任。
Where the insurer knew already that the assured failed to make a truthful disclosure at the time of entering into a contract, the insurer may not avoid the contract; where an insured event occurs, the insurer shall be liable for paying the indemnity or compensation.

保险事故是指保险合同约定的保险责任范围内的事故。
An insured event refers to an event falling within the scope of cover agreed in the insurance contract.

第十七条　订立保险合同，采用保险人提供的格式条款的，保险人向投保人提供的投保单应当附格式条款，保险人应当向投保人说明合同的内容。

对保险合同中免除保险人责任的条款，保险人在订立合同时应当在投保单、保险单或者其他保险凭证上作出足以引起投保人注意的提示，并对该条款的内容以书面或者口头形式向投保人作出明确说明；未作提示或者明确说明的，该条款不产生效力。
Article 17
Where an insurance contract is concluded by way of standard forms provided by the insurer, the standard terms shall be attached to the insurance policy and the insurer shall explain the contents of the contract to the assured.

Where an insurance contract contains terms and conditions concerning exclusion of the liability of an insurer, the insurer shall notify the insured in the proposal form, insurance policy or other insurance documents of such terms and conditions and shall clearly explain orally or in writing such terms and conditions to the assured at the time of concluding the contract. Where such terms and conditions are not clearly explained, they shall be of no effect.

第十八条　保险合同应当包括下列事项:

（一）保险人的名称和住所;
（二）投保人、被保险人的姓名或者名称、住所，以及人身保险的受益人的姓名或者名称、住所;
（三）保险标的;
（四）保险责任和责任免除;
（五）保险期间和保险责任开始时间;
（六）保险金额;
（七）保险费以及支付办法;
（八）保险金赔偿或者给付办法;
（九）违约责任和争议处理;
（十）订立合同的年、月、日。
投保人和保险人可以约定与保险有关的其他事项。

受益人是指人身保险合同中由被保险人或者投保人指定的享有保险金请求权的人。投保人、被保险人可以为受益人。

保险金额是指保险人承担赔偿或者给付保险金责任的最高限额。

Article 18

An insurance contract shall contain:

(1) name and domicile of the insurer;
(2) name and domicile of the assured and the insured and, in the case of a personal insurance, name and domicile of the beneficiary;
(3) subject matter insured;
(4) scope of insurance cover and exclusions;
(5) insurance duration and the time when the insurance attaches;
(6) sum insured;
(7) premium and method of payment;
(8) method of payment of indemnity or compensation;
(9) liability for breach of contract and dispute resolution; and
(10) the day, month and year of signing the contract.

The assured and the insurer may agree on any other matters relating to the insurance.

'Beneficiary' refers to a person who is entitled to claim an indemnity as designated by the insurer or the assured in a contract of personal insurance. The assured or the insured may be the beneficiary.

The sum insured refers to the maximum limit of the indemnity payment or compensation for which the insurer is liable.

第十九条　采用保险人提供的格式条款订立的保险合同中的下列条款无效：

（一）免除保险人依法应承担的义务或者加重投保人、被保险人责任的；
（二）排除投保人、被保险人或者受益人依法享有的权利的。

Article 19

Where an insurance contract is concluded by way of standard forms provided by the insurer, the following terms shall be of no effect:

(1) terms that exclude the obligations of the insurer or increase the obligations of the assured or the insured; and
(2) terms that deprive the assured, insured or beneficiary of their legal rights.

第二十条　投保人和保险人可以协商变更合同内容。

变更保险合同的，应当由保险人在保险单或者其他保险凭证上批注或者附贴批单，或者由投保人和保险人订立变更的书面协议。

Article 20

The assured and the insurer may modify the content of the contract through consultation.

Where an insurance contract is modified, the insurer shall annotate or endorse the policy or any other insurance certificate; or the assured and the insurer shall enter into a written agreement concerning the modifications.

第二十一条　投保人、被保险人或者受益人知道保险事故发生后，应当及时通知保险人。故意或者因重大过失未及时通知，致使保险事故的性质、原因、损失程度等难以确定的，保险人对无法确定的部分，不承担赔偿或者给付保险金的责任，但保险人通过其他途径已经及时知道或者应当及时知道保险事故发生的除外。

Article 21

When knowing the occurrence of an insured event, the assured, the insured or the beneficiary shall notify the insurer in a timely manner. Where the notice fails to be given in time due to wilful misconduct or gross negligence and such failure causes difficulties of ascertaining the nature, cause and loss of the insured event, the insurer is not liable for paying the indemnity or compensation in respect of the portion that cannot be ascertained, unless the insurer knew in time or should have known in time of the occurrence of the insured event through other methods.

第二十二条　保险事故发生后，按照保险合同请求保险人赔偿或者给付保险金时，投保人、被保险人或者受益人应当向保险人提供其所能提供的与确认保险事故的性质、原因、损失程度等有关的证明和资料。

保险人按照合同的约定，认为有关的证明和资料不完整的，应当及时一次性通知投保人、被保险人或者受益人补充提供。

Article 22

After the occurrence of an insured event, the assured, the insured, or the beneficiary, in making claims for an indemnity or compensation, shall, to the best of their knowledge and ability, provide the insurer with evidence and information which are relevant to ascertaining the nature, cause and loss of the insured event.

Where the insurer, in accordance with the contract, considers the relevant evidence and information incomplete, the insurer shall, in a timely manner and once and for all, advise the assured, the insured or the beneficiary to provide supplementary evidence or information.

第二十三条　保险人收到被保险人或者受益人的赔偿或者给付保险金的请求后，应当及时作出核定；情形复杂的，应当在三十日内作出核定，但合同另有约定的除外。保险人应当将核定结果通知被保险人或者受益人；对属于保险责任的，在与被保险人或者受益人达成赔偿或者给付保险金的协议后十日内，履行赔偿或者给付保险金义务。保险合同对赔偿或者给付保险金的期限有约定的，保险人应当按照约定履行赔偿或者给付保险金义务。

保险人未及时履行前款规定义务的，除支付保险金外，应当赔偿被保险人或者受益人因此受到的损失。

任何单位和个人不得非法干预保险人履行赔偿或者给付保险金的义务，也不得限制被保险人或者受益人取得保险金的权利。

Article 23

After receiving a claim for indemnity or compensation from the insured or beneficiary, the insurer shall assess the claim in a timely manner; where the circumstances are complicated, the assessment shall be made within 30 days unless otherwise provided in the contract. The insurer shall notify the insured or the beneficiary of the result of the assessment; where the claim is covered, the insurer shall fulfil its obligation of paying the indemnity or compensation within 10 days after reaching an agreement with the insured or beneficiary on payment. Where the time limit of making payment is specified in the insurance contract, the insurer shall fulfil its obligations thereof in accordance with the provisions in the contract.

Where the insurer fails to fulfil its obligations set out in the preceding paragraph in time, the insurer shall, in addition to the payment of insurance money, compensate the insured or the beneficiary for any loss or damages incurred as a result.

No entities or individuals shall illegally interfere with the insurer's performance of the obligation of paying the indemnity or compensation, or restrict the insured or beneficiary's right of obtaining the insurance money.

第二十四条　保险人依照本法第二十三条的规定作出核定后，对不属于保险责任的，应当自作出核定之日起三日内向被保险人或者受益人发出拒绝赔偿或者拒绝给付保险金通知书，并说明理由。

Article 24

After assessing the claim in accordance with Article 23 of this Act, with regard to claims not covered by the insurance, the insurer shall, within three days from the date of the assessment, issue to the insured or the beneficiary a notice of its refusal to pay the indemnity or compensation and specify the reasons for rejection.

第二十五条　保险人自收到赔偿或者给付保险金的请求和有关证明、资料之日起六十日内，对其赔偿或者给付保险金的数额不能确定的，应当根据已有证明和资料可以确定的数额先予支付；保险人最终确定赔偿或者给付保险金的数额后，应当支付相应的差额。

Article 25

Where the amount of the indemnity or compensation cannot be determined within 60 days from the date of receiving the claim and the evidence and information relevant thereto, the insurer shall effect payment of the determinable amount according to the evidence and information; once the final amount is determined, the insurer shall pay the balance accordingly.

第二十六条　人寿保险以外的其他保险的被保险人或者受益人，向保险人请求赔偿或者给付保险金的诉讼时效期间为二年，自其知道或者应当知道保险事故发生之日起计算。

人寿保险的被保险人或者受益人向保险人请求给付保险金的诉讼时效期间为五年，自其知道或者应当知道保险事故发生之日起计算。

Article 26

For the insured or the beneficiary of insurance other than life insurance, the limitation of action in respect of claims is two years starting from the date when the insured or the beneficiary knows or ought to know of the occurrence of the insured event.

For the insured or the beneficiary of life insurance, the limitation of action in respect of claims for insurance benefits is five years starting from the date when the insured or the beneficiary knows or ought to know the occurrence of the insured event.

第二十七条　未发生保险事故，被保险人或者受益人谎称发生了保险事故，向保险人提出赔偿或者给付保险金请求的，保险人有权解除合同，并不退还保险费。

Article 27

Where no insured event has occurred, and the insured or the beneficiary fraudulently reports that an insured event has occurred and claims an indemnity or insurance compensation, the insurer is entitled to terminate[4] the contract and the premium paid is not refundable.

4 Translators' note: The original terminology does not distinguish between avoidance and termination. We have chosen to use 'terminate' in this Article.

投保人、被保险人故意制造保险事故的，保险人有权解除合同，不承担赔偿或者给付保险金的责任；除本法第四十三条规定外，不退还保险费。
Where the assured or the insured intentionally causes the occurrence of an insured event, the insurer is entitled to terminate the contract and shall not be liable for indemnity payment of insurance benefits; and subject to Article 43 of this Act, the premiums paid are not refundable.

保险事故发生后，投保人、被保险人或者受益人以伪造、变造的有关证明、资料或者其他证据，编造虚假的事故原因或者夸大损失程度的，保险人对其虚报的部分不承担赔偿或者给付保险金的责任。
Where the assured, insured or the beneficiary, following the occurrence of an insured event, provides forged or falsified evidence, information or other proof in order to fabricate the cause of the event or to overstate the loss, the insurer shall not be liable in respect of the portion which is fraudulently claimed.

投保人、被保险人或者受益人有前三款规定行为之一，致使保险人支付保险金或者支出费用的，应当退回或者赔偿。
Where the assured, the insured or the beneficiary is guilty of such conduct as provided in the preceding three paragraphs, and this leads to the insurer's payment of insurance money or expenses, such payments or expenses shall be refunded or reimbursed.

第二十八条　保险人将其承担的保险业务，以分保形式部分转移给其他保险人的，为再保险。

应再保险接受人的要求，再保险分出人应当将其自负责任及原保险的有关情况书面告知再保险接受人。

Article 28

Where an insurer transfers a portion of its underwritten insurance to other insurers in the form of cession, such a transaction is reinsurance.

When requested by the reinsurer, the cedant shall advise the reinsurer in writing of the cedant's own underwriting and relevant information about the direct insurance.

第二十九条　再保险接受人不得向原保险的投保人要求支付保险费。

原保险的被保险人或者受益人不得向再保险接受人提出赔偿或者给付保险金的请求。

再保险分出人不得以再保险接受人未履行再保险责任为由，拒绝履行或者迟延履行其原保险责任。

Article 29

The reinsurer shall not request payment of premium from the assured under the direct insurance contract.

The insured or the beneficiary under the direct insurance contract cannot claim an indemnity payment or compensation from the reinsurer.

The cedant shall not decline or delay performing the obligations under the direct insurance on the ground that the reinsurer fails to fulfil the reinsurance responsibility.

第三十条　采用保险人提供的格式条款订立的保险合同，保险人与投保人、被保险人或者受益人对合同条款有争议的，应当按照通常理解予以解释。对合同条款有两种以上解释的，人民法院或者仲裁机构应当作出有利于被保险人和受益人的解释。

Article 30

With respect to an insurance contract entered into by adopting the standard clauses provided by the insurer, where a dispute between the insurer and the assured, the insured or the beneficiary arises from the understanding of a standard clause, the clause shall be interpreted in accordance with common sense. Where a standard clause has two or more interpretations, the People's Court or arbitration institution shall interpret such a clause in favour of the insured and the beneficiary.

第二节　人身保险合同
Section II: Personal Insurance Contracts

第三十一条　投保人对下列人员具有保险利益：

（一）本人；
（二）配偶、子女、父母；
（三）前项以外与投保人有抚养、赡养或者扶养关系的家庭其他成员、近亲属；
（四）与投保人有劳动关系的劳动者。

除前款规定外，被保险人同意投保人为其订立合同的，视为投保人对被保险人具有保险利益。

订立合同时，投保人对被保险人不具有保险利益的，合同无效。

Article 31

The assured has insurable interests in the following persons:

(1) the assured himself/herself;
(2) the assured's spouse, children and parents;
(3) family members or close relatives other than the above, with whom the assured has a relationship of fosterage, support or maintenance; or
(4) workers with whom the assured has a labour relation.

In addition to the above provisions, where an insured consents to have an insurance contract entered into by the assured on the insured's behalf, the assured is deemed to have an insurable interest upon the insured.

Where the assured does not have an insurable interest in the insured when an insurance contract is concluded, the insurance contract is of no effect.

第三十二条　投保人申报的被保险人年龄不真实，并且其真实年龄不符合合同约定的年龄限制的，保险人可以解除合同，并按照合同约定退还保险单的现金价值。保险人行使合同解除权，适用本法第十六条第三款、第六款的规定。

投保人申报的被保险人年龄不真实，致使投保人支付的保险费少于应付保险费的，保险人有权更正并要求投保人补交保险费，或者在给付保险金时按照实付保险费与应付保险费的比例支付。

投保人申报的被保险人年龄不真实，致使投保人支付的保险费多于应付保险费的，保险人应当将多收的保险费退还投保人。

Article 32

Where the age of the insured is inaccurately declared by the assured, and the actual age of the insured does not fall within the age limit specified in the contract, the insurer may avoid the contract and refund the cash value of the policy in accordance with the contract. Where the insurer avoids the contract, the third and sixth paragraph of Article 16 of this Act shall be applicable.

Where the age of the insured declared by the assured is untruthful so that the assured has paid fewer premiums than he should have paid, the insurer is entitled to rectify the misrepresentation and request the assured to make up the balance, or at the time of claims payment, to pay the indemnity according to the premiums actually paid in proportion to the premiums that ought rightly to have been paid.

Where the age of the insured declared by the assured is untruthful so that the assured has paid more premiums than ought to have been paid, the insurer shall return the overpaid portion of the premiums to the assured.

第三十三条　投保人不得为无民事行为能力人投保以死亡为给付保险金条件的人身保险，保险人也不得承保。

父母为其未成年子女投保的人身保险，不受前款规定限制。但是，因被保险人死亡给付的保险金总和不得超过国务院保险监督管理机构规定的限额。

Article 33

No assured shall apply for personal insurance for a person without capacity for civil transactions under which compensation is payable upon the death of the insured, and no insurer shall underwrite such insurance.

Personal insurance applied for by parents for their underage children shall not be subject to the preceding provision. However, the total amount of death compensation thereunder shall not exceed the limit provided by the insurance regulatory body of the State Council.

第三十四条　以死亡为给付保险金条件的合同，未经被保险人同意并认可保险金额的，合同无效。

按照以死亡为给付保险金条件的合同所签发的保险单，未经被保险人书面同意，不得转让或者质押。

父母为其未成年子女投保的人身保险，不受本条第一款规定限制。

Article 34

An insurance contract under which the indemnity is payable upon death shall be void without the insured's consent and acceptance of the sum insured.

A policy issued under an insurance contract where the indemnity is payable upon death shall not be assigned or pledged without the insured's consent in writing.

Personal insurance applied for by parents for their underage children shall not be subject to the first paragraph of this Article.

第三十五条　投保人可以按照合同约定向保险人一次支付全部保险费或者分期支付保险费。

Article 35

The assured may pay the premiums to the insurer in a lump sum or in instalments in accordance with the contract.

第三十六条　合同约定分期支付保险费，投保人支付首期保险费后，除合司另有约定外，投保人自保险人催告之日起超过三十日未支付当期保险费，或者超过约定的期限六十日未支付当期保险费的，合同效力中止，或者由保险人按照合同约定的条件减少保险金额。

被保险人在前款规定期限内发生保险事故的，保险人应当按照合同约定给付保险金，但可以扣减欠交的保险费。

Article 36

Where the contract specifies that the payment of premium is in instalments and, after paying the first instalment, the assured then fails to pay an instalment over 30 days from the date of the insurer's reminder for the payment, or over 60 days from the agreed time limit, the contract shall be suspended, or the insurer may reduce the sum insured according to the terms and conditions of the contract, unless otherwise provided in the contract.

Where an insured event occurs in respect of the insured within the time limits provided in the preceding paragraph, the insurer shall pay under the insurance according to the contract, but may deduct the outstanding premiums.

第三十七条　合同效力依照本法第三十六条规定中止的，经保险人与投保人协商并达成协议，在投保人补交保险费后，合同效力恢复。但是，自合同效力中止之日起满二年双方未达成协议的，保险人有权解除合同。

保险人依照前款规定解除合同的，应当按照合同约定退还保险单的现金价值。

Article 37

An insurance contract suspended in accordance with Article 36 of this Act is reinstated where the insurer and the assured have reached an agreement through consultation and the assured has paid the overdue premiums. However, the insurer is entitled to terminate the contract if no agreement has been reached by the parties within two years from the date of suspension of the contract.

Where the insurer terminates the contract according to the preceding paragraph, it shall return the cash value of the policy in accordance with the contract.

第三十八条　保险人对人寿保险的保险费，不得用诉讼方式要求投保人支付。

Article 38

With regard to life insurance, the insurer shall not demand the payment of premiums from the assured by means of litigation.

第三十九条　人身保险的受益人由被保险人或者投保人指定。

投保人指定受益人时须经被保险人同意。投保人为与其有劳动关系的劳动者投保人身保险，不得指定被保险人及其近亲属以外的人为受益人。

被保险人为无民事行为能力人或者限制民事行为能力人的，可以由其监护人指定受益人。

Article 39

The beneficiary of a personal insurance shall be designated by the insured or the assured.

The assured's designation of the beneficiary shall be agreed by the insured. Where the assured takes out a personal insurance for a worker with whom the assured has a labour relationship, the beneficiary may not be persons other than the insured or the insured's close relatives.

Where the insured is a person with no or limited capacity for civil transactions, the beneficiary may be designated by the insured's guardian.

第四十条　被保险人或者投保人可以指定一人或者数人为受益人。

受益人为数人的，被保险人或者投保人可以确定受益顺序和受益份额；未确定受益份额的，受益人按照相等份额享有受益权。

Article 40

The insured or the assured may designate one or more beneficiaries.

Where there is more than one beneficiary, the insured or the assured may specify the order of priority and their proportions of the insurance indemnity; in the absence of such specification on the proportions, the beneficiaries share the indemnity equally.

第四十一条　被保险人或者投保人可以变更受益人并书面通知保险人。保险人收到变更受益人的书面通知后，应当在保险单或者其他保险凭证上批注或者附贴批单。

投保人变更受益人时须经被保险人同意。

Article 41

The insured and the assured may substitute the beneficiary by sending written notice to the insurer. The insurer shall endorse or attach an endorsement slip in respect of the change to the policy or other insurance certificate upon receipt of the notice.

Substitution of the beneficiary by the assured is subject to the insured's consent.

第四十二条　被保险人死亡后，有下列情形之一的，保险金作为被保险人的遗产，由保险人依照《中华人民共和国继承法》的规定履行给付保险金的义务：

（一）没有指定受益人，或者受益人指定不明无法确定的；
（二）受益人先于被保险人死亡，没有其他受益人的；
（三）受益人依法丧失受益权或者放弃受益权，没有其他受益人的。

受益人与被保险人在同一事件中死亡，且不能确定死亡先后顺序的，推定受益人死亡在先。

Article 42

Where the insured is dead, the insurance benefits shall be regarded as part of the insured's estate under any of the following circumstances, and the insurer shall pay the indemnity in accordance with the Inheritance Law of the People's Republic of China:

(1) no beneficiary has been designated, or the designation of beneficiary is unclear and cannot be determined;
(2) the beneficiary dies before the death of the insured and there are no other beneficiaries; or
(3) the beneficiary loses the beneficial right by operation of law or abandons the beneficial right and there are no other beneficiaries.

Where the beneficiary and the insured die in the same event and the sequence of their deaths cannot be ascertained, the beneficiary is presumed to die before the insured.

第四十三条　投保人故意造成被保险人死亡、伤残或者疾病的，保险人不承担给付保险金的责任。投保人已交足二年以上保险费的，保险人应当按照合同约定向其他权利人退还保险单的现金价值。

受益人故意造成被保险人死亡、伤残、疾病的，或者故意杀害被保险人未遂的，该受益人丧失受益权。

Article 43

Where the assured intentionally has caused the death, disability or illness of the insured, the insurer shall not be liable for payment under the insurance. Where the assured has paid the premiums for two or more years, the insurer shall, in accordance with the contract, return the cash value of the policy to the other entitled persons.

Where the beneficiary has intentionally caused the death, disability and illness of the insured, or has attempted to murder the insured but failed, the beneficiary shall be deprived of his rights as beneficiary.

第四十四条　以被保险人死亡为给付保险金条件的合同，自合同成立或者合同效力恢复之日起二年内，被保险人自杀的，保险人不承担给付保险金的责任，但被保险人自杀时为无民事行为能力人的除外。

保险人依照前款规定不承担给付保险金责任的，应当按照合同约定退还保险单的现金价值。

Article 44

With regard to a contract under which death is the condition for the payment of the indemnity, where the insured commits suicide within two years from the date of concluding the contract or reinstating the contract, the insurer shall not be liable under the policy, unless the insured has no capacity for civil transactions at the time of committing suicide.

Where the insurer is not liable under the policy in accordance with the preceding paragraph, the insurer shall return the cash value of the policy according to the contract.

第四十五条　因被保险人故意犯罪或者抗拒依法采取的刑事强制措施导致其伤残或者死亡的，保险人不承担给付保险金的责任。投保人已交足二年以上保险费的，保险人应当按照合同约定退还保险单的现金价值。

Article 45

Where the insured's disability or death is caused by his or her own intentional criminal acts or resisting a lawful criminal coercive measure, the insurer shall not be liable for payment under the policy. Where the assured has paid the premiums for two or more years, the insurer shall, in accordance with the contract, return the cash value of the policy.

第四十六条　被保险人因第三者的行为而发生死亡、伤残或者疾病等保险事故的，保险人向被保险人或者受益人给付保险金后，不享有向第三者追偿的权利，但被保险人或者受益人仍有权向第三者请求赔偿。

Article 46

Where an insured event, such as death, disability or illness of the insured, is caused by the act of a third party, the insurer shall have no right of subrogation against the third party after paying the indemnity to the insured or the beneficiary; and the insured or the beneficiary remains entitled to claim compensation from the third party.

第四十七条　投保人解除合同的，保险人应当自收到解除合同通知之日起三十日内，按照合同约定退还保险单的现金价值。

Article 47

Where an assured terminates the contract, the insurer shall, in accordance with the contract, return the cash value of the policy within 30 days from the date of receiving the notice of termination.

第三节　财产保险合同

Section III: Property Insurance Contract

第四十八条　保险事故发生时，被保险人对保险标的不具有保险利益的，不得向保险人请求赔偿保险金。

Article 48

Where the insured does not have an insurable interest in the subject matter insured at the time when an insured event occurs, the insured shall not claim for indemnity payment against the insurer.

第四十九条　保险标的转让的，保险标的的受让人承继被保险人的权利和义务。

Article 49

Where the subject matter insured is transferred, the transferee of the subject matter insured shall assume the rights and obligations of the insured.

保险标的转让的，被保险人或者受让人应当及时通知保险人，但货物运输保险合同和另有约定的合同除外。

Where the subject matter insured is transferred, the insured or the transferee shall notify the insurer in time except for cargo insurance contracts and those contracts that provide otherwise.

因保险标的转让导致危险程度显著增加的，保险人自收到前款规定的通知之日起三十日内，可以按照合同约定增加保险费或者解除合同。保险人解除合同的，应当将已收取的保险费，按照合同约定扣除自保险责任开始之日起至合同解除之日止应收的部分后，退还投保人。

Where the transfer of the subject matter insured increases the level of risk, the insurer may, within 30 days from receipt of the notice provided in the preceding paragraph, increase the premiums according to the contract or terminate the contract. Where the insurer terminates the contract, the premiums paid shall be returned to the assured deducting the premiums for the period from the date of commencement of underwriting to the date of termination in accordance with the contract.

被保险人、受让人未履行本条第二款规定的通知义务的，因转让导致保险标的危险程度显著增加而发生的保险事故，保险人不承担赔偿保险金的责任。

Where the insured and the transferee fail to notify the insurer as provided in the second paragraph of this Article, the insurer shall not be liable under the insurance if the insured event occurs as a result of the increased risk level due to the transfer.

第五十条　货物运输保险合同和运输工具航程保险合同，保险责任开始后，合同当事人不得解除合同。

Article 50

With regard to cargo insurance contracts and voyage hull and machinery insurance contracts, the parties thereto shall not terminate the contracts after the commencement of the insurance period.

第五十一条　被保险人应当遵守国家有关消防、安全、生产操作、劳动保护等方面的规定，维护保险标的的安全。

保险人可以按照合同约定对保险标的的安全状况进行检查，及时向投保人、被保险人提出消除不安全因素和隐患的书面建议。

投保人、被保险人未按照约定履行其对保险标的的安全应尽责任的，保险人有权要求增加保险费或者解除合同。

保险人为维护保险标的的安全，经被保险人同意，可以采取安全预防措施。

Article 51

The insured shall comply with the regulations of the State with regard to fire prevention, safety, production operations, labour protection etc. and ensure the safety of the subject matter insured.

The insurer may conduct safety inspections in respect of the subject matter insured in accordance with the contract and give written recommendations to the assured and the insured for eliminating risky elements and latent defects.

Where the assured and the insured fail to fulfil the duties as agreed to ensure the safety of the subject matter insured, the insurer is entitled to increase the premiums or terminate the contract.

For the purpose of ensuring the safety of the subject matter insured, the insurer may, with the insured's consent, take safety precautions.

第五十二条　在合同有效期内，保险标的的危险程度显著增加的，被保险人应当按照合同约定及时通知保险人，保险人可以按照合同约定增加保险费或者解除合同。保险人解除合同的，应当将已收取的保险费，按照合同约定扣除自保险责任开始之日起至合同解除之日止应收的部分后，退还投保人。

被保险人未履行前款规定的通知义务的，因保险标的的危险程度显著增加而发生的保险事故，保险人不承担赔偿保险金的责任。

Article 52

Where there is a material increase of risk of the subject matter insured during the contract term, the insured shall notify the insurer in a timely manner in accordance with the contract. The insurer can, in accordance with the contract, demand an increase in the premium or terminate the contract. Where the insurer terminates the contract, he will refund to the assured the premiums received after deducting the premiums in accordance with the contract for the period from the date of commencement of the insurance liability to the date of termination.

Where the insured fails to notify the insurer as provided in the preceding paragraph, the insurer shall not be liable for indemnity in the case of the occurrence of an event insured against which is caused by the material increase in risk.

第五十三条　有下列情形之一的，除合同另有约定外，保险人应当降低保险费，并按日计算退还相应的保险费：

（一）据以确定保险费率的有关情况发生变化，保险标的的危险程度明显减少的；
（二）保险标的的保险价值明显减少的。

Article 53

Unless otherwise provided in the contract, the insurer shall reduce the premiums and return the corresponding premiums calculated on the number of days passed, where there is either of the following circumstances:

(1) the basis on which the premium rate is ascertained has changed and the risk level of the subject matter insured has substantially decreased; or
(2) the insurable value of the subject matter insured has substantially decreased.

第五十四条　保险责任开始前，投保人要求解除合同的，应当按照合同约定向保险人支付手续费，保险人应当退还保险费。保险责任开始后，投保人要求解除合同的，保险人应当将已收取的保险费，按照合同约定扣除自保险责任开始之日起至合同解除之日止应收的部分后，退还投保人。

Article 54

Where the assured requests to avoid the contract before the commencement of the insurance liability, the assured shall pay a handling charge to the insurer in accordance with the contract and the insurer shall return the premiums. Where the assured requests to terminate the contract after the commencement of the insurance liability, the insurer shall return the premium paid to the assured deducting the premiums for the period from the date of commencement of insurance liability to the date of termination in accordance with the contract.

第五十五条　投保人和保险人约定保险标的的保险价值并在合同中载明的，保险标的发生损失时，以约定的保险价值为赔偿计算标准。

投保人和保险人未约定保险标的的保险价值的，保险标的发生损失时，以保险事故发生时保险标的的实际价值为赔偿计算标准。

保险金额不得超过保险价值。超过保险价值的，超过部分无效，保险人应当退还相应的保险费。

保险金额低于保险价值的，除合同另有约定外，保险人按照保险金额与保险价值的比例承担赔偿保险金的责任。

Article 55

Where the value of the subject matter insured is agreed between the assured and the insurer and specified in the contract, and loss or damage occurs to the subject matter insured, the value fixed by the policy as the insurable value shall be the basis of the measure of indemnity.

Where the value of the subject matter insured is not agreed between the assured and the insurer, and loss or damage occurs to the subject matter insured, the actual value of the subject matter insured shall be the basis of the measure of indemnity.

The sum insured shall not exceed the insurable value of the subject matter insured. Where the sum insured exceeds the insurable value, the excessive portion is void and the insurer shall return the corresponding premiums.

Unless otherwise provided in the contract, where the sum insured is less than the insurable value, the insurer shall be liable for the indemnity payment in accordance with the proportion between the sum insured and the insurable value.

第五十六条　重复保险的投保人应当将重复保险的有关情况通知各保险人。

重复保险的各保险人赔偿保险金的总和不得超过保险价值。除合同另有约定外，各保险人按照其保险金额与保险金额总和的比例承担赔偿保险金的责任。

重复保险的投保人可以就保险金额总和超过保险价值的部分，请求各保险人按比例返还保险费。

重复保险是指投保人对同一保险标的、同一保险利益、同一保险事故分别与两个以上保险人订立保险合同，且保险金额总和超过保险价值的保险。

Article 56

Where there is a double insurance, the assured shall notify all the insurers concerned of the relevant information with regard to the double insurance. The total amount of the indemnity payment made by all the insurers under double insurance shall not exceed the insurable value. Unless otherwise provided in the contract, the insurers shall be liable for the indemnity payment in proportion to their respective sums insured and the total amount of the sum insured.

With regard to the portion of the sum insured which exceeds the insurable value, the assured under a double insurance may request each insurer to return the premiums proportionately.

Double insurance means the insurance where two or more insurance contracts are effected by the assured in respect of the same subject matter insured, same insurable interest and same insured event and the total sum insured exceeds the insurable value.

第五十七条　保险事故发生时，被保险人应当尽力采取必要的措施，防止或者减少损失。

保险事故发生后，被保险人为防止或者减少保险标的的损失所支付的必要的、合理的费用，由保险人承担；保险人所承担的费用数额在保险标的损失赔偿金额以外另行计算，最高不超过保险金额的数额。

Article 57

Where an insured event occurs, the insured shall take all necessary measures for the purpose of averting or minimising a loss.

After occurrence of the insured event, the insurer shall be liable for any necessary and reasonable expenses incurred for the purpose of averting or minimising any loss of or damage to the subject matter insured; the amount of such expenses born by the insurer shall be calculated separately from the indemnity for the loss of or damage to the subject matter insured and shall not exceed the sum insured.

第五十八条　保险标的发生部分损失的，自保险人赔偿之日起三十日内，投保人可以解除合同；除合同另有约定外，保险人也可以解除合同，但应当提前十五日通知投保人。

合同解除的，保险人应当将保险标的未受损失部分的保险费，按照合同约定扣除自保险责任开始之日起至合同解除之日止应收的部分后，退还投保人。

Article 58

Where there is a partial loss of the subject matter insured, the assured may avoid the contract within 30 days from the date when the insurer makes the indemnity payment; and, unless the contract otherwise provides, the insurer may also avoid the contract, provided that a notice is given to the assured 15 days before the avoidance.

Where the contract is avoided, the insurer shall return the premiums received for the part of the subject matter insured which is not lost or damaged, deducting the portion of premiums earned from the commencement of the insurance liability to the date of avoidance.

第五十九条　保险事故发生后，保险人已支付了全部保险金额，并且保险金额等于保险价值的，受损保险标的的全部权利归于保险人；保险金额低于保险价值的，保险人按照保险金额与保险价值的比例取得受损保险标的的部分权利。

Article 59

Where the insurer has paid the full amount of indemnity after the occurrence of an insured event and the amount of indemnity is equal to the insurable value, the insurer is entitled to take over the interest of the insured in the subject matter insured; where the indemnity is less than the insurable value, the insurer is entitled to take over part of the interest of the insured in the subject matter insured in proportion to the indemnity payment and the insurable value.

第六十条　因第三者对保险标的的损害而造成保险事故的，保险人自向被保险人赔偿保险金之日起，在赔偿金额范围内代位行使被保险人对第三者请求赔偿的权利。

前款规定的保险事故发生后，被保险人已经从第三者取得损害赔偿的，保险人赔偿保险金时，可以相应扣减被保险人从第三者已取得的赔偿金额。

保险人依照本条第一款规定行使代位请求赔偿的权利，不影响被保险人就未取得赔偿的部分向第三者请求赔偿的权利。

Article 60

Where an insured event occurs due to the loss of or damage to the subject matter insured caused by a third party, the insurer shall be subrogated to all the rights and remedies of the insured against the third party from the date of paying the indemnity to the insured.

Where the insured event provided in the preceding paragraph occurs and the insured has already obtained indemnity from the third party, the indemnity obtained shall be deducted when the insurer makes the indemnity payment.

The insurer's exercising subrogation rights according to the first paragraph of this Article shall not affect the insured's rights of claiming indemnity from the third party in respect of the uncompensated part.

第六十一条　保险事故发生后，保险人未赔偿保险金之前，被保险人放弃对第三者请求赔偿的权利的，保险人不承担赔偿保险金的责任。

保险人向被保险人赔偿保险金后，被保险人未经保险人同意放弃对第三者请求赔偿的权利的，该行为无效。

被保险人故意或者因重大过失致使保险人不能行使代位请求赔偿的权利的，保险人可以扣减或者要求返还相应的保险金。

Article 61

Where the insured waives the rights and remedies against the third party after the insured event occurs but before the insurer makes the indemnity payment, the insurer shall not be liable for the indemnity payment.

Where the insured, without the insurer's consent, waives the rights and remedies against the third party after the insurer pays the indemnity to the insured, the act of waiver is of no effect.

Where the insurer is unable to exercise his rights of subrogation due to the intention or gross negligence of the insured, the insurer may deduct from the indemnity payment or demand the return of corresponding indemnity paid.

第六十二条　除被保险人的家庭成员或者其组成人员故意造成本法第六十条第一款规定的保险事故外，保险人不得对被保险人的家庭成员或者其组成人员行使代位请求赔偿的权利。

Article 62

The insurer has no subrogation rights against any family member or a member of the insured's household, unless the family member or member of the household intentionally causes the insured event as provided in the first paragraph of the Article 61.

第六十三条　保险人向第三者行使代位请求赔偿的权利时，被保险人应当向保险人提供必要的文件和所知道的有关情况。

Article 63

Where the insurer exercises subrogation rights against a third party, the insured shall provide all necessary documents or information known to the insured.

第六十四条　保险人、被保险人为查明和确定保险事故的性质、原因和保险标的的损失程度所支付的必要的、合理的费用，由保险人承担。

Article 64

The insurer shall bear any necessary and reasonable costs and expenses incurred in respect of investigating and ascertaining the nature and cause of the insured event as well as the extent to which the subject matter insured is lost or damaged.

第六十五条　保险人对责任保险的被保险人给第三者造成的损害，可以依照法律的规定或者合同的约定，直接向该第三者赔偿保险金。

Article 65

The insurer may indemnify a third party directly for loss or damage caused by the insured under liability insurance in accordance with laws or as provided by the contract.

责任保险的被保险人给第三者造成损害，被保险人对第三者应负的赔偿责任确定的，根据被保险人的请求，保险人应当直接向该第三者赔偿保险金。被保险人怠于请求的，第三者有权就其应获赔偿部分直接向保险人请求赔偿保险金。

Where the insured under liability insurance causes loss or damage to a third party and the liability for compensation to the third party is determined, the insurer shall, upon the request of the insured, make the indemnity payment directly to the third party. Where the insured delays making such a request, the third party is entitled to claim directly against the insurer for its portion of the compensation.

责任保险的被保险人给第三者造成损害，被保险人未向该第三者赔偿的，保险人不得向被保险人赔偿保险金。
Where the insured under liability insurance causes loss or damage to a third party and the insured has not compensated the third party, the insurer shall not make the indemnity payment to the insured.

责任保险是指以被保险人对第三者依法应负的赔偿责任为保险标的的保险。
Liability insurance means the type of insurance where the subject matter insured is the insured's liability to compensate a third party in accordance with law.

第六十六条　责任保险的被保险人因给第三者造成损害的保险事故而被提起仲裁或者诉讼的，被保险人支付的仲裁或者诉讼费用以及其他必要的、合理的费用，除合同另有约定外，由保险人承担。
Article 66
Where arbitration or legal proceedings are instituted in respect of the event insured where the insured under liability insurance has caused loss or damage to a third party, the insurer shall be liable for the arbitration and litigation expenses payable by the insured and any other necessary and reasonable costs and expenses, unless the contract otherwise provides.

第三章　保险公司
Chapter III: Insurance Companies

第六十七条　设立保险公司应当经国务院保险监督管理机构批准。

国务院保险监督管理机构审查保险公司的设立申请时，应当考虑保险业的发展和公平竞争的需要。
Article 67
The establishment of an insurance company is subject to the approval of the insurance regulatory body of the State Council.

When examining the application for the establishment of an insurance company, the insurance regulatory body of the State Council shall take into consideration the need for the development of the insurance industry and fair competition.

第六十八条　设立保险公司应当具备下列条件：
Article 68
The following conditions apply to the establishment of an insurance company:

（一）主要股东具有持续盈利能力，信誉良好，最近三年内无重大违法违规记录，净资产不低于人民币二亿元；

(1) the major shareholders have sustainable profitability and good reputations; have no record of serious violation of laws and regulations within three years; and have more than RMB 200 million net assets;

（二） 有符合本法和《中华人民共和国公司法》规定的章程；

(2) the articles of association comply with this Act and the Company Law of the People's Republic of China;

（三） 有符合本法规定的注册资本；

(3) a registered capital complying with the provisions of this Act;

（四） 有具备任职专业知识和业务工作经验的董事、监事和高级管理人员；

(4) directors, supervisors and senior managers with professional expertise and working experience for their designated positions;

（五） 有健全的组织机构和管理制度；

(5) a sound organisational structure and management system;

（六） 有符合要求的营业场所和与经营业务有关的其他设施；

(6) business premises as required and other facilities relevant to the business; and

（七） 法律、行政法规和国务院保险监督管理机构规定的其他条件。

(7) other conditions as provided by laws, administrative regulations and the insurance regulatory body of the State Council.

第六十九条 设立保险公司，其注册资本的最低限额为人民币二亿元。

国务院保险监督管理机构根据保险公司的业务范围、经营规模，可以调整其注册资本的最低限额，但不得低于本条第一款规定的限额。

保险公司的注册资本必须为实缴货币资本。

Article 69

The minimum amount of registered capital required for the establishment of an insurance company is two hundred million RMB (RMB 200,000,000).

The insurance regulatory body of the State Council may adjust the requirement of the minimum amount of registered capital of an insurance company considering the company's scope of business and size of operation, provided that the amount shall not be lower than the amount provided in the first paragraph of this Article.

The registered capital of an insurance company must be paid-in monetary capital.

第七十条　申请设立保险公司，应当向国务院保险监督管理机构提出书面申请，并提交下列材料：

Article 70

For the establishment of an insurance company, a written application shall be submitted to the insurance regulatory body of the State Council together with the following materials:

（一）　设立申请书，申请书应当载明拟设立的保险公司的名称、注册资本、业务范围等；

(1) an application letter for the establishment of the insurance company on which the name, registered capital, business scope and etc., shall be specified;

（二）　可行性研究报告；

(2) a feasibility study report;

（三）　筹建方案；

(3) a plan for establishment preparation;

（四）　投资人的营业执照或者其他背景资料，经会计师事务所审计的上一年度财务会计报告；

(4) the investors' business licence or background information and accounting reports for the previous year, audited by an accounting firm;

（五）　投资人认可的筹备组负责人和拟任董事长、经理名单及本人认可证明；

(5) a list of the head of the preparation team, the proposed board chairman and general manager approved by the investors, and confirmation from those persons; and

（六）　国务院保险监督管理机构规定的其他材料。

(6) other materials provided by the insurance regulatory body of the State Council.

第七十一条　国务院保险监督管理机构应当对设立保险公司的申请进行审查，自受理之日起六个月内作出批准或者不批准筹建的决定，并书面通知申请人。决定不批准的，应当书面说明理由。

Article 71

The insurance regulatory body of the State Council shall examine the application for the establishment of an insurance company and, within six months from the date of accepting the application, make a decision whether or not to approve the application and notify the applicant thereof in writing. Where the application is not approved, the reasons for rejection shall be specified in the written notice.

第七十二条　申请人应当自收到批准筹建通知之日起一年内完成筹建工作；筹建期间不得从事保险经营活动。

Article 72

The applicant shall complete the establishment preparation within one year from the date of receiving the approval notice; the applicant shall not conduct insurance business during the period of the establishment preparation.

第七十三条　筹建工作完成后，申请人具备本法第六十八条规定的设立条件的，可以向国务院保险监督管理机构提出开业申请。

国务院保险监督管理机构应当自受理开业申请之日起六十日内，作出批准或者不批准开业的决定。决定批准的，颁发经营保险业务许可证；决定不批准的，应当书面通知申请人并说明理由。

Article 73

After completing the establishment preparation, the applicant may apply to the insurance regulatory body of the State Council to commence business operations if the applicant meets the requirements provided in Article 68 of this Act.

The insurance supervision and administration authority of the State Council shall, within 60 days from the date of receiving the application, make a decision whether or not to approve the application for starting business. Where the application is approved, an insurance business permit shall be issued; where the application is not approved, the applicant shall be notified in writing with reasons therefor specified.

第七十四条　保险公司在中华人民共和国境内设立分支机构，应当经保险监督管理机构批准。

保险公司分支机构不具有法人资格，其民事责任由保险公司承担。

Article 74

An insurance company shall obtain the approval from the insurance regulatory body for the purpose of establishing a branch within the territory of the People's Republic of China.

The branch of an insurance company does not have legal personality and the insurance company shall be liable for the civil liability of the branch.

第七十五条　保险公司申请设立分支机构，应当向保险监督管理机构提出书面申请，并提交下列材料：

（一）设立申请书；
（二）拟设机构三年业务发展规划和市场分析材料；
（三）拟任高级管理人员的简历及相关证明材料；
（四）国务院保险监督管理机构规定的其他材料。

Article 75

Where an insurance company applies for the establishment of a branch, a written application shall be submitted to the insurance regulatory body, together with the following materials:

(1) a letter of application;
(2) a three-year business development plan and market analysis materials of the proposed branch;
(3) résumés of the senior managers proposed and relevant evidence; and
(4) other materials provided by the insurance supervision and administration authority of the State Council.

第七十六条　保险监督管理机构应当对保险公司设立分支机构的申请进行审查，自受理之日起六十日内作出批准或者不批准的决定。决定批准的，颁发分支机构经营保险业务许可证；决定不批准的，应当书面通知申请人并说明理由。

Article 76

The insurance regulatory body shall examine the application of the insurance company for the establishment of a branch and make a decision whether or not to approve the application within six months from the date of receiving the application. Where the application is approved, a branch insurance permit shall be issued; where the application is not approved, a written notice shall be sent to the applicant with reasons therefor specified.

第七十七条　经批准设立的保险公司及其分支机构，凭经营保险业务许可证向工商行政管理机关办理登记，领取营业执照。

Article 77

The insurance company and its branches established with approval shall register with the industrial and commercial administration authority on the basis of the insurance business permit, and obtain the business licence.

第七十八条　保险公司及其分支机构自取得经营保险业务许可证之日起六个月内，无正当理由未向工商行政管理机关办理登记的，其经营保险业务许可证失效。

Article 78

Where, without good reason, the insurance company or its branch fails to register with the industrial and commercial administration authority within six months from the date of receiving the insurance business permit, the insurance business permit lapses automatically.

第七十九条　保险公司在中华人民共和国境外设立子公司、分支机构、代表机构，应当经国务院保险监督管理机构批准。

Article 79

Where an insurance company intends to establish subsidiaries, branches or representative offices outside the territory of the People's Republic of China, the approval of the insurance regulatory body of the State Council shall be obtained.

第八十条　外国保险机构在中华人民共和国境内设立代表机构，应当经国务院保险监督管理机构批准。代表机构不得从事保险经营活动。

Article 80

Where a foreign insurance institution intends to establish representative offices within the territory of the People's Republic of China, the approval of the insurance regulatory body of the State Council shall be obtained. The representative offices shall not conduct insurance business.

第八十一条　保险公司的董事、监事和高级管理人员，应当品行良好，熟悉与保险相关的法律、行政法规，具有履行职责所需的经营管理能力，并在任职前取得保险监督管理机构核准的任职资格。

保险公司高级管理人员的范围由国务院保险监督管理机构规定。

Article 81

The directors, supervisors and senior managers shall be of good moral standing, acquainted with laws and regulations relevant to insurance, capable of fulfilling the management and operation duties required by their positions and qualified by the insurance regulatory body before taking up their positions.

第八十二条　有《中华人民共和国公司法》第一百四十七条规定的情形或者下列情形之一的，不得担任保险公司的董事、监事、高级管理人员：

（一）因违法行为或者违纪行为被金融监督管理机构取消任职资格的金融机构的董事、监事、高级管理人员，自被取消任职资格之日起未逾五年的；

（二）因违法行为或者违纪行为被吊销执业资格的律师、注册会计师或者资产评估机构、验证机构等机构的专业人员，自被吊销执业资格之日起未逾五年的。

Article 82

Any person who is under the circumstances provided by Article 147 of the Company Law of the People's Republic of China or any of the following circumstances shall not take the position of a director, supervisor or senior manager of an insurance company:

(1) a director, supervisor or senior manager of a financial institute who was disqualified by the financial supervision and administration authority for illegal activities or disciplinary offences, unless five years have elapsed since the date of disqualification; or

(2) a lawyer, certified public accountant or professional of an asset evaluation agency or certification agency who was disqualified for illegal activities or disciplinary offences, unless five years have elapsed since the date of disqualification.

第八十三条　保险公司的董事、监事、高级管理人员执行公司职务时违反法律、行政法规或者公司章程的规定，给公司造成损失的，应当承担赔偿责任。

Article 83

Where a director, supervisor or senior manager of an insurance company causes losses to the company due to violation of laws, administrative regulations or provisions of the articles of association while performing duties for the company, the director, supervisor or senior manager shall be liable to compensate for such losses.

第八十四条　保险公司有下列情形之一的，应当经保险监督管理机构批准：

Article 84

Where there is any of the following circumstance(s), the insurance company shall obtain the approval of the insurance regulatory body:

（一）　变更名称；

(1) change of name;

（二）变更注册资本；

(2) change in the amount of the registered capital;

（三）变更公司或者分支机构的营业场所；

(3) change of business premises of the company or its branches;

（四）撤销分支机构；

(4) closing a branch;

（五）公司分立或者合并；

(5) demerger or merger of the company;

（六）修改公司章程；

(6) amendment to the company's articles of association;

（七）变更出资额占有限责任公司资本总额百分之五以上的股东，或者变更持有股份有限公司股份百分之五以上的股东；

(7) change of shareholder(s) who controls more than 5 per cent of the total capital amount of a limited liability company, or change of shareholder(s) who controls more than 5 per cent of the total shares of a company limited by shares; or

（八）国务院保险监督管理机构规定的其他情形。

(8) other circumstances provided by the insurance regulatory body of the State Council.

第八十五条　保险公司应当聘用经国务院保险监督管理机构认可的精算专业人员，建立精算报告制度。

保险公司应当聘用专业人员，建立合规报告制度。

Article 85

An insurance company shall employ professional actuaries certified by the insurance regulatory body of the State Council and establish an actuarial reporting system.

An insurance company shall employ professionals and establish a compliance reporting system.

第八十六条　保险公司应当按照保险监督管理机构的规定，报送有关报告、报表、文件和资料。

保险公司的偿付能力报告、财务会计报告、精算报告、合规报告及其他有关报告、报表、文件和资料必须如实记录保险业务事项，不得有虚假记载、误导性陈述和重大遗漏。

Article 86

An insurance company shall, in accordance with the provisions of the insurance regulatory body, submit relevant reports, statements, documents and materials.

The insurance company's solvency report, financial accounting report, actuarial report, compliance report and other relevant reports, statements, documents and materials shall truthfully record the insurance business matters, and shall not have false records, misleading statements or major omissions.

第八十七条　保险公司应当按照国务院保险监督管理机构的规定妥善保管业务经营活动的完整账簿、原始凭证和有关资料。

前款规定的账簿、原始凭证和有关资料的保管期限，自保险合同终止之日起计算，保险期间在一年以下的不得少于五年，保险期间超过一年的不得少于十年。

Article 87

An insurance company shall, in accordance with the provisions of the insurance regulatory body of the State Council, properly keep all the account books, original certificates and other relevant materials.

The keeping period of the account books, original certificates and other relevant materials as provided in the preceding paragraph shall be at least five years in respect of the contracts whose period of underwriting is less than one year, and/or at least ten years in respect of contracts whose period of underwriting is more than one year, starting from the date of the end of the insurance contract.

第八十八条　保险公司聘请或者解聘会计师事务所、资产评估机构、资信评级机构等中介服务机构，应当向保险监督管理机构报告；解聘会计师事务所、资产评估机构、资信评级机构等中介服务机构，应当说明理由。

Article 88

Where the insurance company hires or dismisses the accounting firms, asset evaluation agencies, credit rating agencies or other intermediary service agencies, the insurance company shall report to the insurance regulatory body. Where the insurance company dismisses the accounting firms, asset evaluation agencies, credit rating agencies or other intermediary service agencies, reasons therefor shall be given.

第八十九条　保险公司因分立、合并需要解散，或者股东会、股东大会决议解散，或者公司章程规定的解散事由出现，经国务院保险监督管理机构批准后解散。

经营有人寿保险业务的保险公司，除因分立、合并或者被依法撤销外，不得解散。

保险公司解散，应当依法成立清算组进行清算。

Article 89

Where an insurance company is to be dissolved due to demerger, merger, a resolution by the shareholders' meeting or the shareholders' general meeting, or any causes for dissolution as specified in the articles of association of the company, the company shall be dissolved upon the approval of the insurance regulatory body of the State Council.

An insurance company conducting life insurance business shall not be dissolved unless by reasons of separation, merger or revocation according to the law.

Where an insurance company is dissolved, a liquidation committee shall be formed according to the law to carry out the liquidation.

第九十条　保险公司有《中华人民共和国企业破产法》第二条规定情形的，经国务院保险监督管理机构同意，保险公司或者其债权人可以依法向人民法院申请重整、和解或者破产清算；国务院保险监督管理机构也可以依法向人民法院申请对该保险公司进行重整或者破产清算。

Article 90

Where there is any circumstance provided in Article 2 of the Enterprise Bankruptcy Law of the People's Republic of China, the insurance company or its creditors may, with the approval of insurance regulatory body of the State Council, apply to the People's Court for reorganisation, compromise or bankruptcy liquidation. The insurance supervision and administration authority of the State Council may also apply to the People's Court for reorganisation or bankruptcy liquidation of the company in accordance with the law.

第九十一条　破产财产在优先清偿破产费用和共益债务后，按照下列顺序清偿：

Article 91

The bankrupt's assets shall, after the expenses for bankruptcy proceedings and the debts incurred for the common good of creditors are paid, be distributed according to the following order of priority:

（一）　所欠职工工资和医疗、伤残补助、抚恤费用，所欠应当划入职工个人账户的基本养老保险、基本医疗保险费用，以及法律、行政法规规定应当支付给职工的补偿金；

(1) wages, subsidies for medical treatment, injuries and disability and the pensions for the disabled and the families of the deceased, the basic endowment insurance premiums and the basic medical insurance premiums which the company owes and fails to pay into the employees' personal accounts, and the compensations which should be paid to the employees as provided by the relevant laws and administrative regulations;

（二）赔偿或者给付保险金；

(2) indemnity payments or payment of insurance compensation;

（三）保险公司欠缴的除第（一）项规定以外的社会保险费用和所欠税款；

(3) social insurance premiums and taxes owed by the insurance company other than those provided in item (1); and

（四）普通破产债权。

(4) ordinary bankruptcy debts.

破产财产不足以清偿同一顺序的清偿要求的，按照比例分配。

破产保险公司的董事、监事和高级管理人员的工资，按照该公司职工的平均工资计算。

Where the bankrupt's estate is not sufficient to satisfy all the claims within the same group, the payment shall be distributed on a pro rata basis.

The wages of the directors, supervisors and senior managers of a bankrupt insurance company shall be calculated as the average wages of the employees of the company.

第九十二条　经营有人寿保险业务的保险公司被依法撤销或者被依法宣告破产的，其持有的人寿保险合同及责任准备金，必须转让给其他经营有人寿保险业务的保险公司；不能同其他保险公司达成转让协议的，由国务院保险监督管理机构指定经营有人寿保险业务的保险公司接受转让。转让或者由国务院保险监督管理机构指定接受转让前款规定的人寿保险合同及责任准备金的，应当维护被保险人、受益人的合法权益。

Article 92

Where an insurance company conducting life insurance business is revoked according to the law or declared bankrupt, all of the life insurance contracts and the reserves held by the company shall be transferred to other insurance companies conducting life insurance. Where no agreement of transfer thereof can be reached with other insurance companies, the insurance regulatory body of the State Council shall designate insurance companies conducting life insurance business to accept such transfer.

Where the insurance supervision and administration authority of the State Council designates the acceptance of the transfer of the life insurance contracts and the reserves as provided in the preceding paragraph, the legitimate rights and interests of the insured and beneficiary shall be protected.

第九十三条　保险公司依法终止其业务活动，应当注销其经营保险业务许可证。
Article 93
Where an insurance company ceases its business in accordance with law, the company's insurance business permit shall be revoked.

第九十四条　保险公司，除本法另有规定外，适用《中华人民共和国公司法》的规定。
Article 94
Unless otherwise provided in this Act, the Company Law of the People's Republic of China shall be applicable to insurance companies.

第四章　保险经营规则
Chapter IV: Rules on Insurance Business Operation

第九十五条　保险公司的业务范围：
Article 95
The scope of business of an insurance company shall be as follows:

（一）人身保险业务，包括人寿保险、健康保险、意外伤害保险等保险业务；
(1) personal insurance, including life insurance, health insurance, accidental injury insurance, etc.;

（二）财产保险业务，包括财产损失保险、责任保险、信用保险、保证保险等保险业务；
(2) property insurance, including property loss insurance, liability insurance, credit insurance, guarantee insurance, etc.; and

（三）国务院保险监督管理机构批准的与保险有关的其他业务。
(3) other insurance-related businesses approved by the insurance regulatory body of the State Council.

保险人不得兼营人身保险业务和财产保险业务。但是，经营财产保险业务的保险公司经国务院保险监督管理机构批准可以经营短期健康保险业务和意外伤害保险业务
司经国务院保险监督管理机构批准，可以经营短期健康保险业务和意外伤害保险业务。

No insurer shall concurrently operate personal insurance business and property insurance business. However, upon the approval of the insurance regulatory body of the State Council, an insurance company which operates property insurance business may operate short-term health insurance business and accidental injury insurance business.

保险公司应当在国务院保险监督管理机构依法批准的业务范围内从事保险经营活动

An insurance company shall operate insurance business within the scope of business approved by the insurance regulatory body of the State Council.

第九十六条　经国务院保险监督管理机构批准，保险公司可以经营本法第九十五条规定的保险业务的下列再保险业务：

Article 96

Upon the approval of the insurance regulatory body of the State Council, an insurance company may operate the following reinsurance businesses prescribed in Article 95 of this Act:

（一）分出保险；

(1) outward reinsurance; and

（二）分入保险。

(2) inward reinsurance.

第九十七条　保险公司应当按照其注册资本总额的百分之二十提取保证金，存入国务院保险监督管理机构指定的银行，除公司清算时用于清偿债务外，不得动用。

Article 97

An insurance company shall draw a guarantee fund at the rate of 20 per cent of its total registered capital, deposit it into a bank designated by the insurance regulatory body of the State Council, and use it for no purpose other than repayment of debts at the time of liquidation of the company.

第九十八条　保险公司应当根据保障被保险人利益、保证偿付能力的原则，提取各项责任准备金。

Article 98

An insurance company shall draw various liability reserve funds according to the principle of protecting the interests of insureds and guaranteeing solvency.

保险公司提取和结转责任准备金的具体办法，由国务院保险监督管理机构制定。
The specific measures for insurance companies to draw and carry-over liability reserve funds shall be formulated by the insurance regulatory body of the State Council.

第九十九条　保险公司应当依法提取公积金。
Article 99
Insurance companies shall draw provident funds according to law.

第一百条　保险公司应当缴纳保险保障基金。
Article 100
Insurance companies shall pay the insurance guarantee funds.

保险保障基金应当集中管理，并在下列情形下统筹使用：
The insurance guarantee funds shall be managed centrally and used according to overall planning in the following circumstances:

（一）在保险公司被撤销或者被宣告破产时，向投保人、被保险人或者受益人提供救济
(1) providing remedies for assureds, insureds or beneficiaries, where an insurance company is wound down or declared bankrupt;

（二）在保险公司被撤销或者被宣告破产时，向依法接受其人寿保险合同的保险公司提供救济；
(2) providing remedies for an insurance company which accepts the life insurance contracts of a bankrupt insurance company, where the latter is wound down or declared bankrupt; or

（三）国务院规定的其他情形。
(3) any other circumstances as specified by the State Council.

保险保障基金筹集、管理和使用的具体办法，由国务院制定。
The specific measures for raising, managing and using the insurance guarantee fund shall be formulated by the State Council.

第一百零一条　保险公司应当具有与其业务规模和风险程度相适应的最低偿付能力。保险公司的认可资产减去认可负债的差额不得低于国务院保险监督管理机构规定的数额；低于规定数额的，应当按照国务院保险监督管理机构的要求采取相应措施达到规定的数额。
Article 101
An insurance company shall have the minimum solvency appropriate for its scale of business and degree of risk. The balance of the admissible assets and the admissible liabilities of an insurance company shall not be less than the amount prescribed by the insurance regulatory body of the

State Council; otherwise, the insurance company shall take corresponding measures to reach the prescribed amount according to the requirements of the insurance regulatory body of the State Council.

第一百零二条　经营财产保险业务的保险公司当年自留保险费，不得超过其实有资本金加公积金总和的四倍。

Article 102

The self-retained insurance premium in the current year of an insurance company that underwrites property insurance business shall not exceed four times the sum of its actual capital and provident funds.

第一百零三条　保险公司对每一危险单位，即对一次保险事故可能造成的最大损失范围所承担的责任，不得超过其实有资本金加公积金总和的百分之十；超过的部分应当办理再保险。

Article 103

The liability undertaken by an insurance company for each risk unit, namely, the maximum loss caused by a single insured incident shall not exceed 10 per cent of the sum of its actual capital and provident funds. The excess shall be reinsured.

保险公司对危险单位的划分应当符合国务院保险监督管理机构的规定。

Insurance companies shall classify risk units according to the provisions of the insurance regulatory body of the State Council.

第一百零四条　保险公司对危险单位的划分方法和巨灾风险安排方案，应当报国务院保险监督管理机构备案。

Article 104

Insurance companies shall submit their methods for classifying risk units and catastrophe risk management plans to the insurance regulatory body of the State Council for the purpose of the record.

第一百零五条　保险公司应当按照国务院保险监督管理机构的规定办理再保险，并审慎选择再保险接受人。

Article 105

Insurance companies shall arrange for reinsurance as stipulated by the insurance regulatory body of the State Council, and prudently select their reinsurer.

第一百零六条　保险公司的资金运用必须稳健，遵循安全性原则。

Article 106

Insurance companies must manage their capital according to the principles of stability and safety.

保险公司的资金运用限于下列形式：

Insurance companies may only hold their capital in the following forms:

（一）银行存款；
(1) bank deposits;

（二）买卖债券、股票、证券投资基金份额等有价证券；
(2) trading bonds, equity shares, shares of securities investment funds and other negotiable securities;

（三）投资不动产；
(3) investment in real estate; and

（四）国务院规定的其他资金运用形式。
(4) other forms of investment prescribed by the State Council.

保险公司资金运用的具体管理办法，由国务院保险监督管理机构依照前两款的规定制定。
The specific measures for the administration of the use of funds by insurance companies shall be prescribed by the insurance regulatory body of the State Council in conformity with the preceding two paragraphs.

第一百零七条　经国务院保险监督管理机构会同国务院证券监督管理机构批准，保险公司可以设立保险资产管理公司。
Article 107
Upon the approval of the insurance regulatory body of the State Council in conjunction with the securities regulatory body of the State Council, an insurance company may set up an insurance asset management company.

保险资产管理公司从事证券投资活动，应当遵守《中华人民共和国证券法》等法律、行政法规的规定。
Insurance asset management companies shall engage in securities investment activities according to the Securities Law of the People's Republic of China and other relevant laws and administrative regulations.

保险资产管理公司的管理办法，由国务院保险监督管理机构会同国务院有关部门制定。
The rules for the administration of insurance asset management companies shall be formulated by the insurance regulatory body in conjunction with other relevant departments of the State Council.

第一百零八条　保险公司应当按照国务院保险监督管理机构的规定，建立对关联交易的管理和信息披露制度。
Article 108
Insurance companies shall establish rules for the management and information disclosure of associated party transactions according to the provisions of the insurance regulatory body of the State Council.

第一百零九条 保险公司的控股股东、实际控制人、董事、监事、高级管理人员不得利用关联交易损害公司的利益。

Article 109

The controlling shareholders, actual controllers, directors, supervisors and senior managers of an insurance company shall not damage the interests of the company through associated party transactions.

第一百一十条 保险公司应当按照国务院保险监督管理机构的规定，真实、准确、完整地披露财务会计报告、风险管理状况、保险产品经营情况等重大事项。

Article 110

Insurance companies shall truthfully, accurately and completely disclose their financial and accounting reports, risk management status, insurance product trading information and other major matters according to the provisions of the insurance regulatory body of the State Council.

第一百一十一条 保险公司从事保险销售的人员应当符合国务院保险监督管理机构规定的资格条件，取得保险监督管理机构颁发的资格证书。

Article 111

The insurance salespersons of insurance companies shall meet the qualification requirements of the insurance regulatory body of the State Council, and shall be certificated by the insurance regulatory body.

前款规定的保险销售人员的范围和管理办法，由国务院保险监督管理机构规定。

The meaning of 'insurance salespersons' and rules for management thereof as provided in the preceding paragraph shall be provided for by the insurance regulatory body of the State Council.

第一百一十二条 保险公司应当建立保险代理人登记管理制度，加强对保险代理人的培训和管理，不得唆使、诱导保险代理人进行违背诚信义务的活动。

Article 112

Insurance companies shall set up an insurance agent registration system and strengthen the training and administration of insurance agents, and shall not incite or induce insurance agents to act against the obligation of good faith.

第一百一十三条 保险公司及其分支机构应当依法使用经营保险业务许可证，不得转让、出租、出借经营保险业务许可证。

Article 113

Insurance companies and their branch offices shall use the insurance business permit according to the law, and shall not transfer, lease or lend the insurance business permit.

第一百一十四条　保险公司应当按照国务院保险监督管理机构的规定，公平、合理拟订保险条款和保险费率，不得损害投保人、被保险人和受益人的合法权益。

Article 114

Insurance companies shall, according to the provisions of the insurance regulatory body of the State Council, fairly and reasonably draft the insurance clauses and premium rates, without prejudice to the legitimate rights and interests of assureds, insureds and beneficiaries.

保险公司应当按照合同约定和本法规定，及时履行赔偿或者给付保险金义务。

Insurance companies shall perform the obligation of paying indemnity or compensation in a timely manner according to the insurance contract and this Act.

第一百一十五条　保险公司开展业务，应当遵循公平竞争的原则，不得从事不正当竞争。

Article 115

Insurance companies shall operate business according to the principle of fair competition, and shall not engage in unfair competition.

第一百一十六条　保险公司及其工作人员在保险业务活动中不得有下列行为：

Article 116

In their insurance business operations, insurance companies and their staff shall be prohibited from:

（一）欺骗投保人、被保险人或者受益人；

(1) deceiving an assured, insured or beneficiary;

（二）对投保人隐瞒与保险合同有关的重要情况；

(2) concealing any important information about an insurance contract from an assured;

（三）阻碍投保人履行本法规定的如实告知义务，或者诱导其不履行本法规定的如实告知义务；

(3) obstructing any assured from performing, or inducing any assured not to perform, the obligation of truthful disclosure as prescribed in this Act;

（四）给予或者承诺给予投保人、被保险人、受益人保险合同约定以外的保险费回扣或者其他利益；

(4) giving or promising to give any insurance premium payoff or compensation other than those agreed upon in the insurance contract to an assured, insured or beneficiary;

（五）拒不依法履行保险合同约定的赔偿或者给付保险金义务；

(5) refusing to legally perform the obligation of paying indemnity or insurance money under the insurance contract;

（六）故意编造未曾发生的保险事故、虚构保险合同或者故意夸大已经发生的保险事故的损失程度进行虚假理赔，骗取保险金或者牟取其他不正当利益；

(6) intentionally fabricating an insured incident which has never occurred or an insurance contract or intentionally exaggerating the degree of damage caused by an insured incident which has actually occurred for the purpose of making a false claim, swindling insurance money or seeking other illicit interests;

（七）挪用、截留、侵占保险费；

(7) misappropriating, withholding or pilfering insurance premiums;

（八）委托未取得合法资格的机构或者个人从事保险销售活动；

(8) authorising any institution or individual which has not obtained a legally required qualification to carry out the insurance sales activities;

（九）利用开展保险业务为其他机构或者个人牟取不正当利益；

(9) seeking any illicit benefit for any other institution or individual in the process of insurance business operation;

（十）利用保险代理人、保险经纪人或者保险评估机构，从事以虚构保险中介业务或者编造退保等方式套取费用等违法活动；

(10) conducting any illegal activity such as swindling money in the form of fabricating insurance intermediary business or discharge of insurance through insurance agents, insurance brokers or insurance assessment agencies;

（十一）以捏造、散布虚假事实等方式损害竞争对手的商业信誉，或者以其他不正当竞争行为扰乱保险市场秩序；

(11) damaging the business reputation of competitors by fabricating or spreading misrepresented facts, or disturbing the order of the insurance market by any other act of unfair competition;

（十二）泄露在业务活动中知悉的投保人、被保险人的商业秘密；

(12) disclosing any trade secret of an assured or insured, information of which is obtained in a business context; or

（十三）违反法律、行政法规和国务院保险监督管理机构规定的其他行为。

(13) conducting any other act in violation of law or administrative regulations or the provisions of the insurance regulatory body of the State Council.

第五章　保险代理人和保险经纪人
Chapter V: Insurance Agents and Insurance Brokers

第一百一十七条　保险代理人是根据保险人的委托，向保险人收取佣金，并在保险人授权的范围内代为办理保险业务的机构或者个人。

Article 117

Insurance agents shall be institutions or individuals which charge insurers commission and operate the insurance business to the extent authorised by insurers.

保险代理机构包括专门从事保险代理业务的保险专业代理机构和兼营保险代理业务的保险兼业代理机构。

Insurance agencies shall include specialised insurance agencies which only engage in insurance agency business and secondary insurance agencies which engage in insurance agency as a secondary business.

第一百一十八条　保险经纪人是基于投保人的利益，为投保人与保险人订立保险合同提供中介服务，并依法收取佣金的机构。

Article 118

Insurance brokers shall be institutions which, in the interests of assureds, provide intermediary services for assureds and insurers to conclude insurance contracts, and charge a commission according to law.

第一百一十九条　保险代理机构、保险经纪人应当具备国务院保险监督管理机构规定的条件，取得保险监督管理机构颁发的经营保险代理业务许可证、保险经纪业务许可证。

Article 119

Insurance agencies and insurance brokers shall satisfy the requirements prescribed by the insurance regulatory body of the State Council, and have obtained the insurance agency business permit or brokerage business permit issued by the insurance regulatory body.

保险专业代理机构、保险经纪人凭保险监督管理机构颁发的许可证向工商行政管理机关办理登记，领取营业执照。

A specialised insurance agency or an insurance broker shall register at the administrative body for industry and commerce on the basis of the permit issued by the insurance regulatory body, and obtain a business licence.

保险兼业代理机构凭保险监督管理机构颁发的许可证，向工商行政管理机关办理变更登记。

A secondary insurance agency shall modify the registration at the administrative body for industry and commerce on the basis of the permit issued by the insurance regulatory body.

第一百二十条　以公司形式设立保险专业代理机构、保险经纪人，其注册资本最低限额适用《中华人民共和国公司法》的规定。

Article 120

For a specialised insurance agency or an insurance broker to be formed as a company, its minimum amount of registered capital shall be governed by the Company Law of the People's Republic of China.

国务院保险监督管理机构根据保险专业代理机构、保险经纪人的业务范围和经营规模，可以调整其注册资本的最低限额，但不得低于《中华人民共和国公司法》规定的限额。

The insurance regulatory body of the State Council may adjust the minimum amount of registered capital of a specialised insurance agency or an insurance broker according to its business scope or scale, but the amount shall not be less than the amount set out in the Company Law of the People's Republic of China.

保险专业代理机构、保险经纪人的注册资本或者出资额必须为实缴货币资本。

The registered capital or capital contribution of a specialised insurance agency or an insurance broker must be paid-in monetary capital.

第一百二十一条　保险专业代理机构、保险经纪人的高级管理人员，应当品行良好，熟悉保险法律、行政法规，具有履行职责所需的经营管理能力，并在任职前取得保险监督管理机构核准的任职资格。

Article 121

The senior managers of a specialised insurance agency or an insurance broker shall be of good repute, be familiar with insurance laws and administrative regulations, have the management capability required for performing their duties and have obtained the requisite qualifications designated by the competent insurance regulatory body before holding posts.

第一百二十二条　个人保险代理人、保险代理机构的代理从业人员、保险经纪人的经纪从业人员，应当具备国务院保险监督管理机构规定的资格条件，取得保险监督管理机构颁发的资格证书。

Article 122

Individual insurance agents, practitioners of insurance agencies and practitioners of insurance brokers shall meet the qualifications required by the insurance regulatory body of the State Council and obtain the qualification certificates issued by the competent insurance regulatory body.

第一百二十三条　保险代理机构、保险经纪人应当有自己的经营场所，设立专门账簿记载保险代理业务、经纪业务的收支情况。

Article 123

Insurance agencies and insurance brokers shall have their own business premises and set up special account books to record the revenues and expenditures of the insurance agency or brokerage business.

第一百二十四条　保险代理机构、保险经纪人应当按照国务院保险监督管理机构的规定缴存保证金或者投保职业责任保险。未经保险监督管理机构批准，保险代理机构、保险经纪人不得动用保证金。

Article 124

Insurance agencies and insurance brokers shall deposit guarantee funds or arrange professional liability insurance according to the provisions of the insurance regulatory body of the State Council. The guarantee funds shall not be used by the insurance agency or broker without the approval of the insurance regulatory body.

第一百二十五条　个人保险代理人在代为办理人寿保险业务时，不得同时接受两个以上保险人的委托。

Article 125

No individual insurance agent may represent two or more insurers at the same time when operating life insurance business on behalf of any insurer.

第一百二十六条　保险人委托保险代理人代为办理保险业务，应当与保险代理人签订委托代理协议，依法约定双方的权利和义务。

Article 126

An insurer which authorises an insurance agent to represent it in insurance business operation shall enter into an agency agreement with the insurance agent to agree upon their rights and obligations according to law.

第一百二十七条　保险代理人根据保险人的授权代为办理保险业务的行为，由保险人承担责任。

Article 127

An insurer shall be responsible for its insurance agent's insurance business operation to the extent of its authorisation.

保险代理人没有代理权、超越代理权或者代理权终止后以保险人名义订立合同，使投保人有理由相信其有代理权的，该代理行为有效。保险人可以依法追究越权的保险代理人的责任。

Where an insurance agent enters into an insurance contract in the name of an insurer without authorisation, beyond authorisation or after the termination of authorisation and the assured has reasons to believe that the insurance agent possesses the requisite authorisation, the act of agency shall be valid. The insurer may pursue the insurance agent for liabilities of ultra vires acts according to law.

第一百二十八条　保险经纪人因过错给投保人、被保险人造成损失的，依法承担赔偿责任。

Article 128

An insurance broker which, by its own fault, causes any loss to an assured or insured shall be liable for compensation.

第一百二十九条　保险活动当事人可以委托保险公估机构等依法设立的独立评估机构或者具有相关专业知识的人员，对保险事故进行评估和鉴定。

Article 129

Parties to insurance activities may authorise insurance assessment institutions or other legally established independent assessment institutions or persons with relevant expertise to assess and authenticate insured incidents.

接受委托对保险事故进行评估和鉴定的机构和人员，应当依法、独立、客观、公正地进行评估和鉴定，任何单位和个人不得干涉。

Institutions and persons authorised to assess and authenticate insured incidents shall conduct assessment and authentication in a legal, independent, objective and fair way and free from intervention by any other entity or individual.

前款规定的机构和人员，因故意或者过失给保险人或者被保险人造成损失的，依法承担赔偿责任。

An institution or person mentioned in the preceding paragraph which causes any loss to an insurer or insured intentionally or negligently shall be liable for compensation.

第一百三十条　保险佣金只限于向具有合法资格的保险代理人、保险经纪人支付，不得向其他人支付。

Article 130

Insurance commissions may only be paid to insurance agents and insurance brokers holding the qualifications required by law, and shall not be paid to anyone else.

第一百三十一条　保险代理人、保险经纪人及其从业人员在办理保险业务活动中不得有下列行为：

Article 131

In their insurance business operation, insurance agents, insurance brokers and their practitioners shall be prohibited from:

（一）欺骗保险人、投保人、被保险人或者受益人；

(1) deceiving an insurer, assured, insured or beneficiary;

（二）隐瞒与保险合同有关的重要情况；

(2) concealing any important information about an insurance contract from the assured;

（三）阻碍投保人履行本法规定的如实告知义务，或者诱导其不履行本法规定的如实告知义务；

(3) preventing any assured from performing, or inducing any assured not to perform, the obligation of truthful disclosure as prescribed in this Act;

（四）给予或者承诺给予投保人、被保险人或者受益人保险合同约定以外的利益；

(4) giving or promising to give any reward other than those agreed upon in the insurance contract to an assured, insured or beneficiary;

（五）利用行政权力、职务或者职业便利以及其他不正当手段强迫、引诱或者限制投保人订立保险合同；

(5) forcing or inducing any assured to enter into or restricting an assured from entering into an insurance contract by using any administrative power, position or the advantage of their profession (professional advantage) or by any other illicit means;

（六）伪造、擅自变更保险合同，或者为保险合同当事人提供虚假证明材料；

(6) forging or illegally modifying any insurance contract, or providing any false evidential materials for a party to an insurance contract;

（七）挪用、截留、侵占保险费或者保险金；

(7) misappropriating, withholding or pilfering insurance premiums or insurance money;

（八）利用业务便利为其他机构或者个人牟取不正当利益；

(8) seeking any illicit benefit for any other institution or individual by using business advantages;

（九）串通投保人、被保险人或者受益人，骗取保险金；

(9) colluding with any assured, insured or beneficiary to misappropriate insurance money; or

（十）泄露在业务活动中知悉的保险人、投保人、被保险人的商业秘密。

(10) disclosing any trade secret of an insurer, assured or insured of which information is obtained in a business context.

第一百三十二条　保险专业代理机构、保险经纪人分立、合并、变更组织形式、设立分支机构或者解散的，应当经保险监督管理机构批准。

Article 132

The demerger, merger, change of organisational form, or formation or dissolution of a branch office of a specialised insurance agency or an insurance broker shall be subject to the approval of the competent insurance regulatory body.

第一百三十三条　本法第八十六条第一款、第一百一十三条的规定，适用于保险代理机构和保险经纪人。

Article 133

The provisions of paragraph 1 of Article 86 and Article 113 of this Law shall apply to insurance agencies and insurance brokers.

第六章　保险业监督管理
Chapter VI: Regulation and Administration of the Insurance Sector

第一百三十四条　保险监督管理机构依照本法和国务院规定的职责，遵循依法、公开、公正的原则，对保险业实施监督管理，维护保险市场秩序，保护投保人、被保险人和受益人的合法权益。

Article 134

An insurance regulatory body shall, under the principles of legality, openness and fairness, regulate and supervise the insurance sector according to this Act and the duties prescribed by the State Council so as to maintain the order of the insurance market and protect the legitimate rights and interests of assureds, insureds and beneficiaries.

第一百三十五条　国务院保险监督管理机构依照法律、行政法规制定并发布有关保险业监督管理的规章。

Article 135

The insurance regulatory body of the State Council shall formulate and issue administrative rules on the regulation and supervision of the insurance sector according to laws and administrative regulations.

第一百三十六条　关系社会公众利益的保险险种、依法实行强制保险的险种和新开发的人寿保险险种等的保险条款和保险费率，应当报国务院保险监督管理机构批准。国务院保险监督管理机构审批时，应当遵循保护社会公众利益和防止不正当竞争的原则。其他保险险种的保险条款和保险费率，应当报保险监督管理机构备案。

Article 136

The insurance clauses and premium rates for insurance products which concern public interests, compulsory insurance products and newly developed life insurance products shall be subject to the approval of the insurance regulatory body of the State Council which shall adhere to the principle of protecting public interests and preventing unfair competition in the process of examination and approval. Insurance clauses and premium rates for other insurance products shall be submitted to the insurance regulatory body for record purposes.

保险条款和保险费率审批、备案的具体办法，由国务院保险监督管理机构依照前款规定制定。

The specific measures for the examination and approval and submission of insurance clauses and premium rates shall be formulated by the insurance regulatory body of the State Council according to the preceding paragraph.

第一百三十七条　保险公司使用的保险条款和保险费率违反法律、行政法规或者国务院保险监督管理机构的有关规定的，由保险监督管理机构责令停止使用，限期修改；情节严重的，可以在一定期限内禁止申报新的保险条款和保险费率。

Article 137

Where any insurance clauses or premium rates employed by an insurance company infringe a law or administrative regulation or the stipulations of the insurance regulatory body of the State Council, the competent insurance regulatory body shall order the insurance company to cease their use and make correction within a prescribed time; and if the circumstances are serious, may prohibit the insurance company from applying for new insurance clauses or insurance premium rates for a prescribed time.

第一百三十八条　国务院保险监督管理机构应当建立健全保险公司偿付能力监管体系，对保险公司的偿付能力实施监控。

Article 138

The insurance regulatory body of the State Council shall set up and develop a system for the regulation and supervision of the solvency of insurance companies to monitor the solvency of insurance companies.

第一百三十九条　对偿付能力不足的保险公司，国务院保险监督管理机构应当将其列为重点监管对象，并可以根据具体情况采取下列措施：

Article 139

The insurance regulatory body of the State Council shall regard insolvent insurance companies as key targets of supervision, and may take the following measures as the case may be:

（一）责令增加资本金、办理再保险；

(1) ordering an increase of capital or reinsurance;

（二）限制业务范围；

(2) limiting the scope of business;

（三）限制向股东分红；

(3) restricting the payment of dividends to shareholders;

（四）限制固定资产购置或者经营费用规模；

(4) restricting the purchase of fixed assets or the scale of operational expenses;

（五）限制资金运用的形式、比例；

(5) restricting the forms and proportion of use of funds;

（六）限制增设分支机构；

(6) restricting the formation of additional branch offices;

（七）责令拍卖不良资产、转让保险业务；
(7) ordering an auction of non-performing assets or transfer of insurance business;

（八）限制董事、监事、高级管理人员的薪酬水平；
(8) restricting the level of salaries of directors, supervisors and senior managers;

（九）限制商业性广告；
(9) restricting commercial advertisements; or

（十）责令停止接受新业务。
(10) ordering a company to stop accepting new business.

第一百四十条　保险公司未依照本法规定提取或者结转各项责任准备金，或者未依照本法规定办理再保险，或者严重违反本法关于资金运用的规定的，由保险监督管理机构责令限期改正，并可以责令调整负责人及有关管理人员。

Article 140

Where an insurance company fails to set aside or carry over the reserve funds, or arrange reinsurance in accordance with this Act, or seriously infringes the provisions of this Act on the investment of funds, the competent insurance regulation authority shall order the insurance company to take corrective action within a prescribed period, and may order the replacement of its responsible senior management and the personnel concerned.

第一百四十一条　保险监督管理机构依照本法第一百四十条的规定作出限期改正的决定后，保险公司逾期未改正的，国务院保险监督管理机构可以决定选派保险专业人员和指定该保险公司的有关人员组成整顿组，对公司进行整顿。

Article 141

Where an insurance company fails to make correction within the prescribed time limit after the competent insurance regulatory body makes a decision on correction according to Article 140 of this Act, the insurance regulatory body of the State Council may decide to select insurance professionals and designate the relevant persons of the insurance company to form a reorganisation group to reorganise the company.

整顿决定应当载明被整顿公司的名称、整顿理由、整顿组成员和整顿期限，并予以公告。

A reorganisation decision shall be published containing the name of the company to be reorganised, the reasons for reorganisation, the members of the reorganisation group and the period of reorganisation.

第一百四十二条　整顿组有权监督被整顿保险公司的日常业务。被整顿公司的负责人及有关管理人员应当在整顿组的监督下行使职权。

Article 142

The reorganisation group shall have the right to supervise the ordinary course of business of the insurance company in reorganisation. The person in charge and the relevant managers of the insurance company in reorganisation shall perform their functions under the supervision of the reorganisation group.

第一百四十三条　整顿过程中，被整顿保险公司的原有业务继续进行。但是，国务院保险监督管理机构可以责令被整顿公司停止部分原有业务、停止接受新业务，调整资金运用。

Article 143

In the process of reorganisation, the original businesses of the insurance company in reorganisation shall continue. However, the insurance regulatory body of the State Council may order the company to stop some existing business or stop accepting new business and adjust its use of funds.

第一百四十四条　被整顿保险公司经整顿已纠正其违反本法规定的行为，恢复正常经营状况的，由整顿组提出报告，经国务院保险监督管理机构批准，结束整顿，并由国务院保险监督管理机构予以公告。

Article 144

Where an insurance company in reorganisation has reorganised its violations of this Act and resumed the normal business operation, the reorganisation group shall submit a report thereon, the reorganisation process shall be terminated upon the approval of the insurance regulatory body of the State Council, and the insurance regulatory body of the State Council shall make an announcement to that effect.

第一百四十五条　保险公司有下列情形之一的，国务院保险监督管理机构可以对其实行接管：

Article 145

Where an insurance company falls under either of the following circumstances, the insurance regulatory body of the State Council may administrate the company:

（一）公司的偿付能力严重不足的；

(1) the company is seriously insolvent; or

（二）违反本法规定，损害社会公共利益，可能严重危及或者已经严重危及公司的偿付能力的。

(2) the company damages the public interests by infringing this Act, so as to seriously endanger or to have seriously endangered the solvency of the company.

被接管的保险公司的债权债务关系不因接管而变化。
The debtor-creditor relationships of the insurance company shall remain unchanged after it is taken over.

第一百四十六条　接管组的组成和接管的实施办法，由国务院保险监督管理机构决定，并予以公告。
Article 146
The measures for the formation of an administration group and the implementation of administration shall be determined and announced by the insurance regulatory body of the State Council.

第一百四十七条　接管期限届满，国务院保险监督管理机构可以决定延长接管期限，接管期限最长不得超过二年。
Article 147
Upon the expiry of the administration period, the insurance regulatory body of the State Council may decide to extend the administration period, but the administration period shall not exceed two years at most.

第一百四十八条　接管期限届满，被接管的保险公司已恢复正常经营能力的，由国务院保险监督管理机构决定终止接管，并予以公告。
Article 148
Where an insurance company in administration resumes its normal business operation capacity upon the expiry of the administration period, the insurance regulatory body of the State Council shall decide to terminate the administration and make an announcement to that effect.

第一百四十九条　被整顿、被接管的保险公司有《中华人民共和国企业破产法》第二条规定情形的，国务院保险监督管理机构可以依法向人民法院申请对该保险公司进行重整或者破产清算。
Article 149
Where an insurance company in reorganisation or administration falls under the circumstances prescribed in Article 2 of the Enterprise Bankruptcy Law of the People's Republic of China, the insurance regulatory body of the State Council may apply to the People's Court for subjecting the company to restructuring or bankruptcy liquidation.

第一百五十条　保险公司因违法经营被依法吊销经营保险业务许可证的，或者偿付能力低于国务院保险监督管理机构规定标准，不予撤销将严重危害保险市场秩序、损害公共利益的，由国务院保险监督管理机构予以撤销并公告，依法及时组织清算组进行清算。
Article 150
Where the insurance business permit of an insurance company is revoked due to illegal business operation or the solvency of an insurance company is lower than the standard prescribed by the insurance regulatory body of

the State Council, and the order of the insurance market will be seriously endangered or public interests will be seriously damaged if the company is not put out of business, the insurance regulatory body of the State Council shall put it out of business, make an announcement to that effect, and legally form a liquidation group to conduct liquidation in a timely manner.

第一百五十一条　国务院保险监督管理机构有权要求保险公司股东、实际控制人在指定的期限内提供有关信息和资料。

Article 151

The insurance regulatory body of the State Council shall have the right to require the shareholders and ultimate controlling person of any insurance company to provide the relevant information and materials within a prescribed time limit.

第一百五十二条　保险公司的股东利用关联交易严重损害公司利益，危及公司偿付能力的，由国务院保险监督管理机构责令改正。在按照要求改正前，国务院保险监督管理机构可以限制其股东权利；拒不改正的，可以责令其转让所持的保险公司股权。

Article 152

Where a shareholder of an insurance company seriously damages the interests of the company through associated party transactions, which endangers the company's solvency, the insurance regulatory body of the State Council shall order the shareholder to make correction. Until the shareholder makes such correction, the insurance regulatory body of the State Council may restrict the shareholder's rights of such a shareholder, and, if the shareholder refuses to make correction, order the assignment of the shareholder's shares in the insurance company.

第一百五十三条　保险监督管理机构根据履行监督管理职责的需要，可以与保险公司董事、监事和高级管理人员进行监督管理谈话，要求其就公司的业务活动和风险管理的重大事项作出说明。

Article 153

An insurance regulatory body may, as required for performing its functions of regulation and supervision, hold supervisory talks with the directors, supervisors and senior managers of insurance companies and require them to make explanations of major matters concerning the business operation and risk management of the insurance company.

第一百五十四条　保险公司在整顿、接管、撤销清算期间，或者出现重大风险时，国务院保险监督管理机构可以对该公司直接负责的董事、监事、高级管理人员和其他直接责任人员采取以下措施：

Article 154

During the period of reorganisation, administration, or liquidation as a result of closure of an insurance company or upon the occurrence of any significant risk to an insurance company, the insurance regulatory body of the State Council may take the following measures against the directly liable directors, supervisors, senior managers and other directly liable persons of the company:

（一）通知出境管理机关依法阻止其出境；

(1) notifying the emigration administration authority to prevent them from leaving this country; or

（二）申请司法机关禁止其转移、转让或者以其他方式处分财产，或者在财产上设定其他权利。

(2) applying to the judicial authorities to forbid them from removing or transferring their assets or disposing thereof by other means, or creating encumbrances thereon.

第一百五十五条　保险监督管理机构依法履行职责，可以采取下列措施：

Article 155

For the purpose of performing its functions according to law, an insurance regulatory body may take the following measures:

（一）对保险公司、保险代理人、保险经纪人、保险资产管理公司、外国保险机构的代表机构进行现场检查；

(1) making spot inspections of insurance companies, insurance agents, insurance brokers, insurance asset management companies and representative offices of foreign insurance institutions;

（二）进入涉嫌违法行为发生场所调查取证；

(2) entering a place where the occurrence of an unlawful act is suspected, to make investigation and take evidence;

（三）询问当事人及与被调查事件有关的单位和个人，要求其对与被调查事件有关的事项作出说明；

(3) inquiring the parties concerned and other entities and individuals related to the investigated event, and requiring them to make explanations of the relevant matters;

（四）查阅、复制与被调查事件有关的财产权登记等资料；

(4) reviewing and copying materials related to the investigated event, such as materials on the registration of property rights;

（五）查阅、复制保险公司、保险代理人、保险经纪人、保险资产管理公司、外国保险机构的代表机构以及与被调查事件有关的单位和个人的财务会计资料及其他相关文件和资料；对可能被转移、隐匿或者毁损的文件和资料予以封存；

(5) reviewing and copying the financial and accounting materials and other relevant documents and materials of insurance companies, insurance agents, insurance brokers, insurance asset management companies,

representative offices of foreign insurance institutions and other entities and individuals related to the investigated event; and preserving the documents and materials which may be displaced, concealed or destroyed;

（六）查询涉嫌违法经营的保险公司、保险代理人、保险经纪人、保险资产管理公司、外国保险机构的代表机构以及与涉嫌违法事项有关的单位和个人的银行账户；

(6) obtaining information about the bank accounts of insurance companies, insurance agents, insurance brokers, insurance asset management companies and representative offices of foreign insurance institutions which are suspected of engaging in unlawful business operations and the bank accounts of the entities and individuals related to the suspected illegal matter; or

（七）对有证据证明已经或者可能转移、隐匿违法资金等涉案财产或者隐匿、伪造、毁损重要证据的，经保险监督管理机构主要负责人批准，申请人民法院予以冻结或者查封。

(7) upon the approval of the chief person in charge of the insurance regulatory body, applying to the People's Court for a freezing order or preservation of any illegally obtained funds and other involved property, which can be proved to have been or may be displaced or concealed, or any important evidence, which can be proved to have been or may be concealed, forged or destroyed.

保险监督管理机构采取前款第（一）项、第（二）项、第（五）项措施的，应当经保险监督管理机构负责人批准；采取第（六）项措施的，应当经国务院保险监督管理机构负责人批准。

To take the measure prescribed in subparagraph (1), (2) or (5) of the preceding paragraph, an insurance regulatory body shall obtain the approval of the person in charge of the body. To take the measure prescribed in subparagraph (6), an insurance regulatory body shall obtain the approval of the person in charge of the insurance regulatory body of the State Council.

保险监督管理机构依法进行监督检查或者调查，其监督检查、调查的人员不得少于二人，并应当出示合法证件和监督检查、调查通知书；监督检查、调查的人员少于二人或者未出示合法证件和监督检查、调查通知书的，被检查、调查的单位和个人有权拒绝。

Where an insurance regulatory body conducts a supervisory inspection or investigation according to law, there shall be at least two supervisory inspectors or investigators who shall present their legal credentials and a notice of supervisory inspection or investigation; if there are less than two supervisory inspectors or investigators or they fail to present their legal certificates or a notice of supervisory inspection or investigation, the entity or individual under inspection or investigation shall have the right to refuse the inspection or investigation.

第一百五十六条　保险监督管理机构依法履行职责，被检查、调查的单位和个人应当配合。

Article 156

When an insurance regulatory body performs its functions according to law, the entities and individuals under inspection or investigation shall cooperate with it.

第一百五十七条　保险监督管理机构工作人员应当忠于职守，依法办事，公正廉洁，不得利用职务便利牟取不正当利益，不得泄露所知悉的有关单位和个人的商业秘密。

Article 157

The staff of an insurance regulatory body shall be dedicated, impartial and honest and handle matters according to the rule of law, and shall not seek unlawful benefits by taking advantage of their position or disclose the trade secrets of relevant entities or individuals to which they have access.

第一百五十八条　国务院保险监督管理机构应当与中国人民银行、国务院其他金融监督管理机构建立监督管理信息共享机制。

Article 158

The insurance regulatory body of the State Council shall set up a regulation and supervision information sharing mechanism together with the People's Bank of China and other financial regulatory bodies of the State Council.

保险监督管理机构依法履行职责，进行监督检查、调查时，有关部门应当予以配合。

When an insurance regulatory body performs its functions in the form of supervisory inspection or investigation according to law, the relevant departments shall cooperate with it.

第七章　法律责任

Chapter VII: Legal Responsibility

第一百五十九条　违反本法规定，擅自设立保险公司、保险资产管理公司或者非法经营商业保险业务的，由保险监督管理机构予以取缔，没收违法所得，并处违法所得一倍以上五倍以下的罚款；没有违法所得或者违法所得不足二十万元的，处二十万元以上一百万元以下的罚款。

Article 159

Where someone infringes this Act by forming an insurance company or insurance asset management company without approval or unlawfully operating commercial insurance business, the insurance regulatory body shall ban the business, confiscate the unlawful gains and impose a fine of not less than the amount of but not more than five times the unlawful gains upon it. If there are no unlawful gains or the amount of unlawful gains is less than RMB 200,000, a fine of RMB 200,000 up to RMB 1 million shall be imposed upon it.

第一百六十条　违反本法规定，擅自设立保险专业代理机构、保险经纪人，或者未取得经营保险代理业务许可证、保险经纪业务许可证从事保险代理业务、保险经纪业务的，由保险监督管理机构予以取缔，没收违法所得，并处违法所得一倍以上五倍以下的罚款；没有违法所得或者违法所得不足五万元的，处五万元以上三十万元以下的罚款。

Article 160

Where someone infringes this Act by forming a specialised insurance agency or an insurance broker without approval or carries out insurance agency or brokerage business without an insurance agency or brokerage business operation permit, the competent insurance regulatory body shall ban the entity, confiscate the unlawful gains and impose a fine of not less than the amount of but not more than five times the unlawful gains upon it. If there are no unlawful gains or the amount of unlawful gains is less than RMB 50,000, a fine of RMB 50,000 up to RMB 300,000 shall be imposed upon it.

第一百六十一条　保险公司违反本法规定，超出批准的业务范围经营的，由保险监督管理机构责令限期改正，没收违法所得，并处违法所得一倍以上五倍以下的罚款；没有违法所得或者违法所得不足十万元的，处十万元以上五十万元以下的罚款。逾期不改正或者造成严重后果的，责令停业整顿或者吊销业务许可证。

Article 161

Where an insurance company infringes this Act by operating business beyond the approved scope of business, the competent insurance regulatory body shall order it to make correction within a prescribed time limit, confiscate the illegal gains and impose a fine of not less than the amount of but not more than five times the unlawful gains upon it. If there are no unlawful gains or the amount of unlawful gains is less than RMB 100,000, a fine of RMB 100,000 up to RMB 500,000 shall be imposed upon it. If the insurance company fails to make correction within the prescribed time limit or causes serious consequences, the competent insurance regulatory body shall order it to suspend business for reorganisation or revoke its business operation permit.

第一百六十二条　保险公司有本法第一百一十六条规定行为之一的，由保险监督管理机构责令改正，处五万元以上三十万元以下的罚款；情节严重的，限制其业务范围、理机构责令改正，处五万元以上三十万元以下的罚款；情节严重的，限制其业务范围、责令停止接受新业务或者吊销业务许可证。

Article 162

Where an insurance company commits any of the conduct prescribed in Article 116 of this Law, the competent insurance regulatory body shall order it to make correction and impose a fine of RMB 50,000 up to RMB 300,000 upon it; and, if the circumstances are serious, restrict its scope of business, order it to stop accepting new business or revoke its business operation permit.

第一百六十三条　保险公司违反本法第八十四条规定的，由保险监督管理机构责令改正，处一万元以上十万元以下的罚款。

Article 163

Where an insurance company infringes Article 84 of this Act, the competent insurance regulatory body shall order it to make correction and impose a fine of RMB 10,000 up to RMB 100,000 upon it.

第一百六十四条　保险公司违反本法规定，有下列行为之一的，由保险监督管理机构责令改正，处五万元以上三十万元以下的罚款：

Article 164

Where an insurance company, in violation of this Law, commits either of the following conduct, the competent insurance regulatory body shall order it to make correction and impose a fine of RMB 50,000 up to RMB 300,000 upon it:

（一）超额承保，情节严重的；

(1) providing over coverage with serious circumstances; or

（二）为无民事行为能力人承保以死亡为给付保险金条件的保险的。

(2) providing insurance which takes death as the condition for paying insurance money for a person without the capacity for civil conduct.

第一百六十五条　违反本法规定，有下列行为之一的，由保险监督管理机构责令改正，处五万元以上三十万元以下的罚款；情节严重的，可以限制其业务范围、责令停止接受新业务或者吊销业务许可证：

Article 165

Where someone infringes this Act by any of the following acts, the competent insurance regulatory body shall order that corrective action be taken and impose a fine of RMB 50,000 up to RMB 300,000; and, if the circumstances are serious, restrict the entity's scope of business, order it to stop accepting new business or revoke its business operation permit:

（一）未按照规定提存保证金或者违反规定动用保证金的；

(1) failing to draw the guarantee fund as required or illegally using the guarantee fund;

（二）未按照规定提取或者结转各项责任准备金的；

(2) failing to draw or carry forward any liability reserve fund as required;

（三）未按照规定缴纳保险保障基金或者提取公积金的；

(3) failing to pay the insurance protection fund or draw the provident funds as required;

（四）未按照规定办理再保险的；

(4) failing to arrange for reinsurance as required;

（五）未按照规定运用保险公司资金的；

(5) failing to use the capital of an insurance company as required;

（六）未经批准设立分支机构或者代表机构的；

(6) setting up a branch office or representative office without approval; or

（七）未按照规定申请批准保险条款、保险费率的。

(7) failing to apply for approval of insurance clauses or premium rates as required.

第一百六十六条　保险代理机构、保险经纪人有本法第一百三十一条规定行为之一的，由保险监督管理机构责令改正，处五万元以上三十万元以下的罚款；情节严重的，吊销业务许可证。

Article 166

Where an insurance agency or insurance broker commits any of the acts prescribed in Article 131 of this Act, the competent insurance regulatory body shall order it to take corrective action and impose a fine of RMB 50,000 up to RMB 300,000 upon it; and, if the circumstances are serious, shall revoke its business operation permit.

第一百六十七条　保险代理机构、保险经纪人违反本法规定，有下列行为之一的，由保险监督管理机构责令改正，处二万元以上十万元以下的罚款；情节严重的，责令停业整顿或者吊销业务许可证：

Article 167

Where an insurance agency or insurance broker infringes this Act by any of the following actions, the competent insurance regulatory body shall order it to take corrective action and impose a fine of RMB 20,000 up to RMB 100,000 upon it; and, if the circumstances are serious, shall order it to suspend business for reorganisation or revoke its business operation permit:

（一）未按照规定缴存保证金或者投保职业责任保险的；

(1) failing to deposit the guarantee fund or arrange professional liability insurance as required; or

（二）未按照规定设立专门账簿记载业务收支情况的。

(2) failing to maintain special account books to record its revenues and expenditures as required.

第一百六十八条　保险专业代理机构、保险经纪人违反本法规定，未经批准设立分支机构或者变更组织形式的，由保险监督管理机构责令改正，处一万元以上五万元以下的罚款。

Article 168

Where a specialised insurance agency or an insurance broker infringes this Act by setting up a branch office or changing its form of organisation without approval, the competent insurance regulatory body shall order it to take corrective action and impose a fine of RMB 10,000 up to RMB 50,000 upon it.

第一百六十九条　违反本法规定，聘任不具有任职资格、从业资格的人员的，由保险监督管理机构责令改正，处二万元以上十万元以下的罚款。

Article 169

Where someone infringes this Act by retaining any person without the requisite qualification or practising qualification, the competent insurance regulatory body shall order that corrective action be taken and impose a fine of RMB 20,000 up to RMB 100,000.

第一百七十条　违反本法规定，转让、出租、出借业务许可证的，由保险监督管理机构处一万元以上十万元以下的罚款；情节严重的，责令停业整顿或者吊销业务许可证。

Article 170

Where someone infringes this Act by transferring, leasing or lending its business operation permit, the competent insurance regulatory body shall impose a fine of RMB 10,000 up to RMB 100,000; and, if the circumstances are serious, shall order the suspension of business for reorganisation or revoke its business operation permit.

第一百七十一条　违反本法规定，有下列行为之一的，由保险监督管理机构责令限期改正；逾期不改正的，处一万元以上十万元以下的罚款：

Article 171

Where someone infringes this Act by committing any of the following conduct, the competent insurance regulatory body shall order corrective action within a prescribed time limit; and, in case of failure to take corrective action within a prescribed time limit, shall impose a fine of RMB 10,000 up to RMB 100,000:

（一）未按照规定报送或者保管报告、报表、文件、资料的，或者未按照规定提供有关信息、资料的；

(1) failing to file or keep reports, statements, documents and materials as required or failing to provide the relevant information or materials as required;

（二）未按照规定报送保险条款、保险费率备案的；

(2) failing to file the insurance clauses or premium rates as required; or

（三）未按照规定披露信息的。第百七十条违反本法规定有下列行为之的由保险监督管理机构责令改。

(3) failing to disclose information as required.

第一百七十二条　违反本法规定，有下列行为之一的，由保险监督管理机构责令改正，处十万元以上五十万元以下的罚款；情节严重的，可以限制其业务范围、责令停止接受新业务或者吊销业务许可证：

Article 172

Where someone infringes this Act by committing any of the following acts, the competent insurance regulatory body shall order the entity to take corrective action and impose a fine of RMB 100,000 up to RMB 500,000 upon it; and, if the circumstances are serious, may also restrict its scope of business, order it to stop accepting new business or revoke its business operation permit:

（一）编制或者提供虚假的报告、报表、文件、资料的；

(1) compiling or providing any false report, statement, document or material;

（二）拒绝或者妨碍依法监督检查的；

(2) refusing or obstructing any supervisory inspection conducted according to law; or

（三）未按照规定使用经批准或者备案的保险条款、保险费率的。

(3) failing to use the approved or filed insurance clauses or premium rates as required.

第一百七十三条　保险公司、保险资产管理公司、保险专业代理机构、保险经纪人违反本法规定的，保险监督管理机构除分别依照本法第一百六十一条至第一百七十二条的规定对该单位给予处罚外，对其直接负责的主管人员和其他直接责任人员给予警告，并处一万元以上十万元以下的罚款；情节严重的，撤销任职资格或者从业资格。

Article 173

Where an insurance company, insurance asset management company, specialised insurance agency or insurance broker infringes this Act, the competent insurance regulatory body shall punish it according to the provisions of Article 161 through Article 172, respectively. For its directly responsible person in charge or any other directly responsible person, the competent insurance regulatory body shall reprimand him or her and impose a fine of RMB 10,000 up to RMB 100,000 upon him or her; and, if the circumstances are serious, cancel his or her qualification for holding the position in question or their practising certificate.

第一百七十四条　个人保险代理人违反本法规定的，由保险监督管理机构给予警告，可以并处二万元以下的罚款；情节严重的，处二万元以上十万元以下的罚款，并可以吊销其资格证书。

Article 174

Where an individual insurance agent infringes this Act, the competent insurance regulatory body shall reprimand him or her and may impose a fine of not more than RMB 20,000 upon him or her; or if the circumstances are serious, impose a fine of RMB 20,000 up to RMB 100,000 upon him or her and may revoke his or her practising certificate.

未取得合法资格的人员从事个人保险代理活动的，由保险监督管理机构给予警告，可以并处二万元以下的罚款；情节严重的，处二万元以上十万元以下的罚款。

Where a person who has not obtained the required qualification performs individual insurance agency business, the competent insurance regulatory body shall reprimand him or her and may impose a fine of not more than RMB 20,000 upon him or her; or if the circumstances are serious, impose a fine of RMB 20,000 up to RMB 100,000 upon him or her.

第一百七十五条　外国保险机构未经国务院保险监督管理机构批准，擅自在中华人民共和国境内设立代表机构的，由国务院保险监督管理机构予以取缔，处五万元以上三十万元以下的罚款。

Article 175

Where a foreign insurance institution forms a representative office within the territory of the People's Republic of China without the approval of the insurance regulatory body of the State Council, the insurance regulatory body of the State Council shall ban the office and impose a fine of RMB 50,000 up to RMB 300,000 upon the foreign insurance institution.

外国保险机构在中华人民共和国境内设立的代表机构从事保险经营活动的，由保险监督管理机构责令改正，没收违法所得，并处违法所得一倍以上五倍以下的罚款；没有违法所得或者违法所得不足二十万元的，处二十万元以上一百万元以下的罚款；对其首席代表可以责令撤换；情节严重的，撤销其代表机构。

Where a foreign insurance institution's representative office in the People's Republic of China performs any insurance business activity, the competent insurance regulatory body shall order it to make correction, confiscate the unlawful gains and impose a fine of not less than the amount of but not more than five times the unlawful gains upon it; if there are no unlawful gains or the amount of unlawful gains is less than RMB 200,000, it shall instead impose a fine of RMB 200,000 up to RMB 1 million; may order a replacement of its chief representative; and, if the circumstances are serious, shall order the closure of the representative office.

第一百七十六条　投保人、被保险人或者受益人有下列行为之一，进行保险诈骗活动，尚不构成犯罪的，依法给予行政处罚：

Article 176

An assured, insured or beneficiary who commits any of the following conduct for the purpose of insurance fraud shall be subject to administrative punishment if no crime is constituted:

（一）投保人故意虚构保险标的，骗取保险金的；

(1) intentional fabrication by an assured of a subject matter insured to falsely obtain insurance money;

（二）编造未曾发生的保险事故，或者编造虚假的事故原因或者夸大损失程度，骗取保险金的；

(2) fabrication of an insured incident which has never occurred, fabrication of the cause of an insured incident or exaggeration of the degree of damage caused by an insured incident to falsely obtain insurance money; or

（三）故意造成保险事故，骗取保险金的。

(3) intentional creation of an insured incident to falsely obtain insurance money.

保险事故的鉴定人、评估人、证明人故意提供虚假的证明文件，为投保人、被保险人或者受益人进行保险诈骗提供条件的，依照前款规定给予处罚。

An authenticator, assessor or certifier of an insured incident who intentionally provides a false certificate for an assured, insured or beneficiary to commit an insurance fraud shall be punished according to the preceding paragraph.

第一百七十七条　违反本法规定，给他人造成损害的，依法承担民事责任。

Article 177

Whoever infringes this Act and causes damage to others shall be subject to civil liability.

第一百七十八条　拒绝、阻碍保险监督管理机构及其工作人员依法行使监督检查、调查职权，未使用暴力、威胁方法的，依法给予治安管理处罚。

Article 178

Whoever refuses or obstructs a supervisory inspection or investigation performed by an insurance regulatory body or its staff according to law shall be subject to a punishment in public security administration if no violence or threat is used.

第一百七十九条　违反法律、行政法规的规定，情节严重的，国务院保险监督管理机构可以禁止有关责任人员一定期限直至终身进入保险业。

Article 179

Where a law or administrative regulation is infringed and the circumstances are serious, the insurance regulatory body of the State Council may prohibit the relevant responsible persons from practising in the insurance sector for a prescribed time or for life.

第一百八十条　保险监督管理机构从事监督管理工作的人员有下列情形之一的，依法给予处分：

Article 180

Where any staff member of an insurance regulatory body who undertakes the supervision and administration work commits any of the following conduct, he or she shall be disciplined according to law:

（一）违反规定批准机构的设立的；

(1) approving the formation of any institution in violation of the relevant provisions;

（二）违反规定进行保险条款、保险费率审批的；

(2) examining and approving insurance clauses or premium rates in violation of the relevant provisions;

（三）违反规定进行现场检查的；

(3) making spot inspections in violation of the relevant provisions;

（四）违反规定查询账户或者冻结资金的；

(4) inquiring about accounts or freezing funds in violation of the relevant provisions;

（五）泄露其知悉的有关单位和个人的商业秘密的；

(5) disclosing any trade secret of a relevant entity or individual to which he or she has access;

（六）违反规定实施行政处罚的；

(6) enforcing any administrative punishment in violation of the relevant provisions; or

（七）滥用职权、玩忽职守的其他行为。

(7) any other conduct in abuse of power or dereliction of duties.

第一百八十一条　违反本法规定，构成犯罪的，依法追究刑事责任。

Article 181

Whoever infringes this Act shall be subject to criminal liability if such infringement constitutes an offence.

第八章　附　　则
Chapter VIII: Supplementary Provisions

第一百八十二条　保险公司应当加入保险行业协会。保险代理人、保险经纪人、保险公估机构可以加入保险行业协会。

Article 182

Insurance companies shall join in the Insurance Association of China. Insurance agents, insurance brokers and insurance adjustment institutions may also join in the Insurance Association of China.

保险行业协会是保险业的自律性组织，是社会团体法人。

The Insurance Association of China shall be a self-regulatory organisation for the insurance sector and a social group legal person.

第一百八十三条　保险公司以外的其他依法设立的保险组织经营的商业保险业务，适用本法。

Article 183

Commercial insurance businesses operated by legally established insurance organisations other than insurance companies shall be governed by this Act.

第一百八十四条　海上保险适用《中华人民共和国海商法》的有关规定；《中华人民共和国海商法》未规定的，适用本法的有关规定。

Article 184

Marine insurance shall be governed by the relevant provisions of the Maritime Code of the People's Republic of China; for matters not covered by the Maritime Code, the relevant provisions of this Act shall apply.

第一百八十五条　中外合资保险公司、外资独资保险公司、外国保险公司分公司适用本法规定；法律、行政法规另有规定的，适用其规定。

Article 185

Chinese-foreign joint venture insurance companies, wholly foreign-owned insurance companies and subsidiary companies of foreign insurance companies shall be governed by this Act; except as otherwise provided by laws and administrative regulations.

第一百八十六条　国家支持发展为农业生产服务的保险事业。农业保险由法律、行政法规另行规定。

Article 186

The State shall support the development of insurance business which serves agricultural production. Agricultural insurance shall be governed separately by laws and administrative regulations.

强制保险，法律、行政法规另有规定的，适用其规定。

For compulsory insurance, where laws and administrative regulations provide otherwise, such provisions shall apply.

第一百八十七条　本法自2009年10月1日起施行。

Article 187

This Act shall come into force on 1 October 2009.

Appendix II
CMC Provisions

CHAPTER XII CONTRACT OF MARINE INSURANCE

Section 1: Basic Principles

Article 216
A contract of marine insurance is a contract whereby the insurer undertakes, as agreed, to indemnify the loss to the subject matter insured and the liability of the insured caused by perils covered by the insurance against the payment of an insurance premium by the insured.
The covered perils referred to in the preceding paragraph mean any maritime perils agreed upon between the insurer and the insured, including perils occurring in inland rivers or on land which is related to a maritime adventure.

Article 217
A contract of marine insurance includes:

(1) name of the insurer;
(2) name of the insured;
(3) subject matter insured;
(4) insured value;
(5) insured amount;
(6) perils insured against and perils excepted;
(7) duration of insurance coverage; and
(8) insurance premium.

Article 218
The following items may come under the subject matter of marine insurance:

(1) ship;
(2) cargo;
(3) income from the operation of the ship including freight, charter hire and passenger's fare;

(4) expected profit on cargo;
(5) crew's wages and other remuneration;
(6) liabilities to a third person; and
(7) other property which may sustain loss from a maritime peril and the liability and expenses arising therefrom.

The insurer may reinsure the insurance of the subject matter enumerated in the preceding paragraph. Unless otherwise agreed in the contract, the original insured shall not be entitled to the benefit of the reinsurance.

Article 219
The insurable value of the subject matter insured shall be agreed upon between the insurer and the insured.

Where no insurable value has been agreed upon between the insurer and the insured, the insurable value shall be calculated as follows:

(1) the insurable value of the ship shall be the value of the ship at the time when the insurance liability commences, being the total value of the ship's hull, machinery, equipment, fuel, stores, gear, provisions and fresh water on board as well as the insurance premium;
(2) the insurable value of the cargo shall be the aggregate of the invoice value of the cargo or the actual value of the non-trade commodity at the place of shipment, plus freight and insurance premium when the insurance liability commences;
(3) the insurable value of the freight shall be the aggregate of the total amount of freight payable to the carrier and the insurance premium when the insurance liability commences; and
(4) The insurable value of other subject matter insured shall be the aggregate of the actual value of the subject matter insured and the insurance premium when the insurance liability commences.

Article 220
The insured amount shall be agreed upon between the insurer and the insured.
The insured amount shall not exceed the insured value. Where the insured amount exceeds the insured value, the portion in excess shall be null and void.

Section 2: Conclusion, Termination and Assignment of Contract

Article 221
A contract of marine insurance comes into being after the insured puts forth a proposal for insurance and the insurer agrees to accept the proposal and the insurer and the insured agree on the terms and conditions of the

insurance. The insurer shall issue to the insured an insurance policy or other certificate of insurance in time, and the contents of the contract shall be contained therein.

Article 222

Before the contract is concluded, the insured shall truthfully inform the insurer of the material circumstances which the insured has knowledge of or ought to have knowledge of in his ordinary business practice and which may have a bearing on the insurer in deciding the premium or whether he agrees to insure or not.

The insured need not inform the insurer of the facts which the insurer has known of or the insurer ought to have knowledge of in his ordinary business practice if about which the insurer made no inquiry.

Article 223

Upon failure of the insured to truthfully inform the insurer of the material circumstances set forth in paragraph 1 of Article 222 of this Law due to his intentional act, the insurer has the right to terminate the contract without refunding the premium. The insurer shall not be liable for any loss arising from the perils insured against before the contract is terminated.

If, not due to the insured's intentional act, the insured did not truthfully inform the insurer of the material circumstances set out in paragraph 1 of Article 222 of this Law, the insurer has the right to terminate the contract or to demand a corresponding increase in the premium. In case the contract is terminated by the insurer, the insurer shall be liable for the loss arising from the perils insured against which occurred prior to the termination of the contract, except where the material circumstances uninformed or wrongly informed of have an impact on the occurrence of such perils.

Article 224

Where the insured was aware or ought to be aware that the subject matter insured had suffered a loss due to the incidence of a peril insured against when the contract was concluded, the insurer shall not be liable for indemnification but shall have the right to the premium. Where the insurer was aware or ought to be aware that the occurrence of a loss to the subject matter insured due to a peril insured against was impossible, the insured shall have the right to recover the premium paid.

Article 225

Where the insured concludes with several insurers for the same subject matter insured and against the same risk, and the insured amount of the said subject matter insured thereby exceeds the insured value, then, unless otherwise agreed in the contract, the insured may demand indemnification from any of the insurers and the aggregate amount to be indemnified shall not exceed the loss value of the subject matter insured. The liability of each insurer shall be in proportion to that which the amount he insured bears to the total of the amounts insured by all insurers. Any insurer who has paid an indemnification in an amount greater than that for which he is liable, shall have the right of recourse against those who have not paid their indemnification in the amounts for which they are liable.

Article 226
Prior to the commencement of the insurance liability, the insured may demand the termination of the insurance contract but shall pay the handling fees to the insurer, and the insurer shall refund the premium.

Article 227
Unless otherwise agreed in the contract, neither the insurer nor the insured may terminate the contract after the commencement of the insurance liability.

Where the insurance contract provides that the contract may be terminated after the commencement of the liability, and the insured demands the termination of the contract, the insurer shall have the right to the premium payable from the day of the commencement of the insurance liability to the day of termination of the contract and refund the remaining portion. If it is the insurer who demands the termination of the contract, the unexpired premium from the day of the termination of the contract to the day of the expiration of the period of insurance shall be refunded to the insured.

Article 228
Notwithstanding the stipulations in Article 227 of this Law, the insured may not demand termination of the contract for cargo insurance and voyage insurance on ship after the commencement of the insurance liability.

Article 229
A contract of marine insurance for the carriage of goods by sea may be assigned by the insured by endorsement or otherwise, and the rights and obligations under the contract are assigned accordingly. The insured and the assignee shall be jointly and severally liable for the payment of the premium if such premium remains unpaid up to the time of the assignment of the contract.

Article 230
The consent of the insurer shall be obtained where the insurance contract is assigned in consequence of the transfer of the ownership of the ship insured. In the absence of such consent, the contract shall be terminated from the time of the transfer of the ownership of the ship. Where the transfer takes place during the voyage, the contract shall be terminated when the voyage ends.

Upon termination of the contract, the insurer shall refund the unexpired premium to the insured calculated from the day of the termination of the contract to the day of its expiration.

Article 231

The insured may conclude an open cover with the insurer for the goods to be shipped or received in batches within a given period. The open cover shall be evidenced by an open policy to be issued by the insurer.

Article 232

The insurer shall, at the request of the insured, issue insurance certificates separately for the cargo shipped in batches according to the open cover.

Where the contents of the insurance certificates issued by the insurer separately differ from those of the open policy, the insurance certificates issued separately shall prevail.

Article 233

The insured shall notify the insurer immediately on learning that the cargo insured under the open cover has been shipped or has arrived. The items to be notified of shall include the name of the carrying ship, the voyage, the value of the cargo and the insured amount.

Section 3: Obligation of the Insured

Article 234

Unless otherwise agreed in the insurance contract, the insured shall pay the premium immediately upon conclusion of the contract. The insurer may refuse to issue the insurance policy or other insurance certificate before the premium is paid by the insured.

Article 235

The insured shall notify the insurer in writing immediately where the insured has not complied with the warranties under the contract. The insurer may, upon receipt of the notice, terminate the contract or demand an amendment to the terms and conditions of the insurance coverage or an increase in the premium.

Article 236

Upon the occurrence of the peril insured against, the insured shall notify the insurer immediately and shall take necessary and reasonable measures to avoid or minimise the loss. Where special instructions for the adoption of reasonable measures to avoid or minimise the loss are received from the insurer, the insured shall act according to such instructions.

The insurer shall not be liable for the extended loss caused by the insured's breach of the provisions of the preceding paragraph.

Section 4: Liability of the Insurer

Article 237
The insurer shall indemnify the insured promptly after the loss from a peril insured against has occurred.

Article 238
The insurer's indemnification for the loss from the peril insured against shall be limited to the insured amount. Where the insured amount is lower than the insured value, the insurer shall indemnify in the proportion that the insured amount bears to the insured value.

Article 239
The insurer shall be liable for the loss to the subject matter insured arising from several perils insured against during the period of the insurance even though the aggregate of the amounts of loss exceeds the insured amount. However, the insurer shall only be liable for the total loss where the total loss occurs after the partial loss which has not been repaired.

Article 240
The insurer shall pay, in addition to the indemnification to be paid with regard to the subject matter insured, the necessary and reasonable expenses incurred by the insured for avoiding or minimising the loss recoverable under the contract, the reasonable expenses for survey and assessment of the value for the purpose of ascertaining the nature and extent of the peril insured against and the expenses incurred for acting on the special instructions of the insurer.

The payment by the insurer of the expenses referred to in the preceding paragraph shall be limited to that equivalent to the insured amount.

Where the insured amount is lower than the insured value, the insurer shall be liable for the expenses referred to in this Article in the proportion that the insured amount bears to the insured value, unless the contract provides otherwise.

Article 241
Where the insured amount is lower than the value for contribution under the general average, the insurer shall be liable for the general average contribution in the proportion that the insured amount bears to the value for contribution.

Article 242
The insurer shall not be liable for the loss caused by the intentional act of the insured.

Article 243
Unless otherwise agreed in the insurance contract, the insurer shall not be liable for the loss of or damage to the insured cargo arising from any of the following causes:

(1) delay in the voyage or in the delivery of cargo or change of market price;
(2) fair wear and tear, inherent vice or nature of the cargo; and
(3) improper packing.

Article 244
Unless otherwise agreed in the insurance contract, the insurer shall not be liable for the loss of or damage to the insured ship arising from any of the following causes:

(1) unseaworthiness of the ship at the time of the commencement of the voyage, unless where under a time policy the insured has no knowledge thereof; and
(2) wear and tear or corrosion of the ship.

The provisions of this Article shall apply mutatis mutandis to the insurance of freight.

Section 5: Loss of or Damage to the Subject Matter Insured and Abandonment

Article 245
Where after the occurrence of a peril insured against the subject matter insured is lost or is so seriously damaged that it is completely deprived of its original structure and usage or the insured is deprived of the possession thereof, it shall constitute an actual total loss.

Article 246
Where a ship's total loss is considered to be unavoidable after the occurrence of a peril insured against or the expenses necessary for avoiding the occurrence of an actual total loss would exceed the insured value, it shall constitute a constructive total loss.

Where an actual total loss is considered to be unavoidable after the cargo has suffered a peril insured against, or the expenses to be incurred for avoiding the total actual loss plus that for forwarding the cargo to its destination would exceed its insured value, it shall constitute a constructive total loss.

Article 247
Any loss other than an actual total loss or a constructive total loss is a partial loss.

Article 248
Where a ship fails to arrive at its destination within a reasonable time from the place where it was last heard of, unless the contract provides otherwise, if it remains unheard of upon the expiry of two months, it shall constitute missing. Such missing shall be deemed to be an actual total loss.

Article 249
Where the subject matter insured has become a constructive total loss and the insured demands indemnification from the insurer on the basis of a total loss, the subject matter insured shall be abandoned to the insurer. The insurer may accept the abandonment or choose not to, but shall inform the insured of his decision whether to accept the abandonment within a reasonable time.

The abandonment shall not be attached with any conditions. Once the abandonment is accepted by the insurer, it shall not be withdrawn.

Article 250
Where the insurer has accepted the abandonment, all rights and obligations relating to the property abandoned are transferred to the insurer.

Section 6: Payment of Indemnity

Article 251
After the occurrence of a peril insured against and before the payment of indemnity, the insurer may demand that the insured submit evidence and materials related to the ascertainment of the nature of the peril and the extent of the loss.

Article 252
Where the loss of or damage to the subject matter insured within the insurance coverage is caused by a third person, the right of the insured to demand compensation from the third person shall be subrogated to the insurer from the time the indemnity is paid.

The insured shall furnish the insurer with necessary documents and information that should come to his knowledge and shall endeavour to assist the insurer in pursuing recovery from the third person.

Article 253
Where the insured waives his right of claim against the third person without the consent of the insurer or the insurer is unable to exercise the right of recourse due to the fault of the insured, the insurer may make a corresponding reduction from the amount of indemnity.

Article 254
In effecting payment of indemnity to the insured, the insurer may make a corresponding reduction therefrom of the amount already paid by a third person to the insured.

Where the compensation obtained by the insurer from the third person exceeds the amount of indemnity paid by the insurer, the part in excess shall be returned to the insured.

Article 255
After the occurrence of a peril insured against, the insurer is entitled to waive his right to the subject matter insured and pay the insured the amount in full to relieve himself of the obligations under the contract.

In exercising the right prescribed in the preceding paragraph, the insurer shall notify the insured thereof within seven days from the day of the receipt of the notice from the insured regarding the indemnity. The insurer shall remain liable for the necessary and reasonable expenses paid by the insured for avoiding or minimising the loss prior to his receipt of the said notice.

Article 256
Except as stipulated in Article 255 of this Law, where a total loss occurs to the subject matter insured and the full insured amount is paid, the insurer shall acquire the full right to the subject matter insured. In the case of underinsurance, the insurer shall acquire the right to the subject matter insured in the proportion that the insured amount bears to the insured value.

Index